Owner-occupation in Britain

Two week

By Stephen Merrett

State Housing in Britain (RKP, 1979)

OWNER-OCCUPATION IN BRITAIN

Stephen Merrett

with Fred Gray

Routledge & Kegan Paul
London, Boston, Melbourne and Henley

First published in 1982
by Routledge & Kegan Paul Ltd,
39 Store Street, London WC1E 7DD,
9 Park Street, Boston, Mass. 02108, USA,
296 Beaconsfield Parade, Middle Park,
Melbourne, 3206, Australia, and
Broadway House, Newtown Road,
Henley-on-Thames, Oxon RG9 1EN
Printed in Great Britain by
Billing & Sons Ltd, Worcester
© Stephen Merrett 1982

Library of Congress Cataloging in Publication Data
Merrett, Stephen.
Owner occupation in Britain.

Bibliography: p.
Includes indexes.
1. Home ownership - Great Britain. 2. Housing -
Great Britain. I. Gray, Fred. II. Title.
HD7287.82.G7M47 1982   333.3' 232' 0941   82-12247
ISBN 0-7100-9280-6
ISBN 0-7100-9281-4 (pbk.)

CONTENTS

Contents vii

FIGURES AND GRAPHS

Figures

Graphs

TABLES

PREFACE

This book marks the end of a long journey. In 1973 I took up
an appointment at the Architectural Association in London
to research the process of housing redevelopment and to give
a lecture series on 'the political economy of public housing'.
This was a post for which I had limited qualifications, knowing
as I did absolutely nothing about either subject. But within a
year this chance opportunity had created in me a passionate
fascination for the housing question and this was on two
counts: first, that it is an area of experience which touches
so directly and tangibly on the life of the entire working
people; second, that its subject-matter is so extraordinarily
complex. In 1974 I was appointed to a lectureship at University
College London and decided to attempt to carry through at
this new base a definitive study of the provision of accommodation by local authorities, a research field of great political
importance. *State Housing in Britain* was published in 1979.
In wrestling with the last chapter of that volume - an attempt
to draw up the main features of an alternative housing strategy
- I realised that my grasp of the economic and political relationships within the owner-occupied sector was too weak to permit
more than a preliminary indication of what changes might be
appropriate within that tenure. So in 1979 itself, with more
tenacity than good sense, I resolved to continue my research
in order to complete a study of home-ownership that would be
broadly complementary with the first book. The fruits of that
labour you now hold in your hands.

    Owner-occupation in Britain begins with three chapters,
largely descriptive in nature, that cover the years between
1918 and 1970 and which place the rest of the text within its
historical context. They set out the scale of production of
housing for home-ownership; the changing balance of tenures
within the total stock as a result of new building, clearance
and stock transfers; and the broad evolution of the state's
policy initiatives specifically aimed at stimulating the advance
of this form of property relation.

    The rest of the book, with the exception of the final chapter,
is devoted to an analysis of the system of owner-occupation
in the 1970s and early 1980s. Chapters 4 to 7 begin by treating
the relationships of effective demand. Chapter 4 itself sets out
the main categories of purchasing households and develops a
measure of the principal demographic change which lies behind
the pressure for an increased flow of vacancies. Chapter 5

breaks new ground in understanding the *willingness* of households to purchase for owner-occupation. Chapters 6 and 7 take
up the issue of the *ability* to purchase and are largely concerned
with the sources and distribution of mortgage finance.

The following four chapters explore the supply side, and the
structure of the presentation is quite original here. Chapters
8, 9 and 10 classify the 'stock supply' in terms of its ownership
before sale and examines the distinct motives of the three
dominant groups of vendors, that is, the local housing authorities, private landlords and owner-occupiers themselves. Then
chapter 11 deals with the 'newbuild supply' by the speculative
housebuilding industry, with a particularly strong emphasis on
the land question.

Chapter 12 continues the discussion of housing production by
looking at the rehabilitation of owner-occupied dwellings. The
purchase and sale of such houses and the many interests which
lie behind the exchange process form the subject-matter of
chapter 13. Chapter 14 contains an account of the nature of
vacancy chains as well as a description of the stock of dwellings
and the 'stock' of home-owners, where the distinction between
the mortgagor and the owner unencumbered by debt is highlighted. Chapter 15 launches a fundamental critique of three
distinct but curiously parallel schools of thought on the causal
links between the ownership of domestic property and social
relations.

The penultimate chapter aims at a synthesis of the main text
of the study within a diachronic analysis of the broader economic and political changes of the 1970s and early 1980s. The
final chapter completes my attempt to construct an alternative
housing strategy whilst the appendices include a legislative
chronology of owner-occupation between 1803 and 1981 as well
as some useful time-series.

These two successive volumes, which jointly embrace the
housing situation of some 85 per cent of the British population,
have certain distinctive features which may be worth briefly
mentioning. First, while the subject-matter with which they
deal is essentially the contemporary situation, both set this
within an historical account of the development of the British
housing system and both use past and present, as well as
the author's value-judgments, to propose a positive and con-
structive strategy for the future.

Second, the two studies draw on the language of a number of
'disciplines' in order to advance the analysis. These include
political economy, politics, sociology, philosophy, demography,
geography and law. It is necessary swiftly to add that unques-
tionably the dominant 'discipline' here is that of political economy. Nevertheless, no one can doubt the purpose of breaking
with that terrible intellectual parochialism characteristic of
much Anglo-American literature in this field, i.e. the insistence
on creating an image of this complex reality using only the
language of 'public administration' or 'economics' or 'political

science' or what you will. With respect to political economy itself, the paradigm on which my understanding is based, that of the Anglo-Italian school, comprehensively rejects both neo-classical economics as well as value-theory and yet, curiously, draws as much on Karl Marx as on David Ricardo, John Maynard Keynes and Michal Kalecki.

Third, the analysis in both studies rests on what may be called the four cornerstones of the political economy of the housing question: the subjects of land, production, exchange and consumption. In retrospect, the politically determined choice of an approach based on tenure - state housing and owner-occupation - has fortuitously promoted this holistic approach. For tenure defines ownership and ownership is the pivot between land and production on the one side and exchange and consumption on the other.

It remains for me to acknowledge the assistance I have enjoyed in working on *Owner-occupation in Britain*. My thanks for advice and criticism go to my friends in the Political Economy of Housing Workshop as well as in the Bartlett School of Architecture and Planning at University College London. I am particularly indebted to Sue Field Reid who typed the draft and final manuscripts and to Caroline Jacobs, Anne Grosskurth and Sarah Whatmore who acted as my research assistants at various times. Most important of all my gratitude is extended to my friend Fred Gray who has worked with me on this publication. He is the author of chapters 13, 14 and 15 in their entirety; the rest is my own.

Finally, the reader may find in the remainder of this slim volume a number of neologisms and other terms which are unfamiliar, for example, mortgagee, use-value, realisation and transfer finance, access index, price gain, net worth, impact ratio and income frontloading. In all such cases the index shows clearly where the concept is first defined.

ABBREVIATIONS

BSA   Building Societies Association
BSAP   Bartlett School of Architecture and Planning,
               University College London
CDP   Community Development Project
CEA   Corporation of Estate Agents
CES   Centre for Environmental Studies
CHAC   Central Housing Advisory Committee
CIPFA   Chartered Institute of Public Finance and Accountancy
CLA   Community Land Act
CSO   Central Statistical Office
CRE   Commission for Racial Equality
CURS   Centre for Urban and Regional Studies, University
               of Birmingham
DIY   Do-it-yourself
DLO   Direct Labour Organisation
DLT   Development Land Tax
DoE   Department of the Environment
FES   *Family Expenditure Survey*
GHS   *General Household Survey*
GIA   General Improvement Area
GLC   Greater London Council
HAA   Housing Action Area
HCS   *Housing and Construction Statistics*
HIP   Housing Investment Programme
HMSO   Her Majesty's Stationery Office
HPTV   *Housing Policy Technical Volume*, London, HMSO,
               1977
HSGB   *Housing Statistics Great Britain*
IMF   International Monetary Fund
ISVA   Incorporated Society of Valuers and Auctioneers
JAC   Joint Advisory Committee on Building Society Mortgage
               Finance
LAMSAC   Local Authorities Management Services and Computer
               Committee
MHLG   Ministry of Housing and Local Government
MLR   Minimum Lending Rate
MoH   Ministry of Health
MP   Member of Parliament
na   not available
NAEA   National Association of Estate Agents
NCC   National Consumer Council
NEDC   National Economic Development Council

NEDO	National Economic Development Office
neg.	negligible
NHBC	National House Building Council
NHBRC	National House Builders Registration Council
nk	not known
OPCS	Office of Population Censuses and Surveys
OPEC	Organisation of Petroleum Exporting Countries
PAYE	Pay-as-you-earn
PSBR	Public Sector Borrowing Requirement
PWLB	Public Works Loan Board
RDV	Realised Development Value
RICS	Royal Institution of Chartered Surveyors
SAUS	School for Advanced Urban Studies, University of Bristol
SAYE	Save-as-you-earn
SBC	Supplementary Benefits Commission
SDAA	Small Dwellings Acquisition Act
SDD	Scottish Development Department
SHAC	London Housing Aid Centre
SSRC	Social Science Research Council
TSB	Trustee Savings Bank

1 THE FIRST BOOM

1 INTRODUCTION

Although it was apparent to no one at the time, the year 1914 marked a watershed in the history of housing in Britain. Before that time the vast majority of dwellings, except the largest, had been constructed for private rental. Typically they were erected by builders, large or small, and sold to persons and institutions placing their capital in domestic property, who in their turn rented the houses out to the mass of the population. Of the total stock of dwellings in 1914 perhaps 10 per cent were owner-occupied, less than 1 per cent were in the local authority sector, and the rest were the property of private landlords.[1] After 1914 housebuilding for rental contracted so violently and remained so unattractive for the purpose of the accumulation of capital by private landlords that, except in the 1930s, it has played only the most marginal role in the provision of new housing for the British people until this very day. Instead, housebuilding for owner-occupation and local authority rental became the dominant forms of production.

The explanation of this vast metamorphosis in the system of housing provision constitutes a substantial part of later sections in this chapter. Here I merely want to stress that whilst the extent of home-ownership was relatively narrow in 1914, it was already the case that the policies of the state directly affected the sector in a variety of ways.

With respect to land and planning, intervention was fairly minimal. Transactions in land were basically unconstrained and although a betterment levy of 20 per cent existed, this had been introduced only in the 1910 Finance Act. The first Act explicitly relating to town planning was passed in 1909 and there was further legislation in 1919, 1932 and 1935, the contents of which are briefly summarised in appendix 1. But Cullingworth concludes in a brief review of its implementation that it had little material effect on the scale or location of development.[2]

In reference to housing production, the most significant form of state intervention before 1914 was in regulating the quality of the units erected, principally by means of the building by-laws enacted under the 1875 Public Health Act. Minimum standards were set for newly built houses dealing with sanitation, lighting, ventilation, structural stability and with questions of layout and density such as the width of streets and prohibition of the building of back-to-backs and 'courts'. After the 1870s, new

houses in most towns had to be provided with a piped water
supply and water-borne sanitation.[3]

The role of the state in the field of mortgage finance primarily
consisted in setting the legal framework within which the building
societies operated. These had first emerged out of the variety
of co-operative and friendly societies which arose in the eighteenth
century supporting the uprooted migrants to the new industrial
areas. The Act of 1836 had for the first time accorded them
specific legal recognition. The development of the societies in
their modern form, however, began only in the mid-nineteenth
century and the most important Acts, those of 1874 and 1894,
lay down the foundations in law for their operation.[4] (See
appendix 1 for details.) One must also mention the existence of
the Small Dwellings Acquisition Act of 1899 which permitted the
municipal provision of mortages for owner-occupation. But before
the First World War the sums made available were trifling.

It is necessary also to examine some aspects of government
taxation which had a direct effect on the stream of payments
made by the owner after the purchase of the house had been
completed. Income tax was originally imposed in 1799 and our
present system has grown from the Act of 1803. Under this
certain annual payments, including interest, were paid to their
recipients net of tax. Those persons making the payments, and
deducting tax, could retain the tax so deducted and in this way
would obtain tax relief. Thus in 1914 this relief embraced,
amongst others, owner-occupiers of domestic property making
interest payments on their mortage.

As the author of the *Housing Policy Technical Volume* notes:[5]

> From 1925/26, under a special arrangement, interest on build-
> ing society mortgages was payable in full, without deduction of
> tax. To balance this departure from the normal arrangements
> and to obtain the same relief as would be available if tax were
> deducted and retained, borrowers could set these interest
> payments against their own liabilities for tax. This special
> arrangement was given legislative force in 1951, and consoli-
> dated in the Income Tax Act 1952. Since the introduction of
> PAYE (1944) this relief is normally given to employees through
> the borrower's PAYE coding.

The effect of this was to provide a state subsidy to the home-
owner equal to his (or her) mortgage interest multiplied by his
marginal rate of taxation. Estimates for the aggregate value of
this subsidy exist only since the mid-1960s. (See appendix 4.)
However, before 1939 a married man on average earnings would
have incurred no tax liability, so this subsidy was limited to the
higher income groups.[6]

Thus for mortgagors, i.e. the recipients of loans for house
purchase, income taxation carried with it an automatic subsidy.
But the system also brought with it a most peculiar tax. From its
inception income tax was charged on income from letting proper-

ties, as well as earned income, and this was collected under Schedule A by reference to the assessed rental value of properties. As owner-occupation developed this tax was also charged on home-owners, whose properties clearly could be assessed in terms of their rental value, even though they actually received no rental income. So the Schedule A tax on owner-occupiers (like the subsidy via tax relief described above) was a *by-product* of the general system of income taxation and was not originally introduced as a policy measure designed to impede (or encourage) the growth of this tenure.[7]

Finally, we should note that owner-occupiers have always been liable for the payment of domestic rates, just as council tenants are. Having completed this brief review of the general character of the state's relation in 1914 to the system of owner-occupation, we can turn to consider the extraordinary history of housing policy in the years 1915-21.

2 THE FIRST HOUSING SUBSIDIES

During the First World War housebuilding had come to a virtual standstill, partly because of the war-time building controls. In 1915 the control of rents had also been introduced, in response to working-class agitation in Glasgow. The dwelling shortage, which existed before the war, the accumulated backlog of the war years themselves, and the continued growth of the British population all pointed to the need for a vigorous peace-time housebuilding programme. The government and the civil service realised that the task could not be left to private enterprise, if only because of the fall in real wages in 1914-18 which cut the rent-paying capacity of families, and because of the exceptionally high level of building costs anticipated after the war. Such cool appraisals of the temporary necessity of state intervention were reinforced by the angry social and political climate, for which the appalling housing conditions of British workers were held partly responsible.

In this context the state embarked at the end of the war on a twofold strategy: the stimulation of the state housing sector and the subsidisation of speculative building of small houses for sale or rental. In addition the prolongation of rent control on existing houses was announced in 1920.

Council housing already had a long history and in the half-century preceding 1914 had provided about 24,000 dwellings, of which about 90 per cent had been built after the 1890 Housing of the Working Classes Act. Construction had been carried out both in relation to slum clearance and for general needs purposes. Rents had never been formally subsidised but this too was under consideration in the years before the war's outbreak. The origin of the state sector lay essentially in the failure of both private enterprise and the philanthropic housing movement to provide model dwellings for the working classes at rents they could afford.[8]

In December 1918 Lloyd George, the Prime Minister, promised the building of half a million public sector houses in three years. In July 1919 the Housing and Town Planning Act received the royal assent: it provided a Treasury subsidy sufficient to make possible a huge municipal programme. In the same year the Housing (Additional Powers) Act was passed, which made available a lump sum grant of £130 to £160 to builders constructing small houses for private owners. Marian Bowley has written:[9] 'The subsidy was intended to help the small man who might be in a position to buy a new house if suitably assisted.' In 1920 the 20 per cent betterment levy was terminated; this must have been seen as buttressing the Additional Powers Act by raising the profit element in speculative housing development - as well as in other forms of construction.

Dwellings started within the local authority sector accelerated at such a tremendous rate that in 1921-2, when municipal *completions* reached their first peak, 87,000 council houses were constructed. Unfortunately the movement of speculative building for private owners cannot be traced on a year-by-year basis. However, appendix 2 shows that in the four years 1919-20 to 1922-3 some 26,000 such houses were completed on average each year and we also know that in England and Wales a total of 39,186 dwellings were subsidised under the Additional Powers Act, also peaking in 1921-2.

To understand why these peaks in completions occurred in 1921-2 we must retrace our steps. In the same month in 1918 that Lloyd George was promising the building of half a million homes in a land fit for heroes, the Cabinet also decided to dismantle the war-time system of building licensing. The unrestrained scramble for the outputs of the construction industry created a building boom with a fierce increase in contract prices and soaring wage rates for building workers. The inflation was primarily caused by the private sector's demand for housing and industrial building.[10]

But the boom was short-lived. Indeed, there followed a disastrous slump in the entire economy in 1920-1. The new crisis led the government to seek every means possible to cut public expenditure and the earlier price rises of local authority housing presented the opportunity for attacks on 'municipal profligacy'. With the labour movement enormously weakened by the breakdown of the Triple Alliance of miners, railwaymen and transport workers in April 1921, the government seized its chance to hack back the subsidised housebuilding programme. This dramatic shift in policy was announced in July 1921. No more contracts were to be let for subsidised dwellings in the public sector and the subsidies under the Additional Powers Act were broadly to be limited to certificated houses begun by the end of June 1921. The result of these cutbacks was a very sharp fall in completions by the year 1922-3.[11]

During these years of promise and betrayal in 1918-21, few observers would have noticed that within the state apparatus an

approach to subsidised municipal housing was developing which
thereafter was to be dominant until the present. The clue is
given in a couple of sentences in the first annual report of the
Ministry of Health, the ministry responsible for housing policy.
The 1919 Housing and Town Planning Act required each local
authority to survey the housing needs of its area. The report
pointed out that these estimates of need were to be arrived at
after 'deducting houses likely to be built by other agencies'.[12]
The implication of this should be clear. If we consider the
activity of housebuilding as a circle, the segment of this space
which was to be allocated to the local authority programmes was
what remained *after* the segment likely to be taken up by private
building had first been defined. As time went by this residualist
philosophy, which was already the basis of the small and unsubsidised state programmes before the First World War, was to
assume increasingly sophisticated forms.

3   1921-9: THE BOOM BEGINS

The reversal of the 1918 commitments in July 1921 was not
accompanied by any conviction that housing subsidies could be
completely abandoned. Indeed the view was strongly pressed in
the government and civil service that, for a few years at least,
subsidies were a necessary evil if housebuilding for the respectable working class was to go forward on a substantial scale. As
the economy recovered from the 1920-1 slump, new legislation
was put in train culminating in the Housing Act of 1923 (see
appendix 1).

The Act's central objective was to promote speculative building
of small working-class houses either for sale or rental. The
former was seen as more realistic, at least by Neville Chamberlain, the Conservative Minister of Health, who believed the age
of the small investor in houses had passed. In fact, the great
majority of these dwellings *were* built for sale.[13] Four separate
measures were to be used in implementing the new policy. First,
a lump sum of £75 per unit was payable to builders of approved
houses of modest dimensions completed before October 1925.
Second, the provision of local authority mortgage finance under
the Small Dwellings Acquisition Act was extended. Third, councils
were empowered to guarantee building society advances on small
houses. Fourth, it became possible for local authorities to lend
money to builders constructing modest dwellings.

The 1923 Act was the most important legislative measure specifically concerned with home-ownership before the Second World
War. It made producer subsidies and house purchase finance a
central part of the state's policy, to be placed alongside the
determination of minimum production standards that had followed
the 1875 Public Health Act. Already the ideological purposes of
these developments in policy were becoming clear. Chamberlain
himself, for example, had argued of owner-occupation (in *The*

Times in 1920) that 'every spadeful of manure dug in, every fruit tree planted' converted a potential revolutionary into a citizen.[14]

The 1923 legislation also provided revenue subsidies for local authority housebuilding, at a rate of £6 per house per year for twenty years. But such activity was only to be permitted when the minister was persuaded it was preferable to untrammelled private enterprise. In the same year rent control was extended until 1925, although individual houses were to be decontrolled when sitting tenants vacated them. This, of course, was an incentive to evict. Rent control was later eventually prolonged until 1933 when it was substantially revised.

Table 1.1   Local authority loans sanctioned for the erection or purchase of houses for owner-occupiers in England and Wales 1899-1939

Year	Loans sanctioned (£000)	Dwellings purchasable[a] ('000)
1899-1919	467	na
1919-20	12	neg.
1920-1	203	0.3
1921-2	57	0.1
1922-3	100	0.3
1923-4	1,405	4
1924-5	4,658	13
1925-6	8,613	23
1926-7	9,664	26
1927-8	7,976	23
1928-9	5,664	18
1929-30	5,331	18
1930-1	2,571	9
1931-2	1,737	6
1932-3	1,644	7
1933-4	3,434	13
1934-5	4,155	16
1935-6	5,676	22
1936-7	4,395	17
1937-8	3,410	11
1938-9	2,108	7

Source: MoH *Annual Reports.*

[a] This estimate assumes that 85 per cent cover was provided on the price of each dwelling and that the average price was equal to the average tender price of three-bedroom local authority houses in the same year.

In 1924 John Wheatley, the Minister of Health in the new minority Labour government, raised the subsidies for local authority general needs building as well as those for construction for private rental, but the restrictive rent conditions imposed on the latter had the effect of discouraging speculative builders from taking advantage of the scheme. Wheatley left the 1923 measures intact so that for some time the two Acts operated in parallel. The Labour government also made attempts to change the supply conditions of the industry, which the Conservatives had ignored with the exception of the loans made for builders' working capital. However, the government fell from power before the end of 1924 so rather little was actually achieved here, with the exception of trade union acceptance of apprenticeship dilution.

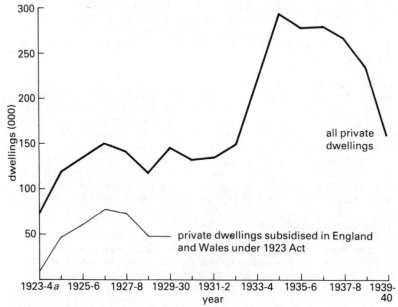

Graph 1.1 Completed dwellings constructed for private owners in Great Britain 1923-40

Source: Appendix 1; MoH, Annual Reports.
a. The figure for 1923-4 is an estimate.

Let us now turn to look at the effects of the 1923 Act. The impact on the supply of local authority mortgages is shown in Table 1.1. The value of loans sanctioned accelerated impressively up to a peak of almost £10 million in 1926-7, although they fell thereafter. Unfortunately we do not know how many advances were actually made. My estimate of the number of dwellings purchasable by this means suggests that it may have risen to as many as 26,000 houses in 1926-7 or 18 per cent of the total number of completions for private owners in that year. Thus the local authorities had come to play an important, if secondary, role in the supply of realisation finance. At the same time, from

1924-5 onwards, councils were guaranteeing 2,000 building society loans each year. The annual loans made available to builders exceeded £4 million only in the two years 1925 and 1926 and never rose above £1 million after 1930-1.

Now let us look at the information on the output of completed houses for private owners. The data are given in Graph 1.1. The movement in output after 1923-4 was absolutely unprecedented on two distinct grounds. First, average annual production was far, far in excess of the pre-war rate of under 100,000 units per year. Second, the great majority of the houses built were for sale to owner-occupiers. Clearly it is of central importance in understanding the housing question between the wars to analyse why so many houses were built for home-ownership. The explanatory factors can be listed under a number of headings.

(a) The rise in real incomes
Personal disposable income per head rose considerably between the wars. In 1920 it stood at £305 and by 1938 had risen to £391 in 1970 prices.[15] Thus *for those in regular employment*, the income available to meet mortgage repayments increased fairly steadily. Because employment growth was most favourable in the south of England and the Midlands with the rise there of motor car and electrical products manufacture, as against the contraction of the coal, textile and ship-building industries in the north, it was in the south that the housebuilding boom was located.

(b) Demographic change
The increase in the part of the population of household-forming age, that most basic of pressures for housing provision, was continuous up to 1914 and reached a peak in the interwar years. In 1921-31, in particular, the annual increase in the adult population exceeded 300,000 persons.[16]

(c) Availability and terms of credit
Almost all households have to rely in part on consumer credit if they buy a house. The amount of mortgage finance increased enormously after 1918. The data on local authority funds are set out in Table 1.1. Much more important were the building societies, whose balances due on mortgages soared from £120 million in 1924 to £636 million in 1937.[17] They survived the depression of the 1930s virtually unscathed. The inflow of funds was maintained both by mortgagors' repayments of principal and interest and by new deposits. Rentiers were attracted by the liquidity of these deposits, the security of the societies' assets and by the relatively high rate of return available compared with company shares and government stock.[18] At the same time the expansion of the building societies was itself dependent on the development of owner-occupation. This constituted a material basis for their professional animosity towards the state housing sector, in so far as it competed with them in meeting housing

need. For the management of the building societies, home-
ownership became the Holy Grail. The desire to expand also led
the societies to devise new ways of facilitating the use of the
abundant savings deposited with them, for example by raising
the ratio of the mortgage advance to the price or valuation of a
house. Moreover, by extending the period of repayment from
an average of 15 years up to 20 to 25 years they raised the total
repaid but cut the *annual* cost. Finally, the fall in rates of
interest after 1931 brought the mortgage rate down from 6 per
cent to 4½ per cent by 1935.[19]

(d) Wage rates and unemployment
Now let us turn from the demand side to the building industry.
Declining money wages in the building materials and construction
sectors meant that costs for the housebuilding firms fell and
subsequently so did house prices. A.L. Bowley's indices of
bricklayers' and labourers' wage rates moved from 104 and 106
respectively in 1924 down to 93 in 1935, then nearly regained
their earlier level by 1939.[20] No data are available on the general
level of house prices for private owners but certainly in the
local authority sector the tender price of three-bedroom non-
parlour houses fell from £408 to £308 in 1924-35.

Wage reductions were in part determined by the high level of
unemployment in Britain between the wars which became particularly severe after the onset of the Great Crash in 1929. The
substantial increase in housing output from 1923-4 shown in
Graph 1.1 was carried out without substantial gains in labour
productivity in speculative building. So the boom could only
take place at all because the sector was able to draw on a vast
reserve army of the unemployed. Far from seeing the movement
of building output as an independent trend tending to moderate
the slump, we should rather see the interwar depression, the
collapse of the great traditional industries, with its multiplier
effects, as a necessary condition on the supply side for the
long construction boom. No slump, no boom. In spite of the
speculative bonanza, unemployment amongst building and contracting workers as a whole was never lower than 10 per cent in
the interwar years and rose to 30 per cent at its peak in 1932.[21]

The quicksilver pace of building for owner-occupation was
matched by tumbling weekly costs of house purchase because of
factors (c) and (d) above. Marian Bowley has suggested that the
cost for a modest but unsubsidised house at a constant mortgage
cover of 70 per cent might have fallen from about 12 shillings
per week in 1925 to less than 8 shillings in 1936, although it
rose sharply again in the following year.[22]

(e) Supply of rental accommodation
Under these conditions the supply of accommodation by rentiers
purchasing new dwellings with their own capital and renting
them out became uncompetitive with home-ownership, *if* the
household had a real choice between the two. After all, the

rentier had management and maintenance costs to bear whilst he could not offer the tenant either the territorial rights or the eventual 'equity' enjoyed by the home-owner. Moreover, the development of the capital market, including the building societies, now offered rentiers a much greater range of placements which, in comparison with 'widowers' houses', were less risky, more liquid, less lumpy and simpler to administer. In brief, if expenditure on rental accommodation were to undercut sufficiently the costs of owner-occupation to make it attractive to the tenant, it would no longer compete with the returns proferred by the money market to the landlord.

The supply of new rental accommodation to those who could *not* afford to buy did take place, as we shall see later, but not on the pre-war scale. Not only was it rather unprofitable, because of minimum use-values in new building, but there was a new form of competition: the rented accommodation vacated by existing households buying their first house! The fear of the introduction of rent control on houses built after 1920 must also have raised the degree of perceived risk.

Having completed this detour through the foundation of home-ownership growth between the wars, I shall now return to policy developments in the period 1925-9.

At the end of 1924 a Conservative government came to power. Within a year it introduced the Land Registration Act which substantially facilitated the growth of owner-occupation by simplifying and cheapening the process of conveying land. (See Appendix 1.) As housebuilding costs fell, and with the labour movement enormously weakened by the smashing defeat of the general strike, Chamberlain in 1926 announced cuts in the subsidies on local authority housing. The reduction took effect on houses completed after September 1927. As a result municipal construction plummeted after 1927-8. Local authority completions had risen from 17 per cent of the total of municipal and private sector output in Britain in 1924-5 up to 46 per cent in 1927-8 because of the vigorous use of the Wheatley subsidies. By 1934-5 it had fallen back to 16 per cent with the reduction in general needs building and the growth of construction for owner-occupation.

Concomitant cuts were made in the subsidies paid to speculative builders. The £75 grant was reduced to £50 with effect from October 1927 and cancelled altogether from October 1929. Graph 1.1 shows that the fall in private dwelling construction in 1927-8 and 1928-9 is accounted for by the sharp drop in subsidised output of some 30,000 units per annum. In England and Wales 1929 was the last year in which the state paid a subsidy direct to builders for housing production for sale. Moreover, 'practically all the houses built by private enterprise with assistance under the Act were built for sale at a price beyond the means of the less well paid workers'.[23]

The Tenth Annual Report of the Ministry of Health, for 1928-9, once again made clear the residualist purpose of local authority

housebuilding. Councils were urged to provide for the needs of
lower-paid workers 'co-operating but not competing with private
enterprise in the provision of houses of the larger and more
expensive types'.[24] Since the ideology of home-ownership embraces
the freedom of choice it purports to introduce in the housing
market, one must point out that in 1929, as in later years, it
was the government's explicit intention to *prevent* such freedom
of choice. The local authorities were *not* to compete with the
speculative builders and building societies. The hostility of the
societies to forms of housing development which would weaken
the demand for mortgage finance interlocked perfectly with the
antipathy of political conservatives in government and the civil
service to capital expenditure by the state, particularly on a
subsidised wage good.

4   1929-39: RESIDUALISM TRIUMPHANT

June 1929 witnessed the installation of the second minority Labour
government. Just like the other parties, Labour had promised
to recommence slum clearance if returned to office. With the
uncontroversial passage of the 1930 Housing Act, the party was
now committed to a twofold objective in its local authority housing programme, redevelopment as well as general needs construction. With respect to owner-occupation, the government
pursued policies no different from those of the Conservatives.
A paragraph in the Eleventh Annual Report of the Ministry of
Health, for 1929-30, which the minister, Arthur Greenwood,
must have either written or approved, gives an insight into the
leadership's attitude to home-ownership and social mix:[25]

> Many local authority and social workers have borne testimony
> to the advantage of having a considerable number of owner-
> occupiers among the working-class population. An interesting
> report received in the course of the year showed one local
> authority, previously sceptical, to have been impressed by
> the improvement in the standard of upkeep of homes on those
> of their estates on which there was a considerable proportion
> of owner-occupiers, and to have found the care and attention
> devoted to the houses owned by their occupiers to have set
> an example which was ultimately followed by their rent-paying
> neighbours. It is, however, generally the case that the need
> of the working class, particularly of the lower paid members,
> cannot be met if they are required to purchase houses. Lack
> of capital, or the need of comparatively frequent removal in
> the course of employment, are in many cases compelling reasons
> for this.

By the summer of 1931 the international economic situation was
at its most critical. In his passion to pursue deflationary policies
the Prime Minister, Ramsay MacDonald, with the connivance of

King George V and Stanley Baldwin, sabotaged his own party's
government and formed what was called a National Government.
In fact, its support relied on the Conservatives and Liberals
in the House of Commons.[26] By 1933 there had been engineered
a dramatic transformation in housing policy. The subsidies
available for general needs building inherited from the Wheatley
Act were abolished. Henceforth councils were to pursue slum
clearance and redevelopment alone, to which was added the task
of overcrowding abatement in 1935. New construction for other
purposes was assigned to the speculative builders.

The basis for this shift back to the sanitary policy of the
1870s was both the perceived state expenditure crisis and the
extraordinary boom in private enterprise construction. As Graph
1.1 shows, private completions virtually doubled in two years
after 1932-3! In 1933, too, rent control was strengthened by
terminating the decontrol provisions of 1923. Presumably this
was in cognisance of the fact that municipal general needs building was being stopped at a time when there was still a huge
housing shortage. The number of households was still 1 million
in excess of dwellings at the 1931 census.

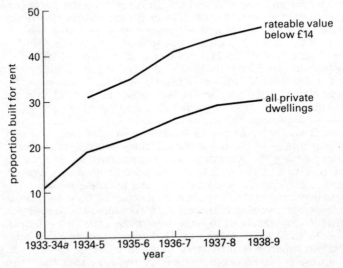

Graph 1.2 Proportion of private dwellings in England and Wales
built for rent 1933-9

Source: MoH, Annual Reports.
a. 1933-4 is for last six months only.

The rationale of the 1933 reorientation included the expressed
belief that the fall in building costs and the rate of interest
would bring back 'investment' in new houses for rental.[27] For

this purpose the Housing Act contained a section intended to raise the building societies' mortgage cover for capitalists buying houses to rent. It appears that this was intended as a cosmetic device to hide the ugly face of the 1933 Act.[28]

Annual data on the proportion of private dwellings built to let appear first only in the second half of 1933-4. They are illustrated in Graph 1.2. The graph suggests the following conclusions: first, throughout the period 1933-9 construction for sale to home-owners far exceeded construction for rental. Second, the proportion of construction for rental did increase during the period, from 11 per cent up to 30 per cent over five years. Third, the rental proportion for the most modest dwellings was higher than the overall proportion and this too increased.

Table 1.2 Increase in private dwellings for sale and rental, and the increase in requirements in England and Wales October 1934 to March 1939 (thousands)

Rateable value of new houses	Additional houses	Requirements[a]	Surplus
Up to £13		300 + 127	433 − 427 = 6
For letting	174		
For sale	259		
£14 to £26		150	748 − 150 = 598
For letting	131		
For sale	470		
£27 to £78			
For sale	147		

Source: Marian Bowley, *Housing and the State*, London, Allen & Unwin, 1945, Table 14.

[a] Requirements for houses for new families were some 450,000 units, divided in the ratio 2:1 below and above a rateable value of £14 (see Bowley, op. cit., p. 13). In addition there was an existing deficit of 127,000 below £14 dwellings.

The private housebuilding boom in the 1930s was very clearly not producing dwellings for those in housing need, that is, the mass of the people who could not afford to buy a house at all. This point is developed in Table 1.2.

Only 26 per cent of aggregate private output was built for rent. It is true that this was supplemented by 84,000 houses put up by the councils under their general needs and decrowding programmes. But this was more than offset by councils clearing more houses than they constructed in their redevelopment activities.[29]

For the more modest houses with an annual rateable value of up to £13, Table 1.2 shows there was an almost perfect balance between output and requirements, although again I must stress that the proportion built for sale was dominant, 60 per cent of

the total. For the more expensive houses there was a huge
surplus of production over requirements. In this situation why
was it that the market did not collapse like a house of cards in
a crisis of over-production?

The answer in general terms is straightforward, although the
detailed mechanics were complex. The bulk of the output of
houses built for sale was purchased by households of a very
mixed social composition including the regularly employed and
better paid skilled manual and clerical workers, teachers,
government employees, families with small and medium-size
businesses, and the class of executive and management personnel.
Some were new households, even more were households moving
out of existing rented accommodation. The finance for house
purchase came largely from the building societies and, as Table
1.1 shows, from an increased provision by the local state in the
four or five years after 1932-3. At the same time, as we have
seen, there was also an increasing provision of new privately
rented houses, about 66,000 per annum between 1934-5 and
1938-9.

The out-migration of existing families generated a huge volume
of vacancies. In some cases the vacancy would be sold off by
the landlord, who might put his capital into a more liquid form.
In the case of large properties, these might be converted, again
either for sale or rental. The vacancies released, where they
were not left empty or converted into offices and other uses,
would be available for the mass of the rent-paying population to
move into. This process would eventually alleviate the degree of
overcrowding and multi-occupation. Redistribution must have
been spatially concentrated and haphazard since vacancies would
be generated only in those areas where substantial out-migration
had occurred. New private building was predominantly in the
Home Counties. The slums were predominantly in the north.

A crucial feature of this process, one that makes impossible
any simple contemporary parallel, is that a very high proportion
of those purchasing houses must have been first-time buyers.
They were therefore not constrained by having to sell their
existing house in order to buy a newly constructed one. It was
the landlord who had to find a new use or a new tenant or himself had to sell. On this score the interests of building capital
and rentier capital were diametrically opposed.

The excess of construction for sale over household formation
amongst the higher income social strata led speculative builders
increasingly to attempt to penetrate more modest income bands
in the later 1930s. In part this was made possible by the return
of rentier capital into the housing market, indicated in Graph
1.2. The perceptible quickening in local authority mortgages
also made some contribution. Another device, already referred
to in the previous section, was an increase in the mortgage cover
provided by the building societies. This was done in the following way. The society advanced 75 per cent cover in the normal
way against the security of the house and a further 20 per cent

against the collateral security of sums deposited with it by the
builder himself. As the buyer repaid the total loan, so too did
he redeem the builder's collateral. Possibly as much as one-half
of the business of some large societies was carried out through
'the builders' pool', as it was known, at the end of the decade.[30]
The drawback for the builder was that in thus moving down-
market he reduced the speed of rotation of his capital. In its
turn this led to jerry-building. The Borders's case, a brilliantly
conducted self-defence by Mrs Elsy Borders of her mortgage
strike on the ground of extensive defects in her new house,
built under the builders' pool, brought the new arrangements
the most unwelcome publicity.[31] Borders's challenge to the
legality of the builders' pool failed in the courts but swiftly led
to the passage of the 1939 Building Societies Act whose stringent
definition of acceptable forms of collateral effectively terminated
the pool arrangements. The state, it seems, had become extremely
sensitive to any threat to the societies' perceived integrity.

It was the insurance companies which provided a second and
more permanent means of increasing what I shall call the cover
ratio, i.e. the proportion of the price (or valuation) of a house
covered by the mortgage loan. In return for a single premium
paid by the borrower to an insurance company, it guaranteed to
compensate the building society for any loss sustained on the
sum loaned which was in excess of the society's normal practice.
This innovation survives today as the Building Societies
Indemnity Scheme.

The rise in employment and wage rates as rearmament got
under way in 1937-8 forced up builders' costs and made their
down-market objectives more difficult to obtain. This explains
the sharp contraction in private housebuilding of 30,000 units in
1938-9. In that year, with the local authorities fully embarked
on slum clearance and redevelopment, the proportion of municipal
building within total private and local authority output had
shifted up again to 34 per cent.

It was only by the end of the decade that we have our first
statistical picture of the importance of owner-occupation within
certain occupational categories. One inquiry in 1937-8 showed
that amongst the families of insured workers in urban areas, i.e.
manual workers, and non-manual workers with incomes up to
£250 per year, 18 per cent were owner-occupiers. In 1938-9 a
sample of budgets of civil servants, local government officials
and teachers recorded that as many as 65 per cent were home-
owners.[32]

The scale of private and public output between the wars meant
that by 1938, in England and Wales, there was an approximate
balance between the number of households and houses. This
was not inconsistent with the continuation of an appalling housing problem since the crude dwelling balance does not indicate
the condition of the stock, nor its distribution between households, nor the number of concealed households, nor the price
and convenience of situation of individual habitations.

Table 1.3 The size and growth of the housing stock and its distribution
         between tenures in England and Wales 1914-38 (millions)

	Owner-occupied	Local authority	Private landlords and miscellaneous	Total
Stock of dwellings in 1914: (units)	0.8	neg.	7.1	7.9
(%)	10	neg.	90	100
1914-38: new building purchases (+),	+1.8	+1.1	+0.9	+3.8
sales (−),	+1.1	neg.	−1.1	0
demolitions/changes of use	neg.	neg.	−0.3	−0.3
Stock of dwellings in 1938: (units)	3.7	1.1	6.6	11.4
(%)	32	10	58	100

Source: HPTV, Part I, Tables 1.23 and 24.

Table 1.3 presents a statistical summary of the events of the
interwar years. The growth in home-ownership was remarkable,
more than quadrupling in absolute terms. Note that almost 40
per cent of the increase derives from 'purchases', that is, sales
of formerly privately rented dwellings. This was the hidden
history of the post 1914 period. The expansion of state housing
was substantial, although the scale was well short of speculative
building for sale. The non-existence of any municipalisation
programme, and therefore no element corresponding to owner-
occupier 'purchases' in the table, also contributed to the absolute
disparity in 1938 between the municipal and owner-occupied
stock. The privately rented sector contracted over this quarter
of the century, of course, but only by 7 per cent of the 1914
total. Building for rental, particularly in the 1930s, had gone
far to offset the sale of previously rented dwellings and the
demolition of the slums.
    These remarks on stock dynamics bring to a close this very
brief review of the situation in 1914, the violent reversals of
interwar housing policy, and the nature of the first long boom
in housebuilding for owner-occupation in Britain. Chapter 2
considers the impact of the Second World War and the period of
reconstruction immediately thereafter.

2 WAR AND RECONSTRUCTION

1 THE WAR YEARS

We have already seen that the approach of war was associated with a sharp fall in private housing completions. As the armed forces and the war-related industries expanded, they bid labour away from the housebuilding industry. Output contracted rapidly, as Graph 2.1 shows. These market forces were under-pinned in October 1940 by the issue of Defence Regulation 56A which specified that it was:

> unlawful to carry out, except under a licence from the Minister of Works, any work of construction, reconstruction, alteration, decoration, repair, demolition or maintenance on a building or on any other fixed work of construction where the cost of the work exceeded the financial limits prescribed from time to time by an order made by the Minister.

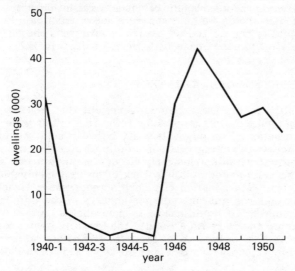

Graph 2.1 Completed dwellings constructed for private owners in Great Britain 1940-51

Source: Appendix 1.
Note: The information on starts does not exist.

17

The effect was that the number of insured male building workers in Britain fell from 1,362,000 in July 1939 to its nadir of 496,000 in July 1944.[1]

The willingness of the state to impose severe cuts in the scale of housing construction in times of war or economic crisis derives from the fact that the annual output of new dwellings is only 1 or 2 per cent of the total stock. Thus production can be virtually eliminated with only a very small *immediate* impact on per capita consumption. This huge disparity between output change and its effect on dwelling consumption is itself a manifestation of the durability of the housing stock.[2]

Thus the war brought a huge reduction in new construction and the routine practices of maintenance and repair, as well, one might add, as the reintroduction of rent control in 1939. But it also brought the Blitz of 1940 and the flying bomb attacks which began in June 1944. These entirely destroyed 200,000 dwellings and damaged 3½ million more, so that the main thrust of the housebuilding work that *did* continue after 1940 was the repair of war damage. This had been put on a sound financial footing in 1941 with the introduction of war damage compensation (see appendix 1).

The grim circumstances of 1945 were exacerbated by the backlog of slum clearance abandoned in 1939. Moreover, there had been a quantum leap in the number of marriages in 1939 and 1940, whilst the number in 1941-50 was greater than in any previous decade. These marriages, of course, raised sharply the number of households seeking separate accommodation.[3] In addition, in spite of the deaths we associate with war, the British population increased by a little over a million in 1939-45.

2   THE FORMULATION OF A STRATEGY

Thus the situation facing the Labour government that came to power after the general election of July 1945 cried out for the most purposive action. The huge disparity between supply and demand, between the existing scale of building materials and construction output in industries stripped of their resources by the war and the demand for building work of every conceivable kind, made a clear determination of priorities necessary. If not, a runaway inflation was guaranteed, particularly in the light of the huge accumulation of liquid assets by households and businesses during the war. As a result, the existing system of building controls was prolonged, at least for the period when aggregate output capacity was being restored to something like its pre-war level.

Let us look briefly at the nature of these controls. In 1945 the Supplies and Services (Transitional Powers) Act renewed Defence Regulation 56A, from which I have already quoted in the preceding section. This regulation established three broad categories of building: licensed work, authorised work and direct

work. Licensed work was done for a private individual or body
and in general these licences were issued by the Ministry of
Works. With authorised work the client was a public body such
as a local authority or a nationalised industry and here the
prior authorisation of the relevant government department was
required. Direct work was done specifically for a government
department and this was excluded from the scope of the regulation. In addition there was all the work done that fell below
the licensing limit. In 1945-8 this was set at £10 in value per
job in any six-month period.[4]

The intention was that an Official Steering Committee would
strike a rough balance between the capacity of the building
materials and construction industry and the aggregate demand
for licensed, authorised, direct and unlicensed building. There
was virtually no control over building labour, whilst before 1947
the allocation of building materials was carried out on a voluntary
basis, with the exception of timber and steel. The latter were
distributed by means of quarterly allocations issued by an inter-
departmental Materials Committee. Evidently the whole system of
control rested on the efficient and effective manipulation of
legally permissible supplies to different sets of clients.

With respect to new housebuilding, speculative construction
was a form of licensed work. The licences were issued on behalf
of the Ministry of Works by officers appointed by the local
authorities. They were authorised to specify a starting date
before which a project could not be begun. The intention was
that close control could be maintained on an area basis over the
volume of work being started in each time period. Similar powers
were exercised from the regional offices of the Ministry of Works
for all other licensed work. Local authority housebuilding fell
under the authorised work category and, of course, was controlled by the Ministry of Health. Only in April 1947 was the
system of earliest starting dates extended to council housing.
With respect to the repair and maintenance of the existing stock
of private housing, this was unlicensed, in principle at least,
only if it fell below the licensing limits.

The government's housing strategy required the distribution
of housing production resources on a planned basis reflecting
Labour's political values. Figure 2.1 illustrates the multiple
forms that housing production can take. Conversion, maintenance and repair were all encouraged where these activities were
seen to promise the restitution of property damaged in the war
and the bringing into use of dwellings that would otherwise be
unoccupied. The improvement of physically sound property was
not encouraged before 1949, and very little slum clearance was
permitted whilst the imbalance between households and occupied
dwellings was so severe. The rebuilding of houses destroyed
by enemy action was, however, unlicensed.

Greenfield site development was the responsibility of both the
local authorities and the speculative builders. The rationale for
the division of output between these two was set out with

unusual clarity and forcefulness:[5]

> As it was impossible to meet all housing needs at once, an
> order of priorities had to be adopted. First and foremost came,
> by Government decision, the needs of those who were living
> under the worst conditions. The great majority of these were
> among the lower income groups of the population, and their
> needs could only be met by an agency which was in a position
> to select occupants according to the degree of hardship they
> were enduring, irrespective of the amount they could afford
> to pay. Local authorities provide such an agency, hence the
> concentration on the building of houses for letting by local
> authorities, with private enterprise, which normally builds
> mainly for sale, playing a subsidiary part.

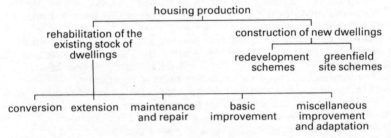

Figure 2.1 A taxonomy of housing production

Housing production as a whole is divided into two fundamental
groups of activity. The first group is the construction of
entirely new dwellings and is itself composed of two families:
the production of houses on sites which have been cleared of a
pre-existing stock of buildings ('redevelopment schemes'); and
housebuilding on other sites ('greenfield site schemes'). The
second group refers to productive activity carried out on the
existing housing stock and I call this rehabilitation. It is composed of five families in this classification. 'Conversion' refers
to changes wrought on an existing structure to change the composition of the dwellings it encloses. 'Extension' embraces the
addition of entirely new living space to an existing house.
'Maintenance and repair' includes a host of small or larger scale
works which attempt to check the process of physical deterioration or to put right or replace parts of the house or its fixed equipment which function imperfectly. 'Improvement' indicates the
addition of entirely new facilities in the house. 'Basic improvement' here includes the installation only of an internal WC, a
bath or shower, a sink, a wash-hand basin, and the supply of
hot and cold water to bath/shower, sink and basin. 'Miscellaneous
improvement and adaptation' embraces all those productive
activities on the stock which do not fall in one of the other five
families. I shall use the term 'housing renewal' to refer jointly
to redevelopment and rehabilitation.

Even what licensed speculative building *was* permitted had to
fall within very modest maximum levels of price and area. The
constraint exercised on private enterprise building made
irrelevant the Pole Committee's recommendations that, as in
1918, it should be subsidised by the Exchequer.[6] By the beginning of 1947 the proportionate contribution of the speculative
sector was set at one-fifth of total new housing output.[7] The
reliance on state housing production was accompanied by central
opposition to any sale of council houses.

3 LAND POLICY

Before we go on to look at the implementation of the government's
housing strategy, it is necessary to look at another dimension of
policy, that concerning the land. The massive and anarchic
growth of the great conurbations in the nineteenth century had
long since convinced Britain's town and country planners that
the spatial pattern of urban growth required to be controlled
and structured. The immense expansion of the owner-occupied
suburbs in south-east England between the wars had served to
buttress this presumption. Moreover the extensive damage and
destruction caused by enemy air attacks on our cities in 1940-5
clearly required government intervention in the land market if
city centre redevelopment was to proceed efficiently in the post-
war years. All of this, as well as the evident injustice of fortunes
being made merely through the ownership of land of appreciating
value, led the Labour government to introduce new legislation
embracing rights in land. Indeed, the manifesto of 1945 had
promised: 'Labour believes in land nationalisation and will work
towards it'.[8]

The 1947 Town and Country Planning Act was a substantial
retreat from this position, but nevertheless it did constitute a
sharp break with the past. Its basis was that landowners would
no longer enjoy the right to develop the land in whatever way
they thought fit, and because of the loss of this right they were
to receive once-and-for-all compensation. Instead, the right to
permit (or to veto) development was vested in the local authorities. Anyone wishing to develop a site had first to secure the
relevant council's planning permission. Where development *was*
permitted, the developer was to pay a development charge equal
to 100 per cent of the increase in the value of the land resulting
from the permission to develop.

At the same time the Act provided for each local authority to
prepare a development plan indicating the manner in which it
proposed that land in its area should be used, including allocat-
ing areas for residential purposes, for about twenty years ahead.
The plan was not binding. In principle it was to promote a spatial
pattern of uses that was both attractive and economically efficient,
to establish a geographical logic within which specific decisions
of development control would find their place.

4   STRATEGY IMPLEMENTATION

Graph 2.1 shows that speculative housebuilding moved off at a
very brisk pace after the war's end, so that by 1947 the annual
number of dwellings completed was already in excess of 40,000
units. In the local authority sector the new programme began
quickly enough but the evidence suggests that the time-lag
between start and completion of the average dwelling was much
slower than with speculative building. As a result, far from
playing its planned subsidiary role, the private sector in 1946
and 1947 provided respectively 55 and 30 per cent of new housing completions. Construction contractors probably chose to
employ fewer men per dwelling under construction in the state
sector than speculative builders did on their own estates. The
reason for this was that the speed of rotation of capital in
speculative building varies inversely with the time-lag between
start and sale, whilst in the local authority sector builders are
paid on a six-week basis for work completed. Therefore builders
have a profit incentive to complete each dwelling quickly only
in the case of speculative development.

By 1947 the strength and the weakness of building controls
were becoming evident. Their main contribution had been to
prevent a runaway post-war inflation in building prices.[9] But
as instruments of economic planning capable of securing a particular volume and structure of production, they had their defects.
For they worked essentially through their negative character:
they sought to *prevent* building companies from carrying out
medium-and large-scale projects that were not licensed or
authorised. Thus the state lacked the ability *positively* to channel
construction work into defined tasks and perforce had to rely on
the response of private companies to the effective demand
exercised by local authorities. In brief, the means of production
in the construction industry still remained in private hands.
This weakness in implementation was not a technical oversight:
it followed directly from the general commitment of the Labour
government to strengthen and expand capitalism in Britain con-
jointly with a major programme of nationalisation and the fiscal
regulation of the macro-economy along Keynesian lines, and
therefore to allow production decisions to be taken largely by
the capitalist class.

However, in the event, even these negative measures worked
unsatisfactorily. There was a political inability to control tightly
the scale of 'direct' and 'authorised' work. There was also a
widespread evasion of controls in construction activities (not
merely in the housing field) expended on the existing stock of
buildings. Individually, these were of modest scale, largely
carried out by the thousands of small and medium building firms,
and, with a low profile in terms of their visibility.

To complete the vicious circle, the mismatch between demand
and supply, that is the overloading of the industry both
nationally and within local sub-markets, actually served to re-

duce the level of labour productivity, most obviously where materials shortages held up work and, as we have seen, in spreading the labour supply over too many council houses 'under construction'. The terrible winter of 1946-7 was a natural disaster which compounded these other difficulties. By March 1947, in an attempt 'to avoid the dissipation of labour and materials over too many houses', the government took up a much more restrictive stance on the approval of state housing tenders and the issue of licences for speculative housebuilding.[10]

In the summer of 1947 the country was confronted suddenly with a major economic crisis, the roots of which can be directly traced to events in 1945. The foreign policy of the Labour administration after the war had been intended to maintain our role as a world power and, with respect specifically to the government's imperialist ambitions, to continue as far as was possible our political, economic and military dominance of dozens of underdeveloping countries. Success in the attainment of this strategic goal, in an age of our own relative decline, was seen to depend critically on our alliance with the United States. As a consequence, when the most violent tensions were generated between the ambition of the state and its means to fulfil it, manifesting itself for example in a balance of payments crisis, it was to the USA and to institutions like the IMF which the USA controlled that the government turned for succour.

In 1945 the USA had made a dollar loan to Britain on the condition that the Bank of England would restore the convertibility of sterling. This was done in July 1947. A massive run-down in our reserves took place so that in August convertibility had to be suspended. Amongst a number of deflationary measures taken during the crisis, a general cut in new housebuilding was decided upon. In the case of speculative building, from mid-August the issue of further licences was suspended save for certain exempted categories.[11] Between December 1947 and December 1948 the number of male employees engaged in the construction of new houses fell by 19 per cent, from 273,000 to 221,000.[12]

The effect of the March and August restrictions and of the 1947 development charges on private sector completions was very marked, as Graph 2.1 shows. But with state housing, the backlog of dwellings under construction allowed completions to rise in 1948 before falling in 1949 with the result that completions in the two sectors were not in the planned 4:1 ratio in 1948 but stood at 5.5:1, from which it shifted only marginally in the following two years.

5 AFTER THE CRISIS

In 1948 the dominant view in the Cabinet was that exports and industrial investment should take precedence over the needs of the family. (The military programme was shielded from the cold wind of austerity and, indeed, in 1948 Britain launched a new war, against the communist-led independence movement in Malaya.) In the spring a decision was taken to maintain the total number of dwellings under construction at 200,000. With a stable rate of starts and an average twelve-month construction period this would have given, curiously enough, an annual rate of completions *also* equal to 200,000. In fact, completed total output in 1949, 1950 and 1951 of private and local authority houses was 193,000, 193,000 and 185,000 units respectively.[13]

After June 1948 the local authorities once again were allowed to issue licences for speculative housebuilding up to one-fifth of their new allocations. They were asked to satisfy themselves that the issue of a licence served a housing need comparable with that served by the erection of a house built by them.[14] As from July the licensing limit itself was eased from £10 in each six-month period to £100 per annum. In November the priority distribution schemes for materials, which had been given statutory backing in 1947, were abolished, steel and timber accepted.[15]

In 1949 a legislative innovation, which in the long term was to be of great importance, was contained in the new Housing Act. For the first time owner-occupiers and all private landlords were eligible to receive, at the discretion of the local authority, grants towards the improvement or conversion of their houses. The total improvement cost was not to fall below £100 nor to exceed £600 but within these limits the state provided a contribution to meet 50 per cent of the costs. The houses had to have a pre-dicted 'life' of at least thirty years and provide accommodation at a sixteen-point standard. This was the first time in Britain that government had made a general commitment to subsidising the rehabilitation of dwellings.

In the same year, 1949, there was a new balance of payments crisis, this time because of the American recession and specu-lation on the devaluation of the pound. Sterling was, indeed, devalued in September. As part of a package of measures the government decided to reduce the housing programme by £35 million through a reduction of the number of dwellings under construction in 1950 by $12\frac{1}{2}$ per cent. The plan was that the sword would fall on the speculative sector and in November 1949 the issue of licences was suspended. In the following February, when Labour fought a general election and barely held on to its overall majority, general issue was resumed. At their discretion the local authorities were to allow up to one-tenth of local new building to be carried out privately. Then, only two months later, the Chancellor of the Exchequer announced that the hous-ing programme was to be restored to its previous level.[16]

As a result of these winter 1949-50 restrictions and the con-tinuing effect of the 100 per cent development charge, private completions fell to only 23,000 units in 1951 and total new dwell-ing output by councils and private builders amounted to only 185,000 units. In contrast with the constraints and cuts in housing, the British engagement in colonial expeditions, the Cold

War and, in 1950, the war in Korea had led to an increase in war expenditure as a proportion of national product from 7 per cent in 1948 to 10½ per cent in 1952.

In October of 1951 a general election took place and a Conservative majority was returned. Harold Macmillan took charge of the Ministry of Housing and Local Government which henceforth was the locus of the state's housing responsibilities. By that year, because of the war-time destruction and the loss of output in the preceding twelve years, the 1938 surplus of dwellings over households in England and Wales of 100,000 had become a deficit of 700,000 units.[17] Many regarded the Tory promise of a magnificent new housing programme as crucial to their electoral success.

The period from the summer of 1945 through to the autumn of 1951 was quite unique in the history of British housing for it witnessed the regulation of aggregate production to meet the housing needs of the mass of the working people. This had never happened before and has not happened since. The circumstances were the marked deterioration in housing conditions as a result of the war; the control of the levers of the state by a party that was profoundly committed to advancing the material well-being of the working class, something Aneurin Bevan symbolised above all; and 'a deep popular expectation of new beginnings'.[18] Bevan had stood the residualism of Chamberlain on its head.

Inevitably the regulatory system suffered from setbacks of a natural or quasi-technical kind, such as the 1946-7 winter, the shortage of indigenous timber and the difficulties inherent in controlling the demand for small-scale rehabilitation. But, in my view, what broke the back of the programme - the cut of August 1947, the 200,000 unit constraint of 1948 and the cut of November 1949 - was the Labour government's unwillingness to expand the public ownership of the means of construction production and its determination to pursue an imperial and world-power role for Britain. These were the maggots in the social democratic apple.

In retrospect the war and the period of Labour reconstruction constitute an interregnum. It follows the first boom in house-building for owner-occupation of the 1920s and 1930s and precedes the second boom which ran from 1951 until the late 1960s. It is this period that is examined in chapter 3.

3 THE SECOND BOOM

1 INTRODUCTION

When Harold Macmillan took office in October 1951, his first
objective was to raise substantially the annual number of housing
starts, predominantly in the local authority and speculative
sectors, until they attained the Conservatives' 300,000 target
for Britain. Thereafter aggregate output was to be held steady.
Council housing starts leapt from 171,000 in 1951 to 231,000 in
1953, although the standards of design were brutally slashed.[1]

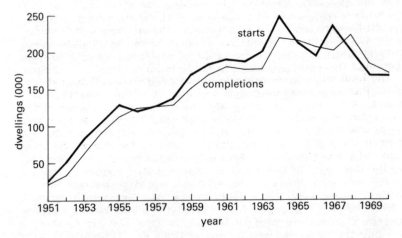

Graph 3.1 Dwellings constructed for private owners in Great
Britain 1951-70

Source: Appendix 2.

With respect to private housebuilding, it was essentially a
matter of unleashing the industry. Licensing was progressively
relaxed and eventually abolished in November 1954 when Defence
Regulation 56A was revoked.[2] Controls on steel and timber had
ended in 1953. Furthermore, there was a most important change
in land legislation. Whilst the system of planning controls was
continued (by the end of 1954 most of the statutory development
plans had been submitted although the bulk were not approved
until 1959), the 1953 Town and Country Planning Act completely

abolished the taxation of development values. In principle this
meant that the difference of the value of the land between, let
us say, its use in farming and its use in housing was no longer
appropriated by the state. Instead it accrued either to the landowner, encouraging land sales, or to the developer, stimulating
land purchases, or both. The local authorities were even cajoled
into purchasing land for resale to speculative builders in order
to provide an adequate supply of construction sites.[3]

The effect of the termination of development land taxation and
of production controls is shown in Graph 3.1. Private housebuilding starts and completions both increased rapidly. The
upward trend was maintained for more than a decade with the
number of units completed curving through its maximum in the
years 1964-8. Thus the period of Conservative power which came
to an end in 1964, largely coincides with the second boom since
1918 in construction for home-ownership. With respect to the
target set in 1951, this was first attained in terms of total housing completions in 1953 and thereafter only in 1958 and 1959 did
they fall substantially short of 300,000 units per year.[4]

Two further aspects of state policy towards owner-occupation
should be mentioned here. The first concerns the sale of council
houses, the second the new building by-laws. In 1945-51, as we
have seen, central policy was to oppose any selling of municipal
dwellings. The first change was announced in recommendations
to the local authorities contained in circular 64/52 of August
1952. Purchase was now possible either by sitting tenants or,
with a vacant house, by a person in need of accommodation for
his or her own use. The 1952 Housing Act repealed the existing
requirement that the best price had to be realised on sale but
allowed the municipalities to prohibit resale or rental within five
years of purchase. Eight years later, in circular 5/60, a minimum
selling price of twenty times the annual rent was recommended
on pre-war houses but the existing restrictions on resale and
rental were dropped on post-war houses. As Table 8.1 on p. 119
shows, the annual sale of council houses in England and Wales
in 1951-64 never exceeded 3,000 units.

The second policy development was the introduction in 1953
of a new set of model building by-laws, the first since 1937.
These marked a break with the past in setting down requirements
functionally; in their much wider use of British standards; in
their insertion of quantitative requirements for fire resistance;
and in their recognition of the need for adequate thermal insulation.[5] Later, in the Public Health Act of 1961, legislation permitted for the first time the drawing-up of *national* building
regulations. This was done in 1965 and they came into force in
1966.

2 THE GRAND DESIGN

For those who believe that the British state has never had a
national housing policy, and there are many, the period 1951-61
perhaps more than any other provides a refutation. These years
witnessed the preparation and then the implementation of a comprehensive strategy of great clarity. The central quantitative
element was to maintain total output at about 300,000 new dwellings each year, a target successfully achieved, as has already
been said. The qualitative dimension concerned the respective
roles of speculative building and state housing construction and
it was this that revealed the essentially residualist nature of the
programme. Private construction was encouraged to surge ahead
whilst public housing was once again confined to making up the
shortfall of speculative output below the aggregate target.
   In order to understand the *nature* of council housebuilding
we must comprehend the Conservative perspective on housing
renewal: renewal was to be partitioned. The local authorities
were to carry through the process of slum clearance, redevelopment and overspill whilst the private sector was to be responsible
for the activities of rehabilitation. In addition the municipalities
were induced to build for the elderly. The common feature of
redevelopment and of building for the mass of the pensioners
was that neither activity would be carried out without state
intervention because neither was profitable to building capital
at the minimum use-values required by the state in its public
health legislation. General needs construction was to be entirely
the preserve of private enterprise. The government, therefore,
had returned to the housing philosophy of Chamberlain in the
golden years of the slump.
   Graph 3.1 shows the irresistible rise of speculative building
after 1951, virtually all of which was for owner-occupation. The
annual compound rate of growth in completions up to 1964 was
19.1 per cent. A necessary condition of this flourishing progress
was for the building society movement to return to its old
strength. In fact advances on mortgages, in terms of their
numbers, increased rapidly after the war until the end of the
1940s when they had reached a figure of some 300,000 (see
appendix 5). Thereafter the number fluctuated around a plateau
(with a particularly sharp fall in 1956) until the late 1950s, after
which advances again soared away, exceeding the half-million
mark for the first time in 1964. The average sum advanced per
loan had risen from £488 in 1940 to £1,950 in 1964. It goes without
saying that the mortgages advanced were not confined to new
developments but were also used for transactions in the existing
stock.
   Loans for house purchase by the local authorities were also
substantially expanded after the war. In England and Wales their
number rose in a volatile progression from 21,000 units in 1951-2
up to 77,000 in 1964 (see appendix 6). The councils provided
over 13 per cent of the total of similar building society advances.

The average sum advanced per loan shifted from £1,102 in 1951-2 up to £2,153 in 1964 whilst total public expenditure on these advances increased from £23 million to £166 million over the same period.

With respect to the interest rate charged on local authority loans, there was an important difference between the principal enabling Acts. Under the Small Dwellings Acquisition Act the rate of interest charged was tied to the local loans rate prevailing one month before the settlement of the terms of the advance. This meant local authorities might make a loss on such transactions in a period of rising interest rates. There was therefore a preference for making loans under the 1949 Housing Act which allowed the local authorities to fix their own rate with the approval of the minister. In 1956 he agreed that under the 1949 Act interest rates set should lie within a range of $\frac{1}{4}$ to $1\frac{1}{4}$ per cent above the PWLB rate at the time the mortgage was signed. In 1957 an increase to $6\frac{3}{8}$ per cent in the Board rate on loans of more than fifteen years led to a reduction in municipal advances. Some feared that when interest rates fell, loans would be prematurely repaid, leaving the authority saddled with debts taken out at a high interest. Other authorities felt it unfair to burden mortgagors for twenty years with a high rate of interest which might prove to be only a transient phenomenon in the money market. The upshot was that in circular 54/57 the minister agreed to consider proposals under Section 4 of the 1949 Housing Act by which the municipalities could issue mortgages at *variable* interest rates. Such rates were not to be less than the current market rate and the scheme was not to be subsidised from the rates.[6] Clearly the shift in government monetary policy after 1951 towards dearer money and the increasing volatility of interest rates on the capital market was forcing the councils to amend their procedures on the money they themselves lent out.

I now turn briefly to the issue of local authority guarantees on building society advances. In the years preceding 1954 there had been negligibly few such arrangements. A new intervention was therefore made in circular 42/54 which suggested two alternative schemes, subsequently fused into a single model in circular 45/55. The councils were to guarantee excess advances by the building societies so that the mortgagor's own deposit on a modest dwelling would be reduced to as little as £125. The new scheme applied to houses costing less than £2,500 and enabled the building societies to advance up to 90 per cent on a pre-1918 house and up to 95 per cent on a post-1918 house. In the years 1954-5 to 1960, the number of such guarantees ran at about 10,000 each year but it declined thereafter, in spite of modifications to the model, and the numbers were negligible in the 1970s.

The objective of the guarantees was, in part, to facilitate purchases of the older stock of housing. In 1958 an entirely new approach to this goal was introduced in the White Paper *House Purchase* and the scheme was embodied in the 1959 House Purchase

and Housing Act. Trustee status was conferred on building
societies entering into certain agreements with the government
and to these societies the Exchequer made twenty-year loans.
Some £100 million was made available for the scheme. The basic
agreement was that the societies in question would use this
extra finance to provide 95 per cent mortgages to credit-worthy
borrowers on pre-1919 houses valued at no more than £2,500.
The societies' advances would normally be over twenty years at
a rate not greater than the BSA recommended rate. The White
Paper had indicated that some £40 to £45 million or 12 per cent
of the total advances against mortgage by the building societies
was on dwellings in this age-cohort. By providing state finance
for this part of the stock it was hoped to boost the resources
available for the next age-cohort of dwellings. 'It is part of the
agreement that within the limit of the enlarged resources thus
available to them, the Building Societies participating in the
scheme will do their best to make advances of up to 95 per cent
for as many purchasers of these 1918-1940 houses as want such
advances.'[7] The purpose of the new measure was, then, both
'to enable more people to buy their own homes' by augmenting
the societies' inflow of funds and, more specifically, by a cascade effect to improve the terms and volume of credit available
for purchase of the interwar housing stock.

The innovation was short-lived. In the years 1959, 1960 and
1961 Exchequer loans claimed by the societies were equal to
£7 million, £38 million and £47 million respectively. The number
of houses purchased under the scheme was about 84,000 units
over the three years. Then suddenly, in the summer of 1961,
the suspension of the scheme was announced as part of the
measures taken in July to restrict public expenditure, and the
last payments were made in December with less than £8 million
of the original £100 million remaining unspent. This extremely
interesting experiment has never since been revived presumably
because it was believed that local authority mortgages could
do a similar job with a greater degree of government control.

It is now an appropriate point to turn away from questions
concerning the flow of speculative developments and the purchase
of the second-hand stock in order to consider the related but
distinct matter of the rehabilitation of private housing. It was in
this sphere that state policy demonstrated its most original and
long-lasting innovations. Much of the ground work was laid down
in the 1953 White Paper *Houses: The Next Step.*

With respect to houses owned by private landlords, rehabilitation was to be stimulated through improvement grants which
reduced the amount of the landlord's outlay; through improvement-
related rent increases which raised the income from his outlay;
and through the general process of rent decontrol, the 1957 Rent
Act being the most important single measure, which was intended
to make private rental more profitable and therefore a more
attractive business. For the most recalcitrant owners, the local
authorities were given powers to compel action. In general these

approaches failed. The size of the privately rented housing
stock continued its pre-war decline - we return to this question
in chapter 9 - and to this day it is heavily over represented in
that part of the stock that is in the poorest physical condition
and with the least adequate facilities.

Now let us consider the rehabilitation of owner-occupied
houses. In the early years of the new administration it was
realised that the implementation of the rehabilitation provisions
of the 1949 Housing Act was proving ineffective.[8] Statistics on
the payment of rehabilitation grants have not been published on
an annual basis before 1960. However, the annual average for
approvals in Britain for *all* private owners in the years 1949-54
was as little as 4,000.

In 1953 Command 8996, *Houses: the Next Step*, set out the
new strategy on renewal, but not before arguing in a lyrical
passage in the preamble that:[9]

> One object of future housing policy will be to continue to
> promote, by all possible means, the building of new houses
> for owner-occupation. Of all forms of saving, this is one of
> the best. Of all forms of ownership this is one of the most
> satisfying to the individual and the most beneficial to the
> nation.

At the same time the government claimed it wished to meet the
requirements for rental 'of the greater part - perhaps necessarily
the greater part - of the population'.[10]

In the analysis of the task of renewal, the White Paper made
a most interesting assumption: renewal was a process that was
largely a matter relating to the privately rented sector. Command
8996 suggested that some 54 per cent of all dwellings in Britain
were privately rented, 18 per cent were publicly rented and 28
per cent were owner-occupied. The implication of the Paper is
that renewal was not a matter of great importance for the local
authority and owner-occupied stock - after all, most of it had
been built after 1918. Thus the advances in legislation in the
owner-occupied sector were a *by-product* of measures taken with
a view to raising the quality of the privately rented stock!

The changes in policy towards rehabilitation that were most
important for the existing or potential home-owner were the
recommendation for a reduction in the minimum length of life of
property qualifying for grants, the complete removal of the
upper limit on the cost of works qualifying for the same and a
relaxation in the standard up to which rehabilitation was to carry
the dwelling. All these proposals were made law in the 1954
Housing Repairs and Rents Act (see appendix 1).

The new legislation acted as a powerful stimulant to rehabilitation. The number of approved grants in Britain jumped to an
annual average of 42,000 in the years 1955-9. Whilst this includes
grants to private landlords, in fact in the 1950s nearly 90 per
cent of all grants went to owner-occupiers.[11] Simultaneously with

the growth of grant approval, the number of local authority
loans made to private owners for dwelling conversion, alteration,
repair and improvement rose from a few hundred each year in
the early 1950s to between 2,000 and 3,000 after 1954.

Although the number of rehabilitation grants rose after 1954,
the government was evidently still dissatisfied with the pace of
improvement. In particular it was unhappy that local authorities
had the right to refuse grants if they so chose. It was also felt
that improvements more modest than those to the twelve-point
standard of the 1954 Act should also be encouraged. As a result
the 1959 House Purchase and Housing Act continued the award
of discretionary grants but introduced new 'standard' grants.
These were claimable as of right on pre-1945 houses for improvement to a five-point standard with a minimum property life of
fifteen years. The maximum grant was £155 or half the cost of
the work, whichever was lower. Moreover, under the scheme
of Exchequer advances to approved building societies already
discussed, the societies agreed to make additional loans over
and above the ordinary mortgage advance in order to enable
owners to meet their share of the cost of these standard improvements. The same Act permitted local authorities to raise their
mortgage cover to 100 per cent. After the Act there was a
tremendous surge in grant approvals which in 1960-4 averaged
90,000 each year. In the same years local authority loans for
dwelling conversion, improvement, etc. were of the order of
10,000 to 15,000 per annum.

3 POLICY RECONSIDERATION

The long boom in speculative building after 1951 and the
associated reduction in the level of state housing construction
had brought a very substantial shift in the proportion of output
built for home-ownership within the total of speculative and
local authority building. The proportion rose from only 16 per
cent in 1952 to between 60 and 63 per cent in 1961-4.

The overall effect of the flow of output, slum clearance and
transfers of ownership in the stock after 1938 are shown in
Table 3.1. During two decades there had been a huge contraction in the size of the privately rented sector as a result of
clearance, the sale of dwellings to owner-occupiers and the
complete failure of landlords to commit capital to new housing
built for rental. As a result, this tenure had diminished so
much as to constitute less than one-third of the stock in 1960
compared with 58 per cent in 1938. The table shows state housing had risen powerfully in relative importance. This was
because the major part of new building resources had flown
into this sector during the 1940s and even the early 1950s. However, the largest absolute increase in terms of tenure was in
owner-occupation because in addition to 1.3 million newly built
houses it ingested 1.5 million dwellings from private rental, a

rate of transfer even greater than that between the wars.

Table 3.1 *The size and growth of the housing stock and its distribution
between tenures in England and Wales 1938-60 (millions)*

	Owner-occupied	Local authority	Private landlords and miscellaneous	Total
Stock of dwellings in 1938: (units)	3.7	1.1	6.6	11.4
(%)	32	10	58	100
1938-60: new building purchases (+),	+1.3	+2.3	+0.1	+3.7
sales (−),	+1.5	+0.2	−1.7	0
demolitions/changes of use	−0.1	neg.	−0.4	−0.5
Stock of dwellings in 1960: (units)	6.4	3.6	4.6	14.6
(%)	44	25	31	100

Source: *HPTV*, Part I, Tables 1.23 and 24.

Now let us look briefly at two important shifts in policy that
took place in 1961-4 and owe their origin to a change in the
government's understanding of the effectiveness with which its
grand design was being implemented. The first concerns the
'voluntary' housing movement and the second is area-based
improvement.

Table 3.1 has shown both that there was a massive transfer
of privately rented dwellings into owner-occupation in the two
decades after 1938 and that there was virtually no new construction for private rental. The civil service had come to recognise
this and admitted as much in the 1961 White Paper *Housing in
England and Wales*.[12] This paper, Command 1290, at the same
time insisted that 'It is not in accord with what people want that
the only building to let should be done by public authorities'.[13]
From this we can infer that a state rental housing monopoly was
something the *Cabinet* did not want. In my view this was the
direct result of its antipathy towards the power which a united
local authority tenants' movement could wield in opposition to
Conservative policies on council housing, amply demonstrated
in the St Pancras rent strike of 1960.[14] The upshot was that
Command 1290 proposed to advance money to non-profit-making
housing associations prepared to build houses to let at economic
rents. The 1961 Housing Act provided a fund of £25 million for
this purpose.

The same Act introduced a new subsidy system for municipal
housing intended to reduce the flow of subsidies received by the
higher wage council tenants and thereby make home-ownership
or non-subsidised rental more attractive to them.[15] The objective

of channelling government subsidies only to households in real
need is reiterated in the 1963 White Paper, *Housing*, in which
the assumption is made that owner-occupiers receive no subsidy:[16]

> In a free country the householder must be prepared to meet
> the cost of his house where he is able to do so. Otherwise he
> will have little freedom of choice. The Government believe
> that most householders are willing to meet the cost - witness
> the growth of owner-occupation - provided that they get a
> good house.

Here, indeed, is an astigmatism serving to verify the most
reductive materialist assertion that the superstructure of ideology
rests on the foundation of material interest. The authors of the
White Paper, whom we can confidently expect were home-owners,
could perfectly well see that the council tenant received a
subsidy but were blind to the very subsidies they themselves
enjoyed, the tax relief on their mortgage payments. It was not
until the Green Paper of 1977 that such 'tax expenditure', as it
is called, was recognised in a government document as possibly
constituting a subsidy.

Returning to the housing associations, the loans they were to
receive under the 1961 Act had been introduced as a pump-
priming operation to demonstrate to potential rentiers that
construction for private letting could be profitable. The demon-
stration effect in this context was negligible: the entrepreneurial
spirit proved exceedingly elusive. As a result the 1964 Housing
Act established the Housing Corporation to promote housing
associations and societies on a permanent basis.

The second shift in Tory policy in the early 1960s concerned
rehabilitation. The experience of Leeds City Council in the
1950s with rehabilitation carried out on an area basis had generated wide interest. The view took shape that private initiative
in house improvement thrives most where the individual household clearly perceives similar changes going on throughout the
neighbourhood. First, there is a psychological stimulus. Second,
so goes the argument, if rehabilitation is carried out to raise
the asset value of the house, such an increase will be more
marked in a residential area where positive environmental
change is widespread. If these arguments are accepted, the
cost effectiveness of public expenditure is greatest when it is
spatially concentrated.

The first official recommendation to local authorities that they
might direct their efforts in promoting rehabilitation on an area
basis was contained in circular 42/62.[17] In 1964 a new Housing
Act made discretionary grants more attractive, as appendix 1
shows, and for the first time introduced the concept of improvement areas into the country's legislation.

Another policy modification in the early 1960s was the abolition
in 1963 of Schedule A taxation of owner-occupiers. In the period
1936-63 the average home-owner's Schedule A income was some

£25 per year. Because payments of mortgage interest and Schedule A income were similar on average, any tax relief on the former would be offset by tax chargeable on the latter. Thus both the first and the second boom in speculative housebuilding for owner-occupation took place over a period when the net subsidy to the tenure in aggregate was negligible! As we saw above, this revision of taxation was not accompanied by the abolition of the tax relief subsidy, that other by-product of the system of income taxation first introduced in 1803.[18] To run on a little, when in 1965 a tax on capital gains was introduced, the government took care to exclude any gain on the taxpayer's sole or main residence and in 1969 when tax relief on loan interest was abolished, specific exemption was given to interest paid on loans used for the acquisition or improvement of property. Throughout the 1960s, then, a number of modifications were made to our system of taxation of income and capital, all of which served to maintain or improve the fiscal advantages of the owner-occupier.

4 THE PARTY OF ALL THE CLASSES

The general election of October 1964 brought a new Labour government to power with a very small overall parliamentary majority. Thirteen long years of exile from government had wrought changes in Labour's stance on many matters of policy and, in particular, had transformed its philosophy with respect to owner-occupation. It was as if the Labour Party, especially in Parliament, had come to regard the British people as stratified into a number of 'housing classes', categorised by their tenure, the form of their consumption of the housing stock. On the basis of this conception of differentiated consumer strata, Labour sought to become the party of *all* the housing classes and thereby isolate the Conservative enemy with its evident contempt for the tenant 'class'.[19] Thus Labour pursued significant reforms aimed at improving the housing conditions of all three of the major tenures: council tenants, home-owners and tenants of private landlords.

Yet the new philosophy went much further than this. The three tenures were certainly not seen to be of equal status and there was no conception that the relative advantages of the groups should be equalised by government intervention. Instead, in a clear convergence with Tory thinking, owner-occupation was presented as the supreme goal in a nation of individual households. This became quite explicit in the government's first housing White Paper, *The Housing Programme 1965 to 1970*:[20]

In the private sector there has been practically no building to let. The conclusion is clear. We are faced with an ever growing shortage of accommodation within the means of poorer families; and the growth of owner-occupation can do

very little to relieve it. The only remedy is an increase in
public sector building . . .
But once the country has overcome its huge social problem
of slumdom and obsolescence, and met the need of the great
cities for more houses let at moderate rents, the programme
of subsidised council housing should decrease. The expansion
of building for owner-occupation on the other hand is normal;
it reflects a long-term social advance which should gradually
pervade every region.

Could Neville Chamberlain have put it more clearly?
Before considering the trajectory of starts and completions in
housing output in 1964-70, let me first give a brief account of
some of the discrete measures adopted during this period to
maintain and extend the advantages of home-ownership and to
broaden its social base. These include the raising of private
housebuilding standards, the introduction of option mortgages,
leasehold reform, and compensation for compulsory acquisition.

(a) Housebuilding standards
Since the 1930s the standards of construction in private housebuilding had been regulated - other than through the building
by-laws - by a voluntary scheme of inspection and certification
operated by the National House-Builders Registration Council.
By 1964 less than 30 per cent of houses built for sale were
covered. As a result of government pressure, 'who made it clear
that if acceptable standards were not achieved by voluntary
means other methods would be tried',[21] in 1964-5 the Council was
reconstituted, its standards raised, and protection for house
purchasers increased by the introduction of a ten-year guarantee
backed by insurance cover against major structural defects.
Apart from workmanship, the NHBRC (later the National House
Building Council) requirements also related to such matters as
layout of kitchen, efficiency of heating, number of power points,
and storage space. Thereafter the government agreed with
the local authorities and building societies that they would make
loans for the purchase of new houses only on condition that such
houses had NHBRC certificates.[22] Here we have an interesting
and unique case of the government regulating production
through informally agreed controls exercised by the suppliers of
realisation finance.
In February 1966, a month before the BSA recommended to its
members that they should insist on certification, there were
2,700 builders registered with the Council.[23] At the end of 1970,
by which time further improvements in standards and protection
had been made, the number of registered builders had risen to
over 14,000, covering about 95 per cent of all houses built for sale.[24]

(b) Option mortgages
By its very nature the subsidy enjoyed by home-owners, i.e.
tax relief on mortgage interest payments, entailed that those

paying tax at less than the basic rate or paying no tax at all received little or no subsidy. Option mortgages were introduced to allow households with low incomes to benefit from subsidy and to broaden the social base of owner-occupation. The new arrangements were announced in the 1966 White Paper *Help towards Home Ownership*, enacted in the 1967 Housing Subsidies Act, and came into operation in April 1968.

With respect to annuity mortgages, initially the system was that the Exchequer paid to the building societies and local authorities interest at 2 per cent per annum on the outstanding capital debt of home-owners opting for the scheme. This permitted the institutions to charge 2 per cent less than the standard mortgage rate on their loans. In January 1970 a revision of the scheme allowed the rate of subsidy to vary upwards and downwards with the standard mortgage rate, thereby ensuring that subsidy to the two sets of home-owners on a mortgage of a given size were roughly equivalent. About 180,000 existing mortgagors changed to option mortgages at the commencement of the scheme and in its first years about 25,000 borrowers a year chose the option mortgage.[25]

It is worth stressing that the new arrangements were proposed not merely on grounds of equity but also in order to widen the social composition of home-owners. (A different way of approaching the same facts would be to say that Labour's confidence in its appeal to all the 'housing classes' permitted it to stimulate a broader 'housing class' composition within the working class.) The 1966 White Paper said:[26]

> The scheme . . . is designed to help those in the lower income groups. . . . Lenders usually fix the sum they are willing to advance on mortgage by reference to the proportion of the borrower's income needed to meet the annual payments on the loan. The option mortgage subsidy will reduce the annual payment a man of modest means has to make for a given amount borrowed and as a result lenders will often be willing to advance a larger sum, or to make advances which would otherwise not have been possible. In this way, home ownership will be open for many more people.

In order to buttress this opening-up of the tenure, the 1967 Act also initiated the option mortgage guarantee scheme. Building societies agreed to entertain applications from option mortgage borrowers buying houses of not more than £5,000 in price, or valuation if that was less, for loans of up to 25 per cent of the valuation of the property over and above the amount normally lent. The additional amount lent was guaranteed by insurance, half provided free by the government and half by insurance companies. Initially about half of all option mortgage borrowers took advantage of the guarantee scheme.

(c) Leasehold reform
In 1967 the Leasehold Reform Act enabled people who had lived
for at least five years in houses within the rateable value limit
of £200 (£400 inside Greater London), which they held on long
tenancies at low rents, to purchase the freehold of their house.
The price payable was to equal the market value of the freehold
interest on the assumption that the lease had been extended for
fifty years. The Act also served, of course, to widen the class
composition of home-ownership. It was particularly important in,
for example, South Wales and the Birmingham area.

(d) Compensation for compulsory acquisition
In 1965 new legislation continued the provision for home-owners
of unfit property purchased between 1939 and 1955 to be compensated at market values during the course of compulsory
acquisition for slum clearance purposes. Other owners of unfit
dwellings received only the site value. In 1968 the MHLG reported
that about one-fifth of all owners of houses in clearance areas
were owner-occupiers[27] and in the 1969 Housing Act the code of
compensation was changed so that henceforth virtually all owner-
occupiers of unfit homes received market value compensation.
   With this description of the major legislative innovations
specific to owner-occupation completed, let me turn back to
consider the progress of housebuilding activity in 1964-70. The
housing strategy for these years was set out in the White Paper
The Housing Programme 1965 to 1970. Therein an overall target
was laid down of 500,000 completions a year in the United Kingdom by 1970. Total output was to be divided in equal amounts
between the private and public sectors. This promised advance
for the municipal tenant and the home-owner was accompanied
by the preparation of a new Rent Act, eventually passed in 1965,
intended to defend the interests of private tenants by a new
system of 'fair rents' and improved security of tenure. Once
again, the appeal was to all the classes.
   The implementation of the public sector programme lay
essentially in the hands of the local housing authorities. Private
output was, of course, the responsibility of the building companies, and their rate of construction was dependent on a
sufficient flow of mortgage funds from the building societies.
How could speculative output be planned? The programme document was full of brave words, no doubt:[28]

> the foundation for a comprehensive national housing plan has
> now been laid . . . for the first time, the Government, the
> building societies and the builders have discussed together
> and agreed on the need for forward planning of house-
> building, and for continuous collaboration to ensure a steadily
> rising programme.

Yet, in practice, no specific measures were taken to realise these
aspirations. Thus, with respect to speculative building, the state

exercised control neither over mortgage funds, which were crucial on the demand side, nor over the rate of housebuilding activity on the supply side.

The inability to implement the plan in the private sector became obvious almost immediately. In early 1965 a sharp decline took place in the building societies' net inflow of funds so that for the year as a whole the amount loaned fell marginally. But the reduction in the *number* of advances was much greater, for the upward trend of house prices, new and second hand, was forcing up the average loan to each mortgagor. Large numbers of unsold houses were the result. From Graph 3.1 we can see that private starts and completions were cut back in 1965 and 1966, doubtless exacerbated by the introduction of a new tax on construction and other non-manufacturing industries, the Selective Employment Tax. In spite of a clear recovery in the money value of the flow of mortgage finance after 1965, and a brief resurgence in speculative housebuilding, private starts had fallen well below 175,000 per annum in 1969 and 1970. In any case, by this stage the national housing programme had already been abandoned after the long drawn-out balance of payments crisis in May-November 1967 had led the government to announce widespread cuts in public expenditure, including local authority housebuilding.[29]

By 1968, the government's macro-economic objectives were primarily oriented towards shifting productive resources so as to raise private investment, increase the volume of exports and cut the volume of imports. This meant that state capital expenditure on a subsidised wage good, i.e. state housing, came under serious attack from within the government and the civil service. Much of the municipal programme was composed of redevelopment and overspill provision, thus every means was sought to reduce this by renewing the *élan* of the rehabilitation programme. Rehabilitation policy itself required public funding. However, at least in the short run, it seemed to require less resources for each dwelling in a renewal project than would redevelopment. Moreover, a substantial proportion of the money necessary would come from the private not the public purse. By now, too, there was much less optimism in official circles about the likelihood of productivity growth in the use of industrialised housebuilding systems in state housing provision.

After 1960 there had been a clear levelling-off in the approval of rehabilitation grants; those to owner-occupiers were running at a level of 54,000 to 65,000 each year and the pace of area improvement had been slower than the government had hoped for. Then, in 1967, the first National Sample Survey of the condition of houses had shown that the scale of disrepair and unfitness was far greater than the authorities had heretofore believed. The government's response to the faltering pace of rehabilitation within the context of the perceived state expenditure crisis in housing renewal was the White Paper *Old Houses into New Homes* and, subsequently, the 1969 Housing Act.

The Act's fundamental objective was to stimulate the process of private rehabilitation on an area basis. Local authorities were given powers to declare general improvement areas in which resources were to be devoted to improving and prolonging the life of a selected residential area as a whole. The emphasis was on voluntary co-operation rather than compulsion. Government grants were made available towards environmental improvement up to an expenditure of £100 per dwelling. At the same time, as appendix 1 shows, the grant levels were raised, the conditions for their approval were relaxed, and approved works of repair and replacement became eligible for grant aid for the first time. Local authorities were also given powers to assist owners to carry out improvement works by taking over the job by agreement. Finally the 'fair rents' machinery of the 1965 Rent Act was used to determine new rents in regulated tenancies following grant-aided improvement: rent decontrol was firmly linked to rehabilitation by the landlord.

The short-run quantitative effects were dazzling: the number of grants approved for home-owners increased from 57,000 in 1969 to 186,000 four years later. The social effects were more complex and I return to these in chapter 12.

The last subject with which I shall deal in this section is the new legislation on land and planning introduced by the Labour government. The appropriation by the state of all or part of increases in land values has always been an element in social democratic philosophy. Since the 1950s 'betterment', as it is called, had escaped taxation other than through death duties. Thus the Land Commission Act of 1967 introduced a betterment levy, initially set at 40 per cent, which was charged on increases in the development value of land and paid by owners when they sold. In order to forestall speculative withholding of development sites the Land Commission was also given wide powers to purchase land by agreement or compulsion, to manage and to dispose of it. With respect to the national housing plan, the 1965 White Paper had promised that where necessary the Land Commission would use these powers to assemble land in quantity for private housebuilding well in advance of need, and said the Commission would be able to dispose of land for owner-occupied housing on favourable terms.[30] The achievements of Labour's land policy during its admittedly short period of operation (the Conservatives were to reverse it in 1971) were meagre, to say the least. By November 1970 the Commission had actually purchased only 2,800 acres of land and collected £46 million from the levy.[31]

Finally we should note that the 1968 Town and Country Planning Act had brought with it substantial modifications to the British planning system. As a result of this Act, and the reorganisation of local government in 1974, both the 'shire' and the metropolitan counties were required to prepare 'structure plans', statements of policy accompanied by diagrammatic illustrations, dealing with broad land-use policies and indicating action areas where major change through development, redevelopment and rehabilitation might be expected. These plans were to be approved by the minister. The district councils were to produce local plans. When development was undertaken privately, the local plan had to provide broad guidelines, as it were a brief to the developer and architect. The Act also provided for planning permissions to lapse if development had not begun within five years and allowed local planning authorities to serve developers with completion notices. This was intended to check speculative land hoarding. After 1974, then, at least in principle, the construction of new housing estates by the private sector had both to conform with the county structure plan as well as secure planning permission from the district authorities.

5 SUMMARY

The period of Conservative government that began in 1951 and lasted for thirteen years was, in retrospect, one of remarkable prosperity. Personal disposable income per head (at 1970 prices) rose from £377 in 1948 to £581 in 1965. The rate of inflation was modest. The scale of unemployment was, and had been since 1945, unprecedentedly low for peace-time. And an 'economic crisis' meant little more than a temporary check to the upward movement of aggregate output as a result of a deficit in the balance of payments. Rates of interest, however, had become more expensive and more volatile in comparison with 1931-51. This was the golden age of Keynesian demand management. It was true: we had never had it so good.

The expansion in real incomes, the overall shortage of dwellings with respect to households in 1951, the huge increase in the flow of funds to the building societies, these were the foundations of a long and remarkably steady boom in speculative building - to the evident delight of the government.

With respect to the scale and composition of new housing output, the policy of the state was crystal clear. The scale objective was to maintain an annual rate of completions in Britain of 300,000 units after 1953 and this was attained. The tenure composition within the total, which defined broadly for whom the dwellings were built, was determined by the speculative boom itself. Building controls over speculative building were relaxed and then abolished and the taxation of development values was rescinded. As the influx of finance to the building societies swelled, the rate of construction rose from 23,000 completions in 1951 to 218,000 in 1964. Local authority mortgage finance simultaneously resumed the minor role it had played between the wars. As speculative production grew, municipal construction was hacked back and channelled largely towards the residualist activities of slum clearance, redevelopment, overspill provision and building for elderly households. The Labour Party's philosophy of directing housing resources on the basis of need had therefore been largely reversed. State housing rent and subsidy policies, particularly after 1961, were integrated with this residualist philosophy, in part with the intention of making owner-occupation more attractive in relative terms for high-wage council tenants.

Turning now to housing renewal, this was conceived of as a very strictly partitioned process. The central initiative was a determined attempt to stimulate housing rehabilitation by private landlords with the incentive of government grants, etc. Indeed it is the interest of the civil service and government in rehabilitation that most distinguish these years from the pre-war era. The new policy failed lamentably amongst the rentier class but was associated with extensive rehabilitation by owner-occupiers of the older housing stock. Approved grants to home-owners were running at a rate of 55,000 to 70,000 per year by the early 1960s, at which time also there develops a belief in the cost-effectiveness of rehabilitation programmes implemented on an area basis.

Very, very slowly the state began to realise that in spite of rent decontrol and government grants, capital was being withdrawn at a precipitous rate from the existing privately rented stock. In order to prevent the dereliction and abandonment of essentially sound houses, and on the contrary to encourage rehabilitation, policy began to show a keener interest in the stock transfer process itself, not merely the realisation of newly constructed houses. That is to say, the unanticipated failures *and* successes of the state's rehabilitation policy demonstrated that the role of the exchange process in switching the category of ownership of a dwelling could prove vital to successful 'improvement'. As a result, local authorities were encouraged to use their mortgage funds on the older housing stock as well as the new; they provided guarantees to the building societies for high mortgage cover on pre-1919 dwellings; and the Exchequer funding experiment of 1959-61 aimed by a cascade effect to increase the finance for the purchase of interwar properties by the order of £30-40 million per year. Finally we should note that the absence of private construction for rental and the antipathy towards the developing state monopoly in rental accommodation led the Conservatives to attempt to revive the housing association movement.

With respect to Labour's policy in 1964-70, we can observe a sharp contrast with its previous periods of office. The main shift was to accept the residualist principle of Toryism. The development of owner-occupation had now become an indicator of a natural advance in social well-being. This shift was associated with the increasing confidence and dominance of social democratic ideas in the party during the 1950s and 1960s, a philosophy that, like Marxism, has been present since the party's foundation. This move towards a greater reliance on the market economy to deal with the housing problem appeared somewhat inconsistent with elaboration of the first national housing plan. It was the plan, not the forces of the market, that broke first. By 1970

large reductions in state housing production had been implemented. Indeed, starts in the two years 1969 and 1970 were less
than those of 1963 and 1964! Moreover, private rehabilitation had
supplanted public redevelopment in the government's housing
renewal strategy. Finally we should note that in 1963-9 both
governments made a number of changes in our taxation system
buttressing the fiscal advantages of home-ownership, and under
Labour in particular a number of initiatives were taken to broaden
the occupational composition of the tenure.

This concise history of the development of owner-occupation
between 1918 and 1970 is now complete. One of the myths of
home-ownership is that the tenure is above all characterised by
its rugged independence. The error is breath-taking if we consider alone that the site must be purchased from the landed
classes, the dwelling is built by a speculative company, the
purchase price is raised by a loan from a building society and
the exchange process is managed by a nest of solicitors, surveyors and kindred gentlefolk. Chapters 1, 2 and 3 have also
attempted to highlight the multiple forms of state intervention,
in the supply of land, in the controls over design standards, in
the subsidies to speculative and rehabilitation production, in
the evolution of sources of mortgage finance, in the subventions
towards consumption payments and, above all, in the residualist
strategy dominant in central government with respect to state
housing production.

In the remainder of this volume, chapter 17 excepted, we
attempt to describe in considerable depth the system of owner-
occupation as it has operated in Britain in the 1970s and early
1980s.

4 THE DEMOGRAPHIC CONTEXT

1 INTRODUCTION

Even the most preliminary inquiry into owner-occupation in
contemporary Britain quickly reveals that the relationships one
is studying are highly interdependent. This poses a problem of
method for it implies there is no obvious starting point to the
analysis. Yet one must begin somewhere and I choose to start
with an account of effective demand, above all in order to be
able to place the chapter on the institutional provision of mortgage finance *before* the description of new housing production.
However, I must stress that we are not dealing with a simple
hierarchy of relationships. There is no fundamental level of
explanation, 'demand' for example, which can be shown to
determine the variables of another level, which themselves fix
those in a third and so on until the pyramid is complete. For
there is no pyramid. In the real system each process, directly
or indirectly, influences every other and at the heart of the
matter lies feedback through time.

Effective demand, in this context, refers to the willingness and
ability of households to purchase dwellings for owner-occupation,
and this flow concept manifests itself concretely by individual
households buying specific dwellings in given locations at
defined prices during known periods of time for their own use.
For each purchasing act there exists a complementary act of
sale and these sales in their aggregate I shall refer to as the
supply of accommodation for owner-occupation. The substance
of any explanation of effective demand must rest on three fields
of inquiry: the households themselves, their desire to purchase,
and their ability to pay the price. The rest of this chapter
treats the purchasing households and the following three chapters
discuss the willingness and ability to purchase.

The set of purchasers in any given time-period - let us assume
it is a year - can be categorised in many different ways. One
basis is in terms of the buyer's existing property relationships
and this will be the most common form of presentation in this
book. Here, four groups are distinguished: sitting buyers,
selling buyers, second-home buyers, and first-time buyers.
Sitting buyers are households that acquire a dwelling which they
already live in and rent. Selling buyers are households that
already own their home, who are acquiring a different house
and, more or less at the same time, selling their existing dwelling.
A single decision process, for example the move by an elderly

couple from suburban London to retire on the Sussex coast, here generates both a purchase and a sale and this is one of the most recurring forms in which the interdependence of supply and demand manifests itself. The third category, second-home buyers, are households that already own their house and who acquire a second (or a third or an *n*-th) home without at the same time selling their existing dwelling. Lastly, first-time buyers are here defined as all other buyers. This categorisation is simple, comprehensive and relevant. More intricate classifications on a property basis would confuse rather than clarify.[1]

A second method of grouping buyers that I shall often use is demographic in nature and divides them into new households, continuing households and immigrant households. The census defines a household as either one person living alone or a group of persons (who may or may not be related) living at the same address with common housekeeping. A new household, then, is one that comes into existence during the year in question. A continuing household is one that already existed at the beginning of that year. Immigrant households are defined here as households arriving in Britain during the year in order to take up residence. Finally, in the case of a married or cohabitating couple who break up during the relevant time-period through separation or divorce, one can call the fragments of that year successor households and treat them as a special case of new households. With some of the groundwork complete, let us look at a selection of demographic statistics.

2 FLOW AND STOCK

One of the most potentially powerful motors in accelerating the effective demand for owner-occupied dwellings is population growth, for in the simplest case where average household size is constant, the rate of growth of the number of households is equal to the rate of growth of the total population. But before looking at the data it is necessary to remember that demand may be strong, may be increasing, even within a population that has a zero growth rate and a stable age composition. Continuing households in owner-occupation may choose to move, continuing households in rented accommodation may choose to purchase, and of course even an unchanging population constantly generates new households.

Since housing is for people, I begin with the size of the total population in Britain. Table 4.1 presents the annual figures for the eleven-year period beginning with the 1971 census. The table shows that the rate of growth of the total was negligible and so no acceleration or deceleration of demand can be sought here. This, however, does not take us very far because there exists no one-to-one correspondence between persons and dwellings. People constitute themselves into households and these are best regarded as the fundamental purchasing units, as I have

already implied. New households are created predominantly by
people between their late teens and (at the latest) their mid-40s.
The size of this group is also included in Table 4.1. Because of
the age structure of the population in 1971, this variable grew
more rapidly than total population, at a rate of 0.91 per cent
per annum. So this measure of the annual rate of growth of the
household-forming population, which has been called the most
basic of pressures for housing,[2] was still extremely modest in
the 1970s.

Table 4.1 Population and households in Great Britain 1971-81 (millions)[a]

Year	Total population	Population aged 15-44	Households
1971	54.2	21.0	18.4
1972	54.3	21.1	18.6
1973	54.5	21.2	18.8
1974	54.5	21.3	19.0
1975	54.5	21.5	19.1
1976	54.4	21.7	19.3
1977	54.4	21.9	19.6
1978	54.3	22.1	19.7
1979	54.3	22.4	19.8
1980	54.2	22.7	20.0
1981	54.2	23.0	20.1

Source: Population: OPCS, *Population Projections*, London HMSO, 1979, Series PP2, no.9,
appendix, Table IVa. Households: private communication from the DoE.

[a] All the data, save for the census figures for 1971, are estimates.

A substantial methodological difficulty must now be considered.
In presenting the demography of the effective demand for housing, in principle we wish to consider only those variables
independent of the supply of housing during the period under
investigation. The size in 1971-81 of the new household forming
population is indeed largely free of supply effects for such
persons were all born before the 1970s began. The only influence
of the house supply that took place during that decade was its
marginal effect on the rates of emigration, immigration and age-
specific mortality.
    Unfortunately, once we move beyond the use of this variable
and turn to consider the number, rate of formation and composition of *households* in Britain, it becomes clear that what is
measured is very closely related to housing supply. For, with the
exception of households that share accommodation in their early
period of existence, the supply of dwelling vacancies, in all its
forms, provides the physical spaces within which new households
are created. The variable 'household', then, is essentially hybrid
in its nature: it is the fundamental unit of demand but is profoundly influenced by housing supply. Once again we see the

interdependence of relationships within the housing system.

So, in order to pursue the analysis, one must look at the last column in Table 4.1, the number of households in Britain in the years 1971-81. The annual rate of growth is 0.89 per cent. This is negligibly different from the rate of increase in the new household forming population, but markedly more rapid than that in total population. As a consequence and allowing for the population not in private households at all but living 'permanently' in hotels, hospitals, schools and other institutions, the average number of persons per household fell from 2.86 in 1971 down to 2.62 in 1981. This decline is, in fact, part of a very long-term trend.

Table 4.2 Households in England and Wales by type of household and age of 'head' of household in 1971 (percentages)[a]

	Under age 30	30-44	45-59 or 64	60-65 or over	Total
Married couple households	9.7	20.5	27.9	10.1	68.2
Lone-parent households	0.4	1.3	2.1	2.6	6.4
Other multi-person households	0.7	0.5	1.4	2.8	5.4
One-person households	1.2	1.4	4.2	13.1	19.9
Total	12.0	23.7	35.6	28.6	100[b]

Source: *HPTV*, Part I, Table II.21. Census-based estimates.

[a] The OPCS assumes there is a meaningful concept of 'head of household' and that men always 'head' married couple households. Column 3 includes households with a female 'head' up to age 59 but male 'heads' up to age 64. The male/female distinction reappears in column 4.

[b] Totals do not add exactly to 100 because of rounding errors.

There were several contributory factors to the fall in this overall average. One was the reduction in the number of con-cealed households, for example single-parent families or married couples living with parents and so not constituting a separate household. Another was the rise in the number of one-person households, particularly elderly persons continuing to live independently in the former family home after the death of a spouse. Thirdly, lower marriage rates and higher divorce rates tended respectively to restrain the increase in married couple households (as against one-person households) and increase the number of lone-parent families with dependent children.

I want now to follow these brief comments on the general rate of growth of population and households in the 1970s with a

description of the *stock* of owner-occupiers at the beginning of
the period I am primarily interested in, that of 1970-81. Thereafter, in section three, I return to the subject of the demography
of purchasers in 1971 as distinct from the set of owners. Table
4.2 sets out the relationship between household type and age of
all households in England and Wales in 1971, whatever their
tenure. It shows very clearly the dominance of the traditional
nuclear family and the importance of elderly one-person households. These groups excepted, no cell in the table has a value
greater than 4.2 per cent. The large number of elderly one-
person households reflects the rising incidence of widowhood
with age, and the much larger proportion of single people at
higher ages as a result of lower marriage rates earlier in the
century.[3]

Table 4.3 gives the household composition of owner-occupiers,
based on GHS classifications and data for England and Wales in
1971. All household types are well represented among home-
owners with the exception of individuals aged less than 60. The
small family is the most important type. In terms of the absolute
difference between owner-occupiers and all tenures, the most
important discrepancies are one-person households, where home-
owners are underrepresented, and small families where owner-
occupiers are overrepresented.

Table 4.3 Households in England and Wales by type of household and tenure
        in 1971 (percentages)

	Owner-occupiers	All tenures
Individuals under age 60	3.8	5.2
Individuals aged 60 or over	9.0	11.8
Small adult households	14.4	14.2
Small families	25.9	22.0
Large families	11.3	12.1
Large adult households	17.8	17.9
Older small households	17.9	16.8
Total	100	100

Source: HPTV; Part I, Table II.22.

Finally, in this brief review of characteristics of the stock of
households at a point in time, Table 4.4 shows the composition
in terms of the age and marital status of the household 'head'
in England in 1971. This confirms the dominance and marginal
overrepresentation of the status of marriage within owner-
occupation. It also shows that 15 per cent of all owner-occupier
households are widowed, divorced or separated. The data also
serve to refute an argument put forward in the *Housing Policy
Technical Volume* that 'There are enough (households headed by
single persons aged at least thirty) to be a significant part of

the demand for owner-occupied housing.'⁴ In fact, that group constitutes only 6 per cent of all owner-occupying 'heads'. The argument so far, then, suggests that marriage is a crucial demographic variable in understanding house purchase.

Table 4.4 Age and marital status of household 'heads' in England by tenure in 1971 (percentages)

Age/status	Owner-occupiers	All tenures
Married, under age 30	9.9	9.9
Married, 30-44	27.6	23.3
Married, 45-59	23.7	22.9
Married, 60 or over	17.5	16.6
Widowed, divorced or separated under 60	4.5	6.3
Widowed, divorced or separated 60 or over	10.6	13.7
Single, under 30	0.3	1.2
Single, 30-59	2.7	3.1
Single, 60 or over	3.3	3.0
Total	100	100

Source: Derived from *HPTV*, Part I, Table II.24.

3 GROSS FLOWS ANALYSIS[5]

Whilst the characteristics of all owner-occupiers at a point in time may be useful in a demographic appraisal of home-ownership, it is most unlikely that the proportionate distribution of these characteristics is identical with their distribution among the set of households that actually purchase dwellings for owner-occupation in any given period of time. The analysis of the flow has to be carried out separately from that of the stock. Let us look, then, at the demography of the flow of purchasing households.

Table 4.5 cross-classifies the property and demographic purchaser categories set down in section one and, for Britain in 1971, puts some figures to the resulting groups. The data are *not* accurate to the nearest thousand and the figure for sitting purchases by former private tenants is a guess (see chapter 9). Let me say something in turn about each of the household groups, starting with immigrant households and ending with continuing households.

The data show that immigrants, in the sense of households arriving in Britain in 1971, constituted only a tiny part of the total effective demand for owner-occupation in that year. The volume of purchases by immigrants of earlier years would be much larger no doubt - after all, in Britain we are all immigrants or their descendants - but they are classified under the other household categories.

New households fall into three groups, married couple new

households, successor households and other new households.
The first of these include both existing married couples formerly
living with relatives or friends and setting up as an independent
household for the first time, as well as newly married couples
setting up house together. Unfortunately, in a blatantly sexist
definition, the DoE does not include in its understanding of
'married couple new households' those newly married couples
where the wife was the 'housewife' in her previous household,
including cases where she was a one-person household! Because
the same woman was 'the person responsible for the household's
domestic arrangements', no new household is regarded as being
formed![6] Thus in interpreting the government's statistical data,
this definitional eccentricity should be borne in mind.

Table 4.5 Estimated purchases of dwellings for owner-occupation in Great
Britain in 1971 (thousands and percentages)

Type of purchaser	Number ('000)	%
Continuing households:		
1 Sitting buyers of rented state housing	18	2
2 Sitting buyers of rented private housing	22	2
3 Selling buyers	410	45
4 Second-home buyers (net)	5	1
5 First-time buyers, formerly state housing tenants	72	8
6 First-time buyers, formerly private tenants		
Under 30	80	
30-44	66	
45 or over	41	
Sub-total %		20
New households/first-time buyers:		
7 Married couple new households		
Marriages where either or both parties not married		
before	145	
Marriages where both parties previously married	20	
Sub-total %		18
8 Successor households from divorce[a]	9	1
9 Other new households	13	1
Immigrant households/first-time buyers:		
10 Households from outside Great Britain	15	2
All households	916	100

Sources: Tables 8.1, 9.1, and *HPTV*, Parts I and II, Tables III.8, III.10 and VI.1.

[a] Excludes households remaining in former matrimonial house.

As Table 4.5 shows, amongst all new households purchasing
dwellings, it is the married couple new household that is
absolutely predominant. The 1971 DoE National Movers Survey
indicated that 56 per cent of all married couple new households

entered owner-occupation immediately. Of these, 68 per cent were childless married couples and 26 per cent were small families.[7]

It must be stressed that not every marriage leads to the immediate purchase of a house: the couple may have been cohabiting and remain where they are; they may constitute a concealed household staying with relatives; or they may go into the privately rented or state housing sectors. Later, of course, concealed households will quite certainly seek to set up house independently, and rented accommodation, particularly in the private sector, is frequently used only as a stepping stone to house purchase. So even in these cases, marriage can lead to house purchase, even if it is a lagged effect.

The predominance of married couple new households amongst all new households purchasing for owner-occupation implies that in looking at the demographic trends of the 1970s with respect to new household formation, the flesh-and-blood basis of effective demand, we can concentrate on those age groups that most powerfully generate marriages.

However, before looking at any data it is vital for me to make two points about the concept of marriage itself. First, most marriages bring into existence a new household. (The marriage of cohabiting couples is the exception.) For this reason the rate of marriage, like the rate of household formation, is a hybrid variable in the sense already expressed above. Newly married couples constitute an importance source of effective demand but the rate of marriage is itself influenced by the supply of dwelling vacancies. Therefore the rate of marriage cannot constitute an independent measure of the demographic pressures behind effective demand.

The second point concerns the distinction between marriages of bachelors to spinsters as against marriages where either or both parties had already been married. Let me call these first and second marriages respectively. These two groups need to be dealt with separately for several reasons. To begin with, in the case of second marriages at least one partner must have already experienced marriage and thereafter widowhood or divorce. So the average age of the partners will be greater than in first marriages; their individual incomes if in employment will be correspondingly different; and they are far more likely than spinsters and bachelors to bring their own children to the marriage ceremony. Moreover if the rate of first marriage dissolution varies between social classes, then so will the ratio of first to second marriages with consequent effects on the class composition of the two groups.

The next issue that differentiates the two marriage types concerns the law. As I have said, it is widowhood or divorce that generates the potential partners of second marriages and so a change in the divorce rate has always been likely to have downstream effects on the second marriage rate. In 1969 the Divorce Reform Act was approved and became operative in

January 1971. It altered the grounds for divorce to irretrievable
breakdown of marriage and led to a sharp increase in the number
of divorces. Nor was this a simple once-and-for-all effect. The
number of decrees made absolute in England and Wales rose
steadily from 58,000 in 1970 to 121,000 in 1975.[8] As a result
there was a corresponding increase in the number of second
marriages which, in Britain, averaged 80,000 per year in the
four years 1968-71 and 121,000 per year in 1972-5. There was
an increase of one-third in 1972 alone with a consequent increase
in the total number of marriages from 447,000 in 1971 to 468,000
in 1972.

The final reason for distinguishing first from second marriages
concerns their net effect on dwelling vacancies. I believe that
in the majority of first marriages, particularly where the partners
are teenagers or in their early to mid-20s, the union is closely
linked in time with the search for a vacant house or flat which
the partners can make their home. In the case of second
marriages, in a large number of cases the partners will settle
in the existing home of one of the two or, even when jointly
moving into a different dwelling, will simultaneously release
their existing homes on to the rental or owner-occupier market.
(This will not happen, of course, with a partner who is sharing
his or her accommodation.) For example, in the case of a divorced
woman with dependent children, living in the former matrimonial
home, who marries a widowed owner-occupier who moves in with
her, the second marriage generates a vacancy with no corresponding house purchase. To sum up this third point, I suggest
that first marriages predominantly bring together partners
each of whom shared their accommodation before marriage (e.g.
with their parents) and thus the marriage has an impact,
immediately or fairly soon, on the pattern of demand and supply
of dwelling vacancies which consists in a net demand effect. On
the other hand, in aggregate, second marriages result in a net
effect that is negligible or is a supply effect.

Because the trend in first marriages is free of any direct
effect of the 1969 Act and because they alone constitute a net
demand effect, I shall use the size and growth of the age group
that generates first marriages as the best non-hybrid measure
of demographic pressure behind the effective demand for owner-
occupation from new households in the 1970s in Britain as a
whole. Since every marriage requires one female and one male,
in this specific case it is necessary to look at the relevant age
group of only one sex, not both, and I shall choose the former.

Examination of the data on first marriages quickly reveals that
the majority of spinsters fall within a very narrow age range.
For example, in England and Wales in 1975 83 per cent of
spinsters marrying bachelors were aged 17-24 inclusive. The
modal age was 19.[9] Graph 4.1 gives the data on the number of
women aged 17-24 in the years 1961-81 and the number of first
marriages in 1961-79. The size of the female 17-24 age group,
the main source of one set of partners in first marriages,

increased very substantially over the years 1961-5, was stable
in the period 1967-71, and thereafter first fell and then rose
in the years 1972-81. The number of first marriages, a hybrid
variable, correlates only loosely with the number of females.
Variations in the ratio of the former to the latter can partially
be accounted for by changes in income over time and in the
difficulty of married couple new households gaining access to
dwelling vacancies. This issue will be taken up again in chapter
16.[10] After 1970, the greater 'availability' of divorced partners
must also be responsible for the huge decline in first marriages.

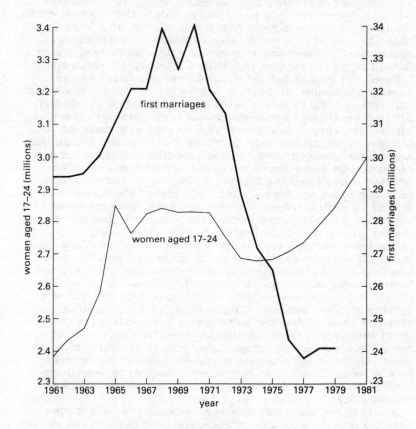

Graph 4.1 The number of women aged 17-24 and the number of
first marriages in England and Wales 1961-81

Source: OPCS and the Registrar General

This discussion of married couple new households is now complete. A little needs to be said next about the two other types of new household listed in Table 4.5. In 1971 neither successor nor 'other new households' played more than the smallest part in the demand for owner-occupied dwellings. The upward trend in divorces since 1970 will have generated more successor purchases but they will never become an important quantitative factor in demand analysis; nor will 'other new households', about half of whom in 1971 were male one-person households.[11] However, it is necessary to remember that both these household types, like immigrant households and married couple new households, have very brief lives for purely definitional reasons. I pointed out above that if an immigrant family buys a house within a year of entering the country, this is indeed counted as a purchase by an immigrant household, whereas if it buys more than one year later it counts as a purchase by a continuing household. This maximum of one year's life applies to all the new household types, for that is how their 'newness' is defined.

Finally let us look briefly at the flow of purchases by continuing households. In Table 4.5 these are broken down into six sub-sets. Sitting buyers of state housing in 1971 made up only a tiny proportion of purchasing households. However, this number can vary violently from year to year as a result of changes in central and local government policies concerning the sale of local authority and new town dwellings. The time-series of these sales and a discussion of the characteristics of those who buy council housing is given in chapter 8. Sitting buyers of housing that was formerly privately rented also appear to be a small sub-set in comparison with aggregate sales for owner-occupation. However, the figure here is no more than an informed guess; chapter 9 deals entirely with this type of sale.

The third category of continuing household is the selling buyer. We can see that this group alone in 1971 made up very nearly half of all purchases for owner-occupation. I return to this group repeatedly in the rest of the volume.

Acquisitions by second-home buyers appear on the face of it to be negligible; however, the figure understates the true situation since, unlike the other rows, it represents not the gross flow of purchases but the gross flow minus the sale of second homes. The true gross figure may be several percentage points higher. Nevertheless the specific sub-sub-set of transfers of second homes from one owner to another is perhaps the least interesting sale/purchase in the entire system of owner-occupation.

The fifth and sixth categories of continuing household purchases are by tenants leaving the state and private rental sectors and together they make up well over one-quarter of all purchases. The age grouping in the private rental case shows that the flow of purchases from these groups declines with age.

This chapter has attempted to give a broad account of the general trend in the size of the population and the number of households in Britain in the 1970s as well as a description of the demographic characteristics of the stock of owner-occupiers at the beginning of the period. It then went on to show that, in 1971 at least, 91 per cent of all purchasers fell into just three groups: continuing household selling buyers, continuing household former tenants, and married couple new household first-time buyers. The net demand effect from this last group derives, I believe, from first marriages and the age group that predominantly provides the female partners for such marriages fell sharply in the years 1971-4 to rise again in 1974-81. Having given an account of the type of household that buys, it is appropriate to consider the second dimension necessary to the analysis of effective demand: the household's willingness to purchase.

5 THE WILLINGNESS TO PURCHASE

1 CHOICES AND CONSTRAINTS

The effective demand for owner-occupation takes its tangible
form in individual acts of purchase, each requiring a household
with the financial ability to buy and the willingness to do so.
This chapter examines why those who acquire a house actually
wish to do so. The existing literature on tenure preference is
marred by an excess of unstructured empiricism or ideological
rubbish, so what follows concentrates largely on laying the
foundation of the analysis of owner-occupier choices and, if it
is thought to be successful, may stimulate the necessary
purposive empirical research. The approach rests on two concepts, predicate and constraint. In the remainder of this section
the second of these is discussed.

Consider the situation of a hypothetical household, a newly
married couple for example, which has purchased a house. Its
final choice will be the outcome of a search process in which
more or less serious consideration is given to the relative merits
of a variety of dwellings that the household sees as available to
it. Three types of constraint restrict the composition of the
couple's feasible portfolio. The first is the flow of vacancies
itself, for the household can only consider dwellings that are
physically available to move into. This flow is the outcome of
complex social processes in which the state has played an
immensely important role, as we saw in chapters 1 to 3.
Individual acts of choice, then, are structured by these processes
and by the history of the state's implementation of its housing
policy. One of the most tangible ways in which the vacancy
constraint reveals itself in contemporary Britain is the extremely
small flow of vacant units for private rental.

The second constraint on feasible choice is the control
exercised by landlords (and others) over access to the vacancy
flow. There is a huge and fascinating literature on this with
respect to state housing. It can be summarised by saying that
in a situation usually marked by excess demand, local authority
management establishes qualification rules applicable to queues
for different dwelling types. These rules, which are often
implemented through points schemes, are based primarily on
length of residence in the district in question and some measure
of the household's existing housing need. These controls are
essentially the product of the total vacancy flow in the sector.[1]
Private landlords also impose rules, though they are less formal-

ised and rarely explicit, and these often discriminate against
black people, adults with dependent children, and households
that might seek to make the accommodation their permanent
home. Lastly, in the owner-occupied sector there have been
many exposures of estate agents preventing the access of ethnic
minorities to houses for sale.

The third constraint is an economic one. Feasible choice for
the household seeking accommodation requires that the stream
of payments for the dwelling are compatible with the household's
current and prospective income. In the specific case of house
purchase, where a loan is usually required, the mortgagee (the
maker of the loan secured against the property) will also
effectively impose constraints on the maximum price of the house
it is prepared to lend on as well as controls on the physical
condition – and possibly also the location of any such house.
The financial constraint is considered at length in chapters 6
and 7.

To sum up, the household's search process will quickly
establish a set of feasible choices in the geographical area relevant
to its decision and it is the vacancy, managerial and financial
controls that determine what dwellings can be entered into this
portfolio. In the worst case a concealed household, say a married
couple living with Mum, will discover that they cannot rent a
private flat for there are none; they cannot get a council house
because they do not have enough points; and they cannot buy a
decent place because they cannot afford it. If the couple then
chooses to acquire a dilapidated house in a decaying road, the
willingness to buy is a product of the poverty, not the freedom,
of choice. Once again the pervasive influence of supply upon
effective demand is clear.

2　THE PREDICATIVE ANALYSIS OF FEASIBLE CHOICE

In the eyes of the industrial classes and their intellectual hand-
maids, the housing conditions of the industrious classes in
nineteenth-century Britain primarily concerned their ability to
reproduce themselves as the diligent 'hands' of industry, as
manual workers. Certainly this conception is a thing of the past,
particularly when there is no work available. In any case, it is
necessary to state at the outset of this 'predicative analysis'
that for working people the dwelling should be understood as an
activity centre required to meet an extremely diverse range of
cultural needs. The house is a place to cook and to eat; a place
to sleep and make love; a place to garden and do carpentry; a
place to suckle babies and rear children; a place to wash and to
defecate; a place to enjoy the company of others, entertain
friends and put up guests; a place to play, read, sew, sing,
make music, study, watch TV, pursue hobbies, and to rest. The
activities pursued will vary, of course, between households and
between individuals within a single household and thus in multi-

person households several activities will often be carried out simultaneously.[2] The house is also a base from which one moves to points in and beyond the neighbourhood in the pursuit of extra-mural activities.

Every dwelling can be described in terms of six major predicates, that is to say, six sets of attributes enjoyed by the house itself or associated with its possession. (By possession, as distinct from ownership, is meant the physical occupation of a dwelling by a household.) The first two predicates specify in turn the physical character of the house and the control exercised over its use by the occupier. They are critical in appraising its function as an activity centre. The third and fourth predicates describe the accommodation's location in space and are critical in appraising its function as a base. The fifth and sixth predicates specify the housing mobility the dwelling offers and its financial attractiveness. Each predicate as a general category of analysis will now be discussed and in section five the relative advantage of different tenures is taken up again.

The physical character of a house can be described in terms of the stability and durability of the dwelling; whether or not it has a garden or garage; its total plot area; its design, including whether it is a flat, bungalow, a terraced, or semi-detached or detached house; the sunlight it receives; its ability to exclude noise, precipitation and dirt; its insulation against heat loss; its ventilation; the internal heating and lighting system; the degree of any condensation; its dryness; the number of rooms and other spaces, their arrangement and type, their area and volume; the fixtures and fittings, storage space and kitchen equipment; the amenities such as water closets, bathroom, washbasin, etc; the state of repair of the whole house, the quality of its materials and the degree of any pest or fungal infestation; and finally, the dwelling's adaptability. Households vary greatly in terms of the number of persons, their age, their sex, their personal relationships, their income and their life-style. Thus the desirability of any single dwelling in terms of its physical predicate will also vary considerably between households.

The second set of attributes relates to the control exercised by the household over its use of the accommodation. This describes the degree of freedom of the occupiers to extend, maintain, repair, improve and adapt the dwelling; the extent of privacy the household has in its use and whether this is limited by involuntary sharing of some of the space; the ability to exclude unwanted intruders; and the degree of security the household enjoys in its possession.

The third and fourth predicates describe the house not as an activity centre in itself but as a base, and I shall refer to them as the environmental and relative loci of the dwelling. Environmental locus here refers to the neighbourhood of the dwelling, the area within a short walking distance. The willingness to live in a house can reflect a number of qualities in the neighbourhood. These include: the volume, danger and noise of local traffic flows;

the physical appearance of the rest of the housing stock and the total built environment; any exposure to natural or industrial pollution, noise or hazards; the availability and quality of local play centres, schools, doctors and clinics; the availability of neighbourhood shops, parks, playing fields, pubs, entertainment facilities, etc.; the scale and nature of any crime in the area; the local residential density; the social class and ethnic origin of one's future neighbours; and whether or not the household already has friends or neighbours living locally.

Whilst these influences can be very strong, they may also be highly subjective with little basis other than, for example, hearsay and estate agents' reports. Moreover, the perceived attractiveness of an area may vary considerably between households. For example, a single person with no thoughts of having children may be quite uninterested in the high reputation of the local primary school whilst for a couple with several young children it is a feature of the neighbourhood of substantial importance.

Now let us turn to relative locus, which is also a spatial concept. It is used here to refer to the availability of alternative transport modes to points in space beyond the neighbourhood, and to the costs in time and money of such journeys. The dwelling here is conceived as a starting point for a number of trips more or less regularly undertaken into the world beyond the neighbourhood. The destinations of these journeys might include the place of work of one or more members of the household; town or city centre shops, restaurants, theatres and cinemas; and areas of natural beauty and recreation.

It is worth pointing to two important relationships between environmental and relative locus. First, the boundary between the neighbourhood and the world beyond it will often be quite indistinct and thus in a Euclidean sense, at least, the two concepts overlap. This methodological difficulty does not seem to be worth making a fuss about. Second, a particular decision to buy or rent a dwelling simultaneously defines one's neighbourhood and one's relative locus.

The fifth predicate, that of housing mobility, relates to the dwelling neither as activity centre nor as base. It describes the relative ease or difficulty that a household encounters after it has taken up occupation of specific accommodation in then moving to a different house which, in terms of the other five predicates, is broadly a good substitute.

3   THE FINANCIAL PREDICATE

The sixth predicate relates to the stream of payments and receipts associated with the possession of the house and it can be referred to as the financial predicate. To prepare the ground a little, the reader is referred to Figure 5.1 which illustrates two concepts, price gain and net worth, that will constantly

recur in the remainder of this volume. Our hypothetical married
couple is assumed to purchase a dwelling in year zero using
finance raised from its own personal assets as well as one or
more loans. After a number of years have elapsed the house is
sold, the outstanding mortgage is paid off and the household
enjoys (however briefly) a cash balance which, as the figure
shows, is equal to the sum of the mortgage principal already
paid off, the personal assets originally ploughed in and the
price gain on the house. The price gain is the selling price of
the house less its original buying price and if the difference is
negative one could speak of a price loss. The cash balance,
the difference between the selling price of the house and the
outstanding loans used to purchase it (or rehabilitate it thereafter), I call the net worth of the house. The net worth can be
estimated even when the house is not sold and so the term
refers to the potential as well as the actual cash balance.[3]

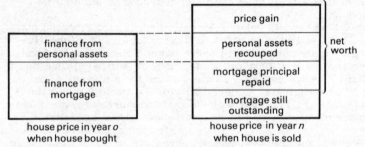

Figure 5.1 The net worth appropriated on the sale of an owner-
occupied house

With these preliminary definitions out of the way, it is possible
to return to the mainstream of the argument. The object is to
establish an analytic method for evaluating the relative financial
advantage of the stream of payments and receipts associated
with the possession of different dwellings, particularly those in
distinct tenures. Moreover, such a method must permit one to
examine critically the very widespread popular view, assiduously
promoted by estate agents, building societies and the state,
that house purchase, in contrast to rental, is a form of 'investment' or a form of 'saving'. To a straightlaced Keynesian
economist this may appear to be a strange paradox for in the
system of Keynes, at least as it is taught by his epigones,
'saving' is precisely income *not* spent on consumption goods and
services. After all, to buy a house is to plunge into a degree
of indebtedness over a period of decades which for most households dwarfs any other debt. How, then, can indebtedness
constitute a form of saving?

A partial answer to this conundrum is that house purchase
brings with it the ownership of an asset the net worth of which
to the buyer can generally be expected to increase continually.

If we assume no fall in house prices, the sale of the house will recoup for the owner his personal assets ploughed in, the money value of his repayments of the principal of the mortgage and any price gains. Even if there is no sale, the household still owns an asset of substantial potential net worth. Admittedly the interest payments on the original mortgage are never recouped but the household may feel compensated for this by the fact that it had the use of the house during the years when these payments were being made. I return to this question overleaf.

Table 5.1   The evaluation of the relative financial advantage of home-ownership and rented accommodation

Option	Row	Annual outlay	Year			
			0	1	2	(n−1)
Owner-Occupation	1	Payment of mortgage interest	i_o	i_1	$i_2 \cdots$	i_{n-1}
	2	Repayments of mortgage principal	p_o	p_1	$p_2 \cdots$	p_{n-1}
	3	Costs of rehabilitation production	c_o	c_1	$c_2 \cdots$	c_{n-1}
	4	Domestic rates and misc. items[a]	d_o	d_1	$d_2 \cdots$	d_{n-1}
	5	Saving from income	s_o	s_1	$s_2 \cdots$	s_{n-1}
	6	Owner-occupation total (rows 1–5)	t_o	t_1	$t_2 \cdots$	t_{n-1}
Rented Accommodation	7	Rental payments	r^*_o	r^*_1	$r^*_2 \cdots$	r^*_{n-1}
	8	Costs of rehabilitation production	c^*_o	c^*_1	$c^*_2 \cdots$	c^*_{n-1}
	9	Domestic rates and misc. items[a]	d^*_o	d^*_1	$d^*_2 \cdots$	d^*_{n-1}
	10	Saving from income	s^*_o	s^*_1	$s^*_2 \cdots$	s^*_{n-1}
	11	Rented accommodation total (rows 7–10)	t^*_o	t^*_1	$t^*_2 \cdots$	t^*_{n-1}

[a] This includes house insurance, leaseholders' ground rents, service charges paid by long-leasehold occupiers of flats, etc.

The particular analytic method I shall use in order to understand the relative financial advantage of different housing options is illustrated in Table 5.1 where two choices alone are considered for the sake of simplicity of exposition. Each option is presumed to meet the accommodation requirements of a hypothetical household; it must be stressed, though, that I am presenting an abstract technique for expressing the meaning and the substance of the financial predicate, not suggesting that any hypothetical or real household is actually carrying out this calculation. At the same time it is worth emphasising that all the variables described have an empirical content and so *in principle* there is no obstacle in estimating their values in specific cases or sets of cases.

The first option is based on house purchase. The finance is raised from the personal assets of the household and a building society annuity mortgage. Possession requires in years zero to $(n-1)$ inclusive a series of payments listed in rows 1-4. Mortgage interest payments and rows 3 and 4 are net of any subsidy received from the state. At the beginning of year n, before the mortgage has been completely redeemed, the house is sold and its net worth appropriated.

The second option is based on rental of a dwelling in the private or public sector. Possession requires in years zero to $(n-1)$ inclusive a series of payments listed in rows 7-9. Rental payments are net of any rebates, subsidies and allowances, as are rows 8 and 9. The rental option permits the household to deposit in an interest-bearing form the personal assets ploughed into house purchase in option 1.

In any single year the payments aggregates of rows 1-4 and of rows 7-9 are unlikely to be equal. In this case the technique calculates the difference and enters it as a potential 'saving from income' in the option with the lower outlay. These streams, rows 5 and 10, are also assumed to be interest bearing. (All interest receipts are calculated net of tax.) A moment's thought reveals that the resultant total for each option in any given year must be identical ($t_0 = t^*_0$ etc.).

The financial evaluation of the two options can now be carried out and consists of the comparison of the potential cash assets in hand at the beginning of year n. In option 1 we have:

$$A_1 = G_1 + Z_1 + P_1 + S_1$$

where A_1 is the potential cash proceeds in total
G_1 is the price gain (untaxed on the household's main residence)
Z_1 is the original outlay of personal assets on the purchase of the house
P_1 is the sum of the mortgage principal repaid
S_1 is the value of the savings stream inclusive of compound interest

Note that the net worth of the house is equal to $G_1 + Z_1 + P_1$. The subscripts refer to option 1 of course. Had the example been based on the simpler situation where the mortgage debt had been completely redeemed, then we would have had:

$$A_1 = X_1 + S_1 \text{ where } X_1 \text{ is the selling price of the house.}$$

In option two we have:

$$A_2 = Z_2 + Z^*_2 + S_2$$

where Z_2 are the personal assets *not* in this case used for purchase but placed in an interest-bearing form ($Z_1 = Z_2$)

$Z*_2$ is the compound interest earned on Z_2

If A_1 exceeds A_2 the evaluation indicates owner-occupation is the more attractive choice in terms of the financial predicate and vice versa where A_2 exceeds A_1.

The technique demonstrates a curious paradox about the financial predicate. It is widely held that owner-occupation alone is a form of saving and this is contrasted unfavourably with rental accommodation where payments, in the popular phrase, are 'dead money'. This is true in the limited sense that the landlord never repays the rent he (or she) receives whereas the owner-occupier does recoup his payments of mortgage principal as well as the price gain on the house, *provided* the gain is positive. The owner-occupier also recovers his personal assets, in the absence of a price loss, but then the tenant never has to disburse these in the first place. However, the technique shows that evaluating the two options in terms of the total savings potential can - under definable circumstances - quite definitely give the advantage to rental, particularly where in each time-period an excess of mortgage payments over rent permits the tenant and not the owner-occupier to save out of income (or simply to save more). In the mature capitalist countries there are a number of cases such as Sweden, Switzerland, West Germany and the Netherlands where the scale of owner-occupation in the early 1970s was at most 35 per cent of all households.[4] Presumably the continued existence of a vigorous rental sector is explained in part by its financial advantages to the possessing households there. The specific approach to the financial predicate adopted here suggests, then, that to represent owner-occupation as a form of saving, and therefore inherently superior in its asset-forming potential to rental accommodation, is entirely false, a modern myth. Yet purchase-as-saving certainly serves to open up the domain of household preference to all those ideological influences associated with the virtues of thrift and 'the prudence of the good householder who saves part of his income to secure the future of his family'.[5] These views are promoted both by the building societies and the state; for example, when the latter intones that the master of the family 'builds up by steady saving a capital asset for himself and his dependants.'[6]

The financial analysis is robust enough for a number of developments. For example, it could treat two home-ownership options in one of which rehabilitation outlays are much higher with a powerful associated advantage in the final price gain. It could also deal with tenure switching during the life time of the household, e.g. a period in rental accommodation followed by entry into owner-occupation. In this case a new row has to be added to the payments stream recording the transactions costs of switches, a subject dealt with at length in chapter 13. Finally the technique can deal with two switching options in which the distinction is based on the date of the switch. Thus in the case of rental followed by house purchase, the financial predicate would favour an earlier rather than a later switch at a time of rapid house price increases, since the earlier switch implies both the appropriation of a greater price gain as well as a lower level of mortgage payments with a corresponding improvement in the potential savings stream.

It is possible to summarise the circumstances that favour one form of tenure against another with respect to their financial evaluation. This is done below.

Circumstances favouring rental	Circumstances favouring owner-occupation
Positive house price changes before entry	Negative house price changes before entry
Negative house price changes after entry	Positive house price changes after entry
High mortgage rates of interest	Low mortgage rates of interest
High rates of interest on personal assets	Low rates of interest on personal assets
Low rents	High rents
High subsidies on rental accommodation	Low subsidies on rental accommodation
Low subsidies on home-ownership	High subsidies on home-ownership

These relationships are self-explanatory with respect to the measurement in each case of A, the potential cash proceeds. It goes without saying that expensive rehabilitation costs and high domestic rates disfavour whichever tenure is worst affected by them in the specific case in question. There is no general rule one can make here since this type of outlay (or subsidy) is not tenure specific. One should also note the contradictory effect of stable but high rates of increase in house prices: they disfavour entry by driving up mortgage repayments, but favour it by promising substantial price gains. However, low rates of interest both on personal assets and on mortgages unambiguously favour entry into owner-occupation.

4　ON USE-VALUE

Much of the basic groundwork in this predicative analysis of the willingness to enter alternative tenures is now complete. Those readers who have been reared in the tradition of neo-classical economics (as I was myself) may well be surprised, even distressed, that I have not yet found it necessary to refer to the 'housing services' provided by a dwelling. This is the fundamental concept of the marginalist analysis of effective demand and is the entity supposed to be purchased through rental or mortgage payments. They are often conceived as homogeneous in their quality but varying in their quantity. Different postulated quantities are then correlated with differences in the stream of payments.

I have searched for these 'services' with patient diligence and regretfully conclude that they do not exist and therefore that all conventional analysis is based on an entity that is purely phantasmal. In the long pursuit of this chimera, the hunter always circles back to his starting point and finds no more, yet no less, than dwelling, located in space, within and beyond which individual human beings grouped into households engage in a complex set of activities.

But house prices, rents and mortgage payments do exist even if they cannot be explained by variations in the quantity of 'housing services' they command. Here, then, it is appropriate to introduce the concept of use-value. By the use-value of a dwelling I mean a holistic conception of the attributes of the dwelling possessed by a household and which can be measured or described in terms of the first four of my predicates, that is, the house's physical character, the degree of control it offers, and its environmental and relative locus.

With respect to my fifth and sixth predicates, I do not sub-sume these into the concept of use-value in deference to Aristotle, Adam Smith and David Ricardo who specifically used the term in contrast to that of 'exchange-value', nor do I use the term in the sense of Marx who employed it to refer to the good itself, viewed in a certain light, rather than the good's attributes.[7]

It is necessary to stress that although one may speak of a house 'having a use-value' this is not in the same sense that it 'has' a garden. A garden exists in space and time. In *this* sense use-values do not exist at all. The concept is employed merely as a way of referring in a holistic manner to four distinct predi-cates specific to the possession of every dwelling and which together constitute the major environmental influence in the life-activities of every household. This permits me to be more precise in the criticism of orthodox demand theory: the difficulty with the concept of the flow of housing services (and also with that of 'utility') is that the neo-classical economists deal with it as if it had the same ontological status as the flow of water. This is illegitimate for water exists but 'housing services' do not. At the same time this philosophical error serves to remind us that since 'use-value' denotes no thing and no activity it has no physical dimension and cannot be measured, although the prefer-ential ranking of dwellings in ordinal terms is possible and statistical descriptions can certainly be given of each of the four component predicates.

So what in the world is the use of 'housing services'? The answer is that the concept serves as a form of commodity fetish-ism; it makes a relation between persons appear as a relation between things. In fact, rent and mortgage payments are not in exchange for 'housing services', they are flows of money paid 'for the permission to inhabit the earth'.[8] Of course, there exists

a very private and complex trade-off between each of the six
predicates; for example, a household may be willing to pay a
much higher price in terms of mortgage payments or rent for a
dwelling with a favourable environmental locus. But these payments are not for a service, they are made so that the household
may possess the dwelling without the owner (in the case of a
tenant) or the mortgagee (in the case of an owner-occupier)
forcing through their eviction. The stream of payments, then,
is a phenomenon of law as well as economics: it is made to secure
certain rights in property. At the same time the household's
willingness to make these payments varies closely and directly
with the dwelling's use-value.

5   THE WILLINGNESS TO PURCHASE

The point has now been reached when it is possible to discuss
in predicative terms why households are willing to purchase
dwellings. Because there is no published evidence collected on
the basis of the foregoing framework, I shall rely on sketching
out what appear to me to be the dominant relationships. Once
again it is assumed we are dealing with a married couple new
household.

In the first place the household may be forced into owner-
occupation because it has no choice. If there is no flow of
private rental vacancies on to the market in the geographical
area relevant to the couple at a rent that they can afford, and
if residential qualifications and points based on need disqualify
them from entry into the council sector, the household will be
forced to buy in order to constitute itself. This point was made
at the beginning of the chapter.

Let it be assumed, however, that the married couple new household *does* enjoy some kind of choice and chooses to buy. This
being so, what is likely to be the basis of that choice? Three
methodological points are of considerable importance. First, it is
assumed that the household earns an average income for its
demographic group, an income that sets an upper limit on the
expenditure it can afford each week or month on accommodation.
Second, one should bear in mind a relationship in this context
that one can call Whitehead's law: in any comparison between
owner-occupation and rental, the lower one's income and wealth
the more likely it is that the appraisal will favour rental, particularly in the state sector.[9] Third, because I assume here that
a genuine choice favours owner-occupation, the predicative
analysis is set out in terms favourable to such a decision. It is
not true, of course, that choice always leads to the selection of
home-ownership.

In terms of the six predicates a choice in favour of owner-
occupation is likely in Britain in the 1970s to have reflected the
following considerations:

(a) Dwelling's physical character

Privately rented dwellings are less likely to enjoy the full range
of the basic internal amenities and are more likely to be in a
poorer state of repair. They are composed overwhelmingly of
flats and therefore have no access to a garden, and in general
have a smaller total area per unit. State housing is very heterogeneous in physical quality. Only if the household were offered
allocations restricted to some of the poorer flatted accommodation
built in the 1930s and 1960s is it likely to have been inferior
to owner-occupation.

(b) Control

In comparison with tenants, the owner-occupier household has
enjoyed very extensive freedom to maintain, repair, improve,
adapt or extend its home. In general, only extensions have
required planning permission. The move towards a tenant's
charter, partially embodied in the 1980 Housing Act, has only
just begun to redress the imbalance in the case of council
tenants. In contrast, both home-ownership and council rental
offer complete privacy inside the house or flat, whilst many
private tenants are forced to share facilities such as a bathroom
or kitchen. Lastly, as owners the household enjoys substantial
security of tenure: it can be dispossessed only in the case of
failure to meet its mortgage repayments or where the district
council compulsorily purchases the property in a slum clearance
scheme or for road-widening purposes, etc. In practice, if not
in law, state housing tenants enjoy as much security as the
owner-occupier, but insecurity of tenure has always been the
bane of the private tenant.

(c) Environmental locus

The relative advantage of owner-occupied housing over rented
housing with respect to environmental locus is difficult to
generalise about but has probably played a major role in the
perceptions and choices of many, many home-owners. If a survey
had been carried out for the country as a whole in any year
during the 1970s, it probably would have shown as a general
truth that neighbourhoods predominantly in owner-occupation
are less exposed to intense traffic flows, industrial pollution
and crime, and that they are environmentally more attractive
and more richly endowed with health and educational infrastructures.

With respect to social class and ethnic origin, we must recognise that in Britain as in the other capitalist countries there
exist unfortunate and disabling divisions between the occupational and ethnic strata of the working people. These manifest
themselves in the housing field as in every other. Neighbourhoods typically in owner-occupation are under represented in
terms of the proportion of manual workers, poor families and
black people. As a result such locations, and thereby house
purchase rather than rental, are probably more attractive to

non-manual workers (at the very least) searching for a home, and more appealing to people with an English, Scottish or Welsh background. If on entry into the state housing sector, a household is likely to be assigned to a flat on one of the least attractive estates, then environmental locus could exert a huge bias in favour of owner-occupation.

(d) Relative locus
In terms of access to city-centre employment, shops and entertainment, private rental is as a general rule superior to either of the other tenures, and on balance state housing is probably superior to owner-occupation. However, in terms of access from the metropolitan conglomerations to the recreational facilities of the countryside, the hills and the sea, the house-owner usually enjoys the superior location.

(e) Housing mobility
With respect to this predicate I know of no hard evidence which demonstrates that relative mobility *is* seen to be greater in owner-occupation but it certainly seems highly likely that that is the way people think. We can simplify the analysis by conceiving households to consider mobility between dwellings within a single tenure category - mobility within the council sector, within owner-occupation, within private rental. The dearth of good quality privately rented property in Britain as a whole in the 1970s surely, on mobility grounds, made this tenure relatively unattractive. Moreover, the low rate of transfers and exchanges and the use of residence qualifications in points systems clearly constrains mobility within and between districts in the council sector.[10] For this reason, owner-occupation may be preferred to a council tenancy, even where owner-occupiers understand the substantial transactions costs that selling buyers have to meet.

Until now, only perceived mobility has been referred to. Is it actually correct to say that housing mobility *is* greater for homeowners? Unfortunately the question admits of no definitive answer. Studies abound of the relative mobility of households and relate this to tenure, distance of the move undertaken, etc. However, the problem is that there exists an association between tenure category and other variables, occupation for example. Therefore, observed differential mobility between tenures may in fact be caused by these other associated variables. To continue the example, the higher mobility, in certain age groups and over longer distances, of home-owners may be explained not by their housing situation but by the fact that a relatively high proportion are professional, managerial and executive workers, occupations characterised by a relatively low spatial density and therefore requiring high geographic mobility.[11]

An exception to any presumption of greater housing mobility for the home-owner arises in the case of factory closures. If this brings about a sharp upward movement in the number of

households wishing to sell their houses within a specific locality
or district, it may prove impossible to close deals in a short
period of time without incurring substantial financial losses. The
surge in supply from the stock here is associated in time and
space with a decline in labour market opportunities and therefore
a deteriorating relative locus. A more general case of restrictions
on owner-occupier mobility is caused by substantial variations
between regions in average house price levels. These make it
difficult for a household to move from a low price to a high price
region. Chapter 14 deals with questions of mobility at greater
length.

(f) Financial evaluation
It goes almost without saying that no study exists that uses the
analysis of section three to describe the relative financial advantage of the three main tenures and until such work is done I
shall remain silent on their real respective relationships. Yet it
is possible to say a little about households' perceptions of the
financial predicate, particularly in a period like the 1970s which,
as we shall see in chapter 16, was marked both by historically
high mortgage rates and a rapid (if uneven) advance in average
house prices.
   The household's actual economic comparison of house-
ownership with rental accommodation is usually carried out in
a rough-and-ready fashion that juggles together five main
elements:

(i)   the relative size in year zero of the rent and the mortgage
       payments on the houses concerned;
(ii)   the possibility of medium - and long-term rent rises;
(iii) the fact that rehabilitation outlays, particularly large ones,
       are borne directly by the home-owner but are usually
       socialised in the state housing sector;
(iv)   the possibility of making substantial price gains through
       owner-occupation;
(v)   the popular (if flawed) notion that rents are simply 'dead
       money' whilst purchase is a form of long-term 'saving' or
       'investment'.

The ownership of the house, probably unencumbered by debt at
the end of twenty or thirty years, also permits the couple to
leave a substantial asset to their children, although Willy Loman's
acerbic comment in *Death of a Salesman* is worth recalling:
'Figure it out. Work a lifetime to pay off a house. You finally
own it, and there's nobody to live in it.'[12]

6 ON OWNERSHIP

The predicative analysis of tenure suggests that the concepts of
'owner-occupation', 'home-ownership' and 'domestic property'
are not as simple and as absolute as is widely believed. These

doubts are reinforced when we appreciate that the juristic
concept of ownership is as a set of specific legal rights governing relations among people with respect to things. As these
rights and their enforcement change, so does the substance of
the concept of ownership.[13]

First, we should recognise that the situation of owner-occupier
and tenant are entirely different from that of the little pig who
had all the roast beef and the little pig who had none, for in the
case of housing tenure *both* parties possess a dwelling. A person
who is literally homeless stands in a situation distinct from
either tenure.

Second, the specific content of owner-occupation itself has
often changed in law. We have seen this in chapters 1, 2 and 3,
for example with respect to the owner's financial rights and
duties - such as the introduction in 1959 of a statutory right to
claim a standard rehabilitation grant and the abolition of Schedule
A taxation in 1963. Most recently there have been important
modifications to the rights of married women living in mortgaged
property.[14]

Third, the social meaning of owner-occupation is structured
by the rights specific to other tenures, for we interpret what it
means to be an owner-occupier in part through its comparability
with other tenures. Thus when the rights of council tenants to
rehabilitate their own dwelling change, for example, so too is
there a shift in the social meaning of home-ownership.

Once the view that owner-occupation has a meaning that is
absolute and static is abandoned, once its essentially relational
and historically specific character is understood, then it follows
that political, psychological and sociological distinctions based on
conceptions of 'housing classes' are likely to be seen as more
tenuous and unstable than at first might be proposed. We return
to a critique of neo-Weberian political sociology in chapter 15.
Nevertheless, in denying it any absolute character it is not
intended to dispute that substantial, though changing, distinctions do exist between tenures. The core of home-ownership
today consists in the very extensive control it gives over the
use of the dwelling to the possessing household and, even more
important, the right to alienate the rights in that property, that
is the right to sell.

These comments lead on to consideration of a motive for purchase that has not yet appeared in this analysis: the motive to
buy merely for the sake of ownership itself. This factor is
repeatedly cited in government White Papers - for example in
1953 as the satisfaction of ownership, in 1971 as 'a deep and
natural desire', and even more definitively in 1977 as 'a basic
and natural desire'.[15] Moreover, the government's empirical
surveys demonstrate with an accuracy to the nearest percentage
point that a majority of former private tenants who decided to
purchase did so because they 'wanted to buy', an exciting if
not totally unexpected result.[16]

In opposition to this regression to the philosophy of property

of John Locke, this abuse of psychology and statistics, I
propose that the evident desire of very substantial numbers of
British working people to own their home rests entirely on an
unmistakable foundation. The material base for the superstructure of the desire for a specific property relation in housing consumption is that owner-occupation, for households on
average or higher than average wages and salaries, in general
gives access to dwellings that are ranked higher in terms of
their use-value and which are perceived to offer greater housing
mobility and long-term financial advantages.

In this interpretation of why people are willing to purchase
dwellings for owner-occupation, the concept of various types of
constraint has appeared, controls that determine household
access to the ever-changing housing stock. The third of these
was referred to very briefly as the financial constraint: it is
clear that a potential choice is only genuinely feasible if the
household enjoys the ability to pay, an ability that marks off the
idea of effective demand from housing need. The next chapter
takes up this question with particular reference to the role of
building societies in the supply of mortgage finance. But before
embarking on that discussion it is as well to make explicit a
distinction that until this point has been only implicit. In this
book the term 'exchange process' is used to describe any situation where the ownership of a dwelling changes from one person
(or institution) to another and the finance necessary for purchase
is referred to as exchange finance. Exchange exhibits two
distinct modes which it is often essential to keep separate. In the
first, a newly constructed dwelling is sold by a developer or
builder; this is called output realisation and the money raised
to buy the dwelling is spoken of as realisation finance. In the
second mode, an owner of an existing dwelling, first sold to him
(or to an even earlier owner) in some previous time-period,
transfers his ownership to another party and in this case one
refers to the transfer process and transfer finance. Exchange,
then, embraces both realisation and transfer. With this clarifi-
cation in mind, we can next consider that most intensively researched of subjects: the building societies.

6 THE CAPACITY TO PURCHASE AND THE BUILDING SOCIETIES

1 INTRODUCTION

Human life comprehends an immense variety of activities. Amongst these is one set of pursuits which, in a material sense, can be regarded as fundamental. It embraces those labours undertaken by the species that bring into existence, develop and maintain the capacity to labour itself. The most significant specific forms of such activities of reproduction are domestic labour and the production of shelter, food and drink, clothing, educational and health services, and some transport services, particularly transport to work. Housing production, then, is a form of what we can call reproductive labour or reproductive production and thus must be analysed within capitalist societies both as a sphere of commodity production in itself and as a source of outputs which, in the long term, are a prerequisite for commodity production in general.

In marked contrast with the consumption of food and drink and clothing, for example, access to housing accommodation by means of outright purchase of the dwelling has never been feasible for the mass of the working people of this country. This follows partly from the material fact that, unlike food and drink and clothing, a house cannot be consumed piecemeal: it is sufficient not merely for a week or a month or a year but, properly maintained, can suffice for the whole of adult life. Moreover, the dwelling as an activity centre must serve a multiplicity of functions which in their turn require certain minimum physical attributes of the structure. These physical predicates of the newly constructed house, together with the productivity and wage rates of workers in the construction materials and building industries, essentially determine the supply price in the long run. As I have said, that price is far too high to make it possible for the majority of households to purchase outright from their income and the formation of married couple new households takes place far too early in their working lives for purchase to be financed wholly out of personal savings.

What a magnificent contradiction! The construction of houses is fundamentally necessary for the survival of the species and the reproduction of the capacity to labour yet those who labour do not receive wages and salaries sufficient for them to purchase those dwellings unless the physical attributes of the houses are so primitive as themselves to constitute a threat in the short or long run to health and to diligent labour.

In the history of British society since the Industrial Revolution, three dominant systems of production, finance and allocation have developed which were capable of overcoming this problem of the realisation of housing output. The first was for particular fractions of the capitalist class themselves to purchase the private housebuilders' supply and then to rent it out to the labouring masses.[1] The second was the development of mortgage finance institutions which provided particular strata of the working population with loans sufficient for house purchase and owner-occupation. The third was for the local state itself to buy the housebuilders' output on a contractual basis and then rent the properties.

The monetary relationships in home-ownership based on mortgage finance are quite simple at the level of the single buyer. The individual household faces a supply price for the new or second-hand property it wishes to purchase plus certain accompanying transaction costs and any major initial rehabili-tation outlays. This lump sum must be raised by combining together: one or more loans from financial institutions; a portion of the household's encashable personal assets, including in appropriate cases the net worth enjoyed by a selling buyer; and finally, any personal gifts or loans from family and friends. However, the correct analytic starting point in understanding the financial costs of owner-occupation to the household is not this lump sum outlay, most of which, after all, is usually borne by the mortgage institutions. Instead we should consider the cost as the continuing expenditure stream composed of the relevant entries listed in Table 5.1, viz. payments of loan interest, repayments of the principal of the loan, continuing rehabilitation outlays and domestic rates, etc., all net of state subsidy.[2] In the great majority of cases this stream of outlays is met out of the household's post-tax income. So the cost of owner-occupation is best measured by the ratio of this flow to the household's post-tax income on a weekly, monthly or annual basis. In passing one can note that because the price of the house is not met out of income, the widely quoted house price-household income ratio is conceptually meaningless. In practice, the ratio appears to be used only because it has a loose relationship with the quotient of annual mortgage repay-ments to annual income.

Moving from the economic to the legal position we find that through home-ownership the occupier obtains legal title to the property as well as the right to use it, but title is usually qualified in that the loan is secured by way of a 'mortgage' on the property, 'a legal agreement giving the lender rights over the property if the borrower defaults on the loan'.[3] When the loan is fully repaid, the purchaser acquires full legal title to the property. In common language the term 'mortgage' usually refers both to the agreement and to the loan made to the mort-gagor. For the mortgage institutions, the security of a loan derives from a double source: the borrower is powerfully

motivated to repay since default will deprive the household of a
basic necessity of life and should default occur, the institution
can resell the property and recoup the outstanding debt.

These economico-legal relationships generate a triple barrier
to house purchase. First, the buyer must secure mortgage
finance and this is likely to be provided only if the ratio of the
net expenditure stream to post-tax income (or some less sophisticated sibling ratio) is perceived as not imposing too risky a
burden on the household's finances. Second, the mortgage
granted will rarely be sufficient to meet the full lump sum of
purchase price, transaction and any initial rehabilitation costs.
This necessitates personal assets or access to private loans.
Third, the mortgage institution must be persuaded that the
property purchased constitutes adequate security for the advance.
The first two explain the enormous limitations of owner-
occupation and mortgage finance in relating housing production
to human need. The third, as we shall see, undermines the
contribution of home-ownership to housing rehabilitation. All
three are specific forms of the 'financial constraint' referred to
in chapter 5.

2   THE SOURCES OF MORTGAGE FINANCE

The relationships described in the previous section suggest that
the starting point of an empirical investigation into the capacity
to purchase is the relative importance of the different sources
of cash raised in order to buy the dwelling. In brief: where
does the money come from for the lump sum payment? Unfortunately no published data exist to allow this question to be
properly answered. Instead we have to rely on the DoE's
National Movers Survey which tabulates the *main* source of
finance for purchase in England and Wales. The survey results
in 1973 are worth summarising briefly.[4] For new households the
building societies were the main source, with local authorities
running a rather bad second. For other first-time buyers, again
the societies were most important and the local authorities
second, the main difference being that for the lowest income
group as many as 28 per cent relied primarily on ready money.
This probably reflects their relatively restricted access to
mortgage finance.

In the case of selling buyers, net worth was almost as
important as society finance; for the lowest income group in
particular, net worth was the primary source for 71 per cent of
them. The DoE argues convincingly that this is correlated with
the buyers' age:[5]

Owner-occupiers at or above retirement age frequently have
fairly low incomes, but correspondingly low outgoings on
their houses through owning outright. When they move, they
are unlikely to trade up, and rather than take on a mortgage,

buy a house that can be afforded from the proceeds of the previous sale.

These data, limited though they are, do demonstrate the fundamental importance of the mainstream mortgage institutions in house purchase. But before continuing, it is useful to recall that the dominance of mortgage loans in the flow of purchases does not imply that the 'stock', so to speak, of owner-occupiers are all mortgagors. This is explained not only by the use of personal assets for purchase, but above all because large numbers of home-owners have fully repaid the loans originally made to them.

Table 6.1 Net advances for house purchase in the UK by main institutional source 1970-80 (percentages)

Year	Building societies[a]	Local authorities[b]	Insurance companies[c]	Banks	Other Public[d]	Total[e]
1970	87	6	3	3	1	100
1971	88	6	1	5	1	100
1972	80	7	neg.	12	1	100
1973	71	12	4	11	2	100
1974	63	24	5	4	5	100
1975	76	17	2	2	4	100
1976	94	2	neg.	2	3	100
1977	96	neg.	1	3	1	100
1978	96	−1	1	5	−1	100
1979	83	5	4	8	neg.	100
1980	78	7	4	9	2	100

Source: HCS.

[a] Includes a small amount for advances other than house purchase.

[b] Includes advances for conversions, improvements, repairs, etc and advances to housing associations and allowances for payments of housing association grants.

[c] Includes topping-up loans. Increased coverage from 1974.

[d] Includes advances by the New Towns and the Housing Corporation.

[e] In fact, due to rounding errors, these totals do not always sum to one hundred.

Now let us turn to consider the relative importance of the mainstream mortgage finance institutions in the supply of funds. Table 6.1 gives a very clear picture of the situation in the 1970s. It shows the annual net amount loaned for house purchase in the UK by the building societies, the insurance companies, the local authorities and the banks. The enormous importance of the societies is evident. Only in 1973 and 1974, when local government lending expanded as that of the building societies contracted, were the latter's net loans less than three-quarters of the grand total. What makes their position so special is not only that they are the heavyweights of mortgage finance but that, unlike the other mainstream lenders, loans for house purchase constitute the dominant entry in their asset portfolio.[6]

So the activities of the building societies, which constitute the subject-matter of the rest of this chapter, are the key to understanding the supply of loans for house purchase. One's inclination is immediately to begin to appraise their lending practices. In order to lend, however, it is first necessary to borrow and it is their position as borrowers that has the prior claim on analysis.

The building societies are amongst the most important institutions of the British financial system and accounts with them are a major form of personal saving. In 1980 more than one-third of the adult population of Britain had money placed with them and there were more than 31 million separate savings accounts. In law the societies are non-profit-making mutual organisations. Their share investors are legally not creditors but members whose financial rights consist of repayment of capital, with interest, according to the rules of the society. Unlike the shareholders of a limited liability company, they have no claim on any surpluses generated by the societies' activities. The societies are statutorily limited in the kind of security on which they can lend which, in general, must consist of land and buildings. They must have the first claim on mortgaged property. The legal framework is largely defined by the 1962 Building Societies Act and is administered by the Chief Registrar of Friendly Societies.

In the 1890s there were as many as 3,500 separate societies but this has fallen continuously in the course of the twentieth century so that by 1980 there existed only 273.[7] From the 1930s the decline primarily reflects the amalgamation of permanent societies to form larger units. The merger process as well as the tendency of smaller societies to grow relatively more slowly has led to a concentration of assets and power in the larger institutions. The proportion of total assets held in the top twenty organisations rose from 65 per cent in 1930 to 84 per cent in 1977.[8]

The major national societies usually have a head office in the town of origin, a number of regional offices, and branches throughout the country, with strong hierarchical control from head office through to the branches. The rapid rate of branch extension in the 1970s was above all aimed at securing an improved cash inflow. Although this has led to a wasteful duplication of facilities by competing societies, the proportion of total assets tied up in premises is relatively low.

Below the level of the branches there is an even more extensive tier of 'agents' who exist in order to channel private wealth and savings into the societies. Official agents are commonly paid a retainer and receive commission from the institutions and/or a quota of mortgage funds earmarked for borrowers nominated by the agents. Most of them are either accountants, solicitors, estate agents or insurance brokers. Commission may be paid at a rate of 1 per cent of the deposits thus channelled and mortgage quotas can operate on a pound-for-pound basis. Boddy writes:[9]

It has been estimated that societies may receive up to forty per cent of their total new investment via agents, and that the proportion of mortgage lending arranged through agents may be even higher. Societies use quotas as a way of procuring investment and often speak of using mortgage funds for 'development purposes'.

3 THE FLOW OF FUNDS

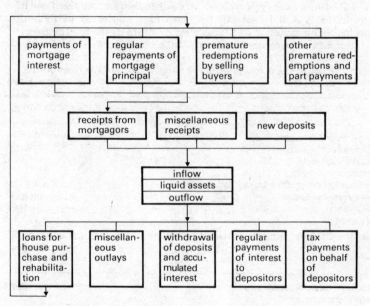

Figure 6.1 The building societies' flow of funds

Before proceeding any further it will be useful to describe the total flow of funds into and out of the building societies. These are set out in Figure 6.1. The inflows comprise only three basic categories. Receipts from mortgagors embrace the regular monthly payments by owner-occupiers of the principal of their loan and interest on the outstanding debt, as well as the premature redemption of mortgage loans either by selling buyers or other home-owners. New deposits I use as a generic term to include the gross inflow of funds in each time-period from 'savers' and 'investors' of all kinds, whatever the type of account in which they are placed. Finally, miscellaneous receipts comprise items such as rents from surplus premises, the interest and profit income from the societies' liquid assets and the commission received from insurance companies for house insurance directed their way by the institutions.

With respect to the outflows, we have five basic categories. Mortgage finance both for house purchase and rehabilitation work obviously is one item. Then there are those categories that relate to depositors: withdrawals of deposits and accumulated interest; the payment of interest on deposits where this is not automatically credited to accounts; and payments made to the Inland Revenue, on the depositors' behalf, of the tax due on their interest receipts. Finally we have miscellaneous outlays which include the wages and salaries of the societies' staff, the rents paid on any office premises not owned, and corporation tax. Table 6.2 presents quantitative information on the flow of funds in 1979 as it is set out by the Chief Registrar of Friendly Societies. The dominant entries are receipts from mortgagors, new deposits, mortgage loans and withdrawals.

Table 6.2 Flow of funds to and from the buildings societies in Great Britain in 1978[a]

In Flow	£m
Receipts from mortgagors:	
Principal repayments	3,615
Interest payments	2,770
Miscellaneous receipts:	
Interest and net profits from cash and investments	733
Insurance commission	65
Other (net)	9
New deposits	16,355
Total	23,547
Outflow	
Loans for house purchase and rehabilitation	8,808
Miscellaneous outlays:	
Management expenses (excluding depreciation)	341
Office premises and other fixed assets	95
Withdrawals	12,820
Interest paid to depositors	660
Taxation (all forms)[b]	817
Total	23,541

Source: Registry of Friendly Societies, *Report of the Chief Registrar of Friendly Societies for the Year 1978, Part 2, Building Societies*, London, HMSO, 1979, p.9.

[a] The nomenclature used is that of Figure 6.1 wherever possible. The discrepancy of £6 million between the two totals was added to liquid assets.

[b] Includes tax payments on behalf of depositors and corporation tax.

Interposed between the inflow and outflow conduits of Figure 6.1 I have drawn a reservoir, so to speak, labelled 'liquid assets'. These are specified categories of assets formally known as 'cash and investments'. They are required so that the societies can be sure of their ability to meet payments due, including both the cheques required when an approved mortgage advance comes to fruition as well as deposit withdrawals on demand or at very short notice. These liquid assets are primarily composed of cash and balances with banks, certificates of deposit, local authority temporary debt, short-term gilt-edged stock and longer-term local authority and central government debt. For all the societies taken together, 15-16 per cent is the effective minimum ratio of these cash and investments to the value of the societies' total assets, below which they go only for short periods whilst measures are taken to raise the ratio.

When a society finds that its outflow exceeds its inflow of funds, then the level in the reservoir of liquid assets can be allowed to fall. Similarly, if the inflow exceeds the outflow it may choose for a time to increase these assets. So the reservoir can be used to permit a substantial differential between the two flows to continue, let us say for weeks or even a few months. But in the long run, the size of the flows must be equivalent.

As we have seen, the building societies are financial intermediaries: they borrow money on the market and on-lend it to house purchasers. Their liquid assets and the fact that no single item among the inflows must equal, pound for pound, any item among the outflows both give the institutions some flexibility in their practices as middlemen. Yet two specific flow relationships are worth highlighting.

First, the gross interest on deposits, that is the sum of the annual interest paid or credited to depositors and the related tax payments to the Inland Revenue, can be thought of as derived from the interest paid to the societies on their loans. As a result the respective rates of interest, the gross interest rate paid to depositors by the societies (the 'deposit rate') and the interest rate paid to the societies by mortgagors (the 'mortgage rate'), must move together, even though some flexibility is permitted. This linkage is reinforced by the importance of the mortgage and deposit rates to the building societies' income and expenditure accounts. Mortgage interest is the dominant form of income and gross interest on deposits is the dominant expenditure item. Income minus expenditure constitutes the societies' gross surplus which, after deduction of corporation tax, mostly goes to their 'reserves'. Legally those reserves are not allowed to fall below about 2 per cent of total assets, the exact figure varying inversely with the absolute value of assets.[10]

The second specific flow relationship concerns what I shall call net deposits, that is new deposits in each time-period minus withdrawals and regular payments of interest to depositors. These flows need to be treated in a unified way, for decisions by depositors to change the flow of new deposits into the societies are related, at least in aggregate, to their decisions to change the scale both of their withdrawals and of the periodic

interest owed to them which they actually take payment of
rather than allow to be credited to their accounts. Net deposits
are a volatile flow and a substantial rise or fall in the value of
this variable will lead to a rise or fall in the flow of mortgage
advances.[11]

In the next section I wish to consider the flow of net deposits
in more detail. But before doing that it is useful to say a little
about the inflow entry referred to in Figure 6.1 as 'receipts
from mortgagors'. Table 6.3 shows the tremendous importance
of repayments of principal as a source of funds for gross
mortgage advances since 1970. The ratio of repayments to
gross advances lay in the range 39-49 per cent throughout the
period.

*Table 6.3   Repayments of principal as a source of gross mortgage advances by
building societies in the UK 1970-80*

Year	Repayments of principal (£m)	Gross advances (£m)	Ratio of repayments to advances (%)
1970	933	2,021	46
1971	1,158	2,758	42
1972	1,434	3,649	39
1973	1,541	3,540	44
1974	1,460	2,950	49
1975	2,197	4,965	44
1976	2,499	6,117	41
1977	2,789	6,889	40
1978	3,619	8,734	41
1979	3,832	9,103	42
1980	3,892	9,614	40

Source: HCS; BSA Bulletin.

Principal repayments fall into redemptions, regular instalments
and part payments: these were in the ratio of 23: 6: 1 for the
period 1970-5 and it can be argued that 'the key to the volume
of mortgage repayments lies in mortgage redemptions'.[12] In order
to understand redemptions, DoE economists have used a concept
drawn from demography which they refer to as age-specific
mortgage attrition rates. The notion is that the 'age' of a
mortgage can be regarded as the number of years that have
passed since it was first issued. It 'dies' when it is redeemed.
For mortgages of any given 'age', the proportionate number of
deaths during the course of a year can be calculated and this is
the attrition rate. Nationwide Building Society data allowed these
rates to be calculated. They vary from year to year depending
on how active the housing market is but broadly we can say
that from the 'age' of 2 onwards the attrition rate runs at
about 10-11 per cent per annum, certainly up to 'age' 13 by

which time only about one-quarter of the original cohort would still be outstanding.

Since only about 7 per cent of owner-occupiers with mortgages moved each year, when these calculations were made in the early 1970s, then redemption by selling buyers does not tell the whole story. It is suggested that perhaps only three-quarters of all redemptions can be accounted for by selling buyers, emigrants, households dissolving through divorce, and redemptions in the cases of married men dying who had previously taken out a mortgage protection policy. The DoE concludes:[13]

> The reality of large numbers of mortgages being redeemed before maturity, for reasons other than sale of a mortgaged house or death of the mortgagor, is thus not in doubt, and calculations for 1971 and 1973 suggest that the number was in the region of 100,000 in each year or perhaps more. . . .
> Nothing is yet known for certain about the reasons for these mortgage redemptions, or the sources from which they are financed. A plausible surmise is that a considerable number of people use capital receipts (e.g. inheritances) to pay off mortgage debts. If so, considerable numbers of householders retain their dislike of debts and do not regard keeping as deep in debt as possible as being a wise thing to do even if that debt bears an interest rate (net of tax relief) well below the rate of inflation.

4   BUILDING SOCIETIES AND THE CAPITAL MARKET

In this section the societies are looked at as financial institutions competing for funds with the rest of the capital market. A brief summary of the legal forms in which money is held with them is therefore a necessary preliminary. In fact there are two main forms: ordinary shares and term shares. With the former, which is dominant, interest is paid at a rate that is variable on notice whilst repayments are made either on demand or after an interval which permits the pass book to be checked. Term shares require a fairly substantial minimum sum to be placed at the outset and in return for guaranteeing the placement for a given period, the lender receives a preferential interest rate. Even higher rates may be paid for sums larger than the minimum and for money held for longer than a two-year term. In addition to these two forms of holding money with the societies there are at least two more: deposits and subscription shares. Neither of them is quantitatively significant within the overall total of the societies' borrowing. (The reader is reminded that, save in the penultimate sentence, deposit is used by me as a generic term for money placed with the societies.)[14]

On the deposits they receive the societies pay an interest rate, a rate that varies over time, between societies and between types of share. For the present let us simplify and

think of it as a single rate, the maximum rate recommended to
the societies by their trade association, the BSA. This rate
and the size of the deposit determine how much interest is earned
by the depositor in each time-period. However, the societies
pay out (or credit to the depositor's account) not the full sum
but the interest earned net of tax. This tax deduction at source
is then paid directly to the Inland Revenue. Let us note in
passing that in general the relation between interest rates before
and after tax is very simple: if we denote the former as i, the
latter as j, and the tax rate paid as t, then:

$j = i \ (1-t)$

Now in the case of the building societies, the rate at which
tax is charged on interest is not equal to the depositor's individual income tax rate but, by a special arrangement with the
Inland Revenue, is a composite rate equal to the weighted
average tax rate of *all* the societies' depositors, excluding rates
above the basic rate. This is done, it is said, to avoid the
record-keeping that would otherwise be necessary for dealing
with small payments of interest on millions of accounts. Because
of this averaging, it follows that the composite rate is less than
the basic rate of tax but, of course, greater than the zero rate.
In the autumn of 1981 the composite tax arrangement only applied
on individual accounts to sums up to £20,000 with one society
but the depositor is permitted to have accounts with more than
one society.

Compositing has certain curious and important effects. First
it robs the poor to pay the rich since zero-rate taxpayers must
pay the much higher composite rate on their deposit interest,
precisely in order to bring down the tax payments of those who
pay income tax at the basic rate. The arrangement redistributes
income in a regressive manner.[15] Second, in the competition for
funds from basic-rate taxpayers, the building societies can offer
a share rate net of tax *equal* to that of the rest of the money
market, even though it promises a before-tax rate that is *lower*
than its competitors. This is simply because building society
interest is taxed at the lower composite rate. To this degree,
then, the arrangement partially shelters the societies from the
bleak winds of financial competition and permits them, in achieving a given flow of net deposits into their accounts, to set a
lower mortgage interest rate for house purchase.[16]

This section began with a brief account of the types of building society accounts and then examined the composite tax
arrangements on deposit interest. It is now time to look at what
constitutes the allure of building societies for depositors. Such
people are tremendously heterogeneous, of course, but one can
posit the existence of two ideal-types present in every depositor,
just as Dr Jekyll and Mr Hyde shared the same human frame.
The first is a 'saver'. For them the societies are attractive
because the multiplicity of branches makes them easy to get to

and the opening hours are convenient; their money seems safe
because they believe the government would never let a society
go under; large cash sums can be withdrawn on demand or with
the briefest delay, although there is no cheque facility; and
finally, 'building societies offer to intending house purchasers
the attraction . . . that building up a fair-sized balance over a
run of years is likely to secure a preferred position in the queue
for mortgages when funds are short'.[17] The societies' extensive
advertising underpins these views. Boddy suggests that they
cultivate their small-saver image to distinguish themselves from
'high finance' and to justify their special tax treatment.[18]

The second ideal-type is a 'rentier'. He (or she) owns certain
assets that must be placed in a form which in a probabilistic
sense maximises the rate of growth in their value net of tax.
The great security of building society deposits and the liquidity
in particular of ordinary shares, should switching be indicated,
are both attractive. The composite tax arrangement is important
for basic-rate taxpayers. Above all, it is the interest rate on the
deposit relative to other interest rates (or other implicit interest
rates where capital gains are part of the accumulation process)
that determine the appropriateness of such a placement. In brief,
we can suggest that for 'rentiers' the relative rate of interest
on society accounts, adjusted for their security, their liquidity
and the tax rate on share interest, crucially affects decisions
to place new deposits with the societies, to withdraw deposits
and accumulated interest and to take payment of interest when
due. Thus the flow of net deposits from 'rentiers' is highly
sensitive to the adjusted relative rate of interest, a variable
open to many forms of calculation. The types of asset that
compete with building society deposits for a place in the
rentiers' portfolio include clearing bank seven-day deposits,
accounts with the Trustee Savings Bank, bank accounts denomi-
nated in a foreign currency, finance house deposits, National
Savings Certificates, other National Savings accounts, gilt-
edged stock, temporary deposits with local authorities, local
government bonds, life insurance, equity shares, unit trusts,
gold, Georgian silver, stamps, commodity futures and - house
purchase!

As I have suggested, the majority of depositors have something
of both ideal-types within them, although one is usually dominant.
People with small accounts tend to be savers and those with
large accounts tend to be rentiers, perhaps largely because the
absolute gains from interest rate maximisation are so much
greater on a fortune than on a widow's mite. So a few words are
in order on the size distribution of building society deposits.

BSA statistics for 1977 demonstrate enormous inequality in
the size of individual accounts. Small accounts make up the
majority of the total number but large ones constitute the lion's
share of aggregate deposits. The statistical proof depends, of
course, on where one draws the line between small and large.
Taking the division at £1,000 the results for 1977 are: deposits

of up to £1,000 made up 67 per cent of the total number of accounts but only 13 per cent of total deposits. More than 40 per cent of deposits were contained in the 7 per cent of all accounts that exceeded £5,000.[19] If the rentier motive is predominant amongst the holders of relatively large accounts, then the societies' deposits are primarily rentier placements and from this we can conclude that they should be sensitive to the adjusted relative interest rate. Let me consider this question next.

The response of the flow of net deposits to shifts in relative interest rates is of great economic and (indirectly) political importance. The relationship has been extensively researched in recent years and the major conclusions of this work are fairly straightforward and can be briefly summarised.[20] First, there does indeed exist a clear positive correlation between the relative rate of interest and the flow of net deposits, where the relative rate is defined as the BSA maximum recommended rate on ordinary shares minus some measure of competing money market rates, such as the interest rate on three-month deposit with the local authorities. Second, this sensitivity is primarily due to flows of funds into and out of the larger accounts. Third, the response appears to derive from two distinct groups: those who have an asset portfolio which they switch between placements and those who are in receipt of substantial financial assets - e.g. from legacies, net worth realised on house sale and maturing insurance policies - who are more likely to place the money with the societies when they offer a relatively attractive rate. Fourth, the opening of a negative differential in interest rates does *not* lead to a transfer of billions of pounds out of the societies' accounts but to more moderate switching and non-placement. Econometric evidence suggests that a 1 per cent deterioration in the relative interest rate in 1973 cost the societies a reduction of something like £35 million per month in net receipts with a time-lag of under one month. By 1976 the figure had risen to between £55 and £60 million.

Fifth and last, whilst the reduced net inflow is insignificant in comparison with the societies' total assets, it can be very substantial indeed in relation to the monthly outflow of mortgage lending. As we have seen, the major sources of money for fresh advances are the repayment of mortgage principal and the flow of net deposits. This vital linkage is explored further in section seven below.

5 MORTGAGE REPAYMENTS AND HOUSEHOLD INCOME

Section four dealt with the principal sources of the building societies' funds. Rather than turn immediately to consider the institutions' lending policies, it is first necessary to say a little about the general nature of loans for house purchase and the relationship of mortgage repayments to household income over time.

From the point of view of the borrower, the mortgage allows him (or her) to spread out the 'capital' outlay on the house over a number of years, although this incurs a cost in terms of the interest charged on the loan. In Britain there are just two basic types of mortgage advance. One is an 'annuity' or 'capital repayment' loan. In this case, setting aside interest rate changes and tax relief, the sum paid each month remains unchanged up to redemption. Initially the payments overwhelmingly consist of interest charges; this slowly changes so that by the end of the loan period they are largely made up of principal repayments. The annual gross sum is fixed when the mortgage is taken out and normally alters subsequently only if the interest rate changes.

The second type of advance is an endowment mortgage on which interest only is paid each year. The principal is repaid when a linked life insurance policy matures. In the event of the mortgagor's premature death, the policy ensures the mortgage is immediately paid off. In the late 1960s endowment mortgages made up as little as 8 per cent of all advances but by 1980 the figure had grown to 23 per cent. Loans to borrowers nominated by insurance companies acting as agents for a society are generally endowment mortgages. The period for which advances of the annuity and endowment type are taken out varies but twenty and twenty-five years are by far the commonest terms. Combination loans of the two types also exist.

We have already seen in earlier chapters that the owner-occupier's mortgage payments are subsidised by the state either through tax relief or the option mortgage subsidy.[21] In the former case the owner's tax payments are reduced by an amount equal to the product of the mortgage interest and his marginal rate of taxation. Since 1974 qualifying interest payments have been restricted, where relevant, to those on the owner's principal house and on the first £25,000 of the mortgage. Tax relief can be seen as reducing the rate of interest the mortgagor pays on his loan. Writing n for the nominal rate charged by the building society, e as the effective rate paid by the borrower after subsidy, and t as the marginal tax rate, it can be shown that:

$$e = n(1-t)$$

Throughout the 1970s the basic-rate taxpayer was taxed at between 30 and 35 per cent in the pound. It follows that the effective rate of interest paid was only about two-thirds of the nominal rate. The subsidy is clearly inegalitarian: the higher the income, the more likely it is to fall in a higher marginal tax rate band, so the higher the subsidy and the lower the effective rate of interest paid.

Tax relief on mortgage interest can be received either with an annuity or an endowment mortgage. In the latter case there is an additional subsidy paid on the insurance premiums, equal to the product of the premiums and half the basic rate of income tax.

The second form of assistance is the option mortgage subsidy, introduced in 1967 for those on relatively low incomes, paying less than the basic rate of tax and therefore receiving less tax relief.[22] This subsidy takes directly the form of a lower rate of mortgage interest charged by the mortgagee, who is compensated for this by the Exchequer. The repayments on an option mortgage remain constant over time if interest rates are unchanged. However, the repayments net of subsidy of an owner enjoying tax relief rise over time, for his tax relief falls each year with the diminishing proportion of interest in his monthly repayments.

Since 1967 governments have made it ever easier for mortgagors to switch from one type of subsidy to the other.[23] In the early 1970s option mortgages made up one-fifth of all mortgages issued by the financial institutions. Thereafter the proportion declined as tax thresholds fell and more and more people decided tax relief suited them best. In 1980 only 11 per cent of building society advances took the option form.

The preceding paragraphs should make it clear that the monthly repayments made on a mortgage are determined by six distinct variables: the size of the mortgage, its type, its term to redemption, the rate of interest charged on it, the form of subsidy received, and the mortgagor's marginal rate of tax. The last factor will reflect both the overall structure of income tax rates in the country as a whole as well as the borrower's income.

Next I wish to look at how the impact of mortgage payments on income changes over time under inflationary conditions. In any single time-period the impact is best measured by the ratio of payments, net of subsidy of course, to household income net of tax. In the case of those receiving tax relief, this is properly treated as a reduction in the numerator of the impact ratio rather than as an increase in the denominator, with care taken not to double-count by doing both!

The 1970s and early 1980s has been a period in which money incomes as well as prices have risen sharply every year, although the annual rate of increase has by no means been a steady one. On the other hand market rates of interest have been extremely volatile. In general the average building society mortgage rate has exhibited a clear upward trend since 1951, as appendix 5 shows.

When mortgage rates are fairly stable, as in 1974-7 for example, when mortgages take an annuity or endowment form and when incomes are sharply rising, a phenomenon of the greatest importance occurs which we can call 'income front loading'. In effect the impact ratio falls sharply over time so that the burden of the repayment of the mortgage is most severe in the first years of the life of the mortgage. It can be shown that for a given absolute disparity between the rate of interest on mort-

gages and the rate of increase of incomes, the higher the rate
of interest then the more severe is the income frontloading
effect.[24]

The value of the impact ratio is determined by the six
variables listed on page 86 and by the household's income net
of tax. The inflationary conditions of the 1970s were associated
both with high mortgage rates of interest compared with previous
decades as well as with a rate of increase in house prices that
tended to outstrip that of incomes. For these two reasons the
initial value of the impact ratio at times reached a very high
level. Yet income frontloading implied that if the barrier could
be surmounted, if the owner-occupier could endure the hard
times of the first two, three or four years of the mortgage period,
thereafter as the impact ratio contracted the economic situation
of the household would substantially improve.[25]

The severity of income frontloading can be moderated in a
number of ways. Low-start mortgages, to which I return in the
next chapter, attempt to do this, and we have already seen that
the tax relief subsidy form does so automatically although the
effect is small. Looking at the numerator of the impact ratio one
can see that the household might choose a down-market house
to keep down the size of the mortgage or lower the cover ratio
by 'saving hard' and ploughing into the purchase as much of
the household's personal assets as could be realised. At the
same time the denominator could be kept as high as possible in
the case of a married couple by ensuring both partners had
full-time jobs. This would imply planning the birth of the first
child to take place only after the impact ratio had fallen. In the
case of unexpected pregnancies, the improved access to abortion
from 1967 onwards would have facilitated 'keeping to the
plan'.

This discussion of income frontloading assumed a stable
mortgage rate. If the rate moves upwards and downwards then
such volatility will produce real distortions in the posited smooth
downward movement of the individual household's impact ratio.
In the situation of the 1970s when the trend of mortgage rates
was quite definitely upward, the income frontloading effect was
partially offset.

The presumed smooth downward curve of the impact ratio
also ignores the situation of selling buyers. In their case the
decision to move may well involve trading up, a phenomenon
we shall look at in more detail in section seven. If this is the
case, it is likely they will take out a mortgage on their new
purchase that is larger than the outstanding mortgage on their
existing dwelling. The result is a step-up in their mortgage
payments. Should the selling buyers behave in this way on a
number of occasions, then the falling arc of their personal
impact ratio is likely to exist as a clear downward trend with
step-ups at each trading-up decision.[26] Trading down, like
falling interest rates, reinforces income frontloading.

6   THE BUILDING SOCIETIES' LENDING POLICIES

How can we understand most effectively the nature of building
society lending behaviour? One route is for the researcher to
build up a substantial portfolio of case-study material, without
any explicit preconceptions, in order to map out a behavioural
pattern within which individual decisions to lend and to borrow
can be located. The chief danger of this empiricist procedure
is that it too easily leads to conclusions that abstract from
the institutional context of the building society managers, the
market context of the mortgagors, and the macro-financial
position of the societies as borrowers themselves. At its worst
it degenerates into substituting in the place of analysis moral
judgments about the spatial, sexual, class, racial and aesthetic
prejudice of management as if a new morality once established
could and would transform their behaviour.

An alternative route begins by locating the societies in their
structural context and then explores lending policies as the
specific manifestation of these structural relationships. The
danger here is that it is too easily assumed that managerial
behaviour can be simply 'read off' from their structural context,
that they are robots motivated only by power sources located in
the macro-economy. It also too easily ignores the preferences
of the mortgagor. I am not here contrasting 'empirical' research
with 'theoretical' research but a fragmentary behaviourism with
a determinist structuralism. Of these the former is, I believe,
by far the less enlightening.

A third route, to combine political economy with social psychology in a holistic contemporary history, is indeed wisdom
itself. In what follows, unfortunately, a structuralist bias will
be as evident to the reader as it is to the author.[27]

First and last the building societies are financial intermediaries.
Fundamentally their activity consists of borrowing on specified
terms from one set of lenders in order to lend these selfsame
funds to another set of borrowers. Success in their competition
for cash inflows is absolutely crucial, as we have already seen.
Every type of financial institution enjoys its own specific strength
and expertise. What is peculiar to the societies is that they
borrow overwhelmingly from private persons sums of money that
can be very rapidly withdrawn, and they lend these funds
predominantly to finance house purchase for owner-occupation
on terms requiring repayment over a period of twenty years or
more. The societies employ liquid liabilities to finance long-dated
assets.

They can, then, be conceived as vast 'money machines' into
which are fed new deposits (and the repayments of existing
mortgages) and from which issue loans for house purchase (and
withdrawals and interest payments). In its advertising material
the Abbey National presents just such a picture. The managerial
elite, based in the societies' head offices, seek above all to
guarantee the machine's financial stability and its financial

growth. This, of course, has made necessary the development
of criteria for the allocation of mortgage finance which will be
implemented at the level of the branch.

From this we can derive a most important conception. When a
would-be mortgagor walks into the office of the branch manager
of a building society, he (or she) exists not only as a person of
flesh and blood intent on buying a house of a given physical
structure in a determined location but he also enjoys a financial
personality as the owner of certain financial assets, as the
receiver of a hypothetical stream of future income from which
the mortgage payments must be deducted, intent on purchasing
a property which has a hypothetical future resale price. To lend
or not to lend? The branch manager's decision principally will
reflect the attributes of the financial personality even though
these attributes may be crucially determined by the physical
and intellectual character of the borrower and the use-value of
the dwelling.

Why is it that the manager must make a business-like assessment of the credit-worthiness of the borrower? First, the
money loop shown in Figure 6.1 that links new mortgage loans
with mortgage repayments is vital to the societies' ability to
repay its own debts. Second, mortgage default on a scale that
caught the eye of the public might lead to a wave of withdrawals
which would soon exhaust the societies' liquid reserves. Third,
even default on a minor scale imposes a burden on management
resources and can blight the career prospects of individual
managers. Default on a loan secured by a property, the resale
price of which is insufficient to cover the outstanding debt,
including mortgage arrears and the transaction costs involved,
is a greater sin - from the point of view of head office - than
default alone.

A sober assessment of the financial personality of borrowers
and the resale prospects of properties inevitably gives rise to
a ranking order, however primitive, in terms of relative risk
with refusal recommended for the highest risk section of the list.
In this situation a permanent shortage of funds is most convenient for the institutions for it is the basis of a rationing or
queueing system. The queue phenomenon is the creation of the
managerial elite, enabling it to impose a permanent set of
constraints on lower-order management and underpinning the
exclusion of high-risk individuals and properties and slower
access for marginal acceptances. The mortgage shortage also
offers a convenient rationalisation for managers' rejection of the
flesh and blood applicants who stand before them and endows
them with a greater sense of power and responsibility. Queuing
and managerial judgment in mortgage allocation are the necessary
conditions that allow institutional prejudice to develop.

But far, far more important than these distortions is the
systematic discrimination that follows from the role of the
building societies as financial intermediaries leading them to
base their mortgage allocation criteria on the financial personality

of the borrowers and not on the needs and existing housing
situation of the household. It is this that must be the first
principle in arguing that the role of the building societies and
speculative housebuilding must be complemented by a vigorous
planned state housing programme of high-quality rehabilitation
and new building.

With few exceptions, mortgage rationing has existed in
Britain now for the last three decades because the BSA has
always set its recommended mortgage rate lower than the market
clearing rate. Simultaneously, careful risk assessment, queueing
systems, the upward trend in house prices and cautious cover
ratios have kept losses on default to a minimum. Moreover before
1981 the societies had faced no real competition in their lending
to mortgagors since the 1930s and 1940s, at which time there
was considerable concern about maintaining 'standards' in
lending.[28]

7 LENDING IN PRACTICE

Given the contextual discussion of the preceding sections,
building society lending practice can be understood by answer-
ing just three questions:

   (i)   In each time-period what determines the mortgage rate of
         interest, the value of funds loaned out on mortgage and
         the number of advances made?
   (ii) To whom do the societies lend and how much do they lend
         to any given mortgagor?
   (iii) On what type of property do they lend and where are
         these properties?

The first question has largely been answered already. The
societies face a known set of market rates of interest with which
they must compete successfully, although the 'reservoir' of
liquid assets permits substantial flexibility in adjusting the
deposit rate to shifts in market rates. The mortgage rate of
interest itself must be kept in line with the deposit rate since
mortgage interest is seen as the source of interest paid on
deposits and an upward shift in the deposit rate not matched
fairly soon by a rise in the mortgage rate could put an unaccept-
able squeeze on the societies' gross surpluses. Nevertheless,
a degree of flexibility exists here too.

Thus the mortgage rate of interest is determined in the final
analysis by market rates of interest although the correlation is
not perfectly linear because of this double element of flexibility
in the linkage. The effective rate of interest paid by the mortgagor, moreover, is substantially below the full market rate
because of the composite tax arrangements and tax relief.

The aggregate value of funds loaned out on mortgage is
determined by the sum of mortgage repayments and the flow of

net deposits plus (minus) reductions (increases) in the stock of liquid assets. The volatile element here is the net deposit flow which, as I have already said, is a function of the societies' adjusted relative interest rate on deposits. Perturbations in this flow can lead to feasts or famines in the supply of mortgage finance. When market rates of interest are low, the societies have no difficulty in setting a deposit rate that attracts net deposits sufficient to build up liquid reserves and provide a liberal flow of mortgage advances. Under these conditions the criteria for the risk assessment of potential mortgagors and properties are relaxed, though not abandoned.

But when market rates are high, particularly when they move *rapidly* to high levels, severe problems can arise. A matching increase in the deposit rate can certainly be made. However, this will require an associated rise in the mortgage rate. This is likely to be strongly resisted by the state. Simultaneously, income frontloading creates severe strains in the household budgets of many recent and potential purchasers. Resistance to a jump in the mortgage rate means the deposit rate increase must be moderated, and therefore the relative rate of interest falls. Now net deposits contract and may become negative, so that even if liquid reserves are run down the flow of mortgage finance is likely to diminish. Correspondingly, risk assessment becomes tougher and marginal owner-occupiers and down-market properties get shunted to the back of the queue.

The cumbersome process by which the BSA changes its recommended rates and the administrative costs of changing the mortgage rates for more than 5 million mortgagors are responsible for the fact that the mortgage rate changes spasmodically whilst market rates change each day, and this may exacerbate the phases of feast and famine.

The question of the number of separate advances has still to be settled. In each time-period it is simply equal to the value of funds loaned divided by the size of the average advance. The latter is equal to the average price of houses purchased with building society mortgages in the relevant period multiplied by the cover ratio. So the number of advances varies directly with the value of funds and inversely with house prices and the cover ratio.

Let me now turn to the second question of the three listed above. This could be treated at great length but I shall be mercifully brief. Much finer detail can be found in Boddy's work. First let us consider the distribution of building society mortgages between selling buyers and first-time buyers. The data are set out in Table 6.4 The falling trend is clear.

Table 6.4 New mortgages by building societies to first-time buyers as a
proportion of all new mortgages in the UK 1970-80 (percentages)[a]

Year	1970	1971	1972	1973	1974	1975	1976	1977	1978	1979	1980
%	61	60	58	52	51	47	49	48	47	45	47

Source: HCS.

[a] The numerator includes some sitting purchasers.

In 1970 first-time buyers made up 61 per cent of all those in
receipt of fresh advances, a figure that had declined to only
47 per cent in 1980. The diminution was particularly sharp in
1972-5 but appears to have stabilised temporarily since then.

Table 6.5 Average advance, price and cover ratio of dwellings purchased with a
building society mortgage by first-time and selling buyers in the UK
1970-80

Year	First-time buyers			Selling buyers		
	Average advance (£)	Average price (£)	Cover ratio (%)	Average advance (£)	Average price (£)	Cover ratio (%)
1970	3,464	4,330	80	3,854	5,838	66
1971	3,914	4,838	81	4,407	6,666	66
1972	4,954	6,086	81	5,538	8,965	62
1973	6,115	7,908	77	6,273	11,900	53
1974	6,568	9,037	73	6,577	13,049	50
1975	7,292	9,549	76	7,409	13,813	54
1976	8,073	10,181	79	8,509	15,160	56
1977	8,515	10,857	78	9,101	16,246	56
1978	9,602	12,023	80	10,611	18,792	56
1979	11,286	14,918	76	11,837	24,074	49
1980	12,946	17,533	74	13,359	28,959	46

Source: HCS.

The position of selling buyers is interesting both because
they now constitute the largest group of purchasers and because
of their appropriation of the net worth generated when they sell
their existing house. In general this allows them to put down a
much larger deposit than a first-time purchaser of similar age
and income level and many societies encourage the selling buyer
to plough back into the house they are purchasing all the net
worth appropriated on the former house. In its turn the higher
absolute value of the deposit can be used either to buy a house
of a similar price (or even less) to the 'old' one but with a lower
level of mortgage debt and therefore a lower impact ratio; or it

can be used to buy a more expensive house, usually with a greater mortgage than the original one.

Table 6.5 shows separately for the 1970s the average cover ratio for selling buyers and first-time buyers. The last statistic is consistently higher. UK data for 1976, when the number of building society advances were almost equally distributed between first-time and selling purchasers, indicate that the latter buy far fewer terraced properties and flats of any age but markedly more bungalows and detached houses. In the same year the price paid by the average selling buyer exceeded that of the average first-time buyer by the huge margin of 49 per cent.[29] Although the selling buyer's cover ratio is smaller, this is more than offset by the higher average price paid on the houses they buy with the result that the mortgage advance they receive exceeds that of the first-time purchaser - 'To him that hath shall be given.'

Selling buyers move for a miscellany of reasons: to trade up, that is to buy a house with a higher-ranked use-value; to move to a new job; to retire, and so forth. Trading up is demonstrably the most important single reason.[30] Since owner-occupiers buy and resell several times during their lives, they are sometimes described as moving up a 'housing ladder' or pursuing a 'housing career', although retirement can lead to the purchase of a dwelling with a lower price than that being sold. Trading up is an enormously important means of concretely taking advantage of the 'paper' price gains described in Figure 5.1 and, as already observed, partially offsets income frontloading.

Before continuing, it is necessary to stress again that even when they can surmount the 'buyer's deposit' barrier both the selling purchaser and the first-time purchaser must be able to demonstrate to the building society that the mortgage they take out bears what the society considers to be a reasonable relation-ship to the mortgagor's income. Boddy discusses this at some length for the mid-1970s.[31] In general a loan to a married couple did not exceed $2\frac{1}{2}$ to 3 times the husband's gross annual income or the criterion was that the monthly mortgage payment did not exceed gross weekly income. One-half of bonuses or overtime earnings were often taken into account and up to one-half of the wife's income. This deserves to be stressed: the woman's wages were treated like the overtime earnings of the man! Alternatively an amount equal to one year's income of the wife was added to the loan size depending on how permanent her employment appeared. In the case of cohabitees and groups of adults, only one person's income was accepted. In all cases a mortgagor offering a larger deposit was likely to be treated with greater liberality.

Clearly women were discriminated against. In large part, I suggest, this is because there are relatively fewer of them in the labour force, those who are employed earn less than men and their incomes usually cease, sometimes for years, after the onset of pregnancy. Discrimination was not - at least, was not purely - an ideological manifestation but reflected the objective circumstance of women's position in the labour market. The passage of the Equal Opportunities Act led to the slow termination of this overt discrimination. The distinctive forms of treatment are now based on the size of each person's income, with the smaller one receiving the treatment a wife's income formerly did. It appears, then, that discrimination has not ended but merely taken a new form.

As we have seen, the maximum size of the mortgage advance is determined by household income. But there are two further determinants of the *actual* advance made. One is whether the household wishes to take advantage of the maximum loan offered and we know that many households prefer a more modest sum. The second determinant is the valuation placed on the property itself. Building societies will not normally advance more than a maximum proportion of this, normally set at 70-80 per cent. So the final advance agreed upon must not only be acceptable to the household concerned, but from the viewpoint of the society must bear a 'proper' relation to household income and the valuation of the property.

The difference between the building society advance and the price of the dwelling is called the purchaser's 'deposit' and, as I have said, constitutes an important barrier to house purchase. As Boddy writes: 'Societies usually prefer that borrowers have demonstrated financial discipline by saving and that they have a significant cash stake in the house from the start to encourage a "responsible attitude".[32] Many buyers raise all or part of the purchase deposit as a topping-up loan from the insurance companies, fringe banks, or finance houses at high rates of interest.

For those borrowers who find it too difficult or too expensive to raise the purchase deposit they require, two schemes exist by which societies provide an advance up to 100 per cent of the valuation of the house. The Building Society Indemnity Scheme is run by the BSA and a number of insurance companies whilst the Option Mortgage Guarantee Scheme is administered by the state, the BSA and some insurance companies. In both cases insurance cover is provided on the excess advance in case of losses incurred through mortgage default.

Let me finally consider the properties on which the societies make advances. The fundamental distinction here is between new and second-hand houses. One of the most important differences between the tenures of owner-occupation and state housing is that 'capital expenditure' in the latter case is almost entirely on new output whilst the exchange finance required for owner-occupation has, in proportionate terms, increasingly shifted away from realisation to transfer transactions, that is, from the purchase of newly constructed dwellings to financing transfers of second-hand houses between owners. As the stock of owner-occupied dwellings has increased and as house prices have risen, a huge volume of funds in gross terms has become necessary to finance transfers alone.

Table 6.6 presents data for the 1970s on the number and gross value of building society advances on new and second-hand housing. Since 1970 building society advances on new property have never exceeded one-quarter of total advances and the balance between new and old had almost halved over ten years.

Table 6.6 Building society mortgage advances on new and second-hand dwellings in the UK 1970-80[a]

Year	New		Second-hand		New as a proportion of total (%)[b]
	Number ('000)	Amount (£m)	Number ('000)	Amount (£m)	
1970	133	510	407	1,492	25
1971	165	713	488	2,016	25
1972	164	862	517	2,752	24
1973	142	903	403	2,601	26
1974	102	700	331	2,220	24
1975[c]	121	946	529	4,003	19
1976	129	1,125	586	4,972	18
1977	122	1,175	615	5,699	17
1978	134	1,504	668	7,205	17
1979	116	1,519	599	7,562	16
1980	95	1,374	581	8,003	14

Source: HCS.

[a] To private persons and housing associations.

[b] Using the number data. Using amount data gives virtually identical results.

[c] Return and coverage revised from January 1975.

Thus between 1970-3 and 1977-80 the flow of new vacancies had fallen by some 34,000 per year whilst the number of second-hand transactions had increased by over 162,000 per year.

These data remind us what a gross misnomer the term 'building society' is. The societies do not, of course, build; moreover, Table 6.6 demonstrates that in 1980 only 14 per cent of their advances were on newly built houses.

It is important to note the rather misleading character of statistics on the gross value of advances on second-hand housing. It is not true that this figure in full represents the demand for new resources from the rest of the British financial system to permit transfers in the existing dwelling stock. In the first place, advances to buyers purchasing from those who sell mortgaged property automatically leads to the recycling into the mortgage institutions of that part of the advance equal to the dwelling's outstanding debt. Admittedly, price increases over time have opened up a substantial gap between the average

advance on a house and the outstanding mortgage redeemed
when the sale goes through. The gross value flow is also self-
financing to the degree that sellers' receipts in excess of any
mortgage redeemed are then placed in a building society account.
As far as I am aware, no longitudinal analysis has ever been
made of the net requirements of financial resources for stock
transfers.[33]

The final issue I wish to deal with in this section concerns
building society attitudes towards older property. By now there
exists a substantial amount of case-study evidence demonstrating that the societies discriminate against older property, particularly unmodernised houses constructed prior to 1918. This
discrimination takes a number of forms: the valuation of the
dwelling is set lower relative to its market price than is normally
the case; the cover ratio offered is lower; the provision of an
'excess' advance under one of the guarantee schemes is more
difficult; and the term of the loan is shorter. When mortgage
finance is relatively scarce, these criteria harden. Since the
prices of older houses tend to be lower than those for new
housing of comparable physical character, the refusal of mortgage facilities on the former may force first-time buyers in
particular to turn to 'starter homes' they regard as qualitatively
inferior.

What explains this discrimination? First we can say that from
the point of view of 'head office' the age of a property is, in a
relative sense, an indicator of a short potential life, a high
rate of future expenditure on maintenance and minor or major
repair, and a high probability of the development of structural
faults.[34] For the society the dwelling has a two fold character,
its physical attributes and its potential rate of increase in
market price. Age is seen to be inversely correlated with the
rate of price increase and therefore with possible losses in the
case of mortgage default. And of course it is precisely the higher-
risk mortgagor who will seek, as a general rule, to purchase
down-market older property since that is the cheapest available.
So age means risk and risk is to be avoided.

But there is a second set of factors shaping this form of
discrimination. Old houses are usually surrounded by old houses
and so are located in 'older areas', often in the inner city. Thus
a view on a single dwelling inevitably is influenced by the
society's rules, however informal, on the environmental and
relative locus of properties that it is prepared to mortgage. This
relationship between space and the property constraint is
developed in chapters 12 and 14.

8   CONCLUSIONS

This chapter has covered a considerable amount of ground. The
text began by suggesting that the supply of mortgage finance
for owner-occupation has been only one of three dominant forms

for securing the realisation of housing output in Britain. The
financial burden that home-ownership imposes on the household
is best understood not as the purchase price of the house but
as the flow of expenditures necessary to pursue this form of
consumption, a flow already described in chapter 5. Thus the
financial constraint on entry consists of three barriers: the
minimum income necessary to meet the expenditure stream, the
purchaser's deposit which must be found, and the agreement of
the relevant mortgage institution to lend on the property in
question.

In Britain in the 1970s the building societies provided the
lion's share of mortgage finance. As financial intermediaries
their liabilities are composed primarily of short-term debts to
individual rentiers and their assets are primarily long-term
loans to house purchasers. The nature of their flow of funds
and the linkage between inflows and outflows was described at
length. Deposits consist largely of ordinary and term shares
and to attract these the societies must pay a rate of interest
which, when adjusted for the high liquidity and security of
these shares and their favourable tax treatment, is competitive
with other forms of holding wealth.

The chapter then went on to describe the main types of
advance and the nature of the state's subsidy payments. For
the basic-rate taxpayer the composite tax arrangements and tax
relief, both of which are regressive fiscal arrangements, reduce
the effective rate of interest paid on mortgage finance below
money market rates. In this sense the owner-occupier is
sheltered from the full effect of market competition for the supply
of funds. This sheltering effect is capable of measurement: in
1981, for example, it reduced the actual mortgage rate of
interest paid to two-thirds of what it would otherwise have
been![35]

Next the lending policies of the societies were considered.
Their managerial elite seeks above all to ensure the institutions'
financial stability and growth. Thus the allocation of mortgage
finance is determined overwhelmingly by the financial 'personality'
of the borrower and the property in question in order to minimise
the risk of default. Risk assessment and selection operate particularly effectively when, as has been the case in Britain since
the early 1950s, the mortgage rate of interest is not a clearing
rate and where rationing is therefore a continuing phenomenon.

Specific aspects of lending practice were examined briefly.
The most important conclusions were that there had been a substantial contraction in 1970-80 both of the relative proportion of
first-time buyers as well as of the relative proportion of realisation as against transfer purchases. Moreover, discrimination
against older property requiring rehabilitation is also a clearly
established building society practice - particularly in 'older
areas' - and takes a number of specific forms. It is explained
largely by the fact that age, poor condition and an 'unattractive'
location reduce the likely price gain on the house and raise the

maintenance and repair costs which, above all in the case of purchase by a marginal owner-occupier, make it a more risky asset in financial terms.

As has already been pointed out, the analysis in this chapter has been intentionally restricted to the operation of the building societies. The next chapter considers the other main sources of mortgage finance. In both these chapters the main objective is to give a still-life picture of the situation in the 1970s. Year-by-year changes are referred to very briefly because they can be understood only when set within their wider political and macro-economic context. It is this diachronic narrative that provides the content of chapter 16.

7 OWNER-OCCUPATION AT THE MARGIN

1 LOCAL AUTHORITY MORTGAGES

Table 6.1 has already shown that, in addition to the building societies, the other most important suppliers of mortgage finance are the district councils, the insurance companies and the banks. In this chapter each of these sources is discussed in turn and the final sections take up the question of marginal owner-occupation.

The early chapters of this book, in treating the evolution of state policy, inevitably paid some attention to the supply of mortgage finance by the state itself. It was shown that the activity of the local state as a provider of house purchase credit began with the Small Dwellings Acquisition Act of 1899; that the supply of funds has always been modest in comparison with the building societies; and that the rate of interest charged, whether fixed or variable, has traditionally been related to the rate at which the local authorities could themselves borrow. All local authority mortgages are funded by means of loans raised directly or indirectly on the capital market and therefore these advances, unlike those of the building societies, add to the public sector borrowing requirement.[1]

Table 6.1 shows that in terms of advances net of principal repayments, the municipal share in the period 1970-80 varied between a peak of 24 per cent in 1974 and a low point of -1 per cent in 1978. Appendix 6 provides the information on gross advances between 1945 and 1980. As Graph 7.1 shows, in 1970-80 the number of loans shifted between a high point of 102,000 in 1975 and a trough of only 16,000 in 1980. These huge proportionate swings in the flow of advances imposed substantial management problems in the efficient staffing of the districts' and counties' mortgage sections and, particularly in a period of upsurge, slowed down the mortgage processing period between application and approval.[2]

With this quantitative information in mind, let me now consider the most important question posed by the existence of local authority mortgages: what is their objective? No one, not even the press officers of the DoE, would wish to argue that this has ever been made crystal-clear. As a starting point one can say this: the powerful upward trend in the supply of credit from the building societies since at least the turn of the century has always permitted the state to conceive the role of municipal mortgage finance as merely complementary to the societies'

activity. Persons of wealth seeking a mortgage have never had
to confront the shuffling and negative face of building society
management.

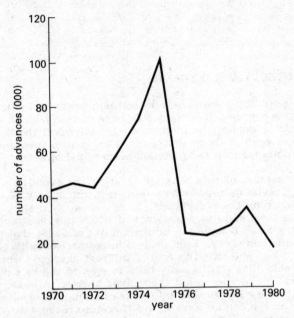

Graph 7.1 The number of local authority advances to private
persons for home purchase in England and Wales 1970-80

Source: Appendix 6.

Yet successive Conservative governments since 1920 and
Labour governments since 1964 have sought to extend home-
ownership from its wealthy core to ever more numerous circles
of the working class. Thus complementarity has been interpreted
as providing house purchase finance to households that find
access to the building societies difficult. But the financial
prudence of the local authority has always required that the
mortgagor and his or her property are considered credit-worthy
risks. The triple barrier of chapter 6 does not disappear, it is
merely modified. The second continuing feature of state mortgage
provision has been the willingness to increase the flow of funds
when society advances were diminishing because of unfavourable
money market conditions.

Once this complementary role became established, it was also
possible to use local authority credit flows as a subsidiary means
of implementing current housing policy objectives. So the
ambiguities of the state role lie both in the indistinctiveness of
complementarity itself, particularly in periods when building

society advances fluctuate, and in the tendency to assign new passengers to the coach as it rolled on its way. This is not criticism but a statement of fact. Perhaps the most important of these passengers was to board in the late 1950s as the civil service came to understand that transfer finance for young first-time buyers could be of great importance in stimulating rehabilitation production on older properties.[3]

The unmistakably down-market character of state lending in comparison with the building societies is illustrated in Table 7.1. The most important feature is the predominance of loans to first-time buyers and this is associated, as one would expect, with a much higher proportion of pre-1919 properties purchased. Even restricting the comparison to first-time buyers, the average price paid is lower in the case of the local authorities whilst their cover ratio is markedly higher. They also supply a significantly higher proportion of option mortgages and low-start mortgages.

Table 7.1 Characteristics of house purchases with local authority and building society mortgages in 1975[a]

| | Mortgage source | |
	Local authorities	Building societies
First-time buyers as a proportion of all buyers (%)	88	47
Pre-1919 properties as a proportion of all properties purchased (%)	62	19
Average price paid by first-time buyers (£)	7,130	9,554
Average cover ratio for first-time buyers (%)	90	76
Proportion of option mortgages (%)[b]	53	20
Proportion of low-start mortgages (%)[b]	11	neg.

Source: *HPTV*, Part II, Tables VII.7 and 8.

[a] Local authority figures are for England and Wales; building society figures are for the UK.

[b] All local authority purchases, but only first-time buyer building society purchases.

These data confirm the complementarity role of the state amongst credit-worthy buyers of relatively modest means. The problem is that it is based on a 'snapshot' of only one year. Nevertheless, government data over a spread of years in the 1970s also show that first-time buyers as a proportion of all buyers lay consistently in the range of 87-90 per cent. Local authority mortgagors also earn lower incomes than building society mortgagors.[4]

Graph 7.1 charts the unsteady course of state mortgage advances in the 1970s. Credit is actually supplied at the local level, predominantly by the district councils but of course central government must interest itself both in the total quantitative flow and in the social groups amongst whom the total is divided.

Particularly in a situation where the flow of building society
advances was fluctuating and yet where, throughout the late
1960s and 1970s, state expenditure was perceived by many to
be 'in crisis', central direction of local supply became more
forceful and comprehensive.

Monetary lending quotas on local authority mortgage finance
were first introduced in 1965. One of the early measures of the
new Conservative government in 1970 was to raise their ceiling
by £155 million. In 1970-1 recommendations were made for the
first time to limit lending to priority categories, which might
change from year to year, and these were the only 'controls'
in the years 1971-2 to 1974-5. The number of advances made
rose very steeply for three years after 1972. New cash restrictions were announced in the second quarter of 1975, to be
tightened again in 1976, and this brought about the municipal
mortgage slump of 1976 and the subsequent years of famine
plotted on Graph 7.1.[5] The 1976 public expenditure White Paper
seems to have been the first central government document to
refer to the local authorities as 'lenders of the last resort'
although the phrase had been used by the GLC in 1971.[6] The
new quotas operated alongside priority categories so that the
centre was attempting simultaneously to control tightly the total
flow from the districts and to establish the rules of the game
for the subdivision within each district. However, it is
necessary immediately to add that it was impossible for the DoE
to force districts to lend more than they chose, where this fell
short of their quota, moreover the priorities established were
neither mandatory nor sufficiently precise to rule out local
'interpretation'. For these two reasons, local implementation of
central policy-makers' wishes varied very considerably in scale
and direction.

The priority categories employed from 1971 onwards included
the following groups:[7]

(i) Existing tenants of a local authority, people who are high
on the authority's waiting list for housing, or people displaced by slum clearance or other public authority development whom the council would otherwise have been obliged
to rehouse.

(ii) Applicants who are homeless or threatened with homelessness, or living in conditions that are overcrowded or
otherwise detrimental to health.

(iii) Individual members of self-build groups when they are
about to occupy the premises as individual mortgagors.

(iv) Applicants who want to buy older and smaller property
unlikely to attract a commercial mortgage advance; and
more particularly persons who want to acquire a house with
a subsequent view to improving it for their own occupation.

(v) Applicants who want to buy larger property for only partial
occupation by themselves, in areas where conditions of
overcrowding seem liable to develop.

(vi) Applicants taking up residence in or around a development or intermediate area or overspill receiving area.

(vii) Staff urgently required where the local authority are satisfied that first they are needed in the interests of the efficiency of the public service and second, that they are unlikely to obtain the requisite mortgage advance from another source.

For 1974-5 only, when speculative builders were having the greatest difficulty in selling their output, a new category was added:

(viii) First-time purchasers of newly built houses from builders or developers where the mortgage transactions may reasonably be expected to be completed by the end of 1974.

For 1976-7 to 1978-9, categories (iii), (vi) and (vii) were dropped and category (i) was extended to cover new-town tenants.

Category (iv) most clearly exemplifies the complementarity of the local authorities' role, associated here quite explicitly with the use of transfer finance to stimulate rehabilitation. In fact DoE data for 1974-5 showed that more than half of all municipal advances fell into this single category.[8] But intervention by the local state to buttress other aspects of housing policy is also clear. Not only do we have the ad hoc innovation of category (viii), but also the much more significant category (i) which attempts to reduce the social and legal pressures for a more vigorous local authority housebuilding programme.

Karn's case study of Birmingham in the first half of the 1970s provides the most valuable insight into local authority practice. Her principal argument is that the priority categories are sufficiently elastic to have contained two quite different policies. The first of these operated up until 1973-4. The second was introduced in 1974 when the Housing Committee took over responsibility for mortgage lending at a point in time when the number of advances increased enormously. The new policy brought a very rapid reduction in the proportion of all advances going to the purchase of pre-1919 property and a major increase in lending to those who, in Karn's eyes, fell into low-priority categories, in particular to young engaged couples with good jobs and thus two incomes. Private tenants and black households correspondingly fell back in terms of the proportionate allocation of state house purchase credit. Karn writes:[9]

From this analysis it emerges more forcefully than one would even have predicted that the group of people who bought newer houses with a corporation mortgage were, with the possible exceptions that they might not have saved very much deposit and may have had slightly lower incomes than average building society borrowers, very similar to any group of first-time buyers going to a building society.

Nothing could demonstrate more clearly than this that whilst in
aggregate local authority mortgage finance has a clearly complementary role, as we saw from Table 7.1, it is possible for
individual councils to interpret their activity in a manner that
veers dramatically from one year to the next.

As we have seen, the decision announced in May 1975 to
reduce local authority lending for house purchase very quickly
took effect. The civil service was well aware that the effect
would be particularly severe in older areas with a higher proportion of property requiring rehabilitation. As a consequence the
DoE attempted, successfully, to persuade the building societies
to engage in a quite novel form of co-operation which became
known as the support lending scheme. The societies agreed to
set aside a specific sum of money each year which would be
available to nominees from the district councils. These were
households applying to the local authority for a loan whom the
district considered would have been successful had there been
no shortage of finance. Their names were forwarded to a building society who would then treat the request under their normal
lending criteria. The objective was that the societies as a body
would thereby switch some of their immense flow of funds into
financing households and properties which in happier times the
municipalities would have catered for. In July 1975 £100 million
was earmarked for the scheme, and later £176 million and £300
million for the financial years 1977/78 and 1978/79. By March
1977 £160 million had been loaned and a further £105 million in
1977/8.[10]

It seems unlikely that we shall ever know just how much success
this innovation has enjoyed, because of the major methodological
difficulty in comparing what *has* happened with what *would have*
happened had there been no scheme. In fact there has been a
great deal of deprecating comment on the outcome. The critics
argue that the sums earmarked were too small in view of the
cut-back in district lending by almost £500 million per annum
between 1975 and 1978, and that the increase in the number of
advances and in the proportion of nominations that were successful merely reflects local authorities learning to sift their own
applicants more vigorously in order to forward nominations that
qualified unambiguously with building society lending criteria.
A 1977 DoE survey showed that in considering applicants for
earmarked funds, the societies continued to offer terms less
favourable than the districts with respect to the cover ratio,
the redemption period and the allowances made for the household's income. At the same time the societies exercised a more
discriminatory attitude against properties requiring rehabilitation,
or without forecourts and front gardens or located in HAAs,
near clearance areas, or in poor areas, or those in part
possession.[11]

Boddy's view in 1980 was that whilst 'societies have increasingly

granted loans to those who would previously have obtained local-
authority mortgages . . . there is little evidence that societies are
now lending on property or to borrowers that previously they
would have refused but that local authorities would have
accepted'. He concludes that:[12]

Much of the replacement would probably have occurred without the elaborate nomination procedures, as happened when
local-authority lending was cut back after 1965 . . . [the
scheme's] main function seems to have been to facilitate the
government cut in local-authority lending and for the
societies to generate goodwill by demonstrating their willingness to cooperate with the government, rather than to fill the
gap left by local authorities.

Even Mark Boleat of the BSA, not a man to understate the
virtues of the societies, conceded that:[13]

It is probably fair to say that the main benefit of the support
scheme should not be measured in terms of the number of
cases but rather in a better understanding by local authorities
and building societies of each other's problems and constraints.

Boleat went on to say that the societies' desire to continue with
the scheme was influenced by their opposition to an alternative
first proposed by Frank Allaun, i.e. the bulk-lending of 10 per
cent of the societies' funds to the local authorities.

2 THE ROLE OF THE INSURANCE COMPANIES AND BANKS

We have seen in Table 6.1 that net lending for house purchase
by the insurance companies was never more than 5 per cent of
the aggregate figure for the main institutional sources in the
1970s. Only since 1976 do we have data for the absolute number
of primary loans made, that is, advances exclusive of 'topping-
up' loans. In 1976-80 these primary mortgages ran at a rate
between 16,000 and 19,000 per annum in the UK.[14] Topping-up
finance, i.e. second mortgages where the first mortgage
usually comes from a building society, constituted in 1978-80
an average of 36 per cent of the insurance companies' total
advances in value. All of their advances are as endowment
mortgages and where they top up a building society loan the
primary loan must also take the endowment form. They base
their rate of interest on what they can earn on long-dated
government securities, although they may lend to their own
employees on special terms. Because the administrative costs of
house purchase credit are high for the companies in comparison
with the other forms of investment open to them, they do not
really seek to compete for this type of business. In fact the
main interest that the companies have in owner-occupation is the

income it provides them from endowment policies on building
society endowment mortgages, from house insurance, from mortgage protection policies and from excess loan guarantees.

Table 6.1 shows that in the years 1970-80 the proportionate
contribution of the banks varied from as little as 2 up to as much
as 12 per cent of the aggregate value of net advances. Until the
late 1970s it was possible to argue that the clearing banks
primarily lent in four distinct markets. The first was to their
own employees at interest rates as low as $2\frac{1}{2}$-5 per cent, an
arrangement designed to underpin loyalty to the firm. The
second was the banks' 'traditional' mortgage business, the bridging loans so often necessary to selling buyers, most commonly to
pay for a 'new' house before they receive the money on the sale
of their existing dwelling. The third was loans to long-standing
customers for terms of up to ten years on up-market properties
at interest rates higher than those of the building societies.
The fourth, surprisingly, was on older, inner-city property.[15]
Before considering the last of these at greater length, it is
necessary to point out that by the early years of the 1980s the
banks had begun to evince a keen interest in the mainstream
mortgage market which made them very much competitive with
the building societies. Since this development is so recent, it is
dealt with fully in chapter 16.

The fourth market for clearing-bank house lending referred to
above is one in which they are joined by the secondary banking
system of the finance houses and merchant banks, and it concerns mortgage provision on down-market properties, typically
pre-1919 property in the inner city of the great conurbations.
I have already remarked that the building societies tend to avoid
this sector. When there is a shortage of local authority mortgage
provision, either because of the policy of specific districts or
because of country-wide state expenditure constraints, a 'permanent mortgage famine', as Karn calls it, can evince itself for
this type of property and area.[16] At this point the banking
system steps in as the *true* 'lender of last resort', as Harloe,
Issacharoff and Minns were the first to demonstrate.[17] One
country-wide survey, conducted in 1975, showed that for the
cheapest category of second-hand houses, those priced at less
than £4,000, only about 10 per cent of sales were financed by
the building societies and 30-40 per cent by the local authorities.
So at least half of all such sales were carried out using the
personal assets of the buyers or mortgages provided by the
clearing banks and secondary financial institutions.[18]

This type of intervention is almost certainly a long-standing
phenomenon. But it became particularly evident in 1972 and
1973 following the introduction by Anthony Barber, the Conservative Chancellor of the Exchequer, of the new regime of
financial competition and credit control in 1971. These policies
terminated a number of existing restrictions on financial activity
and were accompanied by a low level of bank rate which helped
to stimulate an extremely rapid increase in lending from the

banking system, much of which went into real estate in the
notorious 'property boom' of 1971-3. One segment of the property
market affected was the down-market inner areas already
referred to. The clearing banks largely withdrew from this kind
of transaction after 1973 when the property bubble burst,
nevertheless it is likely that the fringe banks etc. still play an
important proportionate role in such areas.

The situation of mortgagors forced by the lack of alternative
sources of house purchase credit to turn to these lenders of
last resort has been vividly described by Valerie Karn in her
account of the owner-occupied housing market in Sparkhill, Soho
and Saltley in Birmingham:[19]

> For the purchasers there are very real financial problems
> about the lack of conventional mortgage lending in older areas.
> The borrowers interviewed were paying about 11 per cent
> interest for building society or local authority loans usually
> for a period of 20 or 25 years. However, if they had a loan
> from one of the clearing banks, the interest rate was about
> 16 per cent for a five-year loan. Fringe banks and finance
> companies usually charged about 2 per cent per month on a
> five- to ten-year loan. Because of these two factors, the
> higher interest rates and the much shorter period of the loans,
> monthly repayments are very much higher for loans than
> those from a building society or local authority. . . . Thus,
> for the same house, those who have to turn to unconventional
> sources of mortgages will have much greater outgoings at
> the start. Such buyers will have very little to spare for
> improving their property or even for routine maintenance.
> Many resort to buying a property jointly with another family
> in order to meet the repayments, sometimes with the result
> that both are overcrowded. Others take in lodgers. These
> expedients help many low and middle income families to get
> out of the cramped furnished rooms in which they have usually
> been living, often with several children, and to get them-
> selves a self-contained house, even if it is of modest quality.
> There they feel free of landlord control and the children are
> able to play where they please. These families feel that they
> have achieved a major break-through in living conditions,
> even if they are exceedingly hard-pressed to meet repayments
> of loans. . . . These buyers also suffer in that there is no
> option mortgage scheme on bank loans and it appears unlikely
> that they claim tax relief. It is yet another case in which 'the
> poor pay more'. In this case too there is added insecurity
> because the banks, fringe banks and finance companies are
> more likely than the local authorities or building societies to
> evict for arrears.

This discussion of the down-market sector of clearing bank
lending has brought us back once again to the specific situation
of the marginal owner-occupier. I define the marginal owner-

occupier as a purchaser or owner whose income is low relative
to other home-owners, or who has relatively meagre financial
assets and thus usually purchases a dwelling with a low use-
value relative to the rest of the owner-occupied stock. I want
to consider this group at greater length before concluding the
chapters on effective demand.

3   MARGINAL OWNER-OCCUPATION AND THE STATE

We have already seen in the historically oriented chapters of
this work that the absolute and relative scale of owner-
occupation in Britain has increased massively during the
twentieth century. The number of dwellings in home-ownership
rose from 0.8 million in 1914 to 9.9 million in 1975, corresponding to 10 per cent of the stock in the former year and 55 per
cent in the latter. The spectrum of socioeconomic classes into
which the British are distributed has always included smaller
or larger numbers of owner-occupiers over its whole range.
However, one can propose as a hypothesis that in the course
of our history the rate of extension of this specific tenure form
has been much earlier and more rapid within those classes and
fractions of classes with more substantial wealth and higher
incomes. This - one can speculate - has had the effect that in
recent decades it is the penetration of home-ownership into the
manual and white-collar groups that has become more significant,
absolutely and in rate of advance.

Of course this process by which the tortoise eventually begins
to catch up with the hare has not altered the fact that at any
point in time - unlike Aesop's fable - for the country as a whole
the proportion of owner-occupying households tends to be
successively greater the higher the income band. Table 7.2
shows this to be broadly true.

The explanation of this differential speed between classes in
their access to home-ownership over time and the consequent
cross-sectional income-tenure association is not hard to find. In
general, as we have seen, house purchase requires either considerable personal assets or access to consumer credit. In the
latter case the mainstream mortgage institutions have always
systematically discriminated in favour of those with cash assets
in hand and relatively high and secure incomes. The simple
purity of the income-tenure association is, however, muddied
both by the evidence of elderly households without an economically
active head owning the dwelling outright, and by the sale to
low-wage earners of cheap, decaying property which was formerly
rented and is situated in areas of poor environmental quality.
The purchase price in this second group is often raised either
through banks of different categories or by means of ready
cash.[20]

The expansion of the owner-occupied sector has been an
objective of government policy since 1919 at the very latest and

this has brought with it recognition by ministers and civil servants that the penetration of classes and fractions of classes on relatively lower incomes might require state support in various ways. The traditional policy measure has been the provision of local authority mortgages. The Labour government of 1964-70 added to this the option mortgage subsidy and lease-hold reform. But by this time policy analysts were beginning to recognise that under inflationary conditions the chief diffi-culty facing the first-time purchaser of new or second-hand property was the income frontloading effect in the early years of the term of the mortgage. Moreover, this particular barrier had been reinforced as a result of a particularly sharp rise both in house prices and the mortgage rate of interest in the early 1970s. This stimulated the exploration of various technical schemes for low-start mortgages in order to offset the income frontloading effect and to attempt to divert consumers' prefer-ences away from state housing.

Table 7.2 *The proportion of households that own their dwelling grouped by gross weekly income in the UK in 1978*

Gross normal weekly income of household	Proportion of households that own their home (%)
Under £20	8
£20 and under £30	22
£30 and under £40	30
£40 and under £50	43
£50 and under £60	41
£60 and under £70	37
£70 and under £80	44
£80 and under £90	46
£90 and under £100	50
£100 and under £110	54
£110 and under £120	62
£120 and under £130	65
£130 and under £150	66
£150 and under £170	69
£170 and under £200	71
£200 or more	81
All incomes	52

Source: Department of Employment, *Family Expenditure Survey: Report for 1978 giving the results for the UK*, London, HMSO, 1980, Table 6.

The first low-start schemes were launched in 1972 by the National Economic Development Office and in 1975 jointly by the DoE and the BSA.[21] Some local authorities and building societies devised their own alternatives. The NEDO scheme, with an option mortgage subsidy, is the simplest. In the first year only the interest on the loan is repaid and thereafter payments build

up at a constant rate in money terms throughout the redemption
period, provided the mortgage rate remains unchanged. If
interest rates are high, e.g. if the option rate stands at $11\frac{1}{4}$
per cent, the reduction in annual payments in the first year is
only 7 per cent. The DoE/BSA scheme is more complicated and
involves a partial deferment of interest payments in the early
years and repayment of the capitalised debt beginning in the
eleventh year of the mortgage. As a consequence, mortgage
repayments rise sharply for five years after year one, and then
jump again in year eleven. Thus, where an option mortgage
subsidy is chosen, the modest beginning and rising repayment
schedule of the low-start mortgage contrasts with the initially
higher but invariant schedule of the conventional capital repayment mortgage.

These forms of low-start mortgage have not proved popular.
Only 11 per cent of all local authority advances in 1975 were of
this type and the building societies had issued very few. No
national statistics are even published on the scale of their use.
Their lack of attraction seems to derive from several causes:
the extra administrative work they impose on the mortgagee; the
fairly modest reduction in outgoings in the early years; the
disinclination of married couple new households earning two
incomes to defer payments when this implies higher money outgoings after they have started a family; and the fear of the
authorities and households that a rising repayment schedule
could cause serious financial difficulties if the mortgage rate
were to rise after the house had been purchased, or if specific
households found that the increase in their money incomes
failed to keep pace with the rate of retail price inflation.

A second type of low-start scheme is the option lease, better
known as 'the half and half mortgage' or as 'equity sharing'.
It appears that this has operated during the 1970s only in the
case of sales of dwellings by local authorities, most of which
were newly constructed houses. The council sells to the
purchaser a 99-year lease on a property for half its freehold
value and at the same time takes payment of a rent equal to
half of the normal council rent on the property. The buyer has
the option to acquire the freehold at any time for half the
current market price. He (or she) is responsible for maintenance
and repair whilst the council continues to receive half the normal
Exchequer subsidy on the house. Leases with an option to buy
the freehold are an old and familiar legal device.[22] What was new
was to set the purchase price at 50 per cent of the freehold
value, although the scheme was also practised on a 40 or 30
per cent basis with a corresponding upward adjustment in the
rent.

Initially the government evinced some enthusiasm for option
leases. In 1976 the Working Group on new forms of social ownership and tenure set up by Reg Freeson, the Minister of Housing,
had supported the idea both with reference to district councils
and housing associations, although not for the sale of the existing

stock of council houses. The housing policy Green Paper
suggested that it could constitute either a permanent tenure
arrangement or a 'stepping stone' to full home-ownership.[23]
And the GLC and Birmingham City Council implemented the idea
in a practical way, the former on a building-for-sale development
at Cheshunt where sales had moved very slowly, and the latter
on an estate originally purchased from a speculative builder.[24]
It was Birmingham, in fact, that had pioneered the option lease.

However, at least by the end of the 1970s, the innovation had
proved to be a damp squib. Local authorities in the six years
1975-80 had sold less than 3,000 dwellings under option lease
arrangements, of which about one-half had been built-for-sale.[25]
The problem seems to have been that the new tenure form applied
only to dwellings disposed of by local authorities. Building-for-
sale schemes were in any case fairly small scale, and any attempt
to expand these on a major scale under option lease arrangements
would have weakened the demand for down-market properties
in the inner city. With reference to sales of the purpose-built
council stock, those authorities that wished to promote this
were precisely those most eager to dispose of the properties
completely, rather than fostering a tenure that was neither fish
nor fowl.

The last low-start scheme I wish to consider is that introduced
by the Home Purchase Assistance and Housing Corporation
Guarantee Act of 1978. The origins of this initiative can be
traced back to the Conservative general election manifesto of
August 1974, although the scheme was thought through and
implemented during the Callaghan administration of 1974-9. Here
is as neat an example as one is likely to find of the Labour Party
stealing the Tory home-owner's clothes. The legislation was
foreshadowed in the housing policy Green Paper in 1977 in the
broader context of the 'natural' desire for home-ownership, and
income frontloading.

The details of the Act can be found in appendix 1. In brief,
first-time buyers who have saved certain minimum sums during
a two-year time-period with a recognised savings institution
are offered a £600 additional loan which is interest free during
its first five years. Purchasers qualifying for the loan also
receive a tax-free grant of £40-110, this varying directly with
the amount saved during the two-year period. The price of the
property bought is not to exceed a regionally calculated
maximum, a limit that can be raised under the Act as time passes.

The housing policy Green Paper assumed that the scheme
would not itself serve to·raise house prices and argues that the
bonus:[26]

> would provide an extra incentive to saving for house purchase,
> especially for those who need a longish period of time to save
> a substantial sum . . . [whilst] the loan would help both
> those who are unable to buy because they cannot raise suffi-
> cient deposit, and those whose problem is the burden of pay-

ments in the early years. The latter would be able to take a
smaller mortgage than otherwise, or might perhaps use the
loan to meet part of the payments in the early years . . . both
methods would effectively provide a low-start mortgage.

Because of the two-year qualifying period, the first loans and
bonuses were not distributed until December 1980. By the
autumn of 1981 the DoE had made available to the recognised
institutions sufficient funds to enable them to provide benefits
to about 25,000 households.

4 MORTGAGE ARREARS

The increasing penetration of owner-occupation amongst
relatively lower-income groups in recent decades - if such has
been the case - suggests that the problem of mortgage arrears
may be slowly becoming more serious, quite apart from short-
run shocks due to rapid upward movements in the mortgage
rate. Unfortunately, once again, no national data exist that
permit us to test this statement. Certainly if we were to base
our understanding on building society losses incurred on
houses that they have repossessed and sold off, the issue
appears to be trivial: at the end of the 1970s such losses ran
at only a few hundreds of thousands of pounds each year, an
infinitesimally small proportion of the annual value of new
advances.
  We do have data on the previous housing situation of households that successfully applied to be considered homeless under
the 1977 Housing (Homeless Persons) Act. In England in the
first half of 1979 as many as 12 per cent of these came from the
owner-occupied sector, although only 4 per cent had lost their
accommodation through a court order for mortgage default.[27]
The problem with these statistics is that they exclude both
those in mortgage difficulties but who remain in possession,
and those who must leave their homes but who enter another
tenure category. Data also exist on county court actions for
the recovery of possession of residential premises in England
and Wales. Unfortunately this lumps together action against
defaulting mortgagors, former licensees and alleged trespassers.
The analysis that follows, then, can make no firm statements on
the national scale or trend in this problem.
  Let me begin with the final sanction the mortgagee wields. A
household normally makes its mortgage payments to a building
society on a monthly basis. If it falls behind with these transfers
then a debt builds up that can be stated as the number of
monthly payments outstanding: this is the arrears problem.
When this becomes acute the mortgagee, be it society, local
authority, bank or insurance company, may take the borrower
to court for having failed to comply with the terms of the loan
agreement. If the action is successful, the court will grant a

possession order to the lender and the building society, for
example, will take possession of the property, sell it, deduct
from the proceeds both its own costs as well as the outstanding
debt, and hand over any funds remaining to the borrower. In
general, however, the societies are reluctant to take default
action: not only is it administratively inconvenient but a court
order that leads to an eviction, particularly if there are children
involved, contrasts brutally with the societies' avuncular image.

Several alternatives to possession exist: the lender may persuade the mortgagor to sell up, repay the outstanding debt,
and move into rented accommodation; the term of the mortgage
may be increased to bring down the monthly payments due;
the arrears may be allowed to accrue until the economic circumstances of the borrower allow them to be cleared off with a
lump-sum payment; the accrued arrears may be added to the
outstanding debt which is then paid off in the normal way over
the remaining period of the loan; or interest-only payments may
be required for an agreed period of time. All of these alternatives, save the first, consist of a rescheduling of the stream
of debt payments. If the mortgagor is in receipt of benefit
from the Supplementary Benefits Commission, he (or she) enjoys
the right to have the state pay the interest on the loan provided
the SBC considers that the claimant's mortgage commitments
were not unreasonable when taken on, that the house is not too
big and too luxurious, and that the neighbourhood is not unduly
expensive.

Let me turn to look at the apparent causes of mortgage
arrears. Here we must rely on a number of case studies and,
in particular, the work of the indefatigable Valerie Karn.[28] The
reasons for arrears cited repeatedly in this literature can be
classified under two heads: first, situations where the household's income broadly remains constant in real terms; second,
situations where there is a sharp and unanticipated fall in
household income.

The constant income case itself contains three sub-categories,
which are perhaps more distinct in logic than in family life:

  (i) The household budget is mismanaged.
 (ii) The household borrows too much when the home is first
      purchased. This can happen with the first mortgage alone
      but is even more likely to occur should the family raise a
      second mortgage. The second mortgage may be sought
      either, for example, to raise the purchaser's deposit
      required by a building society, or to carry out necessary
      rehabilitation work or to purchase furniture, etc. I have
      already referred in section two to the very high costs of
      second mortgages.
(iii) The household may face unavoidable increases in its
      expenditure stream as a result, for example, of a rapid
      rise in the mortgage rate or because of maintenance and
      repair costs in properties with poor physical attributes.

(iv) The reduced income case contains two sub-categories. A
fall in income due to the loss of employment by a woman as
a result of pregnancy or by any member of the household
through death, illness, redundancy or dismissal.

(v) A fall in income as a result of the break-up of the household itself, most commonly through the separation or
divorce of a married couple. This often leads to the man
leaving home and his wife remaining, possibly with one or
more dependent children to care for. If the husband fails
to continue the mortgage payments or fails to provide
sufficient money to the wife for her to do so, and if she
does not secure interest payments from the SBC on the
mortgage, she will have to find other accommodation or be
threatened with a possession order. In all five cases of
arrears a second mortgage from a bank or finance company
may be sought in order to avoid repossession on the first,
to 'buy time' in fact, but unless the underlying problem
is resolved, this merely postpones the evil day.

No quantitative estimates have yet been made of the
relative significance of these factors. Karn calculated that
of 400 local authority mortgages taken out in Birmingham
in 1964-71, almost entirely on pre-1919 property, by 1975
as many as 16 per cent of them had either 'failed', e.g.
through repossession, or were 'at risk', e.g. through
mortgage arrears exceeding six months' payments. Of the
sixty-three mortgages that had 'failed' or were 'at risk',
second mortgages had been taken out in at least twenty-
three cases![29] But no breakdown is given of the causes of
arrears. Finnis has shown in the case of four large building societies with almost 1½ million mortgagors that only
6,215 in April 1976 were in arrears of five months or more
and the number of possession cases in a year equalled
only 1,224. In this case the Abbey National certainly
felt that 'matrimonial problems' account for the major part
of its arrears work.[30] Obviously what we need in this area
is a major national study of the causes of arrears, and the
response processes by households, institutions and the
state, carried out using cohort survival techniques.

5 SUMMARY

Since the 1920s at least, house purchase credit from sources
other than the building societies has always constituted a minor
part of the total flow. Traditionally the local authorities have
provided loans to borrowers who, although 'creditworthy', have
found access to society finance difficult or impossible. Municipal
lending has also been used on a temporary basis to offset sharp
declines in the number of mainstream advances as well as to
assist the implementation of diverse housing policy objectives,
such as those of relieving pressure for local authority construc-

tion and stimulating dwelling rehabilitation. For these reasons councils direct a much greater proportion of their loans to first-time buyers and to pre-1919 properties than is the case with the building societies and their cover ratio is much higher. The growing belief in government since the late 1960s that state expenditure is in crisis has brought with it more forceful and comprehensive controls on local state mortgage lending.

A second alternative source to the building societies has been the insurance companies, which provide both first mortgages and 'topping-up' loans. But they have never exhibited any enthusiasm for expanding their activities in this direction. The third alternative is the banks. They are important in the supply of bridging finance. Moreover in inner-city areas of dwellings with low use-values, banking capital has been shown by several case studies to have played a very substantial role in credit provision to low-income owner-occupiers. The latter may find access difficult even to local authority credit or they may require second mortgages for the purchaser's deposit, initial rehabilitation work or the purchase of furniture, etc.

Owner-occupation in Britain has probably expanded at differential speeds between income groups with the highest earners penetrated earliest and quickest. The direct attempt by the state to extend owner-occupation into successive fractions of the working class has been carried through by local authority mortgages, by the option mortgage subsidy and leasehold reform and, most recently, by a number of measures aimed at reducing income frontloading. But as owner-occupation is expanded in this way it may be bringing with it a worsening problem of serious arrears amongst mortgagors, both those on low incomes and those who experience a sharp contraction in their income, leading at best to a rescheduling of debt payments and at worst to homelessness.

Chapters 4 to 7 have sought to explore the nature of the effective demand for housing for owner-occupation, by looking at the household units themselves and their willingness and ability to purchase. Chapters 8 to 11 that follow examine the supply of dwellings for owner-occupation.

8 THE SALE OF COUNCIL HOUSES

1 INTRODUCTION

The point has come in this volume where it is appropriate to turn from the demand relationships to those of supply, and in this context supply will be understood as the willingness and ability of owners to sell dwellings for home-ownership. This flow concept, in a manner analogous to effective demand, manifests itself concretely by individual persons and companies selling specific dwellings in given locations at defined prices during known periods of time to new owners for their possession. The concept, as employed here, is quite distinct from that of housing production which was defined in Figure 2.1.

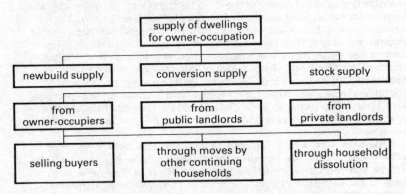

Figure 8.1 The forms of supply of dwellings for owner-occupation

Figure 8.1 provides for Britain in the 1970s a means for the classification of the forms of supply. The fundamental distinction is between the sale in any given time-period of newly produced houses and flats and the sale of dwellings from the already existing stock. Henceforth I shall refer to these forms as new-build supply and stock supply. The supply of converted dwellings, that is, the sale of flats newly created out of the existing stock of dwellings, is *sui generis* and in a sense straddles the other two forms.

The figure implies that stock supply is most effectively understood by a classification based on the sales by different groups of owners. In this chapter I shall deal with sales of previously rented accommodation by public landlords, either to sitting purchasers or of vacant houses. Chapter 9 covers similar sales by private landlords. Chapter 10 deals with the sale of properties already held in owner-occupation. The newbuild supply is treated in chapter 11. This form of supply, one should note, also appears under housing production - usually in the guise of speculatively developed greenfield site schemes.

But before continuing, it is worthwhile noting that there exist certain differences between these categories of supply in their effect on housing mobility, on the aggregate surplus (or deficit) of dwellings over households, and on the relative and absolute extension of the number of owner-occupied houses within the total housing stock. First let us consider the very special situation of landlord stock supply to sitting buyers. This takes place through a metamorphosis in the property rights of a specific household with respect to the house it already occupies. There is no movement *into* the house. (The mobility implications should the household later sell will be considered in section three below.) At the same time the sale has a twofold effect on the scale of home-ownership: the number of rented houses is reduced by one and the number owner-occupied is increased by one.

In all cases other than those of sitting buyers, the housing supply for owner-occupation constitutes the sale of vacant (or partially vacant) properties. When an existing household has bought a vacancy for owner-occupation it then moves out of its former home, thereby leading to a new vacancy. Thus begins a chain of vacancy transfers. The set of such transfers resulting from a single initial move might be thought to be infinite, like the effect of a dull-witted monkey trying to fill all twelve holes in a board with only eleven pegs. In fact the chain is not endless. When a vacancy occurs in a house that thereafter is closed or is demolished or is left permanently vacant, the 'pegs' stop moving. On the other hand when the household that moves into a vacancy is a family newly arrived in the country, or is moving out of shared accommodation or is a newly formed household (but the formation of which itself generated no vacancies), then again the vacancy transfer process within the country stops. The modelling and empirical exploration of vacancy transfer on the basis of matrix algebra, for the country as a whole and for individual districts, counties and regions promises to be an extremely fruitful area of future housing research.

Continuing these remarks on the supply of vacancies, it is worth while noting certain qualitative distinctions between the various categories set out in Figure 8.1, even in the case where we make the assumption (probably unjustified) that the vacancy transfers they generate are essentially the same. In the first place, apart from certain types of conversion, newbuild supply alone adds to the total housing stock. It also specifically adds to the stock of owner-occupied dwellings as does the landlord's stock supply of vacancies, although in the latter case we again see a twofold effect on tenure balance since a gain to home-

ownership is a loss to the rental sector. In contrast, the supply
by selling buyers and the supply from dissolving households and
those moving out of owner-occupation in themselves neither add
to the housing stock in total nor change the tenure composition
of that stock. However, in the case of stock supply by emigrat-
ing households and by dissolving households, particularly with
reference to the death of single-person households, there is a
curious parallel with newbuild supply. In both cases a vacancy
is created without a corresponding necessity for substitute
accommodation to be provided. Newbuild supply increases the
aggregate surplus of dwellings over households by adding
houses; stock supply - because of human mortality - increases
the surplus by subtracting households. The nature of vacancy
creation and vacancy chains is considered at greater length
in chapter 14.

   With these introductory remarks in mind and with this new
representation of the provision of accommodation for owner-
occupation set out, let us turn to consider one element of that
supply, the sale of houses owned by district councils and new-
town corporations.

2   COUNCIL HOUSE SALES AND STATE POLICY: 1875-1970

The issue of the sale of council houses is very nearly as long-
lived as their construction. Indeed the most important nineteenth-
century legislation, the Acts of 1875 and 1890, *insisted* that
council-built dwellings in redevelopment areas should be sold
within ten years of their completion. It was not until the 1909
Housing and Town Planning Act that the obligation to resell was
terminated.

   In practice, local authorities had never been able to find
willing buyers.[1] By the time of the 1936 Housing Act, an amend-
ing and consolidating law, the position was that councils were
merely empowered to sell and all disposals required ministerial
permission. The best price obtainable had to be charged.
However, the onset of the Second World War and the concurrent
fall in housing production led to a ban on sales in 1939 and after
peace was declared the Labour government maintained the
restriction through until 1951, essentially to ensure the availability of houses to let to persons in need.[2]

   A major concept in Conservative political philosophy after
the war had been that of the 'property-owning democracy', a
notion that comfortably embraced owner-occupation. Harold
Macmillan put it thus:[3]

We wish to see the widest possible distribution of property.
We think that, of all forms of property suitable for such distribution, house property is one of the best. Of course, we
recognise that perhaps for many years the majority of families
will want houses to rent, but, whenever it suits them better

or satisfies some deep desire in their hearts, we mean to see
that as many as possible get a chance to own their own house.

Not surprisingly, therefore, the ban on sales was lifted after
the Tory election victory of 1951. Circular 64/52 in effect gave
general ministerial consent to sell in all local authorities in
England and Wales provided that the sale was to a sitting tenant
or, in the case of a vacant property, to a household in need of
a house for its own exclusive use. The Housing Act of 1952
abolished the best price rule but also permitted councils both
to enjoy pre-emptive rights of purchase and to limit the resale
price for five years after the original sale.

Table 8.1 *The sale of dwellings by local authorities and new towns in England and Wales 1939-80[a]*

Year	Local authorities	New towns	Total
1939-52	neg.	neg.	neg.
1953-9[b]	13,103	919	14,022
1960	1,687	74	1,761
1961	2,349	106	2,455
1962	2,828	100	2,928
1963	2,524	329	2,853
1964	2,564	223	2,787
1965	2,216	273	2,489
1966	3,798	483	4,281
1967	3,200	82	3,282
1968	8,571	155	8,726
1969	7,530	260	7,790
1970	6,231	223	6,454
1971	16,851	2,755	19,606
1972	45,058	15,603	60,661
1973	33,720	7,234	40,974
1974	4,153	653	4,806
1975	2,089	175	2,264
1976	4,582	79	4,661
1977[c]	12,020	330	12,350
1978	29,100	449	29,549
1979	40,545	779	41,324
1980	78,535	4,264	82,799

Source: MHLG Reports; HSGB; HCS.

[a] In general, houses and flats built for sale are excluded, as are disposals under option lease arrangements. As far as I am aware, the annual data for sales in Scotland have never been published. During the 1970s perhaps 10,000 were sold in total, the majority in the Scottish new towns.

[b] The annual average equals 2,003 and for these years alone includes houses built for sale.

[c] Local authority figures up to the first quarter of 1977 are of reported disposals. Thereafter the figures are estimates including an adjustment for non-reporting authorities.

Table 8.1 shows that throughout the period 1953-65 sales fell
within the very modest range of 1,000-3,000 units per annum.
The legislation was essentially permissive and one can speculate
that Conservative policy-makers did not seek to force the pace
for fear that it might generate a demand to replace the dwellings
sold from the council stock by means of a higher rate of state
housing construction. The only amendment to policy in these
years occurred in 1960 when circular 64/52 was withdrawn and
replaced by circular 5/60. The latter renewed the general
consent, gave measured encouragement to sales, but modified
procedures so as to check sales at unreasonably low prices. It
also said that interest payments on council mortgages used to
finance such transactions should bear a close relationship to
those on other housing loans and should not represent a concealed subsidy to buyers.

The Labour victory in the general election of 1964 brought
no immediate change in policy. The general ministerial consent
to sell was maintained. After all, as has already been made clear,
the Labour leadership in Parliament was firmly convinced of
the natural superiority of owner-occupation as a tenure form.
In fact the substantial shift in the implementation of policy that
did take place in the late 1960s was engineered by the state at
the local level. In 1966-8 the Conservative Party made very
large electoral gains in a number of metropolitan areas and in
places like Birmingham and London took control of city councils.
They then initiated very aggressive sales policies. Birmingham
was something of a pioneer in all this and its efforts were greeted
with delight in Tory Party circles and were widely publicised.

Pressures within the Labour Party led the MHLG to issue a
new circular in 1967 which, whilst failing to withdraw the general
consent, did argue that sales should not be pursued 'in areas
where there is still an unsatisfied demand for houses to let at
moderate rents'. The general consent in circular 24/67 referred
to sales at full market value where there was no limitation on
resale and specified a reduction of up to 20 per cent of market
value where council pre-emption rights were imposed.

Sales in the late 1960s and the 1970s were usually concentrated
in a very small number of areas: in 1967, for example, those by
Birmingham Corporation accounted for about 40 per cent of the
total in England and Wales![4] At the same time as the minister was
still urging caution, total sales in 1968 leaped to 2.7 times their
level in the previous year. The reliance of central government
on exhortation and advice had clearly failed and in consequence
circular 42/68 was issued. It stated that '. . . the dissipation of
public assets in large-scale disposals must be brought under
control . . .' and limited sales in any one year to one-quarter of
1 per cent of each local authority's housing stock in areas contained in the four conurbations of Greater London, Merseyside,
south-east Lancashire and the West Midlands. Outside of these
areas the general consent of 1967 was renewed. Thus the position
remained until 1970.

3 POLICY AND POLITICS

At this point in the narrative, rather than pressing on with an
account of policy in the 1970s and its implementation, it is preferable first to give an account of what appear to be the principal
arguments underlying the support for and the opposition to
the sale of council houses. Since the driving force for sales has
been the Conservative Party, both within Parliament and in
the powerful local parties, it makes sense to begin on the Right.
We have already seen that since at least 1920 Conservative
political philosophy has welcomed the development of owner-
occupation as a tenure form underpinning social stability in
general and sowing the seed of the Tory vote in particular. For
this reason, since 1951 at least, council house sales have always
been regarded with sympathy. Nevertheless there does seem to
have been a marked shift in the strength of the right's commitment to sales which we can date as commencing from about the
mid-1960s. In part this can be seen as the continuation in tactics
of the owner-occupation strategy: it was believed that such a
policy would have a powerful appeal to high-wage council tenants
who were traditional Labour voters. Yet there is much more to
it than that. The policy shift on sales that became increasingly
evident after the general election of 1964 and reached its apogee
in the 1980 Housing Act manifests the developing hegemony of
a housing philosophy which lies within the ambit of the liberal
rather than the tory tradition of British Conservatism, to use
Budd's distinction.[5] In the text below the attempt is made to sum
up what I believe constitutes such a philosophy with respect to
state housing in general and council house sales in particular.
The paragraph can be taken to represent, then, the very
private views in the late 1970s of an intelligent Conservative
policy-maker who stands firmly in the liberal wing of the party.
I have the views of no specific politician in mind.

> In every political contestation and in every election, local or
> national, Conservative success against labourism in part rests
> on popular perceptions of the nature of the housing question
> and the associated policies and practices of the two major
> parties. It is unlikely that we shall be willing to outbid Labour
> on the scale of housing production or on the channelling of
> output to meet housing need. Therefore it is all the more
> necessary that the perception of the housing question be
> shifted away from production and unsatisfied need and towards
> concepts such as freedom, choice, mobility and subsidy:
> questions of consumption. In this perspective the bureaucracy
> and paternalism of state housing, the squalid environment of
> estates old and new, the vandalism and the huge subsidies
> appropriated by council tenants can be favourably compared
> with the freedom, initiative and mobility enjoyed by the home-
> owner, the tranquillity of the residential suburbs with their
> flowering gardens and the absence of any state subsidies at

all. In fact the substantial increases in real wages during the
1950s and 1960s have made state housing something of an
anachronism; a state sector may have been necessary in the
past but this is no longer the case. Its only function in the
future must be to cater for those dispossessed as a result of
redevelopment, the scale of which must in any case be
reduced, and for those other social categories in special need
such as the elderly poor, the handicapped, the unemployed,
etc. This points to the need for a purposive strategy of
tenure stratification which will assign the middle classes and
the affluent workers to owner-occupation and the residuum to
the council sphere with a subsidiary role for the housing
association movement in order to check the unhealthy development of a local authority rental monopoly and weaken the
potential of political solidarity amongst tenants. In all of this
the role of council house sales assumes some importance. The
sale of the better quality housing stock to sitting purchasers
drawn from high-wage skilled and semi-skilled workers will
further our policy of tenure stratification. Moreover the
expansion of owner-occupation as a result of the disposal of
formerly rented private accommodation must begin to decelerate
as only the rump of private landlordism remains, and therefore the continuing ascent to a 70 per cent level of home-
ownership must increasingly rely on drawing on the reserves
offered by the state housing built over the last century. This
general strategy will win not merely a greater sympathy for
the principles of Conservatism but it will also reduce both the
capital and revenue expenditure on the state sphere and have
the subsidiary advantage of permanently stigmatising the
state sector.

Let us consider next the policy of Labour towards council
house sales. This is much more ambiguous than that of liberal
Conservatism. Acceptance by the Parliamentary Labour Party in
the mid-1960s of the superior virtues of home-ownership made
any principled opposition to sales impossible. As a consequence
Labour ministers accorded local authorities a general consent to
sell throughout their years in office in 1964-70 and 1974-9. This
rather passive support for sales was also buttressed by the
pragmatic reflection that a ban was certain to lose votes but
unlikely to gain many. At the local level, many Labour councils
have actively pursued a policy of selling to sitting purchasers,
in Newcastle, Bristol and Nottingham for example, and in
parliamentary debates Conservative MPs relish the chance of
rolling off the names of Labour councillors who have themselves
bought their own council house.

Yet there has also been considerable opposition from within
the party. In some cases this has taken form as a fundamentalist
appeal against the dissipation of public assets. But certainly
most of the published attacks rest on the arguments that a
policy of *uncontrolled* sales reduces the supply of rented accom-

modation for those in need, diminishes tenant mobility within
the council stock, and creates precisely the stratification of
tenures that I have suggested is a Tory policy objective. A
quotation from Murie gives the flavour of these counter-
arguments:[6]

> If council house sales are to be promoted, then the conse-
> quences should be plainly spelled out. The evidence about
> council house buyers and the properties which are sold offers
> a long term prospect of council housing dominated by the poor
> and elderly poor, living in difficult to let (and to sell) blocks
> of flats and short life properties. The poor will have no real
> choice within a residual 'welfare' council sector as the best
> houses will have been sold to better off tenants. The capacity
> of councils to meet needs will be reduced, opportunities for
> transfer and exchanges will be lost, and the time when the
> supply of adequate properties for rent will be sufficient to
> meet need will be set back still further. Sales diminish the
> capacity to plan and control housing for social ends, reinforce
> social segregation and a sterile tenure system which is geared
> to maintaining housing scarcity. In short, a poor law service
> for housing.

This contrasts sharply with the Conservative stress on choice
rather than on meeting unsatisfied need. A reply to a parliamentary question in May 1979 by the Prime Minister, Margaret
Thatcher, illustrates this:[7]

> Mothers with small children living in tower blocks, just as
> anyone else living in tower blocks will, under a Conservative
> Government, now have three options: to carry on renting, to
> put down an option to purchase the flat within a reasonable
> time, or to purchase the flat. That seems to me to enlarge
> the freedom and possibilities available to such people.

The lines of argument set out above seem to me to have been
the most significant determinants of central and local state
policy. But there have been other lines of attack on or defence
of sales policy which have played a subsidiary role in shaping
government action. These will be dealt with very briefly.
One such argument is that sales will release the council tenant
from a condition of bondage or serfdom. There are few commentators willing to deny the inequality of contract between tenant
and local authority landlord, yet whilst the serfdom argument
constitutes an excellent case for revolutionising state housing
management it is a foolish justification for the sale of council
houses since it is likely precisely to reinforce paternalism within
the residual stock.[8]
A second argument from the defence is that sales can serve
to improve social mix. There may well be some truth in this in
areas where council housing is so predominant that households

wishing to become or to remain owner-occupiers find themselves excluded.[9] However, the work of Forrest and Murie, for example, suggests that the main effect of a policy of unlimited sales is the reverse of that sought by those who wish to encourage social mix. Tenure stratification manifests itself in a spatial dimension by a trend towards restricting council tenantry both to the most disfavoured estates and to those fractions of the population whose levels of wealth and income are lowest.[10] At the same time one must remark that the champions of social mix never argue for the municipalisation of owner-occupied property in the residential suburbs from which council tenants are excluded. Here is another of those extraordinary blind spots in middle-class perceptions of the situation of tenant and owner.[11]

A third argument, one that appears in the armoury of both right and left, is the hypothetical effect on state expenditure of a vigorous sales programme. It is a curious feature of this debate that the right is convinced that sales will reduce expenditure and that therefore the financial facts support a sales policy whilst the Left, usually the first to defend state expenditure, attempts to demonstrate that sales will raise its level and that therefore the financial argument is against sales! I am quite sure, given the very substantial complexities and uncertainties that surround such forecasts and the problematic nature of the criterion used to 'test' policy, that Murie is right to argue: 'In most cases the financial argument has been an additional justification or rationalisation and not a central one.'[12] The main effect of sales in reducing government spending and raising government income is achieved by *cutting* the subsidies paid to council tenants and the outlays on maintenance and repairs and by *gaining* either a stream of mortgage payments, or cash receipts where the house is purchased from personal assets or a building society or bank loan. The main effect of sales in raising expenditure and reducing income is the increased tax relief paid to owner-occupiers and the loss of the tenants' rental payments. The most detailed, careful and honest study so far conducted at the local level shows that the net expenditure effect is likely to be a short-run surplus followed by a more or less permanent deficit.[13]

Finally, the case against unrestricted sales made by some of the rural and coastal councils is worth considering. Not only is their situation a special one but the fact that they are usually Conservative-controlled reminds us that the radical-Right philosophy outlined above has never convinced all sections even of the Tory Party itself that the tenant's right to buy should be untrammelled. These authorities point out that the low availability in villages of rental accommodation for rural workers and their families, the problems in replacing any stock sold off because of planning restrictions and the intense demand for second and retirement houses in the more attractive areas will all lead to substantial medium-term price gains by sitting buyers but a permanent loss of housing to rent for local people in general.[14]

This broadbrush account of the factors determining support for or opposition to the sale of council houses within the major parties and the state is now complete. It hardly seems necessary to mention that sales are seen as an integral part of a rational housing policy by institutions such as the BSA, the RICS and even the CIPFA. The entire commercial lobby of exchange professionals is powerfully motivated to support sales simply because state housing is not bought and sold when its possession changes hands and so there is no transfer of ownership to provide these professionals with their sources of fee income. The general role of this class fraction in owner-occupation is considered at length in chapter 13.

4 POLICY DEVELOPMENTS SINCE 1970

The Conservative victory in the general election of June 1970 was quickly followed by a new communication on sales policy, circular 54/70, which dropped the 1968 quota restrictions, restored the general consent to sell on the terms of the 1967 circular, recognised no substantial conflict between sales and local conditions of housing stress, and encouraged local authorities to do everything in their power to make home-ownership possible. Before 1970 there had been no general consent to sell in Scotland under either Tory or Labour administrations. In Scottish Development Department circular 71/70 local authorities were told that the Secretary of State would now approve all individual applications unless there was special reason for refusing them, although in 1971 this was amended to say that there should be no sales of vacant property in areas where there was a waiting list. Then in 1972 general consent to sell houses to sitting tenants was given in Scotland whilst in England and Wales circular 56/72 regretted that many local authorities were frustrating their tenants' desire to buy and advised that the tenant should only be refused if local circumstances were exceptional. Moreover the government evinced a renewed interest in the discounts being offered tenants: local authorities were told they should give tenants the full benefit of the 20 per cent discount on market value offered where pre-emption clauses existed and that in special circumstances a 30 per cent discount was permissible. Pre-emption terms exceeding five years were introduced under the 1973 Housing (Amendment) Act and this option with a corresponding discount of up to 30 per cent was encouraged by central government in circular 30/73.[15] Finally one should note that the preparation of the Housing Finance Act in 1972, with its prospect of higher rents, also encouraged sitting purchases, particularly by high-wage tenants.[16]

The efforts of the incoming administration to stimulate council house sales at the local level quickly bore fruit. Table 8.1 shows that in England and Wales their volume increased from less than 7,000 in 1970 to more than 60,000 in 1972, at that time the

highest annual rate ever recorded. But the table also shows
they fell like a stone in the following two years. To explain
this we must draw on the language of both economics and politics.
First, the extraordinary price rise in the owner-occupied housing market in general in 1971-3 obviously raised the market
value of dwellings sold from the council stock, thereby making
the trade-off between mortgage payment and rental stream much
less favourable for the sitting purchaser. Also one might add
that from about the middle of 1973 the prospects of quick price
gains were much less evident. Second, local elections throughout the country in 1972 brought Labour to power in a number
of authorities previously held by Tory administrations. I have
already remarked that sales in most years during the 1960s and
1970s were highly concentrated geographically. Thus a change
in power at the local level in even a small number of authorities
could have a significant impact on the national data. So it was in
1972. To give just a single example, in 1972 the Birmingham
Tories were ousted and replaced by a Labour council which
immediately terminated all council house sales save where firm
commitments had been entered into. There was, of course, no
change in the political administration in the new towns and the
54 per cent fall in sales there in 1973 clearly illustrates the
demand phenomenon.

The installation of a Labour minority government in March
1974 once more led to a major revision in government policy.
To be frank, circular 70/74 did not change the terms of the
general consent to sell. Yet the Secretary of State for the
Environment made it clear that in areas where there was a
substantial need for dwellings to let it was generally wrong to
sell for 'The first duty of a local authority is to ensure an
adequate supply of rented dwellings.' The New Town Development Corporations and the Commission for the New Towns were
asked not to sell any more houses to sitting tenants except
where they were under a legal obligation to do so or where
they had obtained special approval, pending review of owner-
occupation in the new towns.[17] With reference to Scotland, SDD
circular 36/74 revoked the general consent to sell although it
was recognised that some sales could be justified to secure
tenure balance in areas with no significant unsatisfied demand
for housing to rent. Five-year pre-emption clauses became
obligatory. With the demand conditions unfavourable and Labour
councils in power in most of the large authorities, the rate of
sales returned to its pre-1968 level, as Table 8.1 shows.

But the new phase was not to last for long. In elections in
May 1976 the Conservatives won control of a large number of
local authorities including fifteen metropolitan districts. The
existence of the general consent to sell permitted them to raise
the rate of sales rapidly over the next three years so that by
the first quarter of 1979 they were running at an annual rate
of 50,000. In 1978 Forrest and the ubiquitous Murie argued in
a politically important article in *Roof* that, by selling dwellings

in areas of housing stress with unmet demands for rented
accommodation, councils in London, Birmingham, Nottingham,
Bradford, Leeds, Derby, Leicester, Bristol, Southampton,
Bolton and Tameside were flouting central government's advice.
In the London Borough of Wandsworth, for example, they produced evidence to show that the sale of vacant newly built and
acquired properties threatened the authority's ability to house
homeless families, to decant households from redevelopment
areas and to continue with its programme of not re-letting to
families with children those casual vacancies arising in multi-
storey blocks.[18] In Nottingham two-thirds of all the council's
houses (rather than flats) coming vacant between February
1977 and March 1979 were sold![19]

Peter Shore and Reg Freeson, respectively Secretary of State
for the Environment and Minister for Housing and Construction,
took no action - as distinct from exhortation - until only a few
weeks before the general election of 1979. They then withdrew
the general consent to sell empty houses built for renting,
restricted sales to sitting tenants under the terms of circular
54/70 to those who had been sitting for at least two years, and
excluded the sale of options to buy at a future date.[20]

The triumph of Mrs Thatcher and her allies in May 1979 has
been attributed, in part at least, to the main plank of her
housing policy, the statutory right of every council tenant to
buy their house at a discount, which was couched in what Jones
has called a 'populist appeal to the anti-bureaucratic, individual-
ist and self-sufficient ideology of home ownership'.[21]

In the short term, whilst the new Housing Bill was under
preparation, a new consent in May restored the situation to what
it had been under circular 54/70 but substantially increased the
permitted discounts. A general consent to sell houses in Scotland
and the new towns was also given on the same terms as those in
England and Wales.

The contents of the 1980 Housing Act can be found in appendix
1. In brief, public sector tenants were given the right to buy
their homes if they had been tenants for more than three years.
A discount on the market price of 33 per cent was available to
tenants of less than four years' standing, rising by 1 per cent
for each further completed year to a 50 per cent maximum. The
statutory obligation of local authorities and new towns to sell
was intended to prevent Labour councils blocking the sales
process. When the dust had settled, no council had shown itself
willing to defy the law on this matter. The objective of the
government's discounts was to give a powerful stimulus to the
rate of sales both by reducing the stream of mortgage payments
on the knocked-down price as well as offering a substantial
price gain should the tenant re-sell. Discounts also place councils
at a financial disadvantage should a new government give them
first refusal on sales of previously rented accommodation if they
must buy back at full market price. Discounts, of course,
seriously undermine the case that sales help reduce public

expenditure and reinforce the view that this argument was a
rationalisation of the true purposes of the legislation.

Royal assent was given to the Act only in August 1980, too
late to affect the volume of sales in that year although in any
case they set a record level, as Table 8.1 shows. In the first
nine months of the scheme 380,000 tenant households had
applied to buy. Local authority ownership of the better quality
housing stock was clearly in the process of being dismembered.

5 THE DECISION TO PURCHASE

The shifts in policy and its implementation that began in 1966
led in the course of time to a number of research studies into
the practice of sales at the local level. Of these Murie's is undoubtedly the outstanding example for its quality and depth.[22]
In this section I shall try to indicate their main conclusions
with respect to the character of the households that buy, the
types of dwelling bought and the motivations for purchase.

A fundamental distinction in classifying buyers of previously
rented accommodation is that between sitting purchasers and
all other purchasers. In the latter case we have a decision that
in general terms does not differ from that of any household
buying any vacant dwelling. It can thus be analysed straight
forwardly in terms of the six predicates set out in chapter 5.
The situation of sitting purchasers is different for they make
a choice not between different properties but between two forms
of tenure of the single dwelling they already possess. The
distinction is also important from the supply side. A sale to a
sitting purchaser has no immediate effect on the availability of
rented accommodation and sales are sometimes defended for that
reason. However, the sale of an empty property implies forth-
with that the house is withdrawn from the supply of vacancies
a district can dispose of, thereby cancelling the move into that
property which would otherwise have taken place as well as any
consequential moves that that move would itself have triggered
off. Unfortunately the DoE have never published any national
data on how disposals break down into these two categories, an
omission that they would do well to make good. Inter-district
variations must be very large: in the past some councils have
sold only to sitting purchasers whilst others such as the GLC,
Nottingham and Wandsworth have actively pursued the sale of
vacant dwellings.[23]

Now let us look at the sources of finance necessary for purchase. Table 8.2 shows that the average valuation of dwellings
sold by district councils in England and Wales in 1977-80 rose
considerably but that this was very substantially moderated by
an increase in the average discount received after 1978. The
combination of discount and local authority mortgage finance

meant that in 1980 on average only 16 per cent of the full
valuation was found from ready cash and personal, building
society or bank loans. Again one would welcome the information
cross-classified by sales to sitting purchasers and to vacancy
purchasers. In the latter case the average discount would
usually be lower and the average initial payment higher. Thus
the data show that the necessary credit comes largely from the
state itself. But this does not mean councils must go into the
capital market to raise mortgage funding. As Aughton writes:
'The universal practice these days is to use a Purchase Agreement, the effect of which is that the housing account receives
mortgage repayments instead of a rent.'[24]

Table 8.2 The valuation, discount and initial payments made on dwellings
disposed of by local authorities in England and Wales 1977-80[a]

1 Year	2 Number of disposals	3 Average valuation before discount (£)	4 Average discount (%)	5 Average valuation after discount (£)	6 Average payment made (£)	7 $\frac{6}{3}$
1977	13,020	8,568	16	7,197	1,959	.23
1978	30,045	10,080	18	8,266	2,676	.27
1979	41,660	12,862	26	9,518	2,534	.20
1980	80,440	15,528	39	9,472	2,547	.16

Source: Calculated using *HCS* data on local authority disposals.

[a] Excludes new towns. The calculation assumes that column four, which is for England
alone, is negligibly different from the England and Wales datum.

Finally, before turning to consider the evidence on the
decision to purchase, it is wise to make explicit an associated
methodological problem. Throughout the years 1966-79 all or
virtually all of those authorities selling council dwellings in
Britain imposed some restrictions on what properties they were
prepared to dispose of. Most commonly, councils refused in
practice to sell flats in multi-storey blocks, maisonettes, single-
bedroom dwellings, sheltered accommodation, dwellings specially
designed for the handicapped and those in the clearance programme. It is therefore dangerous to project what will happen in
the 1980s, with tenants enjoying the *right* to buy, on the basis
of past events when the ability to purchase was restricted. It
is also invalid to state, for example, that 'overwhelmingly it was
tenants living in houses as opposed to flats who chose to buy
in the 1970s' for this implies that flat-dwellers enjoyed the option
and simply failed to exercise it. Similarly, given that there is
an association between the use-value of council dwellings and
the income and occupation of their inhabitants, these past

restrictions also introduce a bias into results describing who chose to buy. The survey results are not false of course; it is simply that they are drawn from a non-representative group of council tenants as a whole.

With respect to the characteristics of buyers, published survey evidence describes the 'typical' purchaser as follows:[25]

> The householder has been a long established tenant, is in middle age with a fairly large family growing up. He is earning above average wages, usually in a skilled manual occupation. The family has often reached the stage in the family cycle where more than one wage-earner is living at home.

Murie's work on Birmingham also shows that small adult households are overrepresented compared to council tenants as a whole, and that a relatively high proportion of purchasers had moved into their house as a result of a transfer application. These traits reflect both the type of property offered for sale by the Conservative administration of that time and the rule that the weekly income of the husband and wife, less 30s per week, should be at least equivalent to the monthly mortgage repayments.[26] In fact the eligibility criteria were slightly less stringent than for other local authority mortgagors both because any discount reduced the purchase price below the market valuation and because in the case of default the council could simply repossess and resume renting the dwelling. The survey results also showed the other side of the coin, that the elderly, the retired, single-parent households, and other households without a wage or with only one wage, were less likely to purchase.

With respect to the characteristics of dwellings, the evidence points overwhelmingly to the sale of houses with gardens on estates where the environmental locus is more favourable.[27] Billcliffe's survey for Shelter in Leeds illustrates this proposition:[28]

> The most popular areas for sales are those overlooking green belts and parkland on the edge of estates, on corner plots or set back from main roads with wide grass verges. Houses sold tend to appear on the map in clusters. Houses are readily sold if they are close to good community amenities such as schools, shopping precincts and bus routes. Houses that are not directly overlooked have a tendency to be sold. Although most houses in the survey area are of a similar type, age, and design, those in streets where there are boarded up and vandalised houses have not been sold.

With respect to the motivation to purchase amongst sitting buyers we can draw on Murie's study of a sample group of 193

households in Birmingham who had bought their houses in
1968-73.[29] The predicates of control, mobility and finance all
appear to have been important. On control, his respondents
clearly identified factors concerning rehabilitation as major
advantages in owning rather than renting. Some 73 per cent
had made a variety of changes since buying. These included
painting the house a different colour; adding a porch or
garage; putting up new garden walls or fences; paving drive-
ways; changes in the kitchen, bathroom, windows and fire-
places; room extensions; moving an outside toilet indoors; the
removal or erection of partitions to alter room layout; the
addition of glass doors, sliding doors and cloakrooms; and the
addition of a water heater. There was a fairly even split
between households paying for work and those carrying it out
themselves. In citing the disadvantages of renting the failure
of the council to do repairs and the lack of freedom to improve
or adapt the dwelling were frequently mentioned. At the same
time the principal advantage of renting was considered to be
that councils *did* carry out repairs and maintenance, especially
of large and external items.[30]

On mobility, only about 3 per cent of purchasing households
had any definite plans to move 'in the foreseeable future'
although 23 per cent thought they might move eventually. The
attractions of moving seemed largely to be to enjoy the same
type of accommodation but in a better area or environment:
quieter spots with more open spaces, less busy roads, better
educational facilities for the children, 'more select areas',
located in the country, on the coast or in suburban areas. There
were a number of references to retirement and, as Murie says,
'the virtual impossibility of council tenants moving to retirement
areas compared with owner-occupiers is an established feature
of the British housing market and actions in anticipation of
retirement are eminently sensible in view of this'.[31]

Finally, on the financial predicate it seemed evident that there
was virtually no intention to sell and realise a short-term price
gain. At the same time, the financial advantages in the medium
and long term were unmistakably present in the minds of purchasers. The short-run financial effect was clearly disadvantageous in spite of the discounts available: the median household
had to face a level of mortgage payments that were more than 50
per cent greater than their council rent when allowance for rate
payments in both tenures is made. Yet the longer-term effects
had outweighed this. Buyers were concerned about the upward
trend in council rents and the major disadvantage of renting
was said to be that it was 'dead money' or paying out continuously with no return. Murie writes:[32]

> Anticipation of retirement, of rent paying capacity in retire-
> ment . . . of children leaving home and security for children

event of death were all mentioned. There was a con-
rable number of references to investment factors. Only
reference was made to tax relief advantages, although
some references were made to the advantage of ownership
in raising additional loans.

The mobility and financial motives are both, I suggest, of
considerable importance in persuading households in the better
rather than the inferior use-value dwellings to buy, since
improved mobility and the realisation of net worth are both
threatened if it proves to be impossible to sell the house at an
advantageous price. Whitehead's law can be applied to the
motivation of sitting purchasers as well as to the general predicative analysis of tenure.

6 SUMMARY

The supply of dwellings for owner-occupation is composed of
two major categories: the newbuild and the stock supply. This
chapter covers the stock supply of formerly rented accommodation
by public landlords. The scale of state disposals was extremely
modest until the late 1960s, since when it has followed a very
marked upward trend, although year-on-year changes have
been extremely irregular. The motivation of recent Conservative
governments in selling off the stock of state housing has been
widely misinterpreted. What lies behind claims such as reduced
public expenditure and the end of tenant serfdom is an iron
determination to expand the owner-occupied stock through
tenure transfers, to stratify the tenure structure of the working
people, and to stigmatise the state sector. All these transformations are believed to bring permanent political advantage to the
Right. With respect to the Labour Party, the last two decades
have witnessed deep ambiguities in its stance, a reflection of
similar uncertainties and divisions about the long-term advantages
of owner-occupied and state housing. The socialist case against
sales is precisely that it will lead to stratification and stigmatis-
ation and that disposals, with respect to the state housing stock,
eventually terminate *social* processes of vacancy allocation and
introduce their privatisation. When sitting purchasers sell, the
dwelling is allocated on the criteria of the market not of social
need.
Research into the motivation of tenants to purchase suggests
that enhanced control of the rehabilitation process, the promise
of improved housing mobility, and the evaluation of the financial
advantages are all central to the decision to buy. Policy developments in the 1970s have generally favoured an increased volume
of sales. The climax to this took place in 1980 when sitting
tenants were accorded the right to buy. With this brief summary

complete, the next chapter takes up the second category of stock supply, the sale of formerly rented accommodation by private landlords.

9 THE SALE OF PRIVATELY
RENTED ACCOMMODATION

1 HOUSES AS CAPITAL

Tenure analysis in Britain traditionally employs three major
categories: accommodation may be rented from local authorities
or new-town corporations; it may be rented from private owners
and in other miscellaneous tenures; or it may be owner-occupied.
The stock supply considered in the previous chapter falls in
the first category. I now turn to the second. Whilst this is
commonly referred to as 'private rental' one should remember
that it is in fact an extremely heterogeneous sector. As the
author of the *Housing Policy Technical Volume* noted:[1]

> It includes housing associations (ranging from the Peabody
> Foundation to much more recently formed associations); dwell-
> ings rented by virtue of employment, both private (e.g.
> agricultural tied cottages, caretakers' flats, vicarages and
> manses) and public (of which armed services married quarters
> are the largest group); accommodation rented with farm or
> business premises (e.g. shops with living quarters over the
> shop); and accommodation rented from private landlords.
> 'Private landlords' range from the Crown Estates Commissioners
> and the Church Commissioners to home-owners going abroad
> for a year and letting their house while they are away.

In Britain in 1976 this second tenure category contained 3
million dwellings, of which 2.79 million were to be found in
England and Wales. Within the latter total it is estimated that
250,000 belonged to housing associations, 700,000 were occupied
by virtue of employment or with farm or business premises,
and 1.84 million were rented from private landlords.[2] It is the
sale to owner-occupiers of accommodation formerly rented out by
private landlords that is the principal focus of this chapter.

An estimate of the scale of sales from category two into owner-
occupation over the years 1914-75 is given in Table 9.1. Rather
sparse evidence suggests that since 1938 some 30 per cent of
purchases were by sitting tenants, many of whom had bought
pre-1914 property at advantageous prices, often for ready
money.[3]

As can be seen, this form of transfer between tenures has
taken place throughout most of the century and on a substantial
scale. The starting point in explaining it is to understand that
for the majority of private landlords in 1914 the houses that they

owned and let to the various classes of British society were a
form of capital. When the landlord first acquired the dwelling,
for example from a builder or from an existing landlord, it was
as a means of placing his (or her) wealth (or funds that he had
borrowed) into a physical object whose ownership generated a
stream of net incomes. This stream consisted of the rents paid
by the owner's tenants in each time-period less expenditures on
maintenance, repairs and the various necessary costs of management. The net income could be calculated before or after tax
and should also have taken into account major rehabilitatory
outlays on the basis of some form of depreciation allowance. In
first considering whether or not to buy the house, its status as
a financial asset could be assessed by the potential landlord as
the rate of return it offered, that is, the ratio of the annual
net income to the purchase price.

Table 9.1 *The sale to owner-occupiers of dwellings formerly privately rented
or in miscellaneous tenures in England and Wales 1914-75*

	1914-37	1938-59	1960-75
Average number of units sold each year	46,000	68,000	69,000

Source: Tables 1.3, 3.1 and 16.2.

a This estimate relies on the assumption that in 1914 10 per cent of the stock of dwellings
were owner-occupied. Unfortunately no direct evidence for this exists.

As time passed the owner was always free to consider the
possibility of asset switching, that is to say, selling his housing
property and using the money received to acquire a different
asset, local authority securities for example, with its own
specific rate of return. The effect of such a switch, in the
simplest case where we ignore capital gains, was to surrender
the net income stream from rents in exchange for the stream of
interest received on the new placement. The amount of interest
received was dependent on two variables: current market rates
of interest and the selling price of the house. Thus the rational
comparison of rates of return was no longer dependent on how
much the owner had paid for the house but on how much he
could sell it for. So asset switching decisions were best carried
out by comparing market rates of interest with the ratio of net
rental income to the dwelling's *selling price*.

Thus, at this fairly abstract level, I would argue that tenure
transfer on the scale and over the time-period indicated in Table
9.1, can be explained in terms of the development of an unfavourable rate of return differential which made asset switching
preferable. I cannot here hope to give an account of the trends
in market rates of interest in the British economy since 1914
but what does require discussion from within the housing system
is, first, some of the determinants of rent levels in privately
rented accommodation and, second, new influences in the twen-

tieth century on the price of secondhand houses.

2   RENTS, HOUSE PRICES AND STATE INTERVENTION

In this section I wish to review very briefly the interventions
of the state in the system of house purchase and consumption
in so far as its actions directly tended to depress the private
landlord's rate of return, that is, the net income/selling price
ratio discussed above. I believe that these interventions have
been crucial in creating a context in which asset switching was
rational. Rental income is dealt with first and the question of
selling prices thereafter.

The concepts of 'property ownership' in general and 'the
ownership of rented accommodation' in particular are not and
never have been ideas that refer to an unchanging social reality.
'Ownership' refers basically to certain rights and duties in law
enjoyed by and required of the owner with respect to what is
owned. These rights and duties change over time as a result of
political struggle - which may be more or less violent - and so
the meaning of 'ownership' changes. One of the most important
legal transformations in British society in the twentieth century
has been the result of the political attack carried out by successive governments - mostly Tory - against that heterogeneous
fraction of the capitalist class that, we believe, owned nine-
tenths of all the dwellings in this country in 1914. The tortuous
history of this long, long war cannot be written here. Suffice
it to suggest that, in a situation where there has been huge
excess demand for privately rented housing, since 1915 successive
Conservative, Coalition, Labour and 'National' governments have
sought to keep private rents below their market clearing rate,
in time of peace and in time of war, in order to head off social
and industrial unrest; and to check the upward pressure of
housing costs on wages which would be inflationary and also
might have the final effect of transforming industrialists' profits
into landlords' rents.

The private landlord, the owner of housing capital, seeks to
maximise his net income by charging rents for his properties as
high as the market will bear. Where his tenants are unwilling
or unable to pay, then he seeks to dispossess them and let to
those who do exercise effective demand. The maximising landlord will also cram as many (or as few) tenants into his properties
as he finds most profitable and will carry out rehabilitation of
the structure on the same principle. It was precisely these
rights of ownership enjoyed by this class fraction that the state
has restricted or abolished.

The most drastic and long-lasting constraint and the one most
injurious to the landlord's interest has been rent control and
the associated guarantees of security of tenure. This was first
introduced during the First World War directly in response to
social and industrial agitation in Glasgow and other cities and

took the form of the 1915 Increase of Rent and Mortgage Interest
(War Restrictions) Act. After modification in 1919 it had the
effect of controlling the rents of all privately rented houses
(within specified rateable value limits) that had been built by
April 1919. In the interwar years successive Acts of Parliament
amended the controls, sometimes to relax them as in 1923, sometimes to make them more restrictive as in 1933, but the controls
were never abolished. Then in 1939, shortly after the outbreak
of war, rents on almost all privately rented houses, including
that very considerable number built in the 1930s, were frozen
at their levels of September 1939.[4]

There was to be no substantial change in rent controlling
legislation until the 1957 Rent Act; this was intended to initiate
a movement back towards much greater freedom for landlords
to make their own decisions unconstrained by the state. However, there is no evidence that the Act reduced the rate of
sales of privately rented accommodation; indeed, in so far as
tenants had to pay higher rents, from their point of view it
made owner-occupation more attractive.

But already by the mid-1960s the new direction in policy
towards *laissez-faire* was abandoned. The Housing Acts of 1961
and 1964 introduced stronger powers for councils to control
the management of multi-occupied houses and to compel landlords to do repairs and undertake improvement. Security of
tenure for most tenants renting unfurnished was reintroduced
and extended in legislation in the years 1964, 1965 and 1973 and
in the Rent Act of 1974 security was given to furnished lettings,
except where the landlord lives in the same building. Rent
control in a new form was reintroduced in the guise of 'fair
rents' through the 1965 Rent Act, although in 1969 and 1972
provision was made under certain conditions for the transfer
of rents that had never been decontrolled to (generally higher)
regulated rents. Moreover there were temporary restrictions
of rent increases as part of general counter-inflation policy in
1969, 1972, 1974 and 1975.[5]

Not until the 1980 Housing Act was there any new attempt to
revive the fortunes of the private landlord. The Act introduced
shorthold tenancies under which landlords were assured of
repossession of a dwelling at the end of a fixed term of 1-5
years. An existing tenancy could not be converted to a shorthold. However, early indications are that the legislation has
completely failed to draw capital back into rented accommodation.
Not only did the Labour Party promise to repeal the Act's
provisions as soon as it was returned to power, but the registration of fair rents, which shorthold requires, has also proved
to be unpopular with landlords.

The general trend of rent controlling legislation since 1915,
then, has been towards constraining the numerator of the landlord's ratio of net income to selling price. But the diminution in
his rate of return can also be approached from the side of the
denominator, the prices of the second-hand stock. Here it is

essential to remember that we are dealing with the selling price only of privately rented houses, which in the last four decades has been composed almost entirely of houses built before 1914 and some 900,000 units constructed for rental between the wars.[6]

The selling prices to owner-occupiers of dwellings coming out of the privately rented sector are prices determined within the housing system as a whole and within the owner-occupied sector in particular. The extraordinarily difficult question of how house prices *are* formed will not be considered until chapter 11. But whatever the determinants may be, we can be quite sure that since the late 1930s the upward trend has been sufficiently rapid that the combination of controlled rents and uncontrolled prices has been sufficient to force the landlord's rate of return to a very low level indeed (see section three below). Here I wish to limit the analysis to just two questions: the specificity of the privately rented stock and the role of the state in stimulating the purchase of dwellings from that stock.

My remarks above on price trends glossed over the fact that at any point in time the average price of houses sold by private landlords has been lower than the average price of all other houses in the total supply. The fact that the selling price was lower implied of course that the landlord's rate of return was that much higher! Whilst this is central to understanding why the rented stock was not sold off completely long, long ago, it does not invalidate the argument that the broad trend of these prices has been upward and in general we can be sure they increased more rapidly than controlled rents.

But why have the prices of the landlord's stock supply been lower? The answer to this question can be couched in the language of the predicative analysis of chapter 5. We have seen that privately rented accommodation has been composed primarily of pre-1914 dwellings. As a result, in general the use-value of these houses has been much inferior to that of houses built for owner-occupation since the 1920s. With respect to their physical attributes fewer have enjoyed the full range of basic amenities and more have suffered from structural faults and major disrepair, in part because of the landlord's perfectly rational neglect. With respect to the control predicate, this form of stock supply is characterised by its high proportion of sitting tenants; the much higher level of prices of properties with vacant possession over those without demonstrates how much this has reduced the willingness of would-be owners to purchase. The fact that houses without vacant possession enjoy a much lower selling price is precisely what has enabled many tenants on relatively low incomes to buy them with cash raised outside of the magic circle of the mainstream finance institutions, With respect to environmental locus, a very large number of properties - in relative and absolute terms, - are located in the older inner areas of our towns and conurbations. This has been perceived by purchasing households, evidently, as a negative feature that is not offset by what appears to be the stock's superior relative locus.[7]

So the relatively inferior use-values of the landlord's stock
has had the perverse effect of setting his rate of return at a
higher level than would otherwise have been the case, thereby
discouraging tenure transfer. At the same time a number of state
interventions in the housing market (which in earlier chapters
I have discussed in a different context) have had the reverse
effect, particularly in the last three decades.

Chapters 4 to 7 of this book explored at some length the
ability and the willingness of households to exercise effective
demand for house purchase for owner-occupation. As part of
this analysis we saw that for many, many years the state has
given its support to house purchase by households with
relatively low incomes and with restricted access to capital,
and has underpinned the purchase by any household type of
down-market properties in disrepair. These policies, partly
purposively and partly as a by-product of the achievement of
other goals, have been of the greatest importance in stimulating
the effective demand for the landlord's stock supply. Some
policies have facilitated potential owners' access to funds and
therefore have strengthened the *ability* to purchase the landlord's supply. Here we can cite the provision of local authority
mortgages, local authority guarantees on building society
advances, the 1959 Exchequer loan programme to the building
societies and the support lending scheme. Moreover, the option
mortgage subsidy as well as the development of low-start mortgages have both been intended to improve in different ways the
specific mortgage repayment situation of the marginal owner-
occupier who would, of course, generally be buying down-
market. Other policies have made the buying of property with a
low use-value a more attractive proposition and therefore have
strengthened the *willingness* to purchase the landlord's supply.
Here we can cite the availability of improvement grants since
1949 and of repair grants since 1969 and the associated area-
based rehabilitation programmes of the municipalities.

In addition to these specific policies, the generalised state
support of owner-occupation, for example through the composite
tax arrangements and tax relief, has certainly gone some way
to bolster the process of tenure transfer by stimulating the
effective demand for every form of supply.

The fairly broad analysis of the landlord and his rate of
return objective in this section needs to be complemented by a
more specific understanding of his position in the 1970s. This is
the purpose of section three which will also serve to correct the
impression earlier paragraphs may have given that the tenants'
world contains only landlords who seek to maximise their rate of
return.

3 THE PRIVATE LANDLORD IN THE 1970s

This chapter by no means pretends to provide a comprehensive
account of the privately rented sector in Britain either in the
past or at the present time. That question is far beyond the
scope of this book. The review of private rental here is strictly
limited to providing a basis for understanding the landlord's
stock supply. But since the concept of the landlord's rate of
return has been central to the argument so far, it behoves me
to refer to a useful calculation carried out by DoE researchers
in 1976-7 on the level of the average rate in 1970 and 1975.[8]

For Britain as a whole no data existed permitting a direct
estimate of the ratio of rents net of expenses to selling prices.
Instead an approach was adopted in which it was 'necessary to
rely on indirect comparisons via the relationship of registered
rents to rateable value, and the relationship of rateable value
to selling price'.[9] It was also thought proper to assume that
formerly rented houses with vacant possession would sell at a
lower price than owner-occupied houses within the same rateable
value range because of their generally poorer state of repair.
On this basis the estimated rate of return in 1970, after provision
for amortisation and major repairs over a forty-year life, and
assuming a selling price at about the lower quartile of all houses
in the rateable value range, was some $3\frac{1}{2}$ per cent.[10] At that
time, long-dated government securities were yielding 9 per cent.
By 1975 the rate of return had fallen to as low as $1\frac{1}{6}$ per cent,
largely because of the relatively rapid increase in house prices
in the intervening years. These data certainly confirm in general
terms the unattractiveness of housing capital in the 1970s and
the fall in the average rate of return under conditions of house
price inflation.

Let us now turn to a different study, which tells us more
about the landlords themselves. In 1976 Paley of the OPCS Social
Survey Division carried out a sample survey of private lettings
in the more densely privately rented areas of England and Wales.
Typically, these were found in cities or in central town areas.
The proportionate distribution of the sample lettings between
landlord types was as follows: 12 per cent were owned by
resident individuals, 35 per cent by non-resident individuals,
25 per cent by companies, 6 per cent by non-charitable trusts
and executors, 15 per cent by charities and housing associations,
and finally 7 per cent were owned by public bodies, etc.[11] The
'private landlords' with which this chapter has been concerned
fall in the first four of these categories, or 78 per cent of the
grand total. Amongst the company lettings, two-thirds were
accounted for by property companies letting mainly residential
accommodation.

Paley's study is as densely packed as the areas she surveyed
and space permits me only to review a fraction of her findings,
the main interest of which lies in the qualitative differences
between landlord types in their attitudes to letting. Two brief

points that confirm certain aspects of the preceding analysis
are that 81 per cent of all the lettings were in buildings constructed before 1919 (and 13 per cent in those built in 1919–44)
whilst as few as 55 per cent of the total enjoyed the exclusive
use of all basic amenities. The properties of resident individual
landlords scored particularly poorly on this variable.[12]

Table 9.2 Lettings by type of landlord and by size of the landlord's holding in
densely rented areas of England and Wales in 1976 (percentages)

Number of lettings in England and Wales in 1976	Resident individual	Non-resident individual	Company	Non-charitable trust/executive
1	36	18	2	–
2-4	42	22	4	15
5-9	10	20	5	4
10-24	12	26	16	14
25-49	–	8	16	17
50-99	–	3	14	19
100-499	–	3	14	25
500-999	–	–	6	6
1,000-9,999	–	–	18	–
10,000 or more	–	–	5	–
All sizes	100	100	100	100

Type of landlord making the letting

Source: Bobbie Paley, *Attitudes to Letting in 1976*, London, HMSO, 1978, Table 2.11.

With respect to letting attitudes and landlord type, we can
start by looking at Table 9.2 which shows clearly that resident
individual landlords predominantly owned 1–4 lettings and non-
resident individuals largely owned 1–24 lettings. The size distribution for companies and non-charitable trusts/executors was
much more widespread and in both cases one-half or more of
these landlords owned at the very least fifty lettings.

As soon as one begins to explore how each landlord conceives
his (or her or the company's) property, the most startling
differences reveal themselves between resident individuals as
a group and the other three categories of Table 9.2. More than
90 per cent of the resident landlords regarded their lettings
essentially as their home or future home. They were not in
general looking to the rent for any financial return on the value
of their property, a relatively high proportion were satisfied
with the rent they received, and such lettings were probably
seen as a means of abating the landlord's own costs.[13] In contrast, little short of 90 per cent of those in the other categories
regarded their properties as financial assets (or liabilities!) and
more than half specifically sought a rate of return on the market
value of the property.[14] This group of what we can call financial
landlords as distinct from resident landlords owned 85 per cent

of all the lettings in the hands of the two groups as a whole.

Three-quarters or more of all the financial landlords felt that the rents they received were insufficient to cover all necessary repairs and give a reasonable return, and more than one-third of them intended, they said, to sell or improve and sell where a vacancy occurred within the sampled address.[15] As one company landlord put it: 'We expect the number of lettings we have to decrease because of the Rent Acts. . . . We get a return on our property of 3-4 per cent, that's the answer. We've sold half in the last two years.'[16] Table 9.3 shows how strongly landlords favoured legislative change to weaken their tenants' security of tenure and to enable them to increase their rents.

Table 9.3 Lettings by type of landlord by the change to existing legislation which the landlord said would help him most (percentages)

Change to existing legislation preferred by the landlord	Resident individual	Non-resident individual	Company	Non-charitable trust/executive
Easier repossession of accommodation	26	32	20	20
Higher rents	11	19	38	29
Rents linked to cost	24	22	13	20
Less tax on rent income	18	15	11	14
More frequent review of rent level	7	5	7	9
Higher improvement grants	7	1	2	2
Other change	1	2	1	–
More than one of the above changes/total repeal of the Rent Acts	3	3	8	4
No change required	3	1	–	2
All responses	100	100	100	100

Source: Bobbie Paley, *Attitudes to Letting in 1976*, London, HMSO, Table 4.21.

So Paley's survey does tend to confirm the line of attack pursued in previous sections. Excluding the miscellaneous tenures referred to on p. 134, the majority of lettings in the hands of private landlords are conceived of as financial assets on which the landlord seeks a return most commonly expressed as the ratio of rent to selling price. When the return is insufficient, in many cases the landlord seeks to sell. Nevertheless the study does show that a substantial minority of privately rented lettings exist that are held by resident individual landlords who appear to seek primarily a flow of income from letting out their future home or a part of their existing home in order to assist them with their own housing costs.

But on all this a word of caution is necessary. The flow of dwellings from private rental to owner-occupation does not mean that the privately rented sector has disappeared nor that there are no re-lettings coming on to the market. Re-letting can be expected for a wide variety of reasons. In tenanted multi-occupied property it may be impossible to secure full vacant possession. Specific properties may be so unattractive in terms of their use-value that it is impossible to sell them for what, to the landlord, seems a worthwhile price. Certain properties, rented out to high-income tenants or to tenants who stay for only brief periods or to tenants who are desperate for accommodation and are unaware of their rights in law, may give a sufficiently high rate of return. And of course in the case of resident landlords, including owner-occupiers who rent out a room, the 'rate of return' simply is not a variable on which decisions are based: re-letting will occur where it does not threaten to inconvenience the owner and where the rental income is sufficient to justify the bother.[17]

4   TENURE TRANSFER AS A SOCIAL PROCESS

The stock supply from private landlords has so far been considered from the point of view of its scale and the landlord's motivations. What has not yet been done is to explore *how* it takes place and what roles various social actors play in carrying it through. Unfortunately the published research into this specific social process in the 1970s is extremely sparse; in particular there is no study parallel to that of Murie for council house sales which seeks to explain the attitudes of the households who purchase.

The most interesting piece of work in this area is a study by Hamnett of the 'break-up' and sale for individual owner-occupation of large blocks of purpose-built, privately rented flats in London owned both by property companies and City institutions, particularly insurance companies.[18] There were two major periods of building such blocks, 1900-14 and the mid- to late-1930s. They are concentrated in the three central London boroughs of Camden, Kensington and Chelsea, Westminster; and some are also to be found scattered in interwar suburbs such as Ealing, Chiswick, Putney and Streatham. They were built for and are still occupied by middle-class households.

The objectives of company landlords in selling are completely consistent with the analysis set out in the preceding sections of this chapter.[19] However, in this case break-up is a fairly recent phenomenon. In 1947 only 5 per cent of all flats in Britain were owner-occupied and Hamnett suggests that the idea of selling evolved from owners witnessing (and sometimes financing) the building for sale to owner-occupiers of flatted blocks in the 1950s. The first break-up in London was in the late 1950s and

there were a few others in the early 1960s. Initially the building
societies had been hostile to providing mortgage finance to purchasing households, but in the 1960s they became increasingly
willing to lend on the security of long-leasehold flats. Company
representatives argued that it was the 1965 Rent Act that
sounded the death knell to their commitment to this form of
asset holding and that the boom in property associated with the
Barber Budget of 1971 led them to switch the money gained from
residential sales into holdings of office and other commercial
premises.

The tenure transfer process can take either of two major
modes: the sale to owner-occupiers by the institutional owner
or, alternatively, the sale by the institution to a company
specialising in break-ups - such as Jim Slater's Strongmead -
which would then carry through the tenure transfer itself. In
the second case, the advantages to the owning institution are
that it immediately benefits from the value of the sale rather
than having to wait whilst individual flats are sold off, possibly
over a long time-period. Moreover any obloquy incurred from
reducing the scarce supply of rented accommodation in London
is avoided by allowing the break-up specialist to play the role
of the scapegoat. Writing of these institutional Tartuffes, Hamnett
comments:[20]

> Many of the insurance companies seek in fact to maintain the
> pretence that they are merely selling flats to another landlord
> who will continue renting, and deny knowledge of any subse-
> quent fate of the property, claiming that they sold in good
> faith and cannot be held responsible.

Let me treat here the case where a specialist company acts as
the intermediary. The existing institutional landlord sells the
block to the intermediary at a valuation that may set tenanted
flats at 25-50 per cent of their market price in vacant possession
and vacant flats at 75-80 per cent of this price. In some cases a
block may require a new lift and new boiler as well as re-roofing
and re-wiring. In addition the new owner spends money on the
decoration of common parts of the block. By this stage the
specialist will have incurred substantial capital outlays, usually
financed by borrowed funds. Since the interest on these borrowings probably exceeds the rental income, there is strong
pressure to sell although inflation in the selling price of flats
(because of external market conditions) may compensate for
delays.

The break-up company then sells a vacancy at as high a figure
as possible to establish a market price from which discounts to
sitting tenants will be deducted. Meanwhile the company will
apply to the rent officer for higher rents both to improve the
cash flow situation and to stimulate the tenant's 'natural desire'
to become a home-owner! The flats are offered to sitting buyers
at, say, two-thirds to three-quarters of their vacant possession

price and even vacancy buyers may get a 5-15 per cent discount.
If the *coup* is successful - and large numbers of poor or elderly
tenants reduce the chances of this - the specialist will be able
to repay the borrowings and any capitalised interest and still
enjoy a handsome profit; if not, the company will face bankruptcy. Time and timing are of the essence.

A second account of the process of landlord's stock supply
can be found in the material on gentrification in London in the
early 1970s. Here we are dealing not with the sale of tenanted
purpose-built blocks of flats but with the vacation and sale of
largely nineteenth-century terraced properties, often in multi-
occupation. The process involves the displacement of the existing
low-income groups of households and their replacement with
higher-income groups. Gentrification, like the flat 'break-up'
market, also takes two modes, the mediated and the unmediated.[21]

In the mediated case, the existing landlords sell to property
developers who displace the tenants by a variety of unsavoury
techniques. The tenant may be 'winkled out' by offers of alternative accommodation and a cash sum; or he or she may be forced
out by harassment and eviction. With the property vacated, the
developers then turn to its conversion into a number of self-
contained dwellings which at the same time are rehabilitated
through extensive repairs and the installation of new basic
amenities. Before the 1974 Housing Act these changes qualified
for local authority grants with no subsequent controls on the disposition of the property.

Conversion could lead to some very dramatic demographic
changes, as the following extract reveals:[22]

. . . in 1-9 Colville Gardens the 'before' population was 210
in 72 units; the 'after' population was 120 people in 93 units.
The 'before' household density in multi-occupation was probably
about the same as the 'after' density in self-contained flats.
The number of children had been reduced from 72 down to zero.
    The gentrifying developer can choose to supply either a
certain number of large units or a greater number of smaller
ones. Presumably the two demand schedules for the two
commodities (small units and large units) are such that whilst
the smaller units bring a lower unit price, this is more than
compensated by the greater number of units, so that total
development receipts are greater. Total costs would also be
greater, the higher the number of units, but then so too
would be the value of any improvement grants received. It is
also likely to be true that a couple with no children can raise
the mortgage finance for a smaller unit more easily than a
couple with children can raise finance for a larger unit at a
correspondingly higher price. This suggests that the turnover
time of capital invested [sic] in small units is faster than in
the case of large units.

Traditionally the building societies have been hostile to flat con-

but there was clear evidence in the 1970s that the
of some at least has been changing.[23]
e case of unmediated gentrification it is the original land-
who seeks full (or partial) vacant possession and sells
directly to the owner-occupier who then rehabilitates the
property.[24] In my study no substantive evidence was produced
on the decisions of owner-occupiers entering an area under
gentrification but the hypothesis was put forward that the
development of inner-London service employment and the rise in
time and money costs of journeys to work might have improved
the relative locus of the inner city. Simultaneously the environmental locus predicate was likely to give gentrification an area-
specific nature which the declaration of general improvement
areas underpinned.

5 SUMMARY

This chapter deals with the second category of stock supply, the
sale of formerly rented accommodation by private landlords. On
average this source has probably provided almost 70,000 units
per annum for owner-occupation in the 1960s and 1970s. The
great majority of rented dwellings held by private landlords are
conceived of as an 'investment' by their owners, as a specific
means of holding capital. The financial return on ownership can
be understood as the ratio of the net rental stream each year to
the selling price of the house. Making the necessary allowances
for central and local government taxation, this ratio can be compared with the annual rate of return on funds placed in the
money market.
    As a very broad truth, one can argue that since the First
World War the comparative rate of return on residential property
has been unfavourable and it is this that has led owners to seek
to sell off their dwellings to the most attractive buyers, predominantly home-owners. In the 1970s the average rate of return
was of the order of 1-4 per cent. In part this low level is the
result of a dramatic weakening in the property rights of landlords
during this century as the state has restricted the rent levels
they could set and has improved tenant security. It is also the
result, in part, of the upward trend in the prices of pre-1919
properties which the development of owner-occupation has encouraged, buttressed by the state's rehabilitation policies and its
attempts to extend the social class composition of home-owners.
    Although work on the break-up market for flatted blocks and
on gentrification has provided many insights, this form of tenure
switching has been sadly under-researched as a social and economic
process. This is despite the fact that in 1914-75 it accounted for
the supply to the owner-occupied sector of some 3.7 million dwellings in England and Wales. The next chapter examines the third
category of stock supply, also an under-researched topic, the sale
of dwellings for owner-occupation by owner-occupiers themselves.

10   THE STOCK SUPPLY FROM OWNER-OCCUPIER HOUSEHOLDS

1   INTRODUCTION

The two preceding chapters reviewed some of the evidence on the stock supply from public and private landlords. This chapter deals with the stock supply by owner-occupier households or their executors. The category is a particularly heterogeneous one and it is best to begin by listing the various circumstances under which such supply takes place. These are:

(a)   a person living alone dies and his (or her) house is sold by the executors of the estate;

(b)   a household, most commonly an elderly person living alone, dissolves as a result of moving in with relatives or moving into a nursing home and in the process decides to sell the existing house;

(c)   a household dissolves as a result of a decision to cohabit, marry or remarry and sells the house it had been living in;

(d)   a household dissolves through separation or divorce and the couple concerned sell up the house and go their separate ways;

(e)   a continuing household decides to move into the rented sector;

(f)   a continuing household emigrates and sells its house;

(g)   a continuing household sells its existing house and buys another.

In Table 10.1 the scale of owner-occupier stock supply is shown for 1971, the most recent year for which the data are available. The published information does not permit types (a) and (b) above to be separated.

2   HOUSEHOLD DISSOLUTIONS AND MOVES INTO RENTED ACCOMMODATION

In this section I want to say a little more about the first five types of stock supply listed above; in the next section the position of the selling buyer will be considered once again.

(a)   Death of one-person households
The most astonishing feature of this form of stock supply and the next one below are their magnitude: the data do not exist but by 1981 the number of dwellings supplied for owner-

occupation in these ways during the year probably exceeded the
number of new houses completed by speculative builders! Perhaps
the datum is less surprising when one considers the number of
owner-occupier households in existence at any point in time and
their demographic composition. It has already been argued in
chapter 4 that the decline in average household size since the
war has been owing, to an important degree, to an increase in
the number of one-person households, particularly elderly
persons continuing to live at home after the death of a spouse.
In the case of home-owners the survivor usually owns outright
and has complete security of tenure.

*Table 10.1 The estimated stock supply by owner-occupier households in Great
Britain in 1971*

Circumstances of supply	Number of dwellings supplied	%
Dissolution of household by death and other dissolutions of elderly households	110,000	17
Dissolution of households owing to marriage and remarriage	14,000	2
Dissolution of households owing to divorce[a]	18,000	3
Continuing households moving into the rented sector[b]	58,000	9
Continuing households emigrating	27,000	4
Selling buyers	410,000	65
Total[c]	637,000	100

Source: *HPTV*, Part I, Table III.8.

[a] Excludes situations where a successor household remains in the former matrimonial home.

[b] 72,000 moves less 14,000 moves where the vacated dwelling was condemned or demolished.

[c] A very small proportion of the total may not have been sold to owner-occupiers.

Between the censuses of 1951 and 1961 the *increase* for all tenures
in the number of men and women over retirement age living as
separate one-person households in England and Wales was of the
order of half a million and in the next decade it was 864,000.[1]
By 1971 there were 8.23 million owner-occupier households and
of these 9 per cent were individuals aged 60 and over. Thus the
ageing of the population, the tendency for the elderly to live
alone after the death of husband or wife, and the increase of the
proportion of the total population in home-ownership had by the
1970s combined to generate a stock of owner-occupiers 'at risk'
at any point in time of well over 700,000. In such a context, the
powerful role of human mortality in determining stock supply of
this type on this scale is easily comprehended.

(b) Dissolution of elderly households other than through death
In 1971 in England and Wales 17.9 per cent or 1.47 million of all
owner-occupier households were older small households. Most of
these were elderly married couples. In the event of the death
of one member of such a household, the survivor may wish either
to stay on in the house; or to move out, sooner or later, and go
to live with relatives or in a nursing home; or to move out and
take rented accommodation, particularly in the local authority
sector. In the first of these three cases they will eventually
reappear in type (a) above of the stock supply. The second
case falls under the sub-heading of this paragraph. In the third
case they appear under type (e) below of the stock supply. The
decision of a survivor to move out is unlikely to be taken primarily
on economic grounds since the house is probably owned outright
and domestic rate rebates for the elderly on low incomes reduce
this form of housing expenditure. The decision to move to
rented accommodation often reflects a desire to be relieved of
the responsibility for maintenance and repair of the owner-
occupied house, or the attractiveness of the special accommodation
provided by district councils for the frail or disabled elderly who
simply cannot survive on their own. The decision to 'dissolve'
the household, by moving in with a married daughter for example,
reflects both the repairs problem as well as the anxiety and
loneliness that many people, young or old, experience when they
live by themselves.

(c) Dissolutions owing to marriage
When an owner-occupier household, for example a single person
or a divorced woman with dependant children, decides to
cohabit or marry or remarry, this brings about the dissolution
of that household. It can also lead to the sale of the existing
home in those cases where the dissolving household moves into
the house of their new partner or the new couple find completely
fresh accommodation. Table 10.1 suggests this is not a
quantitatively significant type of stock supply. However, its
importance may be understated as a result of the sexist definition
of a married couple new household referred to in chapter 4.[2]
Stock supply through dissolutions triggered off by the formation
of new households also derives from persons of the same sex
setting up house together, as in the case of gay couples. A
weakness in the demographic analysis of the *Housing Policy
Technical Volume,* in spite of its many virtues, is that, not
unlike Queen Victoria, it did not recognise the existence of
lesbianism, male homosexuality and heterosexual cohabitation.
Cohabitation is, of course, the scourge and despair of demographic statisticians, something for which many of us in Britain
are to blame at one time or another.

(d) Dissolutions owing to separation and divorce
This is self-explanatory. Table 10.1 shows it makes up only 3
per cent of owner-occupier stock supply. It does not, of course,

include situations where one of the parties concerned stays on
in the former matrimonial home.

(e) Moves by continuing households into rented accommodation
This type itself is composed of two major sub-groups. First we
have moves by elderly persons into rented accommodation. This
was discussed for convenience under type (b) above. Second
we have moves by continuing households who are dispossessed
or who face grave difficulties in meeting their mortgage repayments. This was discussed at length in chapter 7. In total,
Table. 10.1 suggests that moves by continuing households
generated some 9 per cent of the owner-occupier stock supply
in England and Wales in 1971. This includes those 'successor
households' composed of women with dependent children who are
forced to leave their home after the breakdown of their marriage.

*Table 10.2 Tenure by age and marital status of household head in England in
1971 (percentages)*

	Married under 60	Widowed, divorced and separated under 60	Married 60 and over	Widowed, divorced and separated 60 and over
Proportion who are owner-occupiers	56	37	55	40
Proportion who are tenants	44	63	45	60
Total	100	100	100	100

Source: Adapted from *HPTV*, Part I, Table II.24.

Chapter 4 suggested that marriage played a most important
role in the demand for housing. The analysis here demonstrates
that the effective termination of marriage, through the death of
one spouse, through divorce and through separation, also plays
an important part in the stock supply of owner-occupier households. In one way or another it exercises an effect on supply
types (b), (d) and (e) above. Thus the correlation between
marital status and tenure that is evident in Table 10.2 is not
unexpected. However, the data also reflect to a partial degree
other causal relationships: households headed by persons who
are widowed, divorced or separated are less likely to become
owner-occupiers in the first place; the loss of an owner-
occupied house can lead to marital breakdown; finally, the
association of early marriage with tenancy and the higher divorce
rates among those who marry young.[3]

3 SELLING BUYERS

Selling buyers as a group were discussed in chapters 4 and 6
from the point of view of the effective demand for owner-occupied
housing, and much of what was said there is relevant to their
position as stock suppliers. Let us begin by looking again at
their reasons for moving, since this constitutes the motivation
to supply. Table 10.3 shows that in 1971 and 1973 trading up
was by far the most important motive with change of job or a
move to be nearer the work-place running a strong second.
Together they accounted for over 60 per cent of all moves by
selling buyers. However, the evidence is not without its
ambiguities for officers of the DoE, on the basis of data included
in Table 10.3, have suggested that of the 410,000 moves by
selling buyers in Britain in 1971, 41 per cent were in order to
get better housing, 20 per cent were for reasons connected with
employment, and as many as 17 per cent were by retired people.[4]
This suggests the table underestimates the importance of retirement. The number of moves made by selling buyers after they
first entered owner-occupation is uncertain: I suggest the
average lies between two and three.[5]

*Table 10.3 Main reasons for moves by selling buyers in England and Wales in
1971 and 1973 (percentages)*

Main reason for move	
Wanted better dwelling, better area, garden; present house too small or too few rooms.[a]	39
Change of job or to be nearer job	22
Health, bereavement, marriage, to be nearer friends, etc.	15
Present dwelling too large or too expensive[a]	8
Retirement	4
Dwelling condemned or demolished	2
Other	10
Total	100

Source: *HPTV*, Part I, Table II.42.

[a] Present house refers to the house being sold.

Figure 10.1 will assist in understanding the financial position of
the selling buyer; it is developed from Figure 5.1. The household can trade up, or trade down, or 'trade level', i.e. buy a house
of the same use-value as the one sold. When the existing house
is sold, any outstanding mortgage is redeemed. This leaves the
owner with cash proceeds equal to the net worth of the house
sold, that is to say, the sum of the price gain, the personal

assets originally ploughed in and the mortgage principal repaid.
Some of this cash will be required to meet the transactions costs
of the move, such as the payment of fees to the exchange professionals concerned and the transport costs of switching house.
The rest is available to plough into the purchase of the 'new'
house along with any fresh mortgage finance raised. Trading
up usually involves taking out a larger mortgage than the one
outstanding, whilst trading level and trading down most
frequently are associated with a reduction in the mortgage debt.
Chapter 5 discussed this with respect to income frontloading.

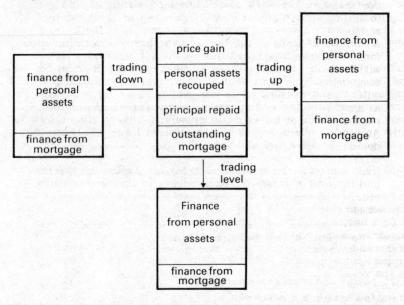

Figure 10.1 The financial situation of the selling buyer (The
height of each rectangle represents the price of the house. The
figure and the text make the simplifying assumption that the
use-values and the prices of dwellings are always positively
correlated.)

The financial assets of the selling buyer, other than those
locked up in the house itself, will rise, fall or stay unchanged
as a result of the move in a way that is determined by the
following equation:

net change in financial assets equals net worth realised on the
existing house plus the new mortgage raised less the purchase
price of the 'new' house and the associated transactions costs
of the move.

Let us consider three feasible examples to illustrate this point.

These can either stand for representatives of different sub-
groups of selling buyers at any point in time or a hypothetical
housing career for a single household.

(i)   A household has lived in a two-bedroom dwelling for ten
      years and decides to trade up to a four-bedroom house
      only twenty minutes' walk away in order to gain more living
      space for their growing family. The price of the 'new' house
      considerably exceeds that of the one sold; moreover, the
      transaction costs are not inconsiderable. As a consequence
      the household ploughs back all its net worth, raises a fresh
      mortgage greater than the sum so recently redeemed, and
      in addition finds its existing financial assets moderately
      reduced.

(ii) A household decides to move house to Milton Keynes in order
      for the husband to take advantage of a promotion offered
      within a new branch-plant owned by the multi-national
      company that employs him. The family trades level, takes
      out a mortgage a little less than its outstanding debt, and
      as a consequence of this and the cost of the move finds its
      personal financial assets temporarily reduced.

(iii) An elderly couple, whose children have long ago left home,
      decide to retire to the north-west coast of Wales and buy an
      attractive new bungalow at a price much less than they sell
      their existing house for. They have no outstanding mortgage
      and in spite of stamp duty, payments to the removals firm
      etc., they make a substantial cash sum out of the trans-
      action.

To a limited extent the dynamic analysis of the selling buyer
can draw on an economic concept known as the income elasticity
of demand. This elasticity is usually employed to measure the
proportionate increase in the quantity consumed of a commodity
as the result of a proportionate increase in real household
income, other things being equal. Unfortunately the published
literature suffers from several weaknesses.[6] First, it fails to
keep firmly separate the longitudinal analysis of individual
households from the cross-section analysis of households in
different income groups. Doubtless the latter can tell us something about the former but there is a substantial translation
problem which needs to be explicitly confronted. Second, the
dynamic relationship betweeen trading up and changes in house
prices and money incomes under inflationary conditions is
treated only by including net worth as an independent variable.
This does not go far enough since, as I argued in chapter 6,
trading up can take place in a context where real income is constant by periodic step-ups in a downward sloping impact ratio
trend. Third, the results exhibit a disturbing volatility: in
1973 it was reported that the lower bound of the income elasticity
was 0.75 whilst four years later 0.75 had become the upper
bound![7] The most interesting result, one that confirms the
analysis of preceding paragraphs, is the powerful effect that
net worth has on price paid: the cross-section data show that

almost one-half of net worth differences are translated into price differences.[8]

4 PAPER GAINS?

The preceding sections provide the basis for exploring a particularly interesting dispute within the economics of home-ownership concerning the benefits to be enjoyed from price gains. Some authors, of whom Topalov is the most eminent, claim that these gains constitute an illusory benefit for the owner-occupier.[9] After all, if the owner does not sell then the increase in the market value of his house is not realised, it is only a 'paper gain'. If, on the other hand he (or she) does sell then the gain is immediately cancelled since the price of the house bought is correspondingly higher.

The proponents of the 'real gains' position argue in reply that price gains are always of genuine advantage to the home-owner and that the benefits accrue in a number of different ways. For the owner-occupier who moves out of the tenure into rented accommodation, the price gain can be encashed. In the case of an owner dying, his (or her) heirs will - usually - encash the gain. For the continuing household that does not move, a price gain can provide the basis for seeking a second mortgage to be employed in a business venture or to finance a substantial consumption outlay. For the selling buyer trading up, the price gain is an essential mechanism in the move; for those who trade down or trade level into a region where house prices are lower, it is possible to encash part of the gain.[10]

In the rest of this section an attempt is made to carry this debate forward a little and in order to do so I shall consider in turn the 'real gains' arguments on encashment and on trading up. The former is easily extended to the inheritance issue. What quickly becomes apparent is that if one does not clarify the nature of the comparisons being made, the inquiry soon flounders in a slough of ambiguity.

The 'real gains' arguments are tested in the following way. It is assumed a certain household in year zero buys a house at a known price using a specific mortgage advance. Two alternative hypothetical futures are then considered. In future one all house prices are assumed to remain constant. In future two all house prices are assumed to increase at a constant rate per year. The term and type of mortgage are identical in each future as is the mortgage rate of interest. The real income from employment is the same in both futures but there exists the possibility of differences in their respective rates of retail price inflation. If it can be shown, in a defined sense, that future two is superior to future one, the 'real gains' proponents have it. If not, not.

Encashment
The mathematics (to give it a grand name) is tucked away in an
annex to this chapter and suggests the following results. First,
if the rate of retail price inflation is equal in futures one and
two, then there is no doubt that future two is preferable. The
advantage in terms of net worth accruing to the household in
constant prices is equal to the price gain of future two deflated
by the retail price index. Second, if the rate of retail price
inflation in future one should exceed that of future two,
obviously the 'real gains' has it for a greater net worth figure
in future two is deflated by a lower retail price index than in
future one. Third, if the rate of retail price inflation in each
future is identical with the rate of house price inflation in that
future, there are again 'real gains' but only during the term of
the mortgage! In this situation the buyer in future two is very
likely to suffer from what I shall call price-gain illusion. If the
annual rate of inflation is not negligible, then the purchaser
will perceive himself to have enjoyed a substantial price gain,
which increases as the years pass. But the mathematics show
that in comparison with a zero price inflation situation the
advantage is *extremely* modest and, as I say, terminates when
the mortgage is redeemed. Fourth, in the case where the rate of
retail price inflation in future two exceeds that of future one
and neither equals its own rate of change in house prices, the
results may favour either the real gains proponents, or the
paper gains proponents, or the real advantage may lie with
future one.

Trading up
Here the original house is sold some years after purchase and
the household trades up into a second house the purchase price
of which, in both futures, is a given multiple of the selling
price of the original house. If we assume that the household
ploughs into the second purchase all the net worth appropriated
on the sale of the first, then we can consider the ratio of this
net worth to the purchase price of the second house as representing, so to speak, a free gift of that proportion of the house.
The mathematical annex shows that, during the life of the
mortgage, the proportion is greater for the future two situation.
Thus trading up *is* a means of making real gains under inflationary conditions compared with zero house price inflation. But
trading up *after* the full term of the first mortgage elapses,
implies the free gift proportion is the same in both cases and is
equal to the reciprocal of the house price multiple already
referred to.

5 SUMMARY

In Britain in 1971 the volume of vacant dwellings supplied from
the existing housing stock by owner-occupier households exceeded

600,000 units. This category of stock supply is particularly heterogeneous. Almost two-thirds of the total in 1971 came from selling buyers but other substantial categories were constituted by the dissolution of elderly households and the movement of continuing households into rented accommodation. The selling buyer supply is principally motivated by decisions to trade up, to change job or move nearer an existing place of employment, or by decisions associated with retirement. The supply from the dissolution of elderly households reflects the growth in house-ownership itself and the increase in the number of elderly one-person households. The supply resulting from moves into rented accommodation probably is composed largely of elderly households moving into the public sector stock and of owner-occupiers moving as a result of difficulties in making regular mortgage payments.

Since trading up is so important as a motive in the stock supply - in 1971 it generated about 170,000 vacancies - a brief account of a move's net effect on a household's financial assets was given. Some trading stereotypes were also described. Finally an attempt was made to clarify the dispute as to whether or not price gains are real or only paper gains. The analysis is only preliminary in nature and could be carried out with a host of varying assumptions at very much greater length. The results here are that, with respect to encashment, price gains are likely to bring real benefits but that there may well be an associated price-gain illusion. With respect to trading up, but excluding cases where the mortgage is fully paid off, price gains are definitely real in permitting the household to pay for a higher proportion of the 'new' house out of net worth.

ANNEX TO CHAPTER 10

1 Encashment

Notation: year o = year in which house is originally bought
year n = year in which house is sold
subscripts one and two indicate futures one and two
W = net worth at out turn prices
Z = net worth at constant (year o) prices
T = original price paid for house
M = outstanding mortgage in year n
c = annual rate of increase in house prices in future two
i = annual rate of increase in retail prices

In year n : $W_1 = T - M$
$W_2 = T(1+c)^n - M$

Thus $$Z_1 = \frac{(T - M)}{(1 + i_1)^n}$$

$$Z_2 = \frac{[T(1+c)^n - M]}{(1+i_2)^n}$$

And
$$Z_2 - Z_1 = \frac{[T(1+c)^n - M]}{(1+i_2)^n} - \frac{(T - M)}{(1+i_1)^n}$$

A Let $i_1 = i_2$ then
$$Z_2 - Z_1 = \frac{[T(1+c)^n - M] - (T - M)}{(1+i_2)^n}$$

$$= \frac{T(1+c)^n - T}{(1+i_2)^n} \qquad First\ result$$

B Now let $i_1 = 0 \quad i_2 = c$

then
$$Z_2 - Z_1 = \frac{[T(1+c)^n - M]}{(1+c)^n} - (T - M)$$

$$= \frac{[T(1+c)^n - M]}{(1+c)^n} - \frac{(T - M)(1+c)^n}{(1+c)^n}$$

$$= \frac{T(1+c)^n - T(1+c)^n - M + M(1+c)^n}{(1+c)^n}$$

$$= M - \frac{M}{(1+c)^n} \qquad Third\ result$$

Note that if $M = 0$, $Z_2 = Z_1$

C Now let $0 < i_1 < i_2\ c$

then
$$Z_2 - Z_1 = \frac{[T(1+c)^n - M](1+i_1)^n - (T-M)(1+i_2)^n}{(1+i_2)^n (1+i_1)^n}$$

$$= \frac{T[(1+c)^n (1+i_1)^n - (1+i_2)^n] + M[(1+i_2)^n - (1+i_1)^n]}{(1+i_2)^n (1+i_1)^n}$$

The numerator's second term is, of course, positive.

If $(1+i_1)^n \geqslant \dfrac{(1+i_2)^n}{(1+c)^n}$

the first term is zero or positive and the real gains proponents have it. If $(1+i_1)^n < \dfrac{(1+i_2)^n}{(1+c)^n}$, then the result could go any way and could even switch over time. $\qquad Fourth\ result$

2 *Trading up*

Notation: as above and in addition

$\qquad u$ = ratio in year n of purchase price of second house to selling price of first house ($u>1$)

p = proportion in year n of purchase price of second house which can be met out of the net worth derived from selling first house.

k = principal repaid by year n on first house plus personal assets originally ploughed into first house purchase

f = $[1-(1+c)^n]<0$

In year n, if we assume that the entire net worth appropriated on the sale of the first house is ploughed back into the purchase of the second,

$$p_1 = \frac{k}{u\,T} = \frac{k\,(1+c)^n}{u\,T(1+c)^n}$$

$$p_2 = \frac{k+\text{price gain}}{u\,T(1+c)^n} = \frac{k+[T(1+c)^n - T]}{u\,T(1+c)^n}$$

Thus $p_2 > p_1$ if $k+[T(1+c)^n - T] > k(1+c)^n$

or if $k-k(1+c)^n + T(1+c)^n - T > 0$

or if $k[1-(1+c)^n] - T[1-(1+c)^n] > 0$

or if $fk - fT > 0$

or if $f(k-T) > 0$

Since during the life of the original mortgage $(k-T)$ must be negative, (see Figure 5.1) and since f is negative, the condition is satisfied and $p_2>p_1$. In the case of trading up after the redemption of the first mortgage, the paper gains proponents win, for $p_1 = p_2 = 1/u$.

11 THE SPECULATIVE HOUSEBUILDING INDUSTRY

1 INTRODUCTION

The analysis of the stock supply is now complete and next I must consider 'supply' in its traditional sense, the production of new units of the housing commodity. To be more precise, this chapter deals with the flow of output of new houses for sale to owner-occupiers. Whilst no hard and fast data exist, it is estimated that as little as 1-3 per cent of this flow is bespoke production, that is, produced in response to a client's specific order. The rest of the output in question is constructed as a speculation, in the belief on the part of the developer that sellers will be found in good time. For this reason the newbuild supply is widely referred to as speculative housebuilding, a term which in this context carries no implicit value-judgment.

A systematic treatment of speculative housebuilding would be a massive work in itself and at the time of writing no such volume has yet been published. Inevitably, since the newbuild supply is only one of many subjects dealt with in this book, the following pages are highly selective. After some brief comments on the construction industry as a whole, I turn in section two to consider the structure of the private housebuilding industry and its output as well as the nature of its economic objectives. In sections three and four the extraordinarily complex question of the supply of land is discussed at some length. Section five deals with the organisation and technology of the labour process and section six sets out my views on the determinants of the long-run trend in house prices.

The construction industry is one of the country's largest economic sectors and in 1980 contributed more than 6 per cent of the UK's gross domestic product.[1] Table 11.1 breaks down output into its component parts and shows that in 1980 recorded housing production made up 39 per cent of the total. Unfortunately no breakdown is published for repair and maintenance to permit us to distinguish that carried out for owner-occupiers from the work done for other housing consumers.

Production is carried on largely by private undertakings or by the local authorities' direct labour organisations. The industry is well known for the multiplicity of its small firms and this is demonstrated in Table 11.2. The data show that whilst the firms with fewer than twenty employees make up 90 per cent of all firms they contribute only 23 per cent of the total net output. At the other extreme the largest twenty firms are the

Table 11.1   Value of output of the construction industry in Great Britain in 1980 at current prices

	(£m)	%
New public housing	1,753	8
New private housing	2,652	12
Housing repair and maintenance	4,113	19
Other public work	6,650	30
Other private work	6,862	31
Total	22,030	100

Source: HCS, Part 2, no. 5, 1981, Table 2.5.

source of 12 per cent of total output. Even this understates the degree of concentration of control in the industry for much of the work done by small firms is on subcontract in the construction projects of the larger enterprises.

Table 11.2   Distribution of number of private undertakings, employment and net output by firm size in the UK in 1978

Firm size by number of employees	Number of undertakings	Employment[a] ('000)	Net output[b] (£m)
0-19	83,338	348	1,717
20-99	7,531	283	1,823
100-2,499	1,322	402	3,125
at least 2,500	20	111	881
Total	92,211	1,144	7,546

Source: Business Statistics Office, 1978 Census of Production.

[a] Excludes labour-only subcontractors.

[b] Unlike Table 11.1, this value is net of the firms payments for goods and services.

It will be noticed that Table 11.2 does not distinguish the housebuilding sector from all other construction activities. This lack of statistical clarity reflects a material fact: there is no housebuilding industry as such. It is not the case that within the construction industry as a whole one set of firms devote themselves to housing work and another set are engaged wholly in non-housing work. A great many firms produce a range of construction 'products', housing products making up only a fraction of the total. In part this is because the technical possibilities of resource switching between product types are manifold; in part it is that, in conditions of volatile demand for any single output, construction of a range of products improves the financial stability of the individual firm.

Yet it would be a mistake to suggest that there is no special-

Table 11.3 Value of housing work done by private contractors in Great Britain by trade of firm in 1978 third quarter (£m)

	New public housing	New private housing	Housing repairs & maintenance	Specialisation index
Main trades: general builders	175.8	284.3	167.2	1.61
Building and civil engineering contractors	109.7	98.3	22.3	0.83
Civil engineers	9.8	18.7	2.3	0.23
Specialist trades: Plumbers	11.8	15.6	25.5	1.84
Carpenters and joiners	4.8	6.1	14.6	1.31
Painters	7.1	5.5	31.0	1.14
Roofers	5.0	10.9	12.5	0.95
Plasterers	11.9	9.9	5.1	1.89
Glaziers	2.6	5.4	10.4	1.74
Demolition contractors	2.5	1.1	0.2	0.99
Scaffolding specialists	5.0	3.0	1.9	0.59
Reinforced concrete specialists	2.4	1.5	1.6	0.63
Heating and ventilating engineers	13.7	11.7	22.7	0.64
Electrical contractors	9.5	7.3	16.2	0.48
Asphalt and tar sprayers	4.2	2.9	1.6	0.33
Plant hirers	19.7	19.5	4.8	0.86
Flooring contractors	1.1	1.6	2.7	0.71
Constructional engineers	0.1	0.1	0.2	0.02
Insulating specialists	0.6	0.6	2.7	0.29
Suspended ceiling specialists	0.1	0.1	0.2	0.08
Floor and wall tiling specialists	1.2	1.4	1.1	0.95
Miscellaneous	1.7	2.1	8.6	0.59
Total all firms	400.5	507.5	355.4	1

Source: DoE, *Private Contractors' Construction Census 1978*, London, HMSO, 1979, Table T.28.

isation whatsoever. Table 11.3 shows the trades into which the industry's firms are conventionally divided and gives the value of the housing work they do. The general builders and the building and civil engineering contractors take the lion's share of the business with 68 per cent of the total. Amongst the specialist trades, the most important are the plumbers, the painters, the heating and ventilating engineers and the plant hirers. A different story is told by the specialisation index which measures the ratio of a trade's housing work to its total

work divided by the same ratio for the entire industry. A
figure of one indicates no relative specialisation whilst higher
values do indicate such specialisation. Thus the plasterers,
plumbers, glaziers, general builders, carpenters and joiners,
and painters specialise most in housing work. Whilst Table 11.3
is useful in indicating the degree of housebuilding specialisation within a trade, it tells us nothing about specialisation
within individual firms and, as far as I am aware, there is no
published comprehensive source that provides such information.

2 THE STRUCTURE OF NEW PRIVATE HOUSING OUTPUT

In this section a fairly descriptive account is given of the output composition of speculative housebuilding with respect to
size of firm and product type. Thereafter the industry is considered both in terms of the activities and skills it embraces
and its financial nature.

Table 11.4 *The distribution of active NHBC-registered companies by size
category in Great Britain 1976-80^a*

Number of private houses started during the year	Active NHBC-registered firms				
	1976	*1977*	*1978*	*1979*	*1980*
1-10	7,812	7,445	7,606	7,271	6,945
11-30	1,218	1,022	1,112	1,015	688
31-50	271	224	230	225	139
51-100	191	158	179	135	89
101-250	108	92	104	114	81
251-500	45	40	48	30	20
Over 500	33	29	29	39	16
Total	9,678	9,010	9,308	8,829	7,978

Source: NHBC.

^{a} The Council improved and revised its classification by size category at the end of this
period and on this new basis their data go back only to 1976. A holding company with
several operating divisions is here, quite properly, classified as one single company.

Table 11.4 and 11.5 provide an excellent picture of how
private housing firms vary in size and how total output is distributed between these firm-size categories. Size is here defined
in terms of the number of housing starts made by a firm in any
given year. The total number of firms that build private houses
is very large indeed, lying in the range of 7,900-9,700 in the
period 1976-80. However, the great majority of these are very
small, starting at most thirty dwellings in any given year. In
1978, for example, such firms constituted 94 per cent of the
grand total of 9,308 active NHBC members. At the other extreme
the number of firms starting more than 500 dwellings lies in

the range of only 29-39 in every year except 1980 when total output was very low and most firms reduced their scale of operations. Cullen, in 1979, suggested that there were only seven 'volume housebuilders' that produced at least 2,500 houses each year. These were Wimpey, Barratts, Broseley, Tarmac, Bovis, Trafalgar House and Christian Salvesen.[2]

Table 11.5 The distribution of private housing starts by size category of company in Great Britain 1976-80 (percentages)

Company size by number of starts during the year	Market share of private housing starts				
	1976	1977	1978	1979	1980
1-10	15	16	15	15	20
11-30	14	13	12	12	13
31-50	7	6	6	6	6
51-100	9	8	8	6	7
101-250	11	11	11	12	14
251-500	10	11	12	7	7
Over 500	34	35	36	42	33
Total	100	100	100	100	100

Source: NHBC.

With respect to output distribution between firms of various sizes, Table 11.5 shows a remarkable spread across the whole size range. In every year even the small firms of at most thirty starts had a market share of more than one-quarter of the grand total. At the same time the share of the 'over 500' category was consistently one-third or more of the total and the thirty or forty largest firms may well have increased their market share in the period covered by the table.

Next I wish to look very briefly both at the way total output is divided between houses and flats as well as the size composition of new houses in terms of their number of bedrooms. Table 11.6 contains the necessary information. Flats make up only 7-12 per cent of total output, peaking in 1975. Amongst houses alone, virtually all have at least two bedrooms. Three-bedroom houses in particular constitute 62-75 per cent of the total. During these years 1969-79 there was a clear upward trend in the supply of houses with at least four bedrooms, which, since 1972, was entirely at the expense of three-bedroom houses.

The larger builders often produce a standard portfolio of house types which cover the first-time buyer, trading-up purchasers and retirement bungalows, 'from cradle to the grave' as one developer put it to me. This particular firm, for example, had gone 'right up-market' when Thomas Cook and Pearl Insurance moved to Peterborough, building five-bedroom houses each in a quarter acre of its own ground so that selling buyers could 'invest' the net worth realised on the sale of

Table 11.6   Flats as a proportion of all dwellings completed for private owners and the size composition of house completions in England and Wales 1969-79[a]

	1969	1970	1971	1972	1973	1974	1975	1976	1977	1978	1979
Houses completed (%)											
1 bedroom	1	neg.	neg.	neg.	1	1	1	1	1	1	1
2 bedrooms	17	17	15	14	12	12	16	18	19	18	16
3 bedrooms	74	73	75	75	74	72	66	64	63	62	63
at least 4 bedrooms	8	10	10	11	13	15	17	17	17	19	20
Total houses	100	100	100	100	100	100	100	100	100	100	100
Flats among all dwellings (%)	7	9	7	8	9	11	12	11	10	9	8

Source: HCS.

[a] A small but unknown number of completed flats are built for sale to private landlords.

their existing houses. At the other end of the spectrum some firms have built low-cost 'starter home' estates for married couple new households and former tenants. A DoE survey has shown that these generate considerable consumer dissatisfaction because of the small size of the houses, the high density and isolation of the estates and the inadequacy of local social services and public transport.[3]

Having completed this brief survey of the size structure of the industry and the composition of its output, next I want to describe the nature of the speculative housebuilding process. This has a twofold character: first, as a sequence of human activities that precede the inhabitation of a newly built estate; and second as a set of financial flows. Let us look at these in turn.

For a single estate the activity sequence in its simplest form can be described as follows:

(i)   carry out market research into trends in the demand for and supply of owner-occupied houses in a specific locality or region;

(ii)   search for and acquire a suitable site;

(iii) Design the estate and seek outline and detailed planning permission for residential construction;

(iv)   Provide for the infrastructural requirements of the site including the water supply, sewerage, gas and electricity connections and prepare the site for construction;

(v)   construct the dwellings;

(vi)   sell the dwellings.

I shall refer to (v) above as the building process and the other five activities as the development process. Development and building may all be carried out within a single firm, as is usually the case with large construction companies. Alternatively the firm may assign the infrastructural provision and the building process to a main contractor for an agreed contract sum, the builder in his turn subcontracting a large part of the work. On large sites, the local authority itself will provide some of the infrastructural requirements.

Corresponding to the activity process, there is a sequence of financial flows. Let us consider these in the case of an established speculative housebuilding firm engaged simultaneously in a number of projects in which it acts both as developer and builder. The financial flows of any *single* project, which are complementary with the activity process described above, may be rather difficult to isolate with any precision and in any case the financial assessment of a single development will in part reflect the accounting conventions specific to the firm, for example on the assignment of overheads. So, for a single firm, the money inflows consist essentially of the income from share issues, borrowing and the sale of output. The outflows consist of the costs involved in operating a national and any regional headquarters, investment in plant and machinery, payments for plant hire, outlays on land purchases, payments for materials and the wages of the site labour force, payments to subcontractors, dividends to shareholders, interest on money borrowed and, finally, tax payments.

The objective of the speculative housebuilder is a financial one: to maximise profits. The activity process is a means to this end and the control the firm's management can exercise over its financial flows is also directed to achieving the same aim. Profit maximisation is interpreted in practice in more than one way: as the highest possible margin of sales income over unit costs, as the highest rate of profit net of tax to capital employed, or as the highest net present value in a discounted cash flow calculation. In seeking to maximise profit on a single project, management must employ a very diverse range of skills with respect to the flow of sales and of costs over time and the interrelation of these two.

On the sales side the crucial elements to financial success are the house-type composition of the development and its density; the choice of an area in which household incomes, mobility patterns and employment trends promise rapid sales of completed output; the selection of a specific site with an attractive environmental locus and a convenient relative locus; and the timing of development and building to meet the market when effective demand throughout the region or country is strong. One of the most effective ways that medium and large companies promote their rate of sales is to have agreed mortgage quotas provided by the building societies for their newly completed estates.[4]

On the cost side management will adopt a land purchase strategy that minimises the outlay on each specific site; it will consider what technological innovations, plant purchase or plant hire decisions and subcontracting arrangements promise lower unit production costs; and it will seek a financial strategy that keeps the cost of capital low and yet does not endanger the stability and integrity of the enterprise should there be a slump in demand or an aggressive takeover bid. The company's gearing and its policy on dividend payments are crucial here.

The sources of capital are diverse. They include ploughed back profits; share issues; overdrafts from the big commercial banks; loans from merchant banks, which may cover as much as 60-80 per cent of capital requirements; short-term mortgages raised on land and half-finished or unsold houses; and suppliers' credits, ranging from 28-day invoices up to bulk orders with deposit and half-yearly payment terms.[5] Small builders are said to be particularly reliant on trade credit and bank overdrafts. Following an upward movement in MLR, interest payments on a land bank, stocks and work-in-progress may be particularly onerous where the firm has relied heavily on loan finance, particularly if sales are sluggish. Cullen has pointed to the need to minimise capital employed in production at the time of a slump in demand.[6] The larger the company, the greater the geographical area it will usually cover and the more likely it is to have specialist divisions, in land purchase or sales for example, at national and regional headquarters. These institutional overheads can create cash-flow problems when output contracts.[7]

Some speculative housebuilders combine housing production with other forms of economic activity which themselves may provide a source of capital. Alternatively the firm may be only one establishment amongst many controlled by a parent company in the wider world of land, property, construction and finance. In this case the housebuilding subsidiary can benefit through transfers from the holding company.[8]

Estimates of the financial performance of private housing firms are scattered and are not always either consistent or comparable. The Economist Intelligence Unit suggested that in 1973-4 average margins were 5 per cent of selling price. They fell to 3 per cent during the years 1974-7. But in 1978 profits rose as selling prices increased more rapidly than costs and Inter Company Comparisons reported that for sixty leading housebuilders in the public and private sector average margins rose from 5.5 per cent in 1976-7 through 6.7 per cent in 1977-8 up to 10.4 per cent in 1978-9. Twenty-four companies doubled their pre-tax profits over this three-year period. Wimpey and Barratts were particularly successful, the latter aiming at first-time buyers with aggressive marketing techniques.[9]

3 LAND PRICES AND HOUSEBUILDERS' PROFITS

In this section I wish to give an account of the importance of
land acquisition to a developer's strategy, to suggest how the
price of land is determined and to carry out a critique of the
very widespread view that housebuilders' profits are based on
speculation in land. For the sake of convenience in exposition
I shall usually assume that development and building are carried out by the same company.

To begin at the beginning: why do housebuilders buy land?
The answer to this is that in order to construct, a builder must
possess a site and the dominant property form in Britain that
permits such possession and also allows the completed units to
be sold for owner-occupation is that of freehold ownership.
Thus, from the point of view of the activity process described
in section two, the housebuilder needs land like a cobbler needs
leather; it is literally his fundamental raw material and ownership through purchase is the legal prerequisite for construction
and sale.

But speculative housebuilding is also a financial process and
indeed I have argued that the developer-builder's critical objective is purely financial. At this level of analysis any simple
simile of land and leather is quite inapposite. Although it does
not do so for all companies, the acquisition of land can play an
extremely important role in a company's financial strategy. This
is because the price of land *at any given point in time* is dependent both on its legal attributes and its development potential;
and also because the price of land changes *over time*, in some
years very violently. Both these characteristics of the price of
land mean that a space is opened up for the speculative builder
to exercise his skills in minimising the cost of his raw material.

Let me next look very briefly at how the company searches
out and secures its land supply. The starting point is the
market research phase of the activity process. A single company, depending on its size, will operate at the national,
regional or local level. Within its geographical field of operations it will attempt to specify areas offering development
potential in the short, medium or long term. The policies of
planners at the district and county level with respect to private
residential construction are of great importance in this search
process. An equally important variable is the changing spatial
pattern of employment and earnings because, given building
society mortgage allocation criteria, this is the most valuable
indicator of effective demand. Of course, car ownership and
the public transport system multiply the feasible residential
locations for a given employment centre but even here transport technology does not generate an unlimited number of possible sites. I was surprised to hear from the managing director
of one major speculative housebuilding company that he believes
'most purchasers of new houses will not travel more than eleven
miles from home to work'. The information flow necessary for

the appraisal of specific sites comes from companies' own
research staff and from a network of contacts including estate
agents, architects, building society managers, surveyors and
solicitors, who work on a commission basis.[10]

The land supply comes predominantly from private individuals
(or institutions) owning farmland. It is most frequently located
on the periphery of existing cities, towns and villages but also
includes infill sites located in the metropolitan suburbs and the
smaller urban areas. Another source of supply is through the
takeover of an ailing company with an attractive landbank, for
example Wimpey's purchase of Moody's in East Anglia and
Barratts's acquisition of E. Barker in North Humberside.[11] A
takeover may permit an expanding firm to move into a region
from which it had previously been excluded. Land may also be
sold by companies specialising in the purchase, 'ripening' and
resale of sites for development purposes. In general, acquisition is done by private negotiation rather than through public
auction.

Vendors may sell their land outright or on the basis of a
conditional contract. To take an example of the latter case, on
land without planning permission for residential development
a sum is paid equal to 10 per cent of the value of the land in its
existing use. Thereafter, when planning permission is secured,
the developer can take up his option at about a 10 per cent
discount on the market value of the land without planning permission. Alternatively the initial contract specifies the price
to be paid when the deal is closed, with a provision for agreed
increments if the exchange is not finalised within, say, 2-3
years.[12] Another arrangement is a 10 per cent down payment
and the rest paid as each plot is developed, either as a fixed
price or as a percentage of the house's selling price.

Land acquisition policy varies substantially between firms.
Some companies purchase their sites in order to proceed with
building work as soon as is practicable. Other firms accumulate
a stock of land sufficient for several years' construction output,
typically four or five. In terms of their legal attributes, these
sites are usually in various stages of 'ripeness' for development.
A part of the landbank may be composed of 'white land', that
is, land not designated for any particular use on a statutory
plan. Part may consist of sites in areas that have been zoned
for residential development by the planning authorities but
which do not yet enjoy even outline planning permission for
housebuilding. Other plots will have such permission and finally
some will have detailed planning approval for schemes comprehensively specified in terms of density, layout, house-type
and infrastructural provision.

The Economist Intelligence Unit in 1975 estimated that perhaps
only 20 per cent of all speculative housebuilders have landbanks and, together with Harloe *et al.*, suggested that in
general it is the larger builders who landbank.[13] The function
of such a bank is primarily to guarantee access to sites for the

building process. Volume builders prefer to plan ahead and
secure their entry rather than to rely on spot transactions in
the months immediately preceding the launching of a new
development. A substantial landbank is particularly useful
should the builder decide to raise monthly starts very sharply
in order to take advantage of a surge in the effective demand
for new private housing. This land reserve needs to be spatially dispersed to avoid glutting local sub-markets. When a
bank loan is used to finance land purchases, the cost of buying
earlier rather than later is particularly evident to management.
But, taking the simplest case, if the rate of increase in the
market value of a site is greater than the rate of interest paid
on the loan, the financial wisdom of early purchase is confirmed.

Small builders, it is argued, find landbanks less attractive.
They tend to build on smaller sites and their requirements are
more flexible than the bigger firms. They appear to be less
willing to lock up loan finance in this real asset. Moreover they
are less eager to take the risks of site purchases that planning
controls may render sterile, particularly since they do not have
the resources enjoyed by a large company for intervening
directly in the 'ripening' process. For the small builder, an
infill development in a quality area with established services is
ideal, promising a rapid rotation of capital.

What determines the price paid for the land purchased by
speculative housebuilders? Let me begin by setting out three
most important distinctions which, in the current literature, are
confused and thrown together in an incredibly higgledy-
piggledy manner. First, differences exist between the prices
paid for a number of sites at a given point in time because of
corresponding differences in their environmental and relative
loci. Second, taking any set of sites with locations that are
equally attractive, differences exist between the prices paid
for them at a given point in time because of corresponding
differences in their legal attributes, and here the gift of planning permission for residential development is the crux of the
matter. Third, the prices buyers are willing to pay for specific
sites of defined loci and attributes will change over time because
of the impact on the housebuilding industry of nationwide
macro-economic developments. These distinctions I shall refer
to as price variations due to locational, legal and temporal
circumstances. Thus the market value of any given site can
change over time for three reasons: because its environmental
and relative locus change, because its legal attributes change,
and because the macro-economic circumstances of the industry
change.

So let us begin again. What determines at a point in time the
price of a site of known location and with a given legal status,
for example outline planning permission? The answer is that
in the bargaining process between landowner and developer
the maximum price that the latter will pay is a residual equal to
the anticipated sales income from the houses that can be

constructed on the site less the costs, exclusive of the site price, necessary for the completion of the development and building processes *including* a sum of money representing the required minimum profit on the development.[14]

With respect to locational circumstances, since dwelling prices vary over space because of house buyers' perceptions of variations in the attractiveness and convenience of different locations, there is a corresponding variation in the residual that determines the developer's bid prices. Spatial differences in the costs of infrastructural provision and of building, for reasons either of physical or human geography, are a second source of bid price variations. There is a strong tendency for the smaller transactions to have relatively high prices per plot and per acre because small sites usually require less expenditure per dwelling on site works and they are more favourably located.[15]

Now let us look at the effect on the residual, and therefore on the developer's maximum offer price, caused by differences in the legal attributes of sites with a broadly similar locational character. In Britain the legal gradations of the majority of our 'greenfield' acreage embrace land located in the National Parks and Areas of Outstanding Natural Beauty, land zoned for agricultural use, white land, land in agricultural use but zoned for residential development, land with outline planning permission for housing construction and land with detailed planning permission for the same. These degrees of ripeness for development should correspond to variations in the developer's offer price. The less ripe the land, the longer the developer will have to hold it before commencing building and therefore the greater the holding costs in financial terms (see above). Moreover the less ripe the land, the greater the resources the developer may have to put into promoting that ripening process within the planning authorities at district, county or ministerial level using the professional skills of architects, lawyers and planning consultants at the builder's financial command. Finally, the less ripe the land the more likely it is that the developer will fail to get planning permission at all and find himself the absentee landlord of a farming tenant, with a very low yield on his land purchase.

The less mature a site is for residential development, the greater is the space opened up for the purchaser's bargaining skills in persuading the landowner of the 'enormous difficulties' that must be faced in pushing a development to fruition. The owner, of course, will have his minimum release price which can hardly fail to exceed the market value of the site in continuing agricultural use. At the same time the owner or his agent should be aware of the market value of land that is fully ripe for residential development and which sells, therefore, at a price close to the full residual between house price and the developer-builder's 'costs' described above. Thus the owner will generally set his minimum release price at higher levels the more mature the land is and may indeed engage in 'ripening' the land himself in order to improve his bargaining power.

The whole argument leads to the conclusion that we can expect a positive correlation between degree of developmental maturity and land price with, possibly, a discontinuity upwards in the function where outline planning permission is granted since this is associated with a marked reduction in developmental risk, a contraction in the planning delays likely to stall the starting date of the building process and, as a consequence, a powerful strengthening of the landowner's bargaining power.

Temporal variation in land prices, with the location and legal circumstances held constant, need not detain us long. Any macro-economic changes that, over a period of time, have the effect of raising house prices more rapidly than building costs will bring about an upward movement in land prices and vice versa.[16] Even equal rates of increase in prices and costs should raise land prices since the absolute size of the money residual will be correlated with these generalised inflationary trends. When house prices rise very rapidly ahead of costs, as they did in the early 1970s, if developers expect costs to 'catch up' in the short to medium term, the maximum offer prices on mature land are likely to be differentially affected.

The rate of change over time in the market value of specific pieces of land will reflect all three of the determinants that I have distinguished, the locational, the legal and the temporal. For example, over a period of three years the price of a site may increase simultaneously because of a substantial inward movement of manufacturing industry to a nearby new town; because the site has moved from the white land category to receiving outline planning permission for residential construction; and because house prices and costs have both experienced similar inflationary trends.

The preceding analysis in this section makes it possible now to destroy a modern myth. On 8 January 1974, the following quotation appeared in the *Investors Chronicle*:

> Despite appearances, housebuilding is only partially the business of putting up houses. The houses are the socially acceptable side of making profits out of land appreciation. In extreme cases ... no houses were built at all, and the profit was taken in the disposal of land bought at much lower cost.

This argument, that housebuilders' profits derive entirely from increases in the market value of the land they own, quickly became accepted amongst a number of authors, including myself, and continues to resonate to this day in discussions of housing and the land question.[17] It now seems to me that the proposition is profoundly mistaken and originates in a misconception and a false generalisation of the experience of speculative housebuilding in 1971-3. The argument has five flaws:

(i)   It fails to explain the profit source of those building firms, possibly four-fifths of the total, that do not engage in landbanking. We do not have any reliable evidence on the output scale of builders that purchase land at or close to its full development value but Andrew Evans points out that the number of plots of land with planning permission for housing sold to private purchasers in England and Wales in 1969-72 was 56 per cent of private housing starts. So for the majority of private housing, at least in that period, maturation landbanking simply did not take place at all.[18]

(ii)   It fails to explain why the profit source tapped by builders that do not landbank cannot be tapped by those that do.

(iii) It fails to recognise that management exercises a very wide range of skills in development and construction, both with respect to the activity process and the financial process, and therefore ascribes all profit to only one of these skills.

(iv)   It fails to indicate that land speculation has its costs and its risks.

(v)   It fails to see that in 1971-3 profits were made by some builders not because the price of their competitors' raw material had risen but because the price of the product of all these firms had soared. The land appreciation argument can be used only to point to the differential effect on profits, favouring those with landbanks as the sudden rise in house prices drove up land prices in a period when interest rates and therefore holding costs were relatively low and the pressure of effective demand enormously assisted the ripening process.

But my evident desire to destroy this myth should not be misinterpreted to imply that land acquisition is merely the physical prerequisite to the commencement of the building process. Throughout, this section has shown that for some firms housebuilding as a financial process can be seen as a practice in which skilful land purchase planning can and does contribute significantly to those companies' financial objectives.

4 THE SUPPLY OF LAND AND THE PLANNING SYSTEM

The preceding section addressed itself largely to questions concerning access to land on the part of the individual housebuilding company. In the following paragraphs I wish to put forward an interpretation of the *general* effects on private housing construction of the planning legislation introduced in Britain through the 1947 Town and Country Planning Act and subsequent Acts.

With respect to residential development, the modern planning

system in Britain rests essentially on a single radical transformation of the rights in land. From 1947 onwards the unfet-
tered right of an owner to carry out a housing development
on his or her land was abolished. The Fabians have argued,
for their own purposes, that the Labour government of the
day had 'nationalised' these rights. This view is almost uni-
versally accepted but is totally false since the state has never
enjoyed the right to develop land owned by a private individual
or company. What actually happened was that an owner could
lawfully develop a site only if he had received prior permission
to do so from the planning authorities of the state. An absolute
right in property had become conditional. Since the 1968
reforms in the nature of the planning process and the 1974
reorganisation of local government, planning permission has
been granted (or withheld) by district councils increasingly on
the basis of their local plans. These plans themselves are
statutorily required to take cognisance of any structural plan
prepared by the county authorities. An individual or company
who is refused permission may appeal in the last instance to the
Secretary of State.

The objective sought by central government through the planning system has never been to restrict the *total* supply of land
purchased by speculative housebuilders and, indeed, has probably never had this effect. Rather, the aim has been to achieve
a spatial disposition of the flow of new output which, in comparison with the *laissez-faire* experience of the interwar years,
would secure a more efficient location of housing estates vis-à-
vis expanding employment opportunities; a reduction in costs
per house of local government expenditure on the physical
infrastructure necessary for an expanding residential population in any specific area; and, in some loosely formulated sense,
a greater harmony between urban and rural land uses. This
revolution in the geography of reproductive production necessitated a legal *coup* against the landowning class. The spatial
achievement, in the broadest terms, has been to contain the
expansion of the great conurbations and, in areas predominantly
of a rural character, to promote housing development within or
on the periphery of the existing towns and villages or within
the designated areas of the new towns.

The individual landowner might grieve over the loss of ancient
rights which, in spite of the planning legislation between the
wars, had in practice remained virtually untrammelled. Yet the
overall effect on landowners as a class has by no means been
disadvantageous and helps explain why the Conservative Party,
in which landed property has a powerful voice, has never
sought to revoke the control of development. Owners of sites
the development potential of which has effectively been terminated by the planning authorities have indeed suffered. But
the aristocracy, the gentry and the multifarious institutional
owners of land that have found their property zoned for residential construction have benefited substantially. For the

restrictive geography of the promise or the gift of planning
permission enormously improves the bargaining power over the
transaction price of the owner relative to the purchaser. This
is confirmed by the price gradient that is reported to exist
for land of varying legal attributes. In this very specific and
restrictive sense the planning system does raise the price of
land, in parallel with its reduction both in the competition
between landowners and in the uncertainty of the development
potential of specific sites. Indeed a hypothesis worthy of test-
ing is that it is the introduction of the planning system that
has led speculative housebuilders to engage in landbanking as
a counter to the strengthened power of specific landowners
flowing from their class losing its absolute rights in land!

One might take the view that since planning raises the price
of land and thereby reduces the proportion of its development
value appropriated by the developer, housebuilding profits
are consequently reduced. This position is accurate as far as
it goes. But, as Edwards points out, the planners create com-
pensating advantages.[19] The control exercised over the flow of
land for residential construction at the local, sub-regional and
regional level provides a more stable marketing context for the
individual builder, helps prevent the glutting of individual
sub-markets by a set of competing firms and links the provision
of public infrastructure to the areas thus zoned. The total
impact may by no means be disadvantageous to housebuilding
capital in its net effect and therefore there is no reason to
suppose that in the total context the planning system creates
barriers to entry for such capitals.

If this line of attack is correct, if the planning system as a
whole does not constitute a barrier to the entry of speculative
housebuilders into profitable development and construction,
why are planners so frequently the subject of attacks from the
industry?[20] Three distinct problems seem to exist, which we
can refer to respectively as proscriptions, delays and inflexibility. Let us take these in turn, beginning first with proscriptions. In any single district or county or in a set of such
areas there exists a price surface for housing of given physical
attributes, the 'hills' and 'dales' of which reflect household
perceptions of the environmental quality and relative convenience of different locations. If housebuilders can secure
development rights at the most favoured points of the price
surface and if construction costs are independent of the price
surface, then both the landowner and the developer-builder
will benefit from higher capital gains and profits respectively.
However, if the aesthetic, social or economic predilections of
the planners generate an evolving settlement pattern which,
through the instrument of planning permission, restricts
developments to the 'valleys' of the price surface then the
economic interests of landed and housebuilding capital are
prejudiced. The cries of anguish from developers are likely to
be particularly acute when they have landbanked with prime

sites of high environmental quality which the planners continue to confine to agricultural use. Any examination in public of a shire county's structure plan throws up examples. The position taken by Costain Homes at the examination in public of the Oxfordshire structure plan in 1977 is a case in point. They wanted Thame included on the very short list of growth towns. Costain owned 313 acres of land south of Thame.[21]

The second problem I referred to concerns delays in securing planning permission, both in outline - the approval in principle for a residential development on site - as well as in detail, the granting of approval in detailed matters concerning the siting and design of the development. The data below indicate the delays experienced by a sample of developers of public as well as private sector sites in south-east England in the early 1970s.[22]

	Average time required in months		
	No special problems	*Problems*	*Delay*
Outline application to outline consent	2	17	15
Outline consent to detailed application	12	29	17
Detailed application to detailed consent	2	10	8
Detailed consent to start	5	17	12
Start to completion	13	17	4

The chief sources of delay were site servicing, the negotiated revision of schemes, and consultation between public authorities and changes of ownership. They affected more than one-half of all the schemes in the survey. The Economist Intelligence Unit suggested:[23]

Developers and builders work in the expectation of some delays and time applications for permissions accordingly. Their forward assessment of demand determines when they want to complete, and applications are fixed in relation to this. It is the unexpected or the over prolonged delays which create the serious problems, and these are clearly frequent, and long.

However, delay was by no means always the fault of the local authorities. Of the lag between outline consent and detailed application it is noted that:[24]

By far the most outstanding characteristic affecting this stage is change of ownership. This occurs in all types of site but is proportionately more frequent in larger sites, and reflects the fact that many owners obtain outline permission in order to establish a value for land which is then sold.

In addition, the hold-up between start and completion reflected developers' decisions to slow down the building rate in order to time completions to suit best the conditions of effective demand.

The third supply problem referred to above was inflexibility. By this I mean a sluggish response in the planners' supply of outline permissions at a time of a rapid surge in effective demand when developers are fast exhausting their stocks of mature sites. On this score the Economist Intelligence Unit report was quite complimentary towards the planners in the south-east at the time of the acceleration in starts in 1971-3 and contradicted reports that it was a land famine that was driving up land prices. In fact the Unit highlighted the authorities' flexibility in their implementation procedures. In Surrey, Buckinghamshire, Kent and West Sussex less than half the sites given outline permission at this time were on land previously listed as likely to come forward for development within five years. Any shortfall of allocated land supply had been compensated by additional allocations and more significantly to granting permissions on new land not previously listed as available in planning terms.[25]

Up to this point I have made no reference to the two major legislative innovations on land supply carried through in the decade following the Heath government's termination in 1970-1 of the betterment levy and the Land Commission.[26] Neither the 1975 Community Land Act nor the 1976 Development Land Tax Act need detain us long and their content is summarised in appendix 1.

The Community Land Act extended the powers of the land authorities to acquire land suitable for 'relevant development', including residential construction, and then to lease it or sell it freehold for development. For a number of reasons the actual impact of the legislation on the industry was minimal, quite apart from the fact that its implementation was ended after Michael Heseltine became Secretary of State for the Environment in May 1979. First, as a result of lobbying by the House Builders Federation during the Bill's progress through Parliament, a number of exceptions were made in defining 'relevant development' and this had the effect of excluding from acquisition builders' landbanks and all land with residential planning permission on 'White Paper day', 12 September 1974. Second, in its early years the Act gave the authorities only the *power* to acquire land. There was no compulsion to do so and many authorities ignored it or merely used it to make purchases that in any case would have gone ahead under their existing powers. Third, Boddy argues that initially there was little financial advantage to implementation in the market conditions of 1975-7 and that the December 1976 state expenditure reductions led to a halving of the acquisition budget and the retention of site-by-site loan sanction.[27]

The Development Land Tax Act of 1976 introduced a tax to be paid by landowners on the realised development value (RDV)

of land, calculated as the difference between a base value and
the selling price of the land when disposed of. When an owner
himself develops a site he is deemed to have disposed of it
immediately prior to the development. There are three methods
of calculating the base value, all of which refer to expenditure
on improvement by the owner plus either its cost of acquisition
or its value in current use. In 1976-9 for a single owner in a
single year the first £10,000 of RDV was tax exempt. The rest
was charged at a rate of 80 per cent save that in the period
up to 31 March 1979 the first £150,000 of RDV carried a $66^2/3$
per cent rate. After their election victory in 1979 the Conservatives exempted the first £50,000 of RDV and reduced the
flat rate tax from 80 down to 60 per cent. What has been the
effect of the Act on the industry? A preliminary point to note
is that development gains in any case had already been taxed
as income since the Finance Act of 1974. In the short run the
new law probably did lead to speculative witholding of land
with development potential from the market in the anticipation
of a Conservative government abolishing the tax or at least
lowering its rate. As we saw above, these hopes were realised
in 1979. The deemed disposal provisions have also caused cash-
flow problems for developers because they have become liable
for tax at the start of the development process before any
houses have been sold. In the long run its most important effect
may be to reduce the net of tax profitability of maturation landbanking and even more to undermine the myth I attacked in
the previous section.

5   THE PROCESS OF PRODUCTION

Until this point the narrative has focused primarily on the land
question. Now I wish to consider the process of production.
The transition to this subject is best achieved through a review
of the nature of the design of private housing, for the activity
of design is both a determinant of the demand for land as well
as an element in the production process itself.

No firm data exist, but the developers, planning consultants
and academics with whom I have talked are agreed that only
a very small proportion of the annual output of private houses
are individually designed. Most firms use pattern books, port-
folios of house-types. The mix of types on a single estate is a
commercial decision that reflects the strength of effective
demand for houses of various sizes in a local market. The role
of the architect is to design the layout of the selected mix and
the corresponding road pattern. A small range of types simplifies site management problems and reduces unit marketing costs.
Dickens suggests that many of the types within these port-
folios are commercialised residual versions of earlier 'progressive' forms of the archetypal rustic hut with its references to
individuality, tradition and rural domestic life.[28] The design

density, i.e. the number of dwellings per acre, is also a
commercial decision, although it must fall within the limits set
by the district planners. Low-density developments are associated with large house-types selling at high prices. For a
given number of annual starts, the greater the average density
of development then the lower the associated demand for housing land.

Thus far the skills of the architect have been represented as
no more than those of an able draughtsman. But an invaluable
article by Harry Gracey makes it clear that creative ability of
a much greater order may be required when developer and
planner conflict over the construction of specific estates.[29] I
have argued above that zoning decisions with respect to residential building, whilst not constituting a barrier to the scale
of speculative housebuilding as a whole, often conflict with the
profit-maximising interests of individual companies. When a
developer purchases land and believes that planning permission
is likely to be refused, he can choose to employ an architect
to assist him in the bargaining process. The function of the
architect and his team is to produce attractive individual house
designs, pleasing landscaping and, in very large developments,
the framework of a planned social infrastructure so that the
planning authorities will be willing to reverse existing spatial
criteria for the control of development. If outline planning
permission is refused, for example because an entirely new
'village' lies squarely within a green belt, the matter can go to
appeal and again the architectural quality of the development
will be used to reinforce the developer's case. The architect
is, in fact, acting as the faithful servant of the company in a
conflict with the state over the legitimacy of a specific instance
of the production of the built environment. A more precise
example could hardly be found of Dickens's proposition that
'design can be envisaged as the resultant of the twin forces:
ideology and production'.[30]

The planners' control of development has also given them the
power to establish certain architectural criteria that take the
form either of design guides, or briefs for specific projects,
or the informal discussions that take place before or after the
application for outline and detailed planning permission. Guidance is carried out both by district officers for individual
schemes and county planning staff for the generality of developments, for example through the famous Essex Design
Guide.[31] Over the decades since the 1947 Town and Country
Planning Act, control has moved far beyond location and density
to embrace site layout, the provision of public facilities, the
protection of local amenities and design details such as materials
and elevations. The development industry has ambiguous attitudes towards design guidance: they perceive it as pushing
up unit costs by raising quality and yet also as providing a
more explicit decision context when planning permission is
sought, with a consequent reduction in the delays inherent in

land maturation.

With this brief discussion of some aspects of design completed, it is appropriate to consider next the organisation and techniques of the building process. The relationship of the developer to construction takes several modes. The developer may act as the main contractor, alternatively he may contract out the entire building process to a separate company for an agreed price. The main contractor, whether coterminous with the developer or not, will let out work to a number of subcontractors and Graham Ive has suggested that subcontracting is more widespread in speculative housebuilding than in any other sector of construction.[32] Subcontracting takes two forms: supply and fix; and labour-only subcontracting or 'the Lump'. With supply and fix, the subcontractors provide materials and equipment as well as the labour required to perform a specific part of the whole task. In the case of the Lump, workers are hired out to the main contractor by the subcontractor and the former provides the materials and most of the equipment. Austrin argues that the Lump, which in effect is a piece-work system, removes from building companies both the necessary responsibilities of organising and controlling labour as well as the social and administrative duties imposed by the state. As Sugden says, by putting trades such as bricklayers, carpenters, plasterers and sometimes labourers on to a self-employed basis, employers avoid national insurance contributions and payments in respect of redundancy entitlement.[33] Many of the workers engaged in the Lump themselves use it, through their self-employed status, to avoid the full payment of income tax.

With respect to the division of labour between general contractor and subcontractors, Hill writes that the responsibilities of the former typically 'consist of preparing foundations and ground slabs, of distributing and storing bulky materials, and of carrying out incidental "builders work" which may be required, for instance by heating engineers or electricians. The rest of the house is built by sub-contract specialist trades.'[34]

Since the nineteenth century the speculative housebuilding industry has witnessed substantial technological advance. This has been composed of two intimately related elements: technical change off-site, in particular through product innovation in materials manufacture; and technical change on-site, particularly as a result of innovation in the supply of plant and equipment of all kinds and in the social organisation of the labour process. In their turn these two types of change produce a new balance within total output between the flow of value-added production on-site as against the off-site flow. Let us next look in turn at each of these two elements.

Richard Hill has provided us with a valuable qualitative insight into innovations in the supply of materials and components. He cites the case of plasterboard and other composite

materials replacing plane surfaces assembled on site from
smaller elements; manufactured concrete roof tiles taking over
from natural split slates and clay tiles; innovations in the
production of timber and aluminium windows; the revolution
in the method of door production since the Second World War;
the deskilling in on-site assembly of pipework as plastic and
copper have replaced lead and cast-iron in pipes; the highly
mechanised flow production of metal lintels; and the supply of
lightweight, factory prefabricated space heating and hot and
cold water services. Finally he writes:[35]

> Changes in the production of components are exemplified
> in the production of prefabricated roof trusses which since
> the early 1960s have been almost universally adopted as
> the means of roofing low-rise housing. These trusses are
> quickly nailed into place and are substitutes for a large
> amount of on-site measuring, cutting, jointing and fixing.

With respect to the on-site labour process, Ive argues that
the construction industry as a whole employs a relatively low
level of fixed capital per unit of output and per person
employed and that within the industry the housebuilding trades
and the general builders are even more undercapitalised.[36] But
we must not allow this to cause us to understate the mechanisa-
tion that has taken place. With respect to the responsibilities
of the general contractor, Hill writes:[37]

> Petrol-driven compressors for pneumatic tools and petrol-
> driven concrete mixers became common in the inter-war
> period but site works have now been revolutionised by
> hydraulically powered small trenching machines, smaller-
> scale tractor-type scrapers and graders and by readymix
> concrete delivery. Materials handling has been partly
> mechanised on larger sites up to the point of consumption
> by individual trades....Small-scale low voltage drills,
> hammers and saws are in extensive use for builders work
> in preparation for specialist trades. One interesting aspect
> of this particular set of changes is that it has happened
> largely by means of the growth of a plant hire trade within
> the building industry.

In spite of the essential similarity of the majority of speculative housing types, permitting certain economies of learning,
it is only in the last few years that a measurable proportion of
output has been based on methods that can be described as
'industrialised', in this case primarily timber-frame housing.
Here timber-framed panels are brought to site and nailed
together on their edges. This quickly provides a light and
temporarily weatherproof framework on which internal and
external work can proceed simultaneously. Moreover labour
can be supervised and controlled much more easily, for a ter-

race of timber-framed houses is a see-through framework for
a large part of the production process. Lastly, what in effect
is the development of factory production of the skeletons of
structural wall elements replaces part of the skilled operation
of bricklaying by unskilled factory assembly of pre-cast timber
sections and sheets.[38]

6 THE DETERMINATION OF HOUSE PRICES

This discussion of the private housebuilding industry has,
until now, largely ignored the question of how house prices
are determined. Price variations within a country can be classified into five fairly distinct categories. The first of these
touches on differences in price at a point in time within a
single travel-to-work area as a result of differences in the
attributes of properties with respect to their physical and control characteristics. The specific content of these characteristics was discussed in chapter 5. The second category of
variation concerns the differences in price at a point in time
within a single travel-to-work area as a result of differences
in the attributes of properties with respect to their environmental and relative loci. The third category refers to spatial
differences in price *between* travel-to-work areas or economic
regions as a result of the specificities of demand and supply in
each area or region. All of these first three categories deal in
variations over space but within a single time-period and can
be referred to under the generic title of predicative differentials. The subject has received very considerable attention in
the British literature, but it is not the focus of my interest in
this section.[39]

The fourth and the fifth categories of price variation both
refer to changes in dwelling prices over time, respectively in
the short run and the long run. Let me deal with these in turn.
When a developer completes an estate, he must decide what
prices to ask for the newly constructed houses. In the normal
case the company will be faced with a number of competitors,
for the estate will lie within one or more travel-to-work areas
and in each of these other developments may be approaching
completion or already have dwellings for sale. Moreover there
will also be competition from the stock supply itself and in
1980 for the country as a whole this exceeded the newbuild
supply in a ratio of six to one if we use building society advances as a guide (see Table 6.6). Housebuilding companies therefore usually regard themselves as price-takers, setting a price
in line with the going-rate suitably adjusted for the predicative
differentials already referred to. Developers do not set their
selling price as a mark-up on prime costs.

In the short run, the movement of price in an upward direction can be very powerfully influenced by the determinants of
demand. An upward shift in demand can take place as a result

of increasing money incomes or through a fall in the mortgage
rate of interest or via a surge in the number of advances being
made by the building societies. Such changes in the conditions
of effective demand are likely to raise the price received by
every supplier, to have a positive but lagged effect on the
number of starts and possibly to speed up the rate of construction on estates where building is already taking place. Such
a price surge permits housebuilding companies to regain any
ground they may have lost in profit margins as a consequence
of earlier upward movements in the cost of materials and site
labour costs.

*Table 11.7 The average price of dwellings for owner-occupation purchased
with completed building society mortgages in the UK 1966-80 (£)[a]*

Year	New dwellings	Other dwellings	All dwellings	All dwellings index
1966	3,953	3,776	3,840	32
1967	4,154	4,001	4,050	34
1968	4,447	4,290	4,344	36
1969	4,690	4,650	4,660	39
1970	4,990	5,010	5,000	42
1971	5,510	5,710	5,650	47
1972	6,920	7,610	7,420	62
1973	9,630	10,170	10,020	84
1974	11,140	11,090	11,100	93
1975	12,234	11,880	11,945	100
1976	13,132	12,679	12,759	107
1977	14,343	13,589	13,712	115
1978	16,792	15,447	15,674	131
1979	21,455	19,886	20,143	169
1980	26,131	23,085	23,514	197

Source: *HSGB; HCS.*

[a] From 1975 the figures are based on a monthly return covering 90 per cent of building
society mortgages. The figures for 1969-74 have been adjusted to be comparable with the
new series. For 1966-8 they are based on approximately comparable *HSGB* data.

However, Table 11.7 shows that, during the last fifteen
years at least, downward shifts in demand as a result of increases in the mortgage rate or reductions in the flow of advances
have never brought with them a fall in country-wide prices
on an annual basis. Admittedly in some areas and for relatively short periods of time prices have fallen and it is certainly
the case that house prices have diminished for longer periods
in relation to the retail price index, for example. This asymmetry in price movement can be explained by the fact that
average money incomes have not fallen since the Second World
War and because when demand conditions turn sour builders

prefer to reduce their output flow, and selling buyers hold
their homes off the market where this is feasible. In the short
run, then, I see effective demand changes as principally
responsible for the periodic acceleration in house prices.

Now let me consider the fifth category of price variation, the
long-run movement in house prices, and here I have in mind
trends taking place over at least a decade. A commonly held
view is that the fundamental determinant of this secular change
comes from the side of effective demand. In the first place, it
is argued, the price of existing houses does not reflect their
historic costs which, for example in the case of older properties, may only be a very small fraction of the current selling
price. Second, it is said that since in any year the sales of
existing dwellings are vastly greater than the output of new
housing for owner-occupation, clearly it is the price of the
stock supply that determines the price of the newbuild supply.
Since the price of the stock is not determined by production
costs, then it is demand that must be the determinant. Household income, the machinations of exchange professionals, the
supply of mortgage credit and the scale of government subsidies
are all cited as shaping effective demand and there may be some
conception of a long-run natural ratio between average house
price and average income.[40]

Unfortunately this thesis has a fundamental weakness. If
demand alone determines the stock supply price trend and this
determines the newbuild supply price trend, then there is no
reason why demand prices should not diverge very substantially from the costs of new construction. If the demand price
is higher we could have very long periods when massive super-
profits are being made in speculative housebuilding. If the
demand price is lower there could be long periods when housebuilding is loss-making so, given the low fixed capital commitment in the industry, leading to the termination of any significant level of output. But in the history of housing in Britain
in this century we have witnessed neither such phenomenon. In
addition, what we require from the demand school is a specification of the quantitative relation between the stock supply price
and the determinants of demand and an explanation as to why
such a relation should hold.

I wish to advance, in a preliminary fashion, an alternative
'classical' thesis that states that the long-run trend in the
price of houses, both existing dwellings and newly built ones,
is determined by the long-run movements in the prices of building materials and components and in the wage rates and productivity of site labour. These prices and labour productivity
on-site are the basis of unit prime costs. The trend in the
prices of materials and the wage rates of building labour are
largely set by factors outside the building industry. The long-
run trend in site labour productivity in speculative housing
construction is something we know very little about.

If the 'classical' thesis does hold then we would expect that

over a long period of time the all-dwellings index of house
prices would intertwine with the index of prime costs. What
leads me to expect such a relationship? Let me set the answer
to this question in an economic context of an upward trend
in the general price level, such as we have experienced in
Britain since the onset of the Second World War. At any point
in time it is perfectly feasible that a substantial disparity might
exist between the indices of prime costs and dwelling prices.
If, for example, the latter exceeds the former, what forces
might bring about convergence? The answer is that such a
disparity reflects a differential between prime cost and selling
price which is very favourable to the developer and thus, as
a consequence, new firms will enter the industry and existing
firms will expand their output. In order to dispose of this
increased level of output as the completed units become available, the ruling level of prices will have to be lower than it
would otherwise have been in order to clear the market at a
lower rate of newbuild supply. This is because effective demand
is a schedule, a set of quantities that households in aggregate
are willing to purchase in a one-to-one correspondence with a
set of prices. Ignoring short-run destabilising price expectations, lower prices are associated with greater quantities
demanded. The schedule shifts from period to period, gently
or violently, as a result of changes in the determinants of
effective demand. These include the size of the population,
particularly in the household-forming age group; the migration
of households with the metamorphosis of employment opportunities and transport systems; the level of money incomes; the
availability and cost of mortgage finance; the pattern of state
subsidies for home-owners; and the relative attributes of
vacancies in different tenures, which itself is powerfully
shaped by the rate and quality of new housing construction for
local authorities and private landlords. Effective demand, as
was stated in chapter 4, concretely manifests itself in any given
time-period as a set of specific purchases.

   As I have said, the increased flow of completions will be
disposed of on the market only at a price that is lower than
that necessary to dispatch a smaller output quantity. But in a
context of marked inflationary price trends, particularly in
money incomes, this relatively lower price is not necessarily
synonymous with an absolute diminution in average selling
prices. However, the moderating influence on the positive rate
of change of price which is exerted by an increase in the flow
of completions certainly does permit materials prices and site
labour wage rates to gain ground on average selling prices and
gives a space for the prime cost index to converge from below
up towards the price index.

   What, then, of a situation in which the disparity between
price and cost indices is unfavourable to the developer? Inevitably, this will be associated with losses in some firms and
uncomfortably tight margins in others. Starts per month can

be expected to fall as some firms go bankrupt, some hibernate and the rest reduce their building rate. As this reduced flow of completions comes on to the market they in their turn will enjoy a higher price than would have been possible in sour market conditions with an unchanged output flow; and developers will hang on grimly until demand, for whatever reason, accelerates again with the *price* index this time converging from below up towards the prime cost index.

The index of costs and the index of prices, then, are like stag and hound in an eternal hunt. The path of the hound veers now to the north, now to the south of the trail of its prey. But it is the flight of the stag that determines the direction of movement.

Graph 11.1 Indices of the cost of housing construction and of home prices in 1969-80

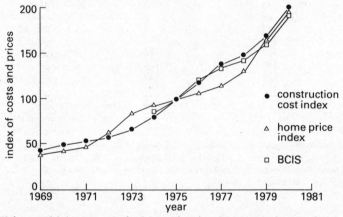

This would be an admirable point in the narrative to insert a long-run data series on unit prime costs in speculative housebuilding in Britain. Unfortunately no such series yet exists. *Building* now publishes a 'housing cost index' prepared by the Building Cost Information Service of the RICS; this is enormously useful but only goes back as far as December 1973. The series is plotted in Graph 11.1.[41] So Table 11.8 is very much second best. The materials index reflects the input requirements of both the private and public housing sectors. The weekly wage index is for the whole of construction. Even with more specific data that took into account the predominance of labour-only subcontracting in the industry, we would still lack a measure of labour productivity to convert wages into unit labour costs. All one can say is that, however crude, it is the only index we have of costs to the builder going back to 1969. Other indicators certainly exist but, that of the RICS excepted, on close inspection these usually turn out to measure prices to clients. Graph 11.1 combines the all-dwellings index

of house prices with the combined cost index. The association
is obviously very close. However, the data are too poor, the
time period is too short and the inflationary trends in prices
of all kinds too general for me to dream of arguing for one
moment that this mere association - however intimate - constitutes statistical confirmation of the 'classical' hypothesis.

*Table 11.8 Indices of material costs and basic weekly wages in the
construction industry in Great Britain 1969-80*

Year	Cost of construction materials for new housing work	Basic weekly wages in construction	Combined cost index[a]
1969	44	42	43
1970	50	47	49
1971	54	52	53
1972	58	59	58
1973	68	65	67
1974	85	76	81
1975	100	100	100
1976	123	115	120
1977	146	125	138
1978	158	135	149
1979	182	149	169
1980	218	174	201

Source: HCS.

[a] Assumes speculative housebuilding prime costs composed of 60 per cent materials and 40
per cent labour. See Roy Drewett, 'The developers: decision processes', in Peter Hall,
Harry Gracey, Roy Drewett and Ray Thomas, *The Containment of Urban England*, vol. 2,
London, Allen & Unwin, 1973, p. 186.

7 SUMMARY

The speculative housebuilding industry is a subject both broad
and complex, well worthy of a volume in itself. In this chapter
a brief sketch was first given of some salient features of the
construction industry as a whole, only 12 per cent of the output of which in 1980 derived from new private dwelling construction. The speculative sector contains many thousands of
firms but the great majority of these start at most only thirty
dwellings in any year. However, small, medium and large companies all make a substantial contribution to aggregate output
with the largest thirty to forty firms providing over one-third
of that total. The archetypical product is the three-bedroom
house but by 1979 dwellings with four or more bedrooms made
up one-fifth of the total exclusive of flats.

Next the physical and financial nature of the industry was
described. The dominant objective is an economic one, the
maximisation of profitability, and this requires the exercise of

a wide range of skills with respect to the raising of capital, the management of production and the specification and marketing of the product.

The importance of land purchases to the success of speculative housebuilding was analysed at some length. The possession of land is, of course, a prerequisite of the development and building process. Furthermore, variations in the unit price of land as a result of locational, legal and temporal circumstances open up a space for the exercise of entrepreneurial ability in land purchase which can have an important effect on the absolute and relative success of the firm. However, a critique was made of those simplistic accounts that have suggested that housebuilding profitability is merely the result of speculating in land price increases, as if dwelling production were little different from the activities of a Dr Mabuse trading in cocoa futures.

The discussion next turned to the land supply and the planning system. The broad objectives of that historical watershed, the 1947 Town and Country Planning Act, were described - as well as its effect on the bargaining power of those landowners who have received or are likely to receive planning permission for housing construction. But no support was given to the view that the planning system constitutes a *general* barrier to housebuilding capital.

The speculative industry's repeated attacks on the control of residential development were explained in terms of the specific proscriptions, delays and inflexibility in land release associated with plan implementation.

A very brief review of the production process followed. The ideological as well as the productive character of design was exemplified. The considerable reliance on subcontracting in general and the Lump in particular was described. The notion that housebuilding is done with traditional materials using few tools was attacked.

Finally, an attempt was made to explain the long-run trend in house prices. In spite of the quantitative dominance of the stock supply over the newbuild supply, it was argued that it is the production costs of the speculative industry rather than demand factors that determine the price trend of owner-occupied dwellings. The core of the analysis was that, with the exception of movements in labour productivity on-site, the trend in unit prime costs is determined outside of the industry, that short-run price movements created by changes in the conditions of demand open up a gap between unit costs and selling prices, and that consequent output changes by developers bring the price back towards the unit prime cost trend. The effect is that the all-dwelling price index 'tracks' the independently determined movement in prime costs. If this is correct, it follows that as an explanation of economic relationships, the so-called long-run ratio of house price to household income, that universal nonsense quotient or coefficient of ignorance, is bunkum.

This chapter is the fourth and last successively to deal with the supply of dwellings for owner-occupation and has specifically considered the production of new dwellings. Before we take up the question of the exchange process - where demand and supply meet - it is convenient first to deal with that other category of housing work that is carried out for owner-occupiers, rehabilitation production.

12 OWNER-OCCUPIER
   REHABILITATION

1 INTRODUCTION

The object of this chapter is to explore the issue of owner-occupier rehabilitation, from the point of view of the effective demand for this category of housing production as well as the supply of such output. Expenditure on the rehabilitation of a specific house by a home-owner requires the fulfilment of two quite distinct preconditions. The first is that of access, in the sense that the owner must first of all have been able to purchase the house in question. The subject of house purchase has already been considered at length in this book, particularly in chapters 5, 6 and 7. The second and subsequent precondition of expenditure is that the owner-occupier both wishes and is able to rehabilitate his (or her) house once purchased. It is that process which is a principal concern of this chapter. The quite distinct act of mediated gentrification by developers and the purchase of houses rehabilitated for sale was examined in chapter 9.

The literature on this important subject is too often marred by linguistic inconsistencies and therefore it behoves me first to adopt certain conceptual conventions. I take it that the original starting point of rehabilitation, a term already defined in Figure 2.1, is the perception of an inadequacy in the physical attributes of the dwelling that the owner-occupier would like to set right. I shall choose to use the term 'obsolescence' to refer to a gap at a particular point in time between the existing physical standard of a house and some perceived alternative. Its connotation here, then, is a state of affairs *not* a process. To understand obsolescence it follows that ideally one should explain both the material conditions of the accommodation and the subjective wishes of the household or (in the context of government policy) the expressed intentions of the planners.

The physical circumstances of the dwelling at a point in time reflect first its original standards of construction; second, the *process* of deterioration resulting from the passage of time and from the occupants' use; and third, rehabilitation itself, which can slow down deterioration or even reverse it and bring improvements in the dwelling. Whether, in general, physical deterioration is a linear function of time, in the absence of rehabilitation, is not clear and probably varies between regions, between houses of different qualities of construction and between the built structure and the mechanical equipment it contains.[1] In any case we can say that for any given house its obsolescence differs between households to the degree that their preferences differ; similarly for any given household obsolescence differs between houses to the degree that their physical attributes differ. Moreover the state of obsolescence grows worse over time as the house deteriorates or as preferred standards rise, for example, because of rising incomes or improved heating technologies. Obviously, for the reverse reasons, the obsolescent state may ameliorate with time.

Our appreciation of the scale of obsolescence is strongly influenced by government departments because it is they who primarily have been responsible for the collection of nationwide data on the problem. *The Housing Policy Technical Volume* suggested the use of three different concepts: lack of amenities, disrepair and unfitness.[2] The first describes a situation where a dwelling lacks (and probably always lacked) a bathroom or an internal WC or central heating or some other facility. The second describes at a given point in time the extent of physical decay in a structure and can be measured by the resources required to 'put it right' in some sense. The third, 'unfitness', is a statutory term that appears in Section Four of the 1957 Housing Act and describes a house judged not to be reasonably suitable for occupation on the basis of a number of criteria such as dampness, lack of natural lighting, instability, etc. The three concepts are reasonably distinct but do, of course, overlap in the actual houses they encompass.

To sum up: the starting point of any decision by an owner-occupier to rehabilitate his house is his perception of the state of obsolescence of the dwelling. This depends on both the physical standards the owner would like to enjoy and the actual material attributes of the accommodation. The latter are determined by the original standards of construction of the house, both with respect to structure and amenities, the process of physical deterioration of the unit over time, and the scale and quality of rehabilitatory work carried out in previous time-periods.

2 HOUSEHOLD DEMAND FOR REHABILITATION OUTPUT

Sections two and three seek to set out what are the primary determinants of the willingness and the ability of owner-occupiers to have rehabilitation work carried out. The question of whether it is done by paying builders or by do-it-yourself (which itself can require substantial cash outlays) is left for consideration in section four. To begin with, it is assumed that the household is able to afford rehabilitation (of an unspecified kind) and that the main task is to explore what motives it has for getting the work done. It is also assumed that the house in question is the principal residence of its occupants, not a second home, although it is worth remembering that in areas such as Wales, Cumbria, Devon, Cornwall and the Cotswolds many second-home purchases are followed by extensive rehabilitatory work.

Rehabilitation changes the attributes of the dwelling and so should be open to an analysis based on the predicative discussion of chapter 5. Two of the predicates presented there are particularly relevant: the physical attributes of the house and the asset valuation. These are now taken in turn.

The labour carried out on an existing house obviously changes it physically and thereby should safeguard or enhance its potential as an activity centre. This is true whether the work refers to an extension that increases the household's living space, external painting that helps protect the brickwork from decay, the repair of the cistern in a water closet, the installation of a bath or central heating, or the erection of a partition to change the layout of a room. Personally, I am convinced that the principal motivation underlying the demand for rehabilitation is the amelioration it promises in the household's internal physical world.

It follows that from this point of view these transformations can only make sense if the family feels a commitment to continue living in that dwelling and in that neighbourhood. If they are already unhappy with the house and its spatial location or if they fear that the neighbourhood may decline or that the house's relative locus may become unfavourable because of the closure of a railway line or a local factory, or if the household feels threatened by the possibility that the district planners may clear and redevelop that area, then the willingness to rehabilitate is enormously undermined. The evidence of numerous case studies points to this unambiguously.[3]

Of course, even from the narrowly physical aspect, rehabilitation is not always an unmixed blessing and the disruption and chaos caused by major works may dissuade many households from undertaking the work in the first place. Kirwan and Martin have also pointed out that in the small terrace houses of northern England, for example, the loss of space as a result of installing a bath or an inside WC may not justify the added 'convenience'.[4] Similarly Peter Cowan has suggested that inflexibility in the layout and construction of a house may generate high production costs for any given physical change and thereby give an initial bias to physical obsolescence.[5] Moreover, owner-occupiers may fear that the final outcome of a small builder's job will fall far short of what their agreement states. One Birmingham study points to the abysmal quality of some work and cites sagging roofs, uncemented ridge tiles and gutters and downpipes dangling in mid-air.[6]

Let me now turn to the question of asset valuation, the last predicate of chapter 5. Rehabilitation, in the comprehensive sense of the term as defined in Figure 2.1, is fundamental in safeguarding or promoting the selling price of a house. Thus every household which, at least in part, conceives the dwelling as a financial asset will recognise that physical deterioration reduces its market value and conversely that improvements or an extension are virtually certain to raise its price. However, empirical research suggests that the statistical relation between the enhancement in price following rehabilitation and the associated expenditure is not simple: in areas of high environmental quality the ratio of the former to the latter often easily exceeds unity but in decaying neighbourhoods the increase may well fall short of the outlays. In the latter case we can speak of a 'valuation gap' since here the post-rehabilitation price of the house falls short of the sum of the total cost of the work and the house's market price prior to the building work. In such cases would-be 'improvers' of obsolescent inner city housing have found their access to mortgage finance for such 'improvement' blocked, for the selling price of the house may be insufficient to repay the loan in the event of mortgage default.[7]

Consideration of these predicates of physical condition and asset value both point to the mutual dependence of the decisions of individual households in an area. Extensions, good quality repairs and improvements in a neighbourhood may serve to raise the perceived obsolescence of the house owned by those who have not yet decided to rehabilitate as well as to underpin their commitment to the area. In addition this visible physical progress stimulates imitation on financial grounds since it directly increases the ratio of price enhancement to contract outlay. Conversely, there are powerful inertial elements in a locality where the dwelling stock is deteriorating.

Before I move on to consider the *ability* to exercise effective demand, one important complication to the argument so far must be introduced. Kirwan and Martin have pointed out that a household's decision whether or not to rehabilitate an old and 'unimproved' inner city house is in part determined by the alternatives, one of which may be the purchase of a newly constructed suburban dwelling. Their view is that in towns like Blackburn, Burnley, Accrington and Nelson, where they carried out their research, distances to the town centre from the suburbs and surrounding urban developments are sufficiently small to give the inner urban areas no serious relative locational advantage. They therefore concluded that peripheral speculative building would definitely weaken the effective demand for rehabilitation.[8]

3   EFFECTIVE DEMAND, INCOME AND CREDIT

In this section I reverse the previous assumption and now take it for granted that the household does wish to undertake rehabilitation (of an unspecified kind). The main task here is to explore whether it enjoys the ability to purchase such outputs. From the point of view of an individual household, the price of a specific job is set by the building firms that are willing to carry out the work. The household's sources of funds to meet this price include cash drawn from current income, past savings, loans from relatives and friends, loans from institutions such as the local authorities, building societies and banks, and government grants.

As far as I am aware no published information exists on the relative importance of these different sources.[9] However, there is plentiful if fragmentary evidence to confirm what one would have in any case presumed: the ability to pay for rehabilitation is determined largely by household income.[10] This is because such income is the source of the family's own cash outlays and because income level is a factor in gaining access to loans for rehabilitation purposes. Already in previous sections of this book we have seen that marginal owner-occupiers, paying high rates of interest on mortgages of relatively short redemption periods, may find their ability to carry out necessary maintenance and large-scale repair on older houses undermined. In other cases unexpected increases in rehabilitation costs amongst such owners, or the burden of repayment of a second mortgage raised to finance a repair and improvement contract, are known to have forced families into mortgage default.[11]

However, the main interest in the British literature has not been the relation between the income and rehabilitation expenditure of established owner-occupier households, but the repair and improvement of specific dwellings consequent upon vertical transpossession, that is the replacement in a house of a low-income household by one with a relatively higher income. This can take the form of the gentrification of houses formerly owned by private landlords, which was discussed in chapter 9; or it can occur when a marginal owner-occupier household moves or is dissolved. Kirwan and Martin's conclusion from their north-east Lancashire study can embrace all these types:[12]

> Put simply, it is clear that the type of people or households involved [in residential rehabilitation] are those that are relatively young, usually with children, usually middle-class, with above average incomes ... most probably undertaking repairs and improvement in connection with a move. The houses involved are certainly not the oldest and tend to be of the period 1900-1940. While some may have lacked some amenities before improvement, most are already reasonably well-equipped, tending to be the larger houses with gardens. The improvements are generally carried out in areas where the general standard of the residential environment is high and where the majority of houses in the area are well maintained and equipped with all amenities.

The quotation above specifically refers to the youth of those who repair and improve. In fact the relation between age and rehabilitation expenditure is referred to very frequently in

the case studies published in Britain.[13] It is said that, as a
general rule, elderly households resist undertaking substantial
rehabilitation. This may be because their incomes are relatively
low and they are unwilling to take on new debts at the end of
their lives. It may be that the perceived obsolescence of their
dwellings is that much the less where they have been used to
conditions at least as bad throughout their working lives. It
may be that they, in particular, hate the disruption and dirt
that a big job always brings. It may be that they feel less able
to cope with the managerial role of employing and paying builders and of seeking local authority grants. No one denies that
many old-age pensioners enjoy doing some DIY in the way of
maintenance, decorating and small-scale repair. Yet even this
has its limits should they topple from a ladder or be warned
by their doctor that, possibly after a lifelong sedentary occupation, putting on the cap of a labourer-cum-craftsman can
endanger their health. To the extent that housing deterioration
is more likely to go unchecked amongst the elderly, the scale
of the problem is huge, for we saw in Table 4.3 that more than
one-quarter of all owner-occupiers are either older small households or individuals aged 60 or over.

Consideration of the constraints imposed by low household
incomes on the effective demand for rehabilitation naturally
leads to the topic of government grants for such work. After
all, if the elasticity of supply of rehabilitation outputs in the
medium and long term is very high, then each pound paid as a
state grant should be accompanied by a reduction little short
of one pound in the cost to the household of any given improvement. Moreover, if the elasticity of demand for this type of
product is high, the operation of a grants system would be
responsible for a much higher level of output purchased.[14]

But before entering into this topic in any detail, it is necessary to make two cautionary propositions. First, there is a
very great deal of rehabilitation work carried out without any
grant assistance whatsoever, although on what scale is not
known because we have no estimates in Britain of the total
volume of such production. Second, grant-aided work itself
is by no means funded 100 per cent by such payments. This
second point requires elaboration.

Let us distinguish in any grant-aided contract two distinct
cash sums: the *total cost* is the entire sum owed to the builder
whilst the *allowable cost* is a sum for the job set by the local
authority's officers on the basis of ministerial guidance which
constitutes the benchmark for their calculation of the grant
payable. The actual grant payment is some defined percentage
of the allowable cost and, as we shall see below, this figure
varies over time and place. Thus the grant paid can and does
fall short of the total cost both because the allowable cost is
less than the total cost and because the grant is less than 100
per cent of the allowable cost. On the former point we have
some useful data. In England and Wales in the years 1969,

1971, 1973 and 1975, with respect to grant-aided work approved for all private owners, the ratio of allowable to total cost was, respectively, 82, 73, 67 and 72 per cent.[15] So in the simple case where this ratio is 70 per cent and where the grant covers 50 per cent of the allowable cost, the ratio of the grant to the total cost is only 35 per cent.

We have already seen something of the origin and development of grant aid for rehabilitation between 1949 and 1969 in chapters 2 and 3 of this book. It was shown that the total number of grants approved had followed an upward trend in those two decades; that two principal types of grant to owner-occupiers had evolved, the original discretionary (or 'improvement') grant for work to a high standard and since 1959 the standard (or 'intermediate') grant for installation of the five basic amenities; and that the 1969 Act had brought Exchequer assistance for environmental work in GIAs and for the first time had included certain repairs amongst items appearing under allowable costs. The new legislation of 1974 and 1980 will be discussed again in section five. Suffice it for the present to say that the 1974 Housing Act contained a number of positive and important innovations from the point of view of the rehabilitating household: housing action areas were created; repairs-only grants were introduced; and the grant was set at 60 per cent in GIAs and 75 per cent in HAAs with rates of up to 90 per cent in hardship cases.

In Britain in the twenty years that have passed since the data first became available the number of grants approved for rehabilitation by owner-occupiers has never fallen below 50,000 per year. The grand total of such grants in the years 1960-79 inclusive amounts to 1.55 million. The scale of production, as a result of grant availability, has almost certainly been substantially greater than would otherwise have been the case. However, it must be stressed that no one knows or has even estimated the net effect in aggregate.

But what the numerous case studies on 'house improvement' make clear is that there are still numerous obstacles to the take-up of grants, especially amongst marginal owner-occupiers. Unfortunately some writers commit the methodological error of concluding that obstacles which have *always* existed, and in some cases in the past to a more serious degree, are the cause of the *decline* in take-up after 1973.[16] In any case, let me look briefly at some of the continuing problems.

In the first place it is widely reported that the application for a grant, particularly for the discretionary grants which constitute more than 80 per cent of all grants approved since 1973, necessitates the home-owner undertaking rehabilitation to a much higher standard and over a far more truncated time-period than would otherwise have been the case. Therefore it is argued that in order to avoid these controls many households repair and improve to their own lower standards and at their own leisurely pace without grant assistance. Such inflexibility in grant approval is then blamed for restricting the amount of rehabilitation production that might otherwise have taken place.

Associated with this question is a second problem. Both economic theory and the empirical evidence suggest that the lower the income of an owner-occupier household, the poorer are likely to be the physical attributes of its dwelling. *Ipso facto*, any attempt to raise house standards to a given level implies greater costs and higher expenditure for the lower income group. Grants can certainly help in making these payments but because the grant is only a percentage of the latter, rehabilitation can require very onerous outlays from households on modest incomes. There is a good deal of evidence that confirms that the level of costs borne by the household is central in constraining the take-up of grants and the scale of rehabilitation. This causal relation was perhaps most evident in the three years following the 1971 Housing Act when grant levels stood at 75 per cent in the intermediate and development areas compared with 50 per cent in the rest of the country. These were boom years for owner-occupier rehabilitation and the collapse in approved grants from 186,000 in 1973 to 71,000 in 1975 certainly coincides with the withdrawal in June 1974 of this temporary additional subsidy.[17]

As I have already suggested, the difference between total cost and grant does not always have to be found from the household's savings. Loans for rehabilitation may be successfully sought and in the case of the elderly, maturity loans are available on which interest only is payable with the principal repaid when the house is sold. But these loans are not a panacea. They do have to be repaid. In case of default, they can and do lead to the family having to leave their home. Finally, amongst old-age pensioners particularly, many people simply do not relish falling into debt on this account.

The third set of problems restraining grant take-up has to do with various bureaucratic controls over their release. These include the complexity of the application process itself and the known delays in the payment of such monies; the introduction in the 1974 Housing Act of rateable value limits on houses for which grants were payable; and the requirement in the same Act for owner-occupiers to repay the grant with compound interest if they sold the house within five years.[18]

This division that I have adopted of the owner-occupier's decision-making process into willingness and ability to pay, and the identification of various analytic categories that explain resistance to the take-up of grants, should not cause us to forget that in the end the decision is made on the basis of a synthetic perception of reality. This point is illustrated beautifully in the work of Monck and Lomas on housing action areas:[19]

Co-ordinating the various initiatives which lead to increased confidence and so to increased investment can be crucial.

What confidence should the building societies have in an area where the council is buying properties but seems unable to improve them? What confidence should the private owner have in an area that is known to be red-lined by building societies? What are elderly owner-occupiers with small resources to feel when they receive virtually no technical (or other) help with grant applications, choosing builders, monitoring the quality of work? What is anyone to think when the zoned housing association buys only three properties in 3 years, and leaves them empty for $2\frac{1}{2}$ years? The investment patterns of home owners in their own housing may seem eccentric to some, but if they choose not to invest in a decaying house in a decaying area after being offered a grant which in reality covers as little as 40%-50% of improvement works, the value of which they could not recoup if they sold the house - this choice cannot be described as peculiar by anyone.

4 THE PROCESS OF PRODUCTION

It is a matter of great regret that no account has yet been written in Britain of the historiography of the housing question, although it goes without saying that we enjoy a rich literature, historical and contemporary, on the housing question itself. A survey of the published work, its relation to policy, its funding sources, the relation between the abstract and the specific, the social science paradigms of the authors and the class interests they serve is long overdue. But what can be said now, I believe, before such an analysis of the production of knowledge is even begun, is that in one specific sense a really disabling misdirection of intellectual resources has long existed. The academic literature on British housing has been dominated, at least until recent years, by three groups of writers: geographers and sociologists with a predominant interest in the spatial pattern of entry to and consumption of the housing stock in different tenures by various social groups; economists with an obsession for models of individual 'utility-maximising' choices, the determination of house prices and the distribution of housing subsidies; and authors in the field of social and political administration with a fabianesque perspective on the formation of central and local government policy. The result has been that the process of housing production has become the neglected child of our research institutions.[20]

This is nowhere illustrated better than in the field of rehabilitation. Conversion, extension, maintenance, repair, improvement and other adaptations *are* production. Yet from the literature on the subject one might have imagined that, once willed and paid for, they appeared out of thin air. In only one of the works cited in this chapter does the process of production appear to be worthy of more than a single paragraph![21] Since

the raw material that I act upon is nothing more nor less than
the published articles, books and statistical series of other
persons and institutions, the upshot is that the coverage of
rehabilitation production is much slighter than I would have
wished.

Rehabilitation is carried out by three sets of workers which
are distinct in an analytic sense even if there is some overlap
in day-to-day practice. Persons working on their own houses
are one such set. Their output does not take a commodity form
since it is not traded and for this reason alone appears in no
statistical measure of housing output. The second set are
workers who, either individually or in groups, carry out
repairs, improvements etc. in exchange for cash but who do
not declare their income so as to avoid tax payments or because
they are 'moonlighting', as happens with some craftsmen and
labourers in DLOs. They constitute an important sector in the
hidden economy. Anyone who has ever seen the ashen face of
a carpenter who is offered payment by cheque is familiar with
this group. Their output also escapes measurement. The third
set are individuals and firms that sell their services to owner-
occupier households as a perfectly legitimate part of their
business activities. This output is just one part of the huge
range of products and services of the construction industry.

From what has already been said it must be clear why no
calculation has ever been made of the relative importance of
these three sets within the flow of rehabilitation production as
a whole. The aggregate measured output of the formal sector
and the scale of rehabilitation within that total was described
in chapter 11, section one. In Britain in 1980 19 per cent of
the output value of the construction industry took the form of
housing rehabilitation and this category made up as much as
48 per cent of total recorded housing output. No breakdown of
work done for owner-occupiers as distinct from other owners
is available. Table 11.3 showed that the lion's share of recorded
rehabilitation work by private contractors, by trade of firm,
comes from general builders, painters, plumbers, and heating
and ventilating engineers.

Some expenditure estimates published in the *HPTV* may help
to fill in the picture a little more and they are set out in Table
12.1. The data are subject to high standard errors and two
points in particular should be noted: first, household purchases
may well include materials for minor alterations and improvements but exclude, of course, the value of the householder's
own labour; second, improvements and extensions carried out
without the aid of a grant are not included.

Two major conclusions can be drawn from Table 12.1. In the
first place, even recognising the exclusion of non-grant-aided
improvement, it seems highly likely that expenditure on repair
and maintenance is much greater than that on improvement as a
whole. Second, cash payments for the purpose of DIY in every
year since 1968 have comfortably exceeded cash payments to

contractors. If we had an estimate of the time spent by house-holds on DIY and if we were to value that on the basis of the income that would be earned by craftsmen and labourers carry-ing out the same functions, it is likely that DIY would make up well over two-thirds of total rehabilitation output in the owner-occupied sector. For example, if our valuation of the owner-occupier's labour-time on average was in the ratio of four to one with his (or her) expenditure on materials, then in 1975 the gross output value of DIY would have exceeded £2½ billion!

Table 12.1 Expenditure by owner-occupiers on repair, maintenance,
decoration and improvement 1967-75 at out-turn prices (£m)

	1967	1968	1969	1970	1971	1972	1973	1974	1975
Payments to contractors for repair, maintenance and decoration:									
owners with mortgages	59	66	68	70	134	149	201	197	279
outright owners	97	105	90	140	113	95	99	208	142
Total	156	171	158	210	247	244	300	405	421
Purchases of materials for house repair, main-tenance and decoration:									
owners with mortgages	96	151	134	165	183	175	272	358	368
outright owners	57	72	61	68	89	84	88	158	134
Total	153	223	195	233	272	259	360	516	502
Grant-aided improve-ment	20	22	22	30	50	95	180	307	178

Source: *HPTV*, Part I, Tables IV.39 and B.1.

The household's choice between DIY and hiring a builder is likely to favour the former the greater the owner's degree of confidence in his own abilities and, *ceteris paribus*, the lower is the family income. This confidence in one's own manual skills is, I suggest, more prevalent among men, among the young and the middle-aged, and among manual workers themselves, especially those from the building industry! Preference for DIY is also likely to be expressed the lighter the physical workload of the task, the less complex it is technically, the more fre-quently it has to be carried out, with associated learning by doing benefits, and the smaller the scale of the task. Thus, as a general rule, one would expect the relative importance of DIY to increase as one moved across the rehabilitation spectrum from conversion, extension and basic improvements through miscellaneous improvements and adaptations to repair and maintenance.[22]

The 1970s saw a huge expansion in large, self-service DIY retail chains associated with names such as Home Charm,

A.G. Stanley and Status Discount. In 1979 in total there were 29,000 'home improvement' outlets in the UK with sales of DIY products at about £1.4 billion, of which paints and wall coverings accounted for about one-third, although the aggregate probably includes some sales of gardening hardware, motor accessories and kitchen furniture. Increasingly easily used materials and tools have been a spur to this development although it needs to be stressed that there is no evidence for an upward trend in the total value of sales at constant prices.[23]

One of the recurrent themes in the case studies of the rehabilitation process is the difficulty owner-occupiers have in getting access to builders that are reliable and yet not expensive, particularly under general conditions of boom in the construction industry. For their part some builders were not willing to carry out work in areas of marginal owner-occupation because the district was regarded as one of 'poor payers'. The supply problem and the failure of local planners to take into account the supply implications of policy change is forcefully illustrated in the following quotation from Paris and Blackaby's Birmingham study:[24]

Little attention had been given to the availability of builders for house rehabilitation before the introduction of large-scale improvement policies. When owners approached the council about grant-aided work they were given a long list of builders who operated in their area. No specific recommendations were made, and owners were left to select their own builders and enter into contracts. Many owners had difficulty choosing a builder and often complained that firms on the council's list were not willing to do improvement work, failed to turn up after verbal agreements, or even had gone out of business many years before.

An implicit assumption of the urban renewal policy was that there existed, within the city, an adequate reservoir of small building firms ready and able to do house improvement work of the scale anticipated in the policy. This, we should recall, involved a *six-fold increase* in grant-aided improvement activity. In practice residents encountered many difficulties finding builders who were prepared to undertake grant-aided work, and frequent complaints were made to voluntary housing advisers as well as council officers.

Our research was constrained by time and personnel from undertaking an extensive analysis of the structure of the local building industry. But our discussions with voluntary agencies, council officers and residents' organisations highlighted the critical importance of the delays and frustrations caused by the general lack of builders willing and able to do improvement work. Given the low level of interest generally, it is extremely unlikely that the local building industry could have been geared up to doing the physical work

necessarily envisaged in Birmingham's urban renewal
policy.

We have seen that for the individual owner-occupier grant-
aided repair and improvement can constitute a considerable
management challenge with respect to assessing what needs to
be done in successfully seeking a grant and in finding and
supervising the work of a building firm. There is no doubt
that the scale and risk of this management task dissuades many
households from undertaking rehabilitation in the first place.
It was for this reason that some district councils introduced
agency agreements. These practices vary in their content from
area to area. In their most comprehensive form (which are
rare) the local authority surveys a property, prepares a schedule of proposed work and working drawings, administers the
approval of a grant and any mortgage facility, lets a contract
to a building firm and supervises the work.
The implementation of agency agreements has met with mixed
success. In Birmingham, for example, the 'urban renewal
agency' lasted only from January 1975 until mid-1976 when the
new Conservative administration scrapped it. Whilst this was
too short a time to judge fully its potential, it is clear that it
had run into a number of difficulties including sluggish processing by the building finance department, a disparity between
the fees charged and the costs to the local authority, an insufficient volume of demand from owner-occupiers, the high level
of inter-departmental co-operation required and, once again,
the shortage of builders. Birmingham did not use its own DLO
because by law, in the absence of specific enabling legislation,
such organisations can only carry out work for their own local
authority. Watkins and Shutt ascribe the scheme's failure above
all to its dominance by architects who could not escape from
their professional model of providing a 'glossy' design solution
to a technical problem rather than a schedule of works which,
given the supply price of rehabilitation work from the industry,
was both desirable and a feasible financial proposition to the
house-owner.[25]
Yet it would be a mistake to imagine that the sufficient condition to solving the production problem is the presence of an
architect with sound technique and a sensitivity to consumer
requirements. Rod Hackney was such a person and he became
deeply committed to the rehabilitation efforts of owner-occupiers
in Saltley. Rather than have work done to second-rate standards, with the consequential cost of setting them right within
a few years, he would choose to miss items out in order to keep
within the government's allowable cost limits. Moreover, as
many items as possible in his designs were to be left to DIY.
In practice, this usually had to be confined to certain convenient or non-essential jobs like decoration and fencing and
rarely saved a lot of money. In spite of his skill and experience,
owner-occupiers found that whilst they got value for money,

good quality work was very costly and, in spite of the government's grant levels, more than they wished to pay for. The
demand for Hackney's services faltered, the cowboys moved in,
and the quality of work diminished enormously. Rehabilitation
of a high standard that would endure had been priced out.[26]

Returning to the discussion of agency agreements, the best-
known success story is that of Newport District Council where
bipartisan political support has long existed for owner-occupier
rehabilitation. Experience had demonstrated to the council that
the household's management problems were a real obstacle and
this led to the introduction of a heavily subsidised fixed-price
package deal. Teething troubles occurred when the authority
took on too many applicants and also employed some incompetent
builders who used the cheapest materials and subcontractors.
As a result the package deal was limited to households living in
GIAs and HAAs, mainly elderly persons or families on low
incomes. Young argues that the results have been impressive,
although not cheap either for the state or for the house-owners
themselves. After several years' experience the time-lag from
application to contract completion had been reduced to nine
months and a group of builders assembled who appeared to be
assured of a steady flow of work at an agreed rate for the
job.[27]

5 REHABILITATION AND THE STATE

The contents of earlier chapters, as well as this one, leave no
room for doubt that rehabilitation of the owner-occupied stock
of dwellings has constituted an ever more important dimension
of the housing policy of the state since 1949. The measures
employed to implement policy can be grouped into two sets:
those intended to stimulate the purchase by owner-occupier
households of down-market second-hand properties; and those
intended directly to promote rehabilitation itself. The first set
embraces the supply of local authority mortgages for house
purchase, leasehold reform, the option mortgage subsidy and
its associated guarantee scheme, support lending and low-start
mortgages. The second set includes the supply of local authority
mortgages to finance large-scale repair and improvement outlays, grants to owner-occupiers, the creation through the
planning mechanism of general improvement and housing action
areas, and the introduction in the 1969 Housing Act of the
councils' right to operate agency services. All of these matters
have been discussed already, particularly in chapters 3 and
7, so there is no need to go over that ground again. Suffice it
to say that the fundamental conception of policy has been to
influence the willingness and ability of individual households
to purchase rehabilitation outputs. Only the agency agreements
are an exception to this. The DLOs, as I have said, have never
been used for repair and improvement of the privately owned

housing stock.

With so much of the groundwork already covered, the principal objective of this section is to review the development of the area orientation in policy. It was in 1967 that the parliamentary leadership of the Labour Party decided to switch the emphasis of its housing renewal policy from redevelopment to rehabilitation. The origins of this enormously important policy shift are various and have been described at length elsewhere.[28] They include the widespread belief that clearance smashed up long-established community networks of personal relationships which it would take years or even decades to renew; the personal distress and the loss of housing accommodation during the long gestation period from the initiation of clearance to the site's re-inhabitation; the popular discontent with the built form that redevelopment took; and the massive reduction in state expenditure promised by the replacement of public redevelopment by private rehabilitation. It was a White Paper disarmingly entitled *Old Houses into New Homes* that publicly signalled the beginning of this sea change, soon to be followed by the 1969 Housing Act. After the general election of 1970, the Conservative government gave its own blessing to the new direction, in the 1973 White Paper *Better Homes: The Next Priorities*.

The innovation of general improvement areas in the 1969 Act seemed at the time to be the full flowering of an area-orientation in policy that can be traced back at least as far as the early 1950s. Yet, in retrospect, perhaps it is an historicist error, a mistaken teleology, to see the GIA (and later the HAA) as the final goal towards which policy had been 'inevitably progressing' in an incrementalist fashion for the preceding twenty years. Perhaps the innovation was promoted in the civil service and the Cabinet, not because a spatially bounded programme was seen to be genuinely more cost effective but because bureaucrats and politicians understood that the policy redirection required, for ideological purposes, tangible symbols of the new humanism in environmental policy. In a situation where the role of the local state was changing from the concrete development of extensive new urban infrastructures towards that of the mere management and co-ordination of a host of decisions made by individual households, private building firms, financial institutions and exchange professionals, the necessity of projecting achievements that could be clearly perceived and believed to be effective required a focusing of the vision of the population. This focus became the specific area, saved from clearance and transformed environmentally by the combination of state and private initiative.

I would not wish to dispute for one moment that the practice of housing policy requires some geographical specificity. Section two above pointed unambiguously to the necessity for each district council to state at the very least which zones are programmed for clearance and which have a long-term future. But

once this is done, in a more or less sophisticated way, it seems
to me to be totally unproven that the specification of areas of
action, scattered about within the zones of a guaranteed future,
promotes private rehabilitation on a scale for the district as a
whole greater than would have been achieved on the same
budget without such areas. The only exception I concede is
where certain congeries of streets and squares are ripe for
gentrification and where an area plan is a precondition in
promising owner-occuper immigrants an environmental locus
apposite to their social values and their desire to live in a
neighbourhood of a certain class. The crucial weakness of the
area approach, as Duncan and Paris and Blackaby have ably
demonstrated is that a vast amount of the limited staff resources of housing, planning and other departments is channelled
into a very limited number of streets in a district, often to
no real effect.

The widespread welcome given to GIAs in 1969 is easily
explained. For some it was a manifestation of the end of the
bad old dogmas of clearance and all the negative experience
that went with it. For the planners it was attractive because
of their unfortunate predilection for any scheme that can be
mapped, the result of the even more unfortunate dominance of
the discipline of geography in their university and polytechnic
education. For local politicians it offered fat prizes to carry
back to their wards. For officers the GIA could become the
show-piece for visiting luminaries. And - not to be too cynical
- doubtless many many people did and do believe that imitative
housing rehabilitation required the seed capital of environmental improvement to be sown only on selected fields.

A second aspect of the physical orientation of state rehabilitation policy was that it was a house - rather than a household-
directed philosophy. Repair and improvement was not seen as
a measure designed directly to meet the unsatisfied needs of
the population but as a means of preserving the housing stock.
To quote Lord Brooke's view: 'the most important thing of all
is to consider the interests of the houses'. The consumption of
these improvements was not seen as problematic and it followed
that the distributional implications of the new policy phase were
ignored.[29] Two developments in the implementation of the 1969
Act forced serious reconsideration. One of these was the low
take-up of grants particularly in the northern regions of the
country. It was this that led to the introduction in the 1971
Housing Act of the 75 per cent grant in the intermediate and
development areas until 1974. The second was the process of
gentrification in which rehabilitation went along with the displacement of existing tenants by higher income owner-occupiers,
often through the intervention of speculative developers.

The 1974 Housing Act contained a number of provisions to
check these negative distributional effects, including the right
of local authorities to reclaim grants from landlords if they
breached the terms of a 'certificate of availability for letting'

and from owner-occupiers if they resold the property within
five years. (The second of these was rescinded in the 1980
Housing Act.) The 1974 Act also sought to stimulate rehabilitation in areas where housing stress was combined with social
problems. In these housing action areas, which were normally
intended to have a five-year life, the emphasis was to be on
house rather than environmental improvement. As we saw in
section three above, the percentage of eligible costs met from
grants was raised, as were the cost limits themselves.

6 SOME RESULTS

In this section I shall set out some of the most important
information available for assessing the scale of rehabilitation
by owner-occupiers and then go on to look very briefly at the
changing scale of unfitness, amenity deficiency and disrepair
in this tenure in the 1970s. Table 12.2 shows the rate of grant
approval to owner-occupiers in Great Britain in the period
1960-79. No more recent data have been published as a result
of an extraordinary decision within the DoE to terminate this
statistical series. The rate of approvals ran at 54,000-67,000
per annum until the very much improved terms of the 1969
Housing Act brought a spectacular trebling of the flow in the
four years up to 1973. This boom was succeeded by an even
more rapid slump back to around 60,000 per annum by 1976-9.
   The other statistic provided by the table is the proportionate
scale of discretionary grants within the total for all grant
types. From less than one-third in 1969 this rose to 84 per
cent in 1973 and has not since fallen below that proportion.
Another point worth noting is that the data up to 1977 are for
grant *approvals*. The *HPTV* has shown that not all grants
approved are actually paid: the relevant ratio stands at approximately 100 : 80.[30] Information that would be extraordinarily
interesting but is not available is the distribution of grants
among income groups.
   With respect to the impact of the action areas since 1969,
curiously enough the DoE does not publish a table demonstrating the relative importance of grant payments within them
vis-à-vis all grant payments. Nevertheless information that has
been published does permit one to make a fairly accurate estimate of the situation in England at least. For owner-occupiers,
grant payments within GIAs and HAAs in the two years 1975
and 1976 were some 7 per cent of all grants paid in the country.
For the two-year period 1977-8 and 1978-9, the proportion had
risen to about 12 per cent.[31] Some 7 or 12 per cent enormously
overstates the specific effect of the importance of the action
area policy if only because some of these grant payments would
have been made even without area declaration. This confirms,
I think, the view expressed in section five above that the area
concept was an ideological rather than a material policy

innovation in 1969.

Table 12.2 Rehabilitation grants approved for owner-occupiers in Great Britain 1960-79[a]

Year	Number of discretionary grants	Number of intermediate repairs and special grants	Total	Proportion of discretionary grants within total (%)
1960	26,192	40,675	66,867	39
1961	24,670	39,037	63,707	39
1962	19,683	37,544	57,227	34
1963	21,458	43,354	64,812	33
1964	21,544	41,976	63,520	34
1965	17,614	42,668	60,282	29
1966	15,823	38,465	54,288	29
1967	16,659	42,156	58,815	28
1968	16,378	42,745	59,123	28
1969	17,144	39,509	56,653	30
1970	33,551	44,463	78,014	43
1971	49,069	41,070	90,139	54
1972	113,330	41,631	154,961	73
1973	156,807	29,290	186,097	84
1974	110,523	15,822	126,345	87
1975	62,480	8,683	71,163	88
1976	52,622	9,030	61,652	85
1977	51,351	8,214	59,565	86
1978[b]	49,838	7,219	57,057	87
1979	56,276	6,522	62,798	90

Source: *HSGB*; *HCS*.

[a] Grants for conversion are included.

[b] From 1978 the data are for grants paid.

Let us look now at the scale of unfitness, amenity deficiency and disrepair in the owner-occupied housing stock. For England alone house condition surveys in 1971 and 1976 showed that the number of unfit dwellings in home-ownership fell from 318,000 to 263,000 over that five-year period. No one understands precisely why this reduction occurred since it is the net result of at least four different movements: the sale of unfit dwellings to other tenures, the demolition of unfit stock, the making fit through rehabilitation of houses previously unfit, and the decay into unfitness of dwellings previously fit. Of the total owner-occupied stock in 1976 only about 3 per cent was unfit and of this probably more than 95 per cent had been built before 1919. The historical origins of this last statistic are well expressed by the author of the *HPTV*:[32]

The present stock of housing and its physical condition are the products of many years of building, of repair, adaptation and improvement, and of progressive structural deterioration and decay. Before the 1870s there were few effective controls to ensure adequate structural standards of building and adequate sanitation. Some 3 million houses were built between 1800 and 1875, of which about half - 10 per cent of the present housing stock - are still standing. By today's standards many of these houses were unfit in the technical sense at the time they were first built; they were built cheaply and at high density, they are inadequate structurally and they lack many of the basic amenities which are today regarded as essential to reasonable standards of living.

Other houses built before 1914 have become unfit through physical decay, often accelerated by years of inadequate maintenance and neglect. Changes in social structure and in patterns of housing utilisation have placed strains upon the physical fabric of many older houses which they were simply not designed to withstand, and this too has contributed to accelerated decay into unfitness.

Whilst unfitness is a relatively insignificant problem *within* the tenure, unfit owner-occupied property is a very considerable part of the unfitness problem as a whole: in 1976 33 per cent of all unfit dwellings were owner-occupied.[33]

Table 12.3 Amenity deficiency in owner-occupied dwellings in England and Wales in 1971 and 1976[a]

	1971 No.	%	1976 No.	%
Dwellings lacking a fixed bath in bathroom	515,000	6	302,000	3
Dwellings lacking an inside WC	711,000	8	407,000	4
Dwellings lacking at least one of the basic amenities	984,000	11	547,000	5
Households lacking central heating (excluding night storage heaters)[b]	5 million	61	4.5 million	51

Source: *HPTV*, Part I, Tables II.4, II.8; Park III, Table A.9.

[a] The percentages are of deficient dwellings within the total owner-occupied stock.

[b] The second two figures are for 1975.

One of the great success stories in our housing history since the Second World War is the huge reduction in the number of dwellings lacking the five basic amenities. This has been the joint outcome of slum clearance and private rehabilitation. It predominantly affected houses built before 1918 because new houses built for private owners since then almost invariably

have had a bathroom and an inside WC. The progress registered
in the period 1971-6 is set out in Table 12.3 and, as can be
seen, has brought with it a reduction of several hundred thousand in the number of houses deficient in the various amenities.
Something like 80 per cent of this advance is the result of
rehabilitation and most of the rest is the result of demolition.
The fall of half a million in the number of households not enjoying central heating is almost entirely owing to the fact that
in the early 1970s such equipment was being installed in owner-
occupied dwellings at a rate of about 150,000 units per year.[34]

Finally we come to the question of the disrepair of houses in
owner-occupation. Table 12.4 shows that the problem is serious
and highly correlated with the age of property. In 1976 houses
requiring repairs costing at least £250 made up two-thirds of
the pre-First World War stock and well over one-third of interwar property. Intertemporal comparisons are particularly difficult here because no specific index of repairs costs exists.
Nevertheless, as far as we can judge, the incidence of serious
disrepair has been growing. In England in 1971 the number of
owner-occupied dwellings needing repairs of at least £500 'at
1971 prices' was 586,000. Five years later it had grown to
832,000.[35]

*Table 12.4 Proportion of owner-occupied dwellings in England requiring
repairs in three cost ranges by age of house in 1976 (percentages)*

	Under £250	£250-499	£500 or over	Total
Pre-First World War	33	32	35	100
Interwar	62	32	6	100
Post-war	97	3	—	100

Source: HPTV, Part I, Table 11.7.

7 SUMMARY

The chapter began by clarifying the relationship between the
state of obsolescence and the twin but opposing forces of
deterioration and rehabilitation. The willingness of owner-
occupiers to engage in the latter was ascribed primarily to
their wish to maintain or enhance the physical attributes of
their dwelling as an activity centre and second, to secure the
asset value of the house. The first motive is conditional on the
household's commitment to the house and neighbourhood in
which it lives. With both predicates, the physical and the
financial, there may exist powerful interdependencies in household decisions within an area. The ability to rehabilitate is
largely determined, directly or indirectly, by household income
and often is associated with vertical transpossession. For a

number of reasons elderly households, more than one-quarter of all owner-occupiers, may be unwilling or unable effectively to maintain or improve their accommodation.

Rehabilitation is a form of housing production, something that social researchers in this country appear to have overlooked. In quantitative terms, it made up about one-half of recorded housing output in Britain in 1980. The workers who produce this output are composed of those in the formal sector, those who engage in DIY and those in the hidden economy, so that it is impossible to measure the true scale of production. One of the biggest obstacles to successful rehabilitation appears to be the shortage of builders who are reliable, efficient, honest and good craftsmen.

The intervention of the state in encouraging owner-occupier rehabilitation has taken two major dimensions: improving the access, particularly of marginal owner-occupiers, to down-market properties; and direct stimulation through grants and loans. Government grants for improvement and/or repair have been available since 1949 and in 1960-79 alone 1.55 million were approved, although a number of obstacles still exist to their take-up. State intervention on the supply side has been minor and fragmentary, whilst local authority DLOs are proscribed from carrying out work for owner-occupiers. I have suggested that the promotion of area-based private rehabilitation since the 1960s, alongside the withdrawal of resources from public redevelopment, is primarily ideological in its motivation. In the 1970s only some 10 per cent of rehabilitation grants were taken up in GIAs and HAAs. During the same decade, for a variety of reasons, there has been a very large net reduction in the number of owner-occupied properties that are unfit or lacking one or more of the basic amenities but there has also taken place an ominous rise in the number of properties in serious disrepair.

Chapters 4 to 11 of this book were all concerned with different aspects of the effective demand for and supply of houses for owner-occupation. It is now time to look at the exchange process, where demand and supply meet face to face.

13 THE EXCHANGE PROCESS

by *Fred Gray*

1 INTRODUCTION: HOME-OWNERSHIP AND THE EXCHANGE PROCESS

In capitalist societies private property is of crucial significance.
It underpins many ideological structures, and in one way or
another legitimates economic processes such as the production
of commodities for 'the market'. Partly because of this, in
Britain transferring the ownership of a dwelling - the single
most valuable piece of property ever likely to be owned by most
people - is generally viewed as a particularly important, complex and potentially hazardous operation. The threat always
exists that if the process is not carried out correctly both
ownership itself and the various rights associated with it may
be challenged.

   This concern about the process of transferring ownership of
a dwelling from one person to another - the exchange process -
has been fed upon and further developed by exchange professionals and, in particular, estate agents, surveyors and valuers,
and solicitors. Exchange professionals have evolved over many
decades to become almost indispensable agents in the process.
The development and use of a specific language and sets of
values, formalities and procedures all act to mystify and obfus-
cate the exchange process to the extent that individual home-
owners usually believe that ownership cannot adequately be
transferred without their assistance.

   The relationships of exchange professionals to the exchange
process are complex. At the level of people buying or selling
dwellings, however, it is helpful to think in terms of three
distinct parts of the overall process: the search process, the
assessment process, and the legal process. The particular
exchange professionals typically associated with each process
are, respectively, estate agents, surveyors and valuers, and
solicitors.

   At this level estate agents function to bring together buyers
searching for a property and sellers seeking a buyer. The
objectives of surveyors and valuers is to provide structural
surveys and valuation reports for (respectively) potential purchasers and building societies wishing to assess the quality and
value of a dwelling. Finally, solicitors are centrally concerned
in the legal process, carrying out conveyancing work for both
purchasers and sellers, and legally securing a mortgage against
a property. It should be stressed that for the variety of reasons

discussed below, this threefold division of function and professional group is not always so clear cut in practice.

Moreover, the perspective developed in this chapter indicates
that exchange professionals do not merely act as passive facilita-
tors, enabling and smoothing the exchange process. The income
of individual professionals is dependent on maximising both
the number of transactions and the fees from each transaction.
This, combined with a unique position in the housing market,
often has a major effect on both the tenure and home-owners.
At an extreme, exchange professionals may directly intervene
as 'merchant capitalists' by using capital to buy and sell property.[1] More typically, as 'merchant professionals' they shape
both the housing market and exchange process in a variety of
ways. The development of professional bodies and sets of rules
and procedures have generally operated to reduce competition
and increase fees. Exchange professionals often function to
channel purchasers towards particular areas, property and
sources of mortgage finance. Through their contacts with building societies and other financial institutions they may help
determine the flow of funds to particular parts of the housing
market or groups of prospective purchasers. They may also be
involved in tenure changes, for instance by encouraging private
landlords to sell, so increasing owner-occupation in particular
areas.[2]

At a broader level exchange professionals have helped per-
petuate the ideology of home-ownership and have particularly
emphasised the value of their role in the exchange process.
The Royal Institution of Chartered Surveyors (RICS), for
example, in a leaflet on *Buying and Selling a House*, argues
that:[3]

> You must be sure to get the full market value for your
> property and the estate agent knows the state of the market
> and the current value of your property. A reputable estate
> agent obtains the best results in the shortest possible time.
> It is his job to put your property immediately before a wide
> range of possible purchasers and what is more, he is in a
> position to find out whether a would-be purchaser is finan-
> cially able to buy. The avoidance of an estate agents fee
> could possibly be a costly mistake, particularly if, by sell-
> ing privately, you fail to negotiate the best price.

Neither the state nor other housing market institutions have
ever radically intervened in the exchange process to question
fundamentally the expertise or worth of exchange professionals.
Housing institutions including most importantly building societies have, over a long period of time, been closely allied with
the exchange professions. In a mutually supporting and self-
sustaining fashion both have maintained *status quo* structures
and processes in the owner-occupied sector to the benefit of
each other. Rather than urging a cheaper, speedier and more

rational exchange system, the influential BSA has long advo-
cated that all home-owners use a full range of exchange professionals. A 1960s guide to house purchase approved by the
BSA argues, for instance:[4]

> Buying a home is worth a great deal of time, thought and
> trouble. Care at the outset will save many headaches or
> even heartbreaks in the future....Right at the outset,
> when looking for a home, you should have it absolutely
> clear in your mind that you will normally need the advice
> of a solicitor about legal matters and formalities (and) the
> advice of a surveyor about the condition and value of the
> house.

Linkages between exchange professionals and other housing
institutions function to channel business from one to another.
Particularly among smaller building societies, directorships
are often held by exchange professionals themselves.[5] There
are also proven links between estate agents and solicitors and
property companies and builders. For example, Benwell CDP
research[6] into thirty-two property companies in Newcastle's
West End revealed that almost half the ninety-six directors
were exchange professionals, and that significant volumes of
funds were lent on mortgage to the property companies by
building societies.

The other side of this coin is that some building societies,
particularly small and medium-sized ones, rely heavily on
exchange professionals for their funds, and in return pay
professionals a commission (1 per cent is typical). Such funds
usually come in the form of single large sums. However, many
estate agents also act as agencies for building societies, collect-
ing small sums from individual savers. Building societies, in
turn, often give the clients of professionals preferential treatment in mortgage allocation, so allowing them to jump the queue
for mortgages.[7]

Building societies employ surveyors (who are usually local
estate agents) to carry out dwelling valuations. Similarly, most
estate agents have at least informal links with specific firms of
solicitors whom they recommend to both buyers and sellers.
Solicitors themselves may have close relationships with building
societies and other financial institutions such as secondary
banks and may be involved not only in conveyancing but also
in arranging loan finance. These complex webs of functional
relationships appear to work well, particularly in business and
financial terms, for all but home-owners themselves.

The support of the orthodox exchange process by other agents
in the housing market is, then, understandable. However, the
attitudes and activities of the state over the exchange process is less easy to explain. The exchange process in the owner-
occupied tenure is neither particularly beneficial nor efficient
for individual home-owners. It tends to be costly, time-

consuming and restrictive. Similarly, the present process is often detrimental to the overall functioning of the tenure. Who lives where, in what type of housing and under what conditions is partly determined by the exchange process. Consequently, the inegalitarian and inequitable nature of the exchange process becomes solidified in the form of housing market outputs. These outputs pose increasing problems in terms of access to home-ownership; the expansion of the tenure; flexibility and move-ment within the sector; and so on. It is in this context that since the late 1960s governments have sanctioned a series of reports aimed at understanding and questioning the exchange process. In practice, however, reform has tended to be minor and, if occasionally potentially far reaching, quickly neutral-ised and turned to the best interests of the exchange profes-sionals themselves. Indeed, over a long period of time the state has at least conceded, typically passively condoned, and often actively abetted the position and power of the established exchange lobby.

The paradoxical support of the state provided to exchange professionals whose activities pose increasing problems to the tenure appear to arise from a number of factors. At one level, the interests of the state and the exchange lobby *do* coincide in that both wish to expand owner-occupation. Moreover, *were* the state to intervene radically (for instance, to allow local government to provide rival non-profit-making exchange services) this might bite at the very ideology of owner-occupa-tion with its stress on notions such as the worth of the private market, and the value of the freedom and choice allowed to individual home-owners.

At a more direct level, the exchange *status quo* is protected by often very powerful professional bodies (such as the Law Society and the RICS) which have acted as influential pressure groups, usually successfully representing the interests of their members in Parliament, central and local government, and the media. In addition, exchange professionals are well represented in Parliament. Law, for example, has consistently provided one of the largest single occupational backgrounds of Members of Parliament. Many local and county councils have strong exchange profession lobbies.[8] Indeed occupations such as being a solicitor or estate agent are amongst the few to provide the income and allow the time to enter politics with ease. The well-documented cases of corruption involving land and property[9] within local authorities are but one aspect of the informal and formal net-works and contacts continually used to further the interests of exchange professionals. Furthermore, the press and particularly the local press (which derives a sizeable proportion of advertis-ing revenue from estate agents) rarely mounts any opposition to the exchange process as it presently exists. The withdrawal or restriction of property for sale advertisements is one sanc-tion estate agents may employ to influence the press if informal lobbying is unsuccessful.

Despite the generally supportive role played by the state
and housing institutions, it should not be assumed that the
exchange *status quo* remains unchallenged. The very nature
of the process at times creates pressures that do not favour
the professional orthodoxy. For example, because of their different functions, the various groups of exchange professionals
have different opportunities to maximise their income. Indeed,
a conflict of interests may exist between estate agents and
solicitors. Estate agents are able to assume a comprehensive
perspective on the total housing market in which they work. As
we shall see, they have various opportunities to increase the
total number of transactions that take place and to maximise
their income. Solicitors, in contrast, have less opportunity to
intervene directly in the housing market, and are more dependent on maximising the fees they derive from each individual
conveyance. To do this they need to demonstrate their expertise and worth, typically by ensuring that the process is as
long, complex and time-consuming as possible. This activity
may clearly conflict with an estate agent's desire to maximise
the rate and speed of sales.

Another potential difficulty for the exchange professions is
that maximising both the number of transactions and the level
of fees is not always compatible. High transaction costs may
stop some people from moving, and provides an incentive for
home-owners to use cheaper exchange services. For example,
the development of do-it-yourself conveyancing and cut-price
estate agents both threaten the position and income of established exchange professionals, and may be seen as a backlash
against the high level of exchange fees typically endured by
home-owners. Similarly, exchange professionals gain from
escalating house prices since their fees are generally proportionately related to the level of house prices. However, high
house prices may reduce the total number of transactions and
affect the income of exchange professionals. This appears to
have been the case following the house price boom of the early
1970s, for in 1974 solicitors' fees from conveyancing slumped
dramatically.[10]

It is to transaction costs, one of the central issues in the
exchange process, that this chapter now turns.

2   TRANSACTION COSTS

As home-ownership has expanded so too have the number of
individuals and firms involved in the exchange process. Huge
sums of money, in the form of fees for services rendered,
flow from home-owners to exchange professionals. These
amounts have tended to escalate rapidly over time (Table 13.1)
as a result of inflation, the continued expansion of the tenure,
and the general increase in house prices.

Table 13.1 Housing Policy Review estimates of owner-occupier transaction
        costs

Type of transaction cost	Year	
	1967 (£m)	1975 (£m)
Solicitors' fees for conveyancing		
buyers	40	102
sellers	17	51
Solicitors' fees for work on mortgages		
building societies	9	16
others	1	2
Estate agents' commissions	17	73
Fees for building society valuations by surveyors	5	18
Advertising directly by vendors	4	10
Building societies' indemnity policies (single premiums)	3	11
Stamp duty on conveyances	12	45
Land registry fees	3	10
Total transaction costs	111	338

Source: HPTV, Part I, Table C.4, p. 230.

By far the single most important reason for ownership of a
dwelling to be transferred is household movement. This accounts
for about nineteen out of every twenty conveyancing transactions by solicitors.[11] Every move by an owner-occupier from
one dwelling to another involves two sets of ownership transfers, and for both dwellings a full set of exchange professionals will hope to become involved. However, exchange professionals may also be involved in other circumstances. On
the death of a male married home-owner a solicitor is generally
involved in transferring ownership to the wife. Usually the
sale of council houses to sitting tenants also involves solicitors
and, in some situations, estate agents. For example, in 1981
one estate agent offering a nationwide 'comprehensive service'
was reported to be charging council tenants £160 for seemingly
dubious assistance in buying their home.[12]

Similarly, exchange professionals are typically used if an
existing occupier of a property held on leasehold purchases
the freehold of his or her home. The work by Green[13] and
Stewart[14] for Birmingham CDP shows that solicitors, surveyors
and estate agents (many of whom own intermediary interests
as head or under leaseholders themselves) may all make considerable sums in this situation. Sometimes the charges for
professional services more than doubles the cost of the total
transaction. In the mid-1970s residents buying their freeholds
in Saltley, Birmingham paid fees to an average of four solicitors

and three valuers.

The most widely quoted estimate of the transaction costs borne by owner-occupiers are those of the *Housing Policy Review*[15] (Table 13.1). The *Review* estimates suggest that in 1975-6 the exchange process in the UK provided solicitors with a gross income of £170 million, estate agents £73 million, and surveyors £18 million. The state also gained significant financial returns from the process: £55 million in the form of stamp duty and land registry fees. These figures indicate that the total transaction costs amounted to £338 million; almost 10 per cent of the total current expenditure of £3,640 million by home-owners on items such as the payment of mortgage interest, principal repayments and expenditure on repairs, maintenance and decoration.[16]

There are, however, good reasons for arguing that the figures provided in the *Housing Policy Review*, although generally accepted, are in fact grossly inaccurate underestimates of the transaction costs experienced by home-owners. The *Review* does not provide detailed information on how the figures were compiled or on their accuracy. Indeed, there are significant gaps in the data. For example, no estimate is provided of the revenue obtained by the state through the imposition of value added tax on the various transactions involved in the exchange process. Similarly, information is not provided about the sums paid by the three in ten buyers who commission independent structural surveys.[17]

More significantly, the figures for estate agents' commission seems likely to be hugely inaccurate for a number of reasons. The £17 million for 1967 is hardly believable if the Monopolies Commission research is accepted.[18] This indicated that estate agents' fees for domestic property transactions totalled £50 million two years earlier in 1965. Assuming the latter figure to be more realistic, and the *Housing Policy Review* underestimate was of a similar proportion in 1975, the figure of £73 million should be increased to about £215 million. There is other support for this view. The 1979 Price Commission report on estate agents indicates that in 1978 a *conservative* estimate of the average income from domestic property sales per estate agents office was £25,000.[19] The number of estate agents offices in Britain is at least 11,500 and perhaps in excess of 20,000 (see section three below). This suggests a gross income from domestic property sales for estate agents of between £287 million to in excess of £500 million. Even the lower estimate is four times the *Housing Policy Review* figure.[20]

A similar gross underestimate for solicitors' fees also exists in Table 13.1. Following detailed research, the Benson Committee[21] reported that the gross fees earned by solicitors firms in England and Wales for conveyancing in 1975-6 was £300 million. This figure greatly exceeds the *Housing Policy Review* estimate for the UK as a whole. When Scotland is taken into account the aggregate of solicitors' fees from conveyancing in 1975-6 was probably more than double the Table 13.1 estimate of £170 million.

To summarise the argument, even ignoring VAT or fees arising from independent surveys of dwellings, the total of owner-occupied transaction costs in the UK in 1975 varied from between £610 million to in excess of £900 million. Both amounts constitute a very significant proportion of the total current expenditure of home-owners. The upper estimate rivals the £1,015 million estimated to have been spent by owner-occupiers on repairs, maintenance and decoration in 1975-6, and is in excess of the regular payments of mortgage principal (of £672 million) made by home-owners. It is also greater than the tax relief on mortgage interest of £856 million granted to households in the tenure.

Table 13.2 Estimated average transaction costs for the sale of a £23,000 house and the purchase of a £28,000 house in 1979

Type of transaction cost	£
Purchase of £28,000 house	
Solicitors' fees (including building society work)	245
Building society valuation fee	44
Survey	83
Land registry fee	70
Stamp duty	420
VAT	31
Total cost	893
Sale of £23,000 house	
Solicitors' fees	176
Estate agents' commission	463
VAT	51
Total cost	690

Source: Consumers' Association, 'Moving home', *Which?*, May, 1979, pp. 305-13. Table from p. 306.

Another way of looking at transaction costs is in terms of the average costs experienced by home-owners moving from one dwelling to another. The Consumers' Association 1979 survey[22] (Table 13.2) provides information about a typical transaction involving a selling buyer moving from a dwelling sold for £23,000 to another purchased for £28,000. From both sale and purchase solicitors obtained 27 per cent of the total charges, estate agents 29 per cent, and surveyors 8 per cent. The state itself extracted 36 per cent of transaction costs in the form of VAT, stamp duty and land registry fees. Since many home-owners wishing to move spend money on transactions that turn out to be abortive,[23] the figure of £65 estimated for failed transactions should also be added. Transaction costs then total £1,648, or 7 per cent of the house price.

Such sums may clearly be a hindrance to residential mobility in the tenure. Those who do move will often be forced to borrow money or to eat into savings or whatever price gains they make on the sale of their existing home. The level of transaction costs is a particularly heavy burden for those on low incomes and for the significant proportion who do not derive net worth in selling their existing dwelling. For example, since in the late 1970s over a third of home-owners had incomes of less than £3,000 per year, high transaction costs may actually prohibit the movement of substantial numbers of owner-occupiers. Moreover, the likely transaction costs for potential first-time buyers may be the final straw in excluding those on low incomes from entering the tenure.

The exchange process experiences of home-owners is in direct contrast to the situation in the public sector. Here, not only because ownership remains the same whoever occupies a dwelling but also because local authorities are more concerned to minimize the costs and time involved in exchange rather than extract a profit, the exchange process is simpler, quicker and significantly cheaper.[24]

Furthermore, individual council tenants who move within the tenure do not bear the brunt of exchange costs themselves. Those least able to afford the costs incurred in exchange are not barred from joining in the process. Perhaps the best example of the far greater efficiency of state housing in this respect is when tenants agree to exchange or swop the dwellings they occupy. Such an event is almost unheard of in the owner-occupied sector, yet happens frequently in local authority housing with no greater costs than those incurred in physically moving between houses.

A relatively similar argument may be made about the differences in the exchange process in the owner-occupied as opposed to the private rented sector. Green argues in discussing the move away from private renting to owner-occupation in Saltley that:[25]

> Solicitors, estate agents, surveyors and mortgage brokers only do well out of property transactions. Yet tenants came and went without any change in ownership....Owner-occupation changed all this. Not only does property change hands more frequently, but in smaller parcels so that the ratio of exchange value to professional services decreases. And additionally, within Saltley, the new tenure generates additional services out of the separation of building from land ownership....Clearly, owner-occupation directly increases the volume of property transactions.

Having discussed some general features of the exchange process and the issue of transaction costs, the remainder of this chapter is devoted to examining in turn estate agents, sur-

veyors and valuers, and solicitors, and their role in the management of the exchange process and the structuring of the
housing market.

3 ESTATE AGENTS AND THE SEARCH PROCESS

Estate agency in its present form is very much a phenomenon
linked to the expansion of owner-occupation. However, the
initial emergence of estate agency can be traced back to the
nineteenth century. A publication from the Chartered Auctioneers' and Estate Agents' Institute explains its development
as follows:[26]

> Real estate practice is one of a number of professions that
> have grown out of England's industrial development; and
> it is in the upheaval of the nineteenth century, with its
> redistribution of ownership and its multiplication of pro-
> blems affecting property, that can be traced the evolution
> of the vocation of auctioneer and estate agent.
> The increasing responsibilities attaching to real estate
> practice by degrees reached a stage when they required
> the undivided efforts of men prepared to undertake them,
> and when they could no longer be discharged by lawyers,
> whose purely legal work was making more and more insis-
> tent demands upon their attention....It followed of neces-
> sity that the responsibility for the practical as distinguished
> from the legal business attaching to real estate gradually
> shifted from lawyer to layman.

Nonetheless, the fact that in Scotland estate agency is still
often provided by solicitors suggests that in England and
Wales estate agents were in a better position to separate out
the two roles. There appear to be at least two reasons for
this difference. One is simply that the more advanced development of owner-occupation in England and Wales has allowed
estate agency to prosper more easily.[27] The other reason concerns fundamental differences in the laws of Scotland and
England and Wales.[28]

> In England and Wales an offer to purchase a property is
> usually made 'subject to contract'. This means that neither
> the offer nor its acceptance is legally binding ... until
> formal contracts have been prepared and exchanged. In
> Scotland, however, if a formal offer to purchase is made
> in writing and is formally and unconditionally accepted in
> writing, a contract, legally binding on both parties, exists
> from the date of acceptance. Solicitors may sign an offer
> or acceptance on behalf of their clients.

Estate agents clearly have much more opportunity to intervene in the exchange process in England and Wales since legal formalities are introduced at a much later stage. In contrast, the Scottish system allows solicitors to maintain a more complete monopoly over the exchange process.

Access to estate agency has always been very open. Indeed, until the implementation of the Estate Agents Act of 1979 anyone could set up as an estate agent without previous experience, qualification or regulation. This, when combined with the opportunity to obtain a considerable income and the very small amount of capital necessary to start an estate agency, has undoubtedly made the occupation one of the most attractive and accessible of all in the housing market. By the late 1970s about one-third of agencies had existed for no more than ten years, and one in five for no more than four years.[29]

For a long period estate agents have been centrally involved in the growth of owner-occupation. This involvement has not only been in terms of acting as intermediaries bringing seller and buyer together with the appropriate financial and legal organisations (activities that are central to the work of all estate agents) but also in propounding the very ideology of owner-occupation and, for instance, suburbanisation. One historical illustration is the following extract from an estate agent's description extolling the virtues of living (and buying a house) in Crawley in 1920:[30]

> Crawley as it appears today is not the sudden creation of the jerry-builders' magical wand, but a slow and leisurely growth of more than half-a-century.
>
> Crawley today is no longer a village but the abode of numbers of gentlemen of leisure and of others whose avocations are in the City, and who find themselves the better for residing in this bracing spot, the air of which, sweeping over the South Downs, is impregnated with the ozone of Brighton's sea.

In a similar vein is literature of the same period from an estate agent attempting to attract people to buy homes planned for a new estate.[31]

> Every house is to have a different elevation or finish to give a pleasant variation in keeping with the Estate, every care being taken to preserve the natural beauties; so there will be no fear of Balham or Tooting being planted in this sylvan spot.
>
> As to terms - well, don't worry! They are as flexible as one could wish, for we never turn away a friend. Every client is a friend, and we want YOU to join our happy circle on this wonderful Estate of ours.
>
> The property is freehold, there is no title or land taxes payable, no architects fees, surveyors fees, or any of

those annoying extras which are usually associated with
house purchase; in fact, you can purchase your house
through us with the minimum of trouble.

It is particularly difficult to estimate accurately the number of
estate agents in Britain today. Two official reports have suggested figures of about 10,000 separate estate agents offices
in 1968[32] and 11,500 in 1979.[33] In contrast Williams[34] quotes the
estimate provided by the *Estate Agents Directory* of 24,000
estate agencies in 1974-5. The problem can also be approached
by looking at the situation in particular places. For example,
in 1981 there were fifty-eight estate agents offices located in
Brighton, a town with 28,000 owner-occupied dwellings. On
average each office in Brighton survives on the income derived
from whatever sales occur amongst less than 500 dwellings. If
the same figure is generally applicable, the 10 million owner-
occupied dwellings in England and Wales in 1976 would support
over 20,000 separate estate agents offices.

Estate agents nowadays handle about 70 per cent of domestic
property sales in England and Wales.[35] However the use of
estate agents varies from area to area, and according to the
characteristics of property and household involved. For example, the Price Commission reported that the percentage of
purchasers buying via estate agents varied from 49 per cent
in the Midlands and Wales to 87 per cent in London.[36] Similarly,
64 per cent of vendors sold through agents in the north of
England compared with 79 per cent in the south. Dwellings with
higher prices are more likely to be sold by estate agents than
those with below average prices.[37] In addition, households in
non-manual socioeconomic groups with above average incomes
and relatively young heads are likely to make greater use of
estate agents than households with the reverse of these characteristics.[38]

In the late 1970s an average of 60 per cent of the income of
all estate agents was in the form of fees charged for house
sales.[39] Estate agents are concerned to maximise the number of
selling and buying home-owners using their services, and also
the level of fees extracted through the exchange process. These
two guiding principles – attracting clients and maximising fees –
provide the keys to understanding the present structure and
practices of estate agency and its impact on the housing market
in Britain.

Estate agents often develop particular strategies to attempt
to maximise their business. In particular circumstances these
strategies may help structure the housing market in ways
that lead to fundamental change in specific places. A case in
point is gentrification.[40] The *London Property Letter*, privately
circulated to estate agents and property interests, provides
ample illustrations of how in the early 1970s London agents
viewed gentrification as a means of increasing both house prices
and the number of transactions in an area, both to estate

agents' own financial benefit. For example, in February 1970
Barnsbury was recommended as 'a chicken ripe for plucking,
thanks mainly to Islington Borough Council's environmental
improvement plans for the area'.[41] Similarly, 'properly done,
conversions are the next best thing to counter-feiting for
making money'.[42]

Williams, in his research into Islington,[43] argues that estate
agents aided gentrification through their financial links with
landlords, who were encouraged to sell to reap the gains from
disposing of their capital asset.[44] Estate agents also showed the
representatives of building societies around houses and neighbourhoods in order to demonstrate the potential for mortgage
lending. In addition, in stepping outside their roles as merchant
professionals to act as merchant capitalists, some estate agents
were involved in property companies that participated in buying,
converting and improving homes for sale to higher-income
households.

Green[45] provides a somewhat different illustration of the activities of estate agents, this time in acting as agents for a major
change of housing tenure in Saltley, Birmingham. He argues
that estate agents shaped the market, acting both as agents
for the seller and brokers for the buyer. Because of the reluc-
tance of building societies and local authorities to lend mortgage
funds, estate agents were able to 'orchestrate buyer and finan-
cier' by introducing clients to other financial institutions, such
as secondary banks and finance houses, prepared to lend sufficient funds for house purchase. Such arrangements disadvantaged buyers in a number of respects. Interest rates were high,
and the general conditions of loans severe. Estate agents themselves obtained commissions of between £50 and £100 from
buyers, either directly or indirectly, for arranging the mortgage.

The preceding examples illustrate the sometimes fundamental
influence of estate agents on the structure and character of
the housing market itself. More generally estate agents have
considerable power to regulate the exchange process in a variety
of ways. In order to hasten a particular sale, they may introduce buyers to other exchange professionals such as solicitors
and surveyors, or to mortgage-lending institutions. The Price
Commission research indicates that estate agents introduced
13 per cent of buyers to solicitors, 10 per cent to surveyors,
and 12 per cent to mortgage-lending agencies.[46] In lubricating
other aspects of the exchange process, estate agents may
receive some financial reward in the form of commissions for
introductions to other firms.

Attracting clients and maximising fees can also be aided by
agents specialising in a relatively small geographical area or on
one type of property. Similarly, estate agents may attempt to
match buyers to particular areas and sorts of property and,
by implication, exclude some potential purchasers from certain
sorts of dwelling or location. Providing partial, inaccurate or

biased information to potential buyers are typical means of
managing demand for property. The most extreme and well
documented example of such activities are the actions and behaviour of estate agents towards black people. In her 1960s study
Burney quotes estate agents as saying

> ... it is supposed to be part of the skill of the business to
> know what sort of property appeals to that sort of person.[47]

> I would do my best to head off coloured buyers from a good
> suburban area or a new estate.[48]

> In fact it would be my duty to do so in the interests of the
> community and for the sake of the people who have bought
> houses in good faith.[49]

Estate agents do not simply assume the values and prejudices
held by white house vendors. For example, in his Bristol study
Hatch notes that while agents generally agreed that the 'obligation to vendor' ethic was of paramount importance in their
operation, of those

> who received a relatively 'low' level of discriminatory instruc-
> tions from vendors, 23% nevertheless admitted that they dis-
> criminate on a racial basis. Similarly, 45% of those receiving
> a 'high' number of these instructions did not discriminate.[50]

In practice the obligation to vendor appears less important than
the other beliefs and assumptions, including the desire to
attract clients and maximise fees, that individual agents hold.
    Since the 1968 Race Relations Act the available evidence indi-
cates that the level of racial discrimination in house purchase
has decreased to a considerable extent, particularly in its
most blatant and explicit forms.[51] However, it still occurs in
many cases. Smith reports a series of house purchase tests
carried out in the early 1970s, where 12 per cent of Asian and
West Indian potential purchasers were offered definitely inferior
dwellings, and 5 per cent a different 'but not obviously inferior
range'.[52] In 1980 the Commission for Racial Equality[53] provided
a detailed report on the extensive, long-standing and explicitly
planned racial discrimination by a single firm of London estate
agents.
    Although invariably it will be less extreme and less explicit
than for black people, when the opportunity arises (and is
thought to be in the general interest of the business) estate
agents may also attempt to manage the demand from white clients.
This may be by selecting and fitting prospective purchasers
to particular areas and types of property. As a result estate
agents exert a sometimes powerful force on access to housing,
although in general it is likely that they act to reinforce existing socio-spatial patterns. Williams, for example, argues that

in order to protect their business many estate agents believe
that 'the safest response is to keep like with like and to deter
persons from moving to areas occupied by persons "unlike"
themselves'.[54]

Turning to the central issue of fees, estate agents are typically paid by the vendor of a property, usually on a 'no sale,
no commission' basis. There are, however, some major exceptions to this generalisation. For instance, if a vendor gives
an agent 'sole selling rights', he must pay the agents' fees
and expenses even if the dwelling is sold by the vendor himself.
About one in five sales in the UK is on this basis.[55] Even more
stringent conditions sometimes exist. Some agents use a clause
in their business terms whereby commission is payable merely
on the introduction of a person who is 'ready, willing and able'
to purchase, even if completion of the transaction does not,
in fact, take place.[56] Similarly, more than one in ten buyers
(as opposed to vendors) are charged fees by the agents they
use, although the actual reason for the charge is rarely known
by the buyer.[57]

Over 95 per cent of estate agents charge fees as a proportion
of the selling price of a dwelling.[58] This has the obvious advantage that as house prices escalate so too does the income of
estate agents. Estate agents may have some impact on house
prices, at least in the short term.[59] Indeed, in 70 per cent of
transactions estate agents suggest the asking price of a property, sometimes in consultation with the vendor, more often
independently.[60] Moreover, for a long period of time established
estate agents have formed themselves into local or national
associations, and have tended to utilise standard rates of fees,
sometimes formally set out, on other occasions informally accepted.[61]

Such activities clearly operate in the best interests of groups
of estate agents by tending to maximise the commission they
receive, but against the interests of home-owners. The practice
was the subject of a Monopolies Commission investigation in the
late 1960s, which found that 'in charging fees or commission
at standard rates estate agents are so conducting their affairs
as to restrict competition'.[62] Following the report of the Commission, the government imposed an Order designed to stop
national bodies laying down standard charges. Despite this,
although there are sometimes substantial variations in fees
nationally,[63] the majority of estate agents still charge very
similar fees within local markets. This has the consequence of
increasing the number of separate estate agents offices.

> With all firms charging at standard rates there is no price
> incentive for clients to go to the firm with lowest costs;
> consequently all offices tend to have an equal chance of
> attracting clients and a firm may attract a larger share of
> the business with two small offices than one large office.
> As in the sale of goods, if price competition is prevented,

outlets tend to be more numerous.[64]

The management of the exchange process is, however, fraught
with potential difficulties. As we have seen, a significant percentage of home-owners through choice or lack of any alternative do not use estate agents. Clearly, a general acceptance
amongst owner-occupiers that estate agents were not necessary
intermediaries in buying and selling dwellings would quickly
destroy the profession. Similarly, other housing institutions
or the state could, in theory, radically intervene to demystify
the role of estate agents, and provide non-profit-making property exchanges. However, at present the very attractiveness
and openness of estate agency holds out perhaps the greatest
threat to the continuation of the profession in its present form.
In recent years there has been a proliferation of firms charging
low standard fees for registration (rather than sale) of property,
and utilising computer matching techniques and various other
recently developed sales methods such as the use of video-
tapes of vendors' properties.[65] For example, in 1981 one firm
with nine branches across England and Wales levied a £60
registration fee and charged no commission on the sale of a
property. Their publicity stressed they provide 'The real
alternative to estate agents, and their fees.'
   Against such attacks on their position, established estate
agents respond in a number of ways. In general they attempt
to reassert the worth of their present function and role in the
exchange process. Of particular importance in the process are
national professional bodies and local associations aimed at
safeguarding and enhancing the general interests of estate
agents. The three largest organisations are the Royal Institution of Chartered Surveyors (RICS), The Incorporated Society
of Valuers and Auctioneers (ISVA) and The National Association
of Estate Agents (NAEA). Numerous smaller bodies exist, such
as the Corporation of Estate Agents (CEA), the Rating and
Valuation Association, and the Institute of Auctioneers and
Appraisers in Scotland. The conditions of entry into these
bodies vary greatly. The RICS and ISVA both require members
to have practical experience and to have passed a prescribed
examination. In contrast, practical experience is the only
requirement for membership of the NAEA. Agents can become
'professional members' of the NAEA by completing a course of
study, although there is no requirement to pass examinations
to gain this status.
   Some bodies attempt to demonstrate to home-owners the professionalism of their members. For example the RICS tell vendors:[66]

   It is essential to employ a properly qualified agent. A
   member of the Royal Institution of Chartered Surveyors
   who will have the letters FRICS or ARICS after his name
   has been professionally trained and his first class advice

and top business ability will be based on sound knowledge. He also has to observe a code of professional conduct which requires from him high standards of ethics and service. In addition, he is covered by an indemnity scheme which provides cover against loss of deposits due to fraud, dishonesty or misappropriation.

Despite such statements, the sanctions available to national or local associations are not particularly powerful. At worst, an individual agent may be excluded from membership. None of the organisations publicise the extent of unprofessional conduct by their members, the steps taken to counter it, or the effectiveness of the sanctions that exist.

In essence, both local and national organisations function to foster the interests of estate agents themselves, invariably through sets of rules encouraging mutual backscratching of members. In its rather reserved fashion, the Price Commission report argues that in some respects 'these rules of conduct have an adverse effect on competition between estate agents'.[67] For example, rules and codes of conduct of local and national organisations cover such items as 'touting' (contacting home-owners trying to sell privately), 'canvassing' (blanket coverage of home-owners in a particular area), and 'putting' (advertising themselves as 'the leading property seller' and so on).[68] The following are illustrations of the national and local rules that have an effect on competition between agents:[69]

No advertisements about the achievement or success of a firm.

Restrictions on the number, size and appearance of 'for sale' boards.

No soliciting by personal call or telephone.

No non-member of the profession to share in remuneration.

Having regard to the relevant scale of charges and to charge fairly and in consonance with the reputation of the profession.

No commission to be unfair to other members.

Only combined advertisements of members wishing to participate may be inserted in official town guides; publishers shall agree not to permit the inclusion of the advertisements of non-members without the approval of the chairman.

No seeking of instructions by circulars.

No co-operation with any agent in the district who is not a
member.

From the evidence provided above, it is apparent, that established estate agents have so far successfully repulsed fundamental reform of their work and the exchange process. Since
1888 there have been repeated private members' attempts in
Parliament to introduce legislation to control estate agency,
typically either through compulsory registration or by constraints on the practice of the work. These attempts have all
been unsuccessful.[70] However, during the 1970s the government
itself introduced some minor reforms. The restrictions on imposing standard fees for commission have already been described.
The general continuation of standardised fees since then illustrates both the weakness of the government involvement and
the strength of the estate agency lobby and practice nationally.
Some broader based legislation also has at least potential rele-
vancy to estate agents. The 1968 Race Relations Act is one
example. The Restrictive Trade Practices Act of 1976 is another,
although to date the Act does not appear to have had any
significant impact on the practice of estate agency either locally
or nationally.

The most explicit and broad legislative control so far was
contained in the Estate Agents Act of 1979. The Bill received
Royal Assent as one of the last Acts of the Labour government
that left office in 1979. The Act is, in fact, limited and restrictive in scope. Rather than fundamentally altering the practice
of estate agency, it aims to protect home-owners in their involvement with agents; protection is provided for clients' deposits;
the Director General of Fair Trading is enabled to warn or
prohibit 'unfit' persons from working as estate agents. The
Act also attempts to make the dealings of estate agents with
their clients more open, for example by requiring agents to
give vendors details of the basis of their charges.

Although on the statute book, the Act was not implemented
during the first two and a half years of office of the Conservative government elected in 1979. In the autumn of 1981, the
Secretary of State for Trade announced that commencement
orders for certain Sections of the Act would be made the following spring. Two Sections (16 and 22) were not included in
this announcement. These two Sections require that estate
agents insure against failing to account for clients' deposits,
and, reach a 'minimum standard of competence'. The two exclu-
sions mean that the impact of the Act even as a measure of
consumer protection against 'rogue' estate agents will be
weakened. Interestingly, the RICS was particularly unhappy
that the measure to ensure standards of competence was
excluded.[71] This Section of the Act would have allowed the RICS
and other organisations greater power and influence, and would
perhaps have ultimately welded estate agents into a stronger
and more unitary professional group able to exclude deviant

practitioners.

Given that the raison d'être of professional organisations is to maintain the interests of members who conform to mainstream assumptions and practices, policies increasing the power and influence of professional bodies will not result in fundamental reform of the exchange process. Seen in this light, the Estate Agents Act - whether fully or partially implemented - will help maintain, indeed enhance, the professional *status quo*.

4   SURVEYORS, VALUERS AND THE ASSESSMENT PROCESS

In the exchange process both surveying and valuing are activities carried out by professionals (typically the same individuals) to assess the quality and worth of dwellings. In essence both activities require a similar range of expertise and knowledge, although professionals in the field make every effort to distinguish the two. Indeed conceptually it *is* possible to distinguish between surveying - examining and assessing the physical structure and condition of a dwelling - and valuing, which takes the process a step further by placing a value on a dwelling assessed according to both the quality of the building and the environment in which it stands.

The attempt by surveyors and valuers in the domestic property field to make a clear contrast between the two activities is closely related to the two sets of possible clients that such professional services are aimed at. One group of clients are potential purchasers of dwellings who may wish to have the structure and condition of a building assessed, and consequently commission independent structural surveys. The second set are building societies, which are legally required to have a valuation carried out on a dwelling to ensure it represents 'adequate security' for a mortgage.

The emergence of surveying in its present form is, like estate agency, very much linked to the growth of modern capitalism and increased importance of private property in Britain.

> With the development of an industrial society the acquisition of land for canals, roads and railways created fresh needs and opportunities for exercise of surveyors' skills. At the same time the growth of a market in property led surveyors to diversify their activities to include services in connection with buying, selling and letting property of all kinds.[72]

No accurate estimate of the number of surveyors involved in the exchange process is available. Most surveyors are engaged in a number of different forms of surveying and a series of related activities (for example, estate agency, commercial property work and auctioneering). However, a majority of the

18,000 chartered surveyors in private practice in the late
1970s derived some of their income from surveying and valuing
domestic property.[73] The numbers of surveyors working in
this area has rapidly escalated with the growth of owner-
occupation,[74] although firms tend to remain small, 'the majority
having one to five people engaged in business'.[75]

At least as it pertains to the exchange process, surveying
is closely related to estate agency in a number of ways. As
with estate agency, neither statutory registration nor specialist
qualification is required. Anyone may work as and call himself
or herself a surveyor.[76] Most surveyors engaged in the
exchange process are also estate agents. Surveying and valuation tends to be a significant, although minor, source of income
for estate agents: in 1978 it provided an average of 12 per cent
of the total income of agents.[77] In a similar fashion to estate
agency, regulation of surveying has largely been undertaken
by those working in the field, rather than by the state.

Estate agency and surveying tend to share the same professional bodies. This is particularly true of the RICS, which
serves an especially important function for surveyors. As one
illustration, it is the major body involved in regulating fees for
surveyors' services.[78] The RICS, along with the ISVA, negotiate
the scale of fees for building society valuations with the BSA.
The fees charged are a proportion of the value of the property.
In contrast to such *ad valorem* scales, the RICS recommends
that the fees for structural surveys should be 'by arrangement
according to the circumstances'.

Of the two sets of clients, building societies constitute the
most steady and sure demand. Since the 1962 Building Societies
Act, societies have been required to obtain valuation reports
in order to assess the adequacy of the security for the mortgage. Societies base the amount loaned on the valuer's assessment of the property's value, rather than the price agreed
between vendor and purchaser. Most valuations (about 85 per
cent) are carried out by surveyors in private practice who,
it is argued by building societies, have intimate knowledge of
local housing markets.[79]

Building societies invariably accept their valuer's assessment
in deciding whether to offer a mortgage and, if so, the amount
and conditions attached to it (for example, whether specific
repair work has to be undertaken). A valuation is essentially
an assessment of the demand for a dwelling based not only on
the quality of a specific building, but also the present and
presumed future 'market' for a dwelling of that type in the
particular area. Such activity has a clear subjective element,
and is often important in helping to shape the structure of
local housing markets and the nature of housing opportunities
available to people. Its potentially contentious and contro-
versial nature is a major reason for building societies' reluc-
tance to disclose valuations to mortgage applicants.[80]

Lambert[81] has provided the most comprehensive discussion of

the work of surveyors in building society valuations, specifically in the older areas of Birmingham. Local building society
managers appear heavily dependent on valuers in deciding
which areas and property are suitable for their funds. Dwellings in the older areas of Birmingham were seen to be poor
risks because of both limited demand and the uncertainties
created by local authority housing policies. Surveyors understood and shared building societies' often implicit assumptions
about property values, future security and sound 'investment'
practice, and hence also the range of dwellings and areas
acceptable to societies. To a large degree both tend to hold
'conservative and cautious values' about the housing market:
'...surveyors are taught to fear the worst and assume that
unless there are absolutely no signs to the contrary values
and house prices *may* not be sustained'.[82] Valuations consequently reflect existing lending situations and practices.

Seen in this light, surveyors are not passive actors but have
a central if not an independent role affecting and structuring
housing demand, and the housing market itself – for instance
on property values and house prices. In the case of inner-city
housing and red-lining they '...by and large have a sustaining
effect on preventing the expansion of the market for older
housing'[83] financed by building societies. In such situations
surveyors may simply change hats to become estate agents,
manipulating the exchange process further by encouraging
those households forced to purchase in the inner city to use
highly disadvantageous sources of alternative finance.

The confidentiality of building society valuations to the
society concerned not only operates in the best interests of
societies but also in favour of surveyors and valuers. It
encourages potential purchasers to commission independent
(and more expensive) structural surveys. In addition, particularly in Scotland[84] and also to a lesser extent elsewhere in
Britain, potential purchasers often have to pay for multiple
building society valuations if a proposed transaction fails. In
these circumstances the same dwelling may be surveyed several
times, and on each occasion a surveyor receives a fee.

As with all aspects of the exchange process, surveyors'
professional organisations have sought to propagate amongst
home-owners a belief in the importance and value of the services offered. For example, in a leaflet, *Purchaser Beware*,
the RICS argues the case for independent structural surveys:[85]

Homes are expensive....You simply cannot afford to make
mistakes. It is only sensible therefore to find out all you
can beforehand about the property you intend to buy....
The only safe way to find out about the structural condition is to have a structural survey carried out by an expert.
With the many other expenses involved you may be tempted
to cut corners and save on this item but it would be false
economy and in any case don't think of a structural survey

as an extra expense: it could save you money.

However, surveyors and valuers have not been particularly successful in managing the demand for structural surveys from potential purchasers. Most people see this as one of the least essential and most avoidable elements in the exchange process, it being pointless to pay even more fees given the other already burdensome transaction costs. Moreover, purchasers appear to accept that the property is bound to be secure if a building society accepts it as adequate security. This is despite publicity from both building societies and surveyors and valuers suggesting the limited nature of building society valuations:[86]

> The sole purpose of the building society's inspection is to satisfy the society that the property you propose to mort-gage to them is a good security for the loan and that, if you fail to keep up your payments, they will be able to recover their money by selling the property; the building society's surveyor is not required to make a structural survey and his report is confidential to the society.

This argument clearly does not hold water. A building society valuation showing that a property was 'good security' followed by an independent survey revealing that the 'property is unsound' is both extremely unlikely and would also invalidate the building society valuation process.

The value of independent surveys can also be attacked because in reality there is no certainty that either survey or valuation would uncover all defects. Despite stressing the expertise of the professional (the surveyor '...can see and understand the sometimes minute signs and clues to major struc-tural defects which would be overlooked by the untrained') the RICS admits to potential inadequacies. For example, 'Do remem-ber, however, that your surveyor cannot take the house to pieces and look at every single part'. Indeed, a clause is usually inserted into a survey report to cover the surveyor from such eventualities:[87]

> We have not inspected woodwork or other parts of the structure which are covered, unexposed or inaccessible and we are therefore unable to report that such parts of the property are free of rot, beetle or other defects.

The dissatisfaction of potential purchasers with the work of surveyors and valuers in the domestic property field appears widespread. Less than 30 per cent of purchasers commission independent surveys, indicating the failure of the profession to demonstrate its worth. Moreover, there is immense dis-satisfaction amongst home-owners about multiple building society valuations and the confidentiality of valuation reports.[88]

Partly because of the failure of the profession to ensure

demand from potential purchasers for its services, but also because of increased competition amongst building societies and adverse criticism from the Royal Commission on Legal Services in Scotland, cracks have appeared in the wall of traditional surveying and valuation practice. In 1980 the Abbey National building society announced that it would allow mortgage applicants to see, for an extra fee, some details of the society's valuation report. Some other societies also subsequently moved away from the non-disclosure practice, although contentious comments from the valuer are typically excluded from the report given to the mortgage applicant. In 1981 the RICS also introduced a cheaper alternative to the structural survey 'designed to give home-buyers an accurate idea of the condition of the property and what it is worth'.[89]

This response from building societies and the professional organisations to increasing criticism may head off more fundamental reforms. One alternative (already common in the United States[90]) that would strike at traditional practices is for a single survey and valuation report on each dwelling for sale to be made available to all prospective purchasers and the building societies they approach.

5 SOLICITORS AND CONVEYANCING

Solicitors, like all exchange professionals, have a variety of opportunities to mediate the exchange process. At times they may act for or work as merchant capitalists through their links with estate agents, property companies and builders. They tend to have informal relationships with building societies[91] and other financial institutions, and are centrally involved in the channelling of commissions for various exchange activities from home-owners to exchange professionals (including themselves). However, the particular concern of this section is the involvement of solicitors in the conveyancing process.

'Conveyance' means the transfer of property rights by written document, and includes the activities involved in examining the title deeds and preparing the transfer documents for the sale and purchase of dwellings.[92] Conveyancing is the single most important aspect of the exchange process. This is true financially, and more importantly, in a legal sense. Without conveyance a transaction will fail whatever the preceding involvement of estate agents and surveyors.

Solicitors hold a virtually complete professional monopoly over conveyancing. Yet because of the nature of the process, being the final set of actions before the completion of an exchange, solicitors depend on the activities of other exchange professionals for the amount of business they receive.[93] Unlike estate agents and surveyors who prosper on maximising the rate and speed of sales, solicitors have a marked interest in demonstrating the complexity, importance and length of time each con-

veyance takes. This interest not only allows solicitors to maximise fees, but also acts to sustain their monopoly. A pertinent
comment is one made by the Royal Commission on Legal Services
in Scotland: 'The difficulties and complexities of the legal procedure (have) helped maintain a monopoly for solicitors in conveyancing work which is in practice more extensive than that
conferred by the state'.[94] Conveyancing is the most lengthy
of all the activities carried out by exchange professionals,
taking an average of four months[95] and often substantially
longer.[96]

The solicitors' monopoly over conveyancing parallels the
growth of British capitalism during the nineteenth century.
Before solicitors achieved their present monopoly in the late
nineteenth century, the 1804 Stamp Act had restricted the
activity to the legal profession in general. In earlier centuries
conveyancing was frequently carried out by laymen. The
underdeveloped nature of conveyancing in the nineteenth century which lagged behind the growth of capitalism and the
increasingly fundamental importance of private property in
society, led to considerable problems in proving ownership
(or title). In 1830 the Real Property Commission described
the issue as follows:[97]

> ...of the real property of England a very considerable pro-
> portion is in one of these two predicaments: either the want
> of security against the existence of a latent deed renders
> actually unsafe a title which is marketable or the want of
> means of procuring the formal requisites of title renders
> unmarketable a title which is substantially safe.

It was imperative that evidence of ownership was clear and
legally demonstrable. Consequently the state encouraged the
development of a specific professional group, solicitors, to
carry out conveyancing. Moreover, in doing so the state allowed
solicitors a monopoly over the process that pre-dates the
evolution of owner-occupation as the major tenure form in
Britain. However, partly because of the crucial significance of
private property, this monopoly was combined with a degree
of state control. For instance, unlike the titles 'estate agent'
and 'surveyor' which can be used by anyone without regulation,
qualification or control, the term 'solicitor' is legally restricted
to qualified practioners on the Roll of Solicitors maintained by
the Law Society.

The Law Society is perhaps the most respectable and influential of all professional bodies. With the backing of the state
it regulates entry into the profession, sets standards of practice and governs the conduct of solicitors. However, despite
the seeming power and authority of the Law Society, individual
solicitors sometimes ignore either the spirit or the letter of the
rules that exist to protect clients. Moreover, in these situations
the Law Society itself may appear loath to commit itself in favour

of the client. With the state itself, the Law Society governs
solicitors' remuneration. Fees for conveyancing are controlled
(although, as we shall see, only in a very general fashion) by
orders made by a statutory committee whose members include
the Lord Chancellor, other senior members of the judiciary,
and the President of the Law Society. The Law Society itself
may prosecute outsiders who endanger the status and position
of solicitors; the legal actions over cut-price conveyancing
being a prime example. It acts as an influential and usually
successful pressure group in Parliament, government and elsewhere. Finally, the Society has published a variety of material
aimed at the general public and supporting the profession.
In the case of conveyancing, it has stressed the professionalism
and expertise of solicitors, and the utmost necessity of home-
owners employing them in the supposedly hazardous, difficult
and complex process. For example, in the pamphlet *Buying
a House? See a Solicitor* the Law Society states:[98]

> The land your house is built on can involve you in disputes
> over boundaries, fences, rights of way, rights of light,
> road charges or compulsory acquisition....It is no good
> leaving these things to chance and then learning the hard
> way, either by expensive quarrels with neighbours or by
> having to move out all together at a thumping great loss.
> These are just some of the reasons why the FIRST PERSON
> you should go and see as soon as you think of buying a
> house is a solicitor.

Critics, however, argue that in carrying out conveyancing
solicitors may well not be able either to discover or solve such
difficulties: 'under the conveyancing system as traditionally
operated, practically everything of any importance about a
house, and its transfer from vendor to purchaser, is left to
chance'.[99]
  Conveyancing is of crucial importance to solicitors as it is
by far the single most important source of their income. The
Benson Committee[100] reported that in 1975-6 the £299.7 million
derived by solicitors from conveyancing constituted 47 per
cent of their gross income. Conveyancing is by far the most
important source of income for small firms. However, small
firms are relatively unimportant in the total conveyancing
business. The reverse tends to apply to large firms. Apart
from providing the major source of income for solicitors, conveyancing also tends to be more profitable than other categories of work. It provided 45.8 per cent of their total fee
income, but only 37.2 per cent of fee-earners were engaged in
conveyancing. The Benson Report here echoes the more direct
findings of the 1968 Prices and Incomes report which showed
that conveyancing accounted for 55.6 per cent of solicitors'
income, but only 40 per cent of their total expenses. The
opportunities for conveyancing (i.e. the number and turnover

of owner-occupied dwellings) appears to be a major explanation
of the total number of solicitors and their geographical location.
For example, between 1966 and 1976 the number of solicitors in
private practice in England and Wales increased from 18,600
to 27,200. This growth is in part related to the increase in
home-ownership during the period, particularly so since by
far the heaviest concentration of solicitors in private practice
are in areas where owner-occupation dominates and has been
expanding.

Solicitors' firms spent an average of 6.2 hours on the conveyance for sales and 6.8 hours on the conveyance for purchases.
Partners worked on the conveyance for between an average of
53 and 58 per cent of the time, assistant and trainee solicitors
(i.e. those on salaries) for between 16 and 21 per cent of the
time, and other fee-earners such as unqualified clerks for
between 25 and 27 per cent of the time. The amount of time
increases with the price of property involved. For conveyancing sales it rose from an average of 4.2 hours for dwellings
costing no more than £5,000 to 9.7 hours for dwellings priced
at over £30,000. The hourly average charge made was £24.80
for sales and £22.50 for purchases. However, the hourly charge
varied from £20.20 for purchases between £10,000 and £15,000
to £26.50 for properties costing between £20,000 and £30,000.

Despite the status of the Benson Committee, some of the data
it collected should, however, be treated with caution. There
was no independent check or confirmation made of the validity
of the information provided by solicitors who responded to
the Committee's questionnaires. For instance, the practical
reason for the time spent on a conveyance to be related so
closely to the price of property involved remains unclear. More
probably, it may simply be a means by which solicitors justify
their use of scale fees linked to the value of the property involved. In addition, one critic, Joseph,[101] argued in 1976 that the
time spent on a conveyance is, in fact, a maximum of 1.5 hours
for sales and 2.0 hours for purchases. As such, 'the conveyancing solicitor charges at a basic rate of about £80 an hour,
and this is probably a minimum'.[102] Moreover, 'the bulk of
house conveyancing which comes out of solicitors' offices is
not done by solicitors. It is done by unqualified clerks
employed by a solicitor or a firm of solicitors.'[103] The Hughes
Report[104] provides some confirmation of Joseph's arguments.
For example, on the subject of the amount of fees per hour,
some categories of transactions were recorded as being charged
at an average of at least £78 an hour for sales and at least
£92 an hour for purchases.

The main criticisms of the conveyancing process as it presently
exists are that solicitors have an unjustifiable monopoly; the
fees charged are excessive and bear no relationship to the
work done; the process is made unduly complex and obfuscatory
when much of the work is, in fact, routine and simple; conveyancing generally takes too long; neither vendors nor

purchasers have any realistic choice in or control over the
process; despite solicitors' claims to professional expertise
and skill, there is no guarantee that a conveyance will necessarily be satisfactory with their involvement; and, finally,
because of professional self-interest, a variety of reforms that
could rapidly change conveyancing to a quick, simple and
cheap process with maximum security stand little chance of
being implemented.

As with other exchange professions, challenges to the position of solicitors come from three fronts: home-owners themselves, from individuals and organisations working in the
legal process, and the state.

Despite the immense amount of publicity from the profession
warning against the supposed dangers of owner-occupiers
doing their own conveyancing, there has been some increase
in do-it-yourself conveyancing in recent years. This development has largely occurred because of the publication of a
variety of material demystifying conveyancing and the solicitors'
monopoly over it. However, most evidence suggests that do-it-
yourself conveyancing is still on an extremely small scale, and
that the ideology surrounding the legal aspects of the exchange
process still exerts an immense influence on most home-owners.

The greatest challenge to the position of solicitors has come
from within the exchange process itself. During the 1970s there
was a steady growth in companies offering cut-price or fixed-fee
conveyancing. For example, early in 1976 five such firms were
operating with more than twenty separate offices.[105] The legal
monopoly of solicitors is bypassed by using someone who drafts
the crucial instrument of transfer free, or by employing an
outside solicitor. The profession clearly sees this development
as the greatest threat to its monopoly. The Law Society, in
attempting to neutralise the threat, has undertaken a number
of prosecutions of cut-price firms, although interestingly these
prosecutions have sometimes been ultimately unsuccessful. Such
alternatives to the traditional means of conveyancing are still
in their infancy. The profession will undoubtedly do everything
possible to ensure that the alternatives do not develop further,
although at present it remains unclear whether the *status quo*
will be maintained.

With regard to the role of the state, over a long period of time
it has tended to show two Janus-like faces. On the one hand
it has implemented a number of reforms that, although sometimes potentially far reaching, have quickly been neutralised
by solicitors and the Law Society. On the other hand, it has
carried out other activities that have protected and enhanced
the solicitors' monopoly. One illustration of the state working
against the interests of solicitors is land registration. This was
first introduced by statute in 1897. By 1978 the area of compulsory registration covered 74.2 per cent of the population of
England and Wales.[106] Following the 1979 Land Registration
(Scotland) Act a similar system is to be introduced into that

country. Land registry by the state simplifies the conveyancing process by registering and recording details of the ownership of land and guarantees the owners security of title. In theory, registration could minimise conveyancing to a merely technical matter and so undermine the present role of solicitors. Despite immense and long-term opposition to land registration, nowadays solicitors have virtually monopolised the right of search (although, in fact, anyone with a registered interest may search the register) and so have nullified the threat the reform posed.

Another form of state intervention has been over fees for conveyancing. Following three reports from the National Board for Prices and Incomes between 1968 and 1971, stating that solicitors made excessive profits from conveyancing, statutory scale fees and a formal rule against solicitors undercutting each other were abolished by the Solicitors Remuneration Order, 1972. The Order provided that solicitors 'shall charge such sums as may be fair and reasonable having regard to all the circumstances of the case'. It was thought that the Order would result in increased fee competition and reduce the differences in the fees charged for conveying unregistered as against registered titles. Since 1973, however, rather than the fees for unregistered titles being reduced, the amount charged for registered titles has been increased to be on a par with the former. The available evidence indicates that competition over fees remains minimal. The Law Society has done little to encourage fee competition. For example, *A Guide to the Professional Conduct of Solicitors* says:[107]

> The Council are of the opinion that the public interest requires that solicitors should not use the giving of quotations or estimates of their fees as a means of attracting professional business since, whilst this may provide a cheaper service it would almost certainly lead to a diminution in the quality of that service.

As both the Benson and Hughes Reports demonstrate, scale fees based on the price of property still generally apply. As such, solicitors gain from house price inflation and have an interest in maximising property values.

In contrast to attempts by the state at reform, in a somewhat contradictory fashion the state has also acted to maintain the profession's power and influence. This appears as true today as in the past. For example, the Solicitors Act 1974 excludes anyone but solicitors from carrying out conveyancing work 'unless he proves that the act was not done for or in expectation of any fee, gain or reward'.[108]

Nonetheless, the state has been increasingly aware of the criticisms made of the conveyancing process and the solicitors' role in it. This is most evident by the setting up in the 1970s of Royal Commissions on Legal Services, one for England, Wales and Northern Ireland, and one for Scotland.[109] The Commissions were required by their terms of reference to consider a number of general issues concerning legal services, but in particular 'whether any, and if so what, changes are desirable in the public interest...in the rules which prevent persons who are neither barristers nor solicitors from undertaking conveyancing and other legal business on behalf of other persons'. Conveyancing was the only activity identified by name and clearly illustrates the concern of the state.

The Benson Report is a prime example of the state's own machinery failing to provide the basis for much needed effective reform. Following highly organised, well-presented and very effective lobbying by the Law Society to retain the *status quo*, the Royal Commission recommended not only that solicitors should keep their conveyancing monopoly, but also that it should be extended to include the sale contract. This extension aimed at removing the competition from non-solicitor conveyancing organisations. Other recommended reforms of conveyancing were minimal, directed at encouraging competition over fees and acting against excessive fees. The extremely weak nature of the proposals suggests that major changes in conveyancing or in conveyancing costs are most unlikely.

In contrast to the Benson Report, the Hughes Report for Scotland made much more radical recommendations.[110] It proposed that a standing committee (including members of 'the general public') should examine among other things, 'the feasibility of introducing a simpler system of transferring property which might be provided by the State at a reduced cost to the public'; that conveyancing documents should be simplified and standardised and 'written so far as possible in simple language'; that the solicitors' monopoly should not (as the Law Society wished) be extended; and, that 'domestic conveyancing should no longer be restricted exclusively to the legal profession'. The implementation of this set of proposals would provide the basis for the radical reform of the conveyancing process, although at present there is no indication that the proposals will, in fact, be acted on.

Fundamental reform of conveyancing is, arguably, in the state's best interest. The current role of solicitors poses a threat both to the exchange process itself and the full development of owner-occupation as a tenure form; second, it imposes an undue financial burden on home-owners; third, the time-consuming nature of conveyancing slows the exchange process; fourth, it can be argued to restrict residential mobility and the free functioning of the tenure, and may reinforce the exclusion of particular groups of people from home-ownership; and finally, the solicitors' stress on the complex, legal and almost mystical nature of ownership may actually work against the full popular acceptance of property ownership.

Whatever the need for considerable reform, one may doubt the likelihood of it occurring. Not least this is because solicitors

are closely involved in and exert a variety of pressures on
the state. Because of their position and power, and the unique
status of the Law Society as a professional body of seemingly
unimpeachable respectability and standing, solicitors have always
been able to avoid, delay, challenge and neutralise fundamental
reform from the state. Indeed, the profession has been able
to use the state to enhance further its role in the exchange
process.

14 STOCK AND FLOW

by Fred Gray

1 INTRODUCTION[1]

The expansion of owner-occupation has been the single most important change - at least in quantitative terms - in the British housing system during the twentieth century. Before the First World War less than one in ten of dwellings in England and Wales were owner-occupied. By 1950, the figure had increased to 29 per cent, and to 49 per cent by 1970. In 1976 more than half (55 per cent) of households in the UK were home-owners.[2]

This chapter describes some of the features of the people and dwellings in the owner-occupied sector. Effectively it deals with the outputs and consequences of the processes analysed elsewhere in this book. Two particular themes are developed. One concerns the stock of dwellings and their inhabitants. The other deals with the process of movement in the tenure and the flow of households between dwellings.

In the following two sections information is provided about the dwellings and households in the owner-occupied sector. Here the discussion largely revolves around isolating some of the major contrasts *between* the owner-occupied and other tenures (section two) and *within* the owner-occupied tenure itself (section three). Typically, many commentators treat owner-occupation as a monolithic and homogeneous tenure. The usual image associated with owner-occupation is that of the suburban ideal of affluent white-collar workers in nuclear family units of husband, wife and children, living in detached or semi-detached dwellings of a high standard. As we shall see, particularly in comparison with other tenures, owner-occupation does indeed tend to be the tenure of the relatively well-off, associated with middle-class suburbia.

However, it is particularly important not to take this treatment of owner-occupation too far. Indeed in many respects the contrasts *within* the sector, in terms of both household and dwelling characteristics, are greater than those between the owner-occupied and other tenures. Major differences in housing opportunities and standards exist between specific groups of home-owners, themselves differentiated according to a variety of household characteristics. Very significant minorities of home-owners deviate from what might be expected given the image of the sector. Indeed, some home-owners are greatly disadvantaged low-income households, living in extremely low-quality dwellings. This tendency for the tenure to be regressive in its operation, with the already privileged gaining access to the best housing, and the poor having little opportunity to improve their inferior dwellings, is exemplified in section three.

Sections four and five move on to the other principal theme of the chapter, examining flow and movement in the tenure. The focus is on residential mobility (section four) and housing chains and filtering (section five). Residential mobility - the movement of people from one dwelling to another - is in an immediate sense an important process of change, through which individuals and households are matched (or mismatched) with dwellings, and socio-spatial patterns created and changed in residential areas. The evidence provided in sections four and five demonstrates that the contrasts within the tenure, in terms of who moves, when, why, and to what sort of dwelling, assume crucial significance, particularly in helping to explain the perpetuation of major inequalities between different groups of home-owners.

2 STOCK: CONTRASTS BETWEEN TENURES

Behind the fact that the majority of households in Britain now live in owner-occupied dwellings lie often immense spatial variations in the extent of owner-occupation from place to place. Nationally, the degree of home-ownership varies from 35 per cent in Scotland to 59 per cent in Wales.[3] As Table 14.1 demonstrates, there are also considerable differences at finer spatial scales. In general, a greater proportion of households are owner-occupiers in the more affluent southern regions and in suburban and rural areas. Other tenures tend to be more dominant in northern regions and older and larger urban areas, particularly inner cities. These variations in the extent of owner-occupation from area to area are reflections of a myriad of processes operating over various spatial scales and historical periods. Some processes are unique to relatively small local areas, others more general to certain regions or Britain as a whole.

For example, in the case of Tower Hamlets which borders central London (with the extremely low level of owner-occupation of 2.4 per cent of all households) this area has deviated from the national trend because of a relatively unique mix of factors. Longer-term economic and social processes resulted in a dominance of working-class rented housing in the locality. The class and income distribution of the resident population, both in the past and today, precluded home-ownership as a realistic tenure choice. The political control of the local authority has emphasised council housebuilding since the First World War. In any event, patterns of land ownership and control have minimised the opportunities available to private builders and developers to construct houses for sale. Even with land

availability, production agencies would have been unlikely
to see the area as suitable for owner-occupation. Furthermore,
the decisions of building societies and other mortgage-lending
agencies will have excluded both dwellings and households in
the area from loan finance.

Table 14.1 Extremes in owner-occupation in various administrative areas,
late 1970s (percentages)

| Administrative areas | Households in owner-occupation as a percentage of all households | | |
	Outright owners	Mortgagors	All owner-occupiers
Regions			
Greater London	16.6	27.6	44.2
Northern	19.2	25.2	44.4
East Anglian	27.7	29.1	56.8
South West	31.2	30.6	61.8
Shire Counties			
Northumberland	19.1	26.4	45.5
Lancashire	36.8	34.9	71.7
Metropolitan districts			
Knowsley	7.5	21.4	28.9
Stockport	26.9	43.3	70.2
Non-metropolitan districts			
Nottingham	12.9	21.0	33.9
Epsom Ewell	32.4	47.7	79.1
London			
Tower Hamlets	1.2	1.2	2.4
Harrow	26.3	46.6	72.9

Source: Derived from DoE (1979), *National Dwelling and Housing Survey*, and DoE (1980),
National Dwelling and Housing Survey, Phases II and III.

In contrast, Harrow (72.9 per cent owner-occupation) and
Epsom and Ewell (79.1 per cent owner-occupation) are archetype
London suburbs developed during the housing boom of the
interwar period, and added to since 1945. Land was available
to builders and developers eager to build for home-ownership.[4]
The changing employment profile of the London region and
developing class structure of the south-east both acted to
ensure a ready supply of actual or potential home-owners over
a sustained period of time. Both the dwellings and households
willing and able to occupy them constitute ideal avenues for
building society loans. The political complexion of such areas,
itself closely related to the dominance of home-ownership,
mitigates against large-scale public sector housebuilding,

Table 14.2 Dwelling characteristics by tenure, late 1970s (percentages)

Dwelling characteristics	Tenure			
	Outright owners	Mortgagors	All owner-occupiers	Other tenures
Rateable values				
Up to £100	17.7	7.7	12.0	17.1
£101 to £200	36.0	35.7	35.9	56.3
£201 to £300	30.4	39.1	35.4	20.1
£301 and over	15.3	16.8	16.2	5.1
Information unavailable	0.5	0.6	0.6	1.5
Type of accommodation				
Detached	30.5	27.1	28.6	4.5
Semi-detached	32.0	42.4	37.9	27.2
Terraced	28.9	25.3	26.8	31.4
Purpose built flat/maisonette	3.0	2.5	2.7	22.7
Other flat/room	3.8	2.3	2.9	12.9
Other	1.8	0.5	1.1	1.4
Age of building				
Before 1919	45.0	23.0	32.5	20.5
1919-44	28.0	25.0	26.3	21.0
1945-64	17.0	22.0	19.8	36.3
1965 or later	10.0	30.0	21.4	22.2
Basic amenities				
Sole use of all	92.1	98.0	95.4	86.7
Some shared, none lacked	1.0	0.6	0.8	5.1
At least one lacking	7.0	1.4	3.8	8.2
Central heating				
Yes	53.5	72.2	64.3	39.0
No	46.5	27.8	35.7	61.0
Number of rooms				
1	0.1	–	–	2.6
2	0.6	0.2	0.4	5.1
3	3.4	1.7	2.4	15.1
4	22.3	13.4	17.2	26.0
5	29.6	36.7	33.6	31.4
6	30.7	31.6	31.2	16.5
7 or more	13.4	16.4	22.4	3.5
Persons per room				
Under ½	67.0	28.0	44.6	37.9
½ but under ⅔	20.0	28.0	24.4	24.0
⅔ but under 1	10.0	36.0	24.7	23.7
1	2.0	7.0	4.8	9.6
Over 1	1.0	2.0	1.7	4.7

Source: Derived from DoE (1979), *National Dwelling and Housing Survey*, and OPCS (1980), *General Household Survey 1978*.

as shown by recent work on Bromley[5] and Croydon.[6]

Cumulatively, the processes described in this book and *State Housing in Britain* have created a situation of considerable contrasts in dwelling characteristics between the owner-occupied dwelling stock, and those of other tenures. Table 14.2 illustrates some of these contrasts. A particularly important feature is that the dwellings of home-owners tend to be of a higher quality than those of tenants. Rateable values, which reflect both dwelling and neighbourhood amenities and standards, are, on average, higher. Similarly, a greater proportion of home-owners live in detached or semi-detached houses, have sole use of all amenities, central heating, and occupy large houses with adequate and often extremely generous room standards for household members.

On all these counts, people who become owner-occupiers have a much better chance of living in higher-quality dwellings than if they become tenants. Home-ownership tends to be associated with good dwellings, other tenures with somewhat inferior dwellings. Moreover, the highest quality housing is concentrated in the owner-occupied sector.[7] The reverse is also true in that despite the dominance of the tenure nationally, *relatively* few owner-occupied dwellings fall into what may be considered indices of inferior quality and standards. Nonetheless, it should be stressed that in *absolute* terms, because of the overall size of the tenure, the number of inferior owner-occupied dwellings is considerable.

This differential dwelling quality between tenures helps explain the preferences for owner-occupation expressed by many people when questioned in housing surveys. As Harrison and Lomas note, 'the available survey evidence does on balance suggest that people prefer owner-occupation; that is, they would like to be in that tenure if financial constraints could be assumed away'.[8] Given the dwelling quality expectations associated with the tenure (and the favourable financial subsidies) it would be surprising indeed if many people did not wish to become home-owners. Clearly, though, such advantages are not inherent to owner-occupation *per se*, since housing policy could change in such a way to bring rented housing up to and even above the standards typical of owner-occupied dwellings.[9]

One exception to the relationship between dwelling characteristics and tenure is the age of buildings. Despite the massive growth of home-ownership since the war, home-owners are more likely to live in older dwellings than other households. An explanation of this seeming paradox is that the expansion of the tenure has, in part, resulted from tenure transfers. For example, of the extra 7 million owner-occupied dwellings created between 1938 and 1978, about two-fifths were previously in the private rented sector.[10] In addition, the massive post-war slum clearance campaigns and building of public sector dwellings helps account for the relative dominance of newer dwellings in the rented tenures.

Table 14.3 Household characteristics by tenure, late 1970s (percentages)

Household characteristics	Outright owners	Mortgagors	All owner-occupiers	Other tenures
		Tenure		
Type of household				
One person aged under 60	4.5	4.0	4.2	8.8
Small adult	9.2	22.9	17.0	13.2
Small family	6.7	37.0	24.0	16.6
Large family	3.4	12.8	8.8	9.7
Large adult	16.8	18.4	17.7	16.4
Older small	35.7	3.8	17.5	16.8
One person aged 60 or over	23.6	1.1	10.8	18.5
Age of head of household				
Under 25	0.5	4.5	2.8	7.0
25-44	9.3	60.9	38.7	28.0
45-64	39.4	32.1	35.2	35.4
65 or over	50.9	2.5	23.3	29.7
Socio-economic group of head of household				
Professional	4.9	10.4	8.0	1.6
Employers and managers	17.9	21.2	19.8	6.7
Other non-manual	18.9	22.3	20.8	14.2
Skilled manual	24.9	32.4	29.1	31.7
Semi-skilled manual	9.6	8.0	8.7	18.0
Unskilled manual	3.1	1.8	2.4	8.2
Other	20.8	4.0	11.2	19.8
Qualifications held by head of household				
Degree or equivalent	7.0	12.0	10.3	3.2
Other higher or equivalent	10.0	22.0	18.0	7.3
Other	28.0	32.0	30.7	23.2
None	55.0	34.0	41.1	66.3
Activity status of head of household				
Economically active	43.4	94.2	72.3	57.5
Economically inactive	56.6	5.8	27.7	42.5
Gross annual income of economically active heads of households				
Less than £1,500	4.0	–	1.0	5.4
£1,500 but less than £3,000	24.0	10.0	13.3	32.1
£3,000 but less than £4,000	27.0	25.0	25.5	32.6
£4,000 but less than £6,000	28.0	44.1	40.3	25.6
£6,000 or more	16.0	21.0	19.9	4.3

Continued ...

Table 14.3 continued . . .

Gross annual income of economically inactive heads of households				
Less than £1,500	58.0	40.2	57.0	73.6
£1,500 but less than £3,000	29.0	36.1	29.9	23.5
£3,000 or more	12.0	23.7	13.1	3.0
Number of earners in household				
None	50.8	5.2	24.5	37.3
One	26.9	34.3	31.1	30.4
Two	16.2	48.6	34.9	23.6
Three or more	6.2	11.9	9.5	8.5
Number of cars available to household				
0	42.1	14.8	26.5	61.0
1	46.1	63.8	56.2	34.0
2 or more	11.8	21.4	17.3	5.0
Consumer durables				
Washing-machine	73.0	90.0	82.7	66.6
Deep freezer	34.0	51.0	43.7	19.2
Vacuum cleaner	95.0	97.0	96.1	87.5
Colour TV	62.0	75.0	69.4	51.8

Source: As for Table 14.2.

Apart from these contrasts in dwelling characteristics, there are also (as Table 14.3 demonstrates) important differences in the characteristics of households between the owner-occupied and other tenures. A broad, but nonetheless accurate, generalisation is that home-ownership tends to be associated with 'middle-class', economically active, nuclear family units, and other tenures with 'working-class', economically marginalised, 'unorthodox' households. Table 14.3 presents a variety of information to support this view.

For example, when compared with renting households, owner-occupiers are less likely to be at the extremes of the 'household type' and 'age of head of household' spectrums. It is relatively unlikely for young single people to be home-owners. Instead they typically enter the tenure at around the time of marriage. Indeed, many households in the owner-occupied sector are 'families' at the child-rearing stage with middle-aged heads. Table 14.3 also indicates that owner-occupiers are more likely than tenants to be drawn from the various non-manual and white-collar socioeconomic groups. Furthermore, there is a greater probability of home-owners being educationally successful, economically active, and earning relatively high incomes. Income level is particularly important. For instance, the higher a head of household's income, the greater the likelihood that they will be home-owners.

The reverse of these generalisations tends to apply to households in other tenures. For example, the rented tenures are more likely to house 'working-class' households, manual workers, the economically inactive, those on low incomes, and the educationally unsuccessful. Similarly, a larger proportion of households in other tenures consist of older people living on their own. This highlights the social need function of the public sector - the housing of old people by local authorities - and also the existence of a significant group of older people, in the private rented sector, who were unable to take part in the expansion of home-ownership during earlier decades.

Apart from the data provided in Table 14.3, on other grounds too it may be argued that owner-occupation caters for the 'typical' family unit, with other tenures tending to house different 'unorthodox' household units. In 1977, whereas 64 per cent of two parent families were in the owner-occupied sector, this was so for only 34 per cent of single-parent families.[11] Similarly, only 30 per cent of unemployed heads of households, 50 per cent of retired heads and 43 per cent of 'housewife' heads are home-owners.[12]

An important conclusion emerges from this assessment of the differences in household and dwelling characteristics between tenures. Housing policy fostering home-ownership over and above other tenures often operates to allocate the better dwellings to the economically advantaged, with relatively secure and good occupations and high incomes. In turn, many of these households are also what are generally conceived of as 'normal' family units of two parents and children with male income earners. Consequently, because of the associations between dwelling quality and tenure, households that are economically disadvantaged and marginalised, and which deviate from the orthodox family type, tend to be excluded from home-ownership and may be effectively penalised with lower-quality dwellings. Yet during the post-war period, and particularly in the 1970s, such households - whether single-parent families, young or old single people, or those on relatively low incomes and the unemployed - have vastly increased in number and now constitute significant sections of the population.[13]

Despite the general validity of this conclusion, it should be emphasised that it applies only as a general trend. Many households do not conform to the trend. For instance, some tenant households are relatively affluent nuclear family units. Similarly, the owner-occupied sector is not homogeneous and significant numbers of home-owning households are not economically active, middle-class, orthodox family units.

Indeed, an undue emphasis on the homogeneity of the owner-occupied sector may lead to errors in understanding and explanation. A case in point is the far greater car ownership and use of consumer durables amongst home-owners (Table 14.3). This is to be expected given the various contrasts in

household characteristics between tenures. However, some
authors have gone further and argued that a causal relationship exists with owner-occupation itself leading to the use
of more consumer durables. Pawley, for instance, states that[14]

> the manufacturers, importers and retailers of cars, freezers,
> washing machines, colour television sets, sound systems,
> furniture, garden accessories and so on in their turn rely
> on the appreciating value of houses to maintain demand for
> their products.

The implication is that if other tenures were more dominant
there would be a reduced sale of such products. Harvey, in
a considerably more refined analysis, argues that the growth
of home-ownership combined with suburbanisation, has been
of crucial importance in capitalist societies such as the USA.
In particular, this is so because it partly resolves the threat
of an underlying 'overaccumulation crisis' by sustaining and
expanding consumption. He suggests that[15]

> the whole structure of consumption in general relates to
> the form which housing provision takes. The dilemmas of
> potential overaccumulation which faced the United States
> in 1944 were in part resolved by the creation of a whole
> new life style through the rapid proliferation of the sub-
> urbanization process.

The analysis laying behind statements of this kind has been
subject to a number of essentially theoretical criticisms[16] that
need not detain us here. More relevant in the present context
is that the argument of authors such as Pawley and Harvey
tends not to be supported by the empirical evidence. For
example, it ignores the considerable proportion of people in
other tenures who do have access to cars or use consumer
durables. More important, economic activity, number of earners
in a household, and income levels vary from tenure to tenure
in much the same pattern as the use of consumer durables. At
its simplest, then, home-owners consume more not because of
their tenure, but because of their higher incomes.
Furthermore, the use of consumer durables and cars within
the owner-occupied sector is far from being homogeneous.
For example, as Table 14.3 demonstrates, outright owners
(despite presumably having complete control of their financial
asset unlike mortgagors) make less use of cars and consumer
durables than those in the process of buying. This theme of
the contrasts within the owner-occupied tenure is developed
in the following section. The interpretation presented below
indicates that mortgagors have the greatest access to cars and
use of consumer durables not because they are mortgagors,
but because of their already advantaged economic position when
compared with both outright owners and people in other tenures.

To sum up this section, the data provided in Tables 14.2 and 14.3 support the view that a significant proportion of home-owners are relatively affluent, 'middle-class', 'family' households. The equation of home-ownership with 'suburbanisation', and all the latter term implies about life-styles and patterns of behaviour and consumption, has some general validity (although we should not put causal primacy on home-ownership to explain household characteristics). As we shall see in section three, however, this should remain nothing more than a broad generalisation. In absolute terms large numbers of dwellings and households deviate from this generalisation. Indeed, in many respects the dwelling and household contrasts *within* the owner-occupied sector are more significant and extreme than those, isolated above, that exist between tenures.

3 STOCK: THE CONTRASTS BETWEEN HOME-OWNERS

This section emphasises the importance of contrasts and differences within the owner-occupied tenure. These contrasts sometimes have a clear spatial manifestation. Particular owner-occupied sub-markets deviate dramatically from the norm for the tenure discussed in the previous section.

Perhaps the most clear example of this concerns race and owner-occupation. Because most black households do not have the characteristics that generally apply to those in the tenure, we should expect relatively few black people to be home-owners. Yet the Political and Economic Planning 1974 survey[17] indicated that 50 per cent of West Indian households and 76 per cent of Asian households were home-owners. Since black people are more than proportionately represented amongst manual socio-economic groups, these percentages are much higher than would be expected if the association between tenure and socio-economic group applying to white people also held true for black people. Indeed, as Table 14.4 demonstrates, for both Asians and West Indians, the reverse trend applies, with owner-occupation being greater amongst manual rather than non-manual groups, and tending to increase the less skilled the head of household.

Significantly, owner-occupation for black people is no guarantee of good-quality housing. Instead dwellings tend to be old (only 8 per cent built since 1940), up to five times more likely to lack basic amenities than the dwellings occupied by white people, and are much more often shared and/or overcrowded.[18] The general explanation put forward by authors such as Smith[19] and Rex and Tomlinson[20] is that various processes such as local authority selection and allocation policies and building society mortgage-lending criteria (both at times influenced by racial discrimination) tend to act to exclude black people from adequate housing in all tenures. The particular demands of their family and community structure (especially in the case of

Asians), when combined with their general class position,
pushes them into low-quality owner-occupation.

Table 14.4 Owner-occupation by race and socioeconomic group in 1974

| | Socioeconomic group (% of owner-occupiers) | | | |
	Non-manual	Skilled manual	Semi-skilled manual	Unskilled manual
General population	67	45	33	20
Asians	59	81	82	85
West Indians	35	59	53	39

Source: Derived from D.J. Smith (1977), *Racial Disadvantage in Britain*, Harmondsworth, Penguin.

Nonetheless, more recent survey results indicate that the
relationship between tenure and race is not fixed, but may
undergo rapid change. The 1979 National Dwelling and Housing
Survey[21] (Table 14.5) when compared with the 1974 PEP survey
mentioned above suggests that, much against the general trend,
the proportion of both West Indians and Asians owning dwellings fell during the 1970s. The greatest change was amongst
West Indians; by the late 1970s only 36 per cent were home-
owners, compared with about one in two a few years earlier.
Assuming that both surveys are statistically accurate, the evidence suggests that West Indians are (unlike the situation in
the 1960s) increasingly being admitted to the public sector. The
same trend, although to a much lesser degree, may also be
discerned for Asian households.

Table 14.5 Tenure by race in 1978 (percentages)

| Tenure | Ethnic group of head of household | | |
	White	West Indian	Asian
Owned outright	23.8	4.5	17.0
Mortgagors	30.8	31.4	52.9
Other tenures	45.4	64.1	30.1

Source: DoE (1979), *National Dwelling and Housing Survey*.

Clearly this process, if it continued over a sustained period of time, would challenge the views of race and housing typically held by academics writing on the subject. It appears to be the case that the relationships between race and tenure are being realigned. On one hand, an increasing proportion of West Indians are becoming public sector tenants, although often living in inferior and low-quality inner-city estates.[22] On the other hand, a majority of Asian households, because of the nature of their family and community structure and general class position in the context of a racially hostile society, remains in low-quality owner-occupied housing.

Both in the recent past and today owner-occupation has filled a particular role for black people, much against the general trend applicable to white middle-class families. However, even the norm for white home-owners hides often widely divergent circumstances. The most well-documented instance of this, discussed in more detail in chapters 13 and 15, concerns white home-owners in the inner city. Such people tend to form low-income, economically marginalised, working-class households who live in old and often extremely inadequate dwellings. Because of building society lending policies, many home-owners in the inner city are unable to draw on the usual sources of mortgage finance available to the better-off. Consequently, they suffer the double disadvantage of living in low-quality housing and paying relatively large sums to purchase and maintain their homes. For these people the ideal of suburban home-ownership is indeed an ideal, with little chance of it becoming a reality.

The household and dwelling characteristics of home-owners also vary at other spatial scales. For example, as Townsend notes,[23]

in Wales, a very high proportion of owner-occupied accommodation is in terraced housing, much of it relatively poor quality and low value. Such housing assumes functions in the local economy and community structure fulfilled elsewhere by privately rented housing.

At the regional level, differences in housing markets, the stock available and the level of house prices, has an impact on who is able to enter the tenure, and consequently on the regional socioeconomic and age profile of home-owners. For example, in 1978 in Greater London, of first-time buyers 9 per cent bought dwellings costing under £10,000, 7 per cent had incomes of under £4,000 per annum, 21 per cent were aged under 25, and 17 per cent paid a deposit of under £1,000 to secure the house they purchased. In contrast, of first-time buyers in Yorkshire and Humberside, 65 per cent bought houses costing less than £10,000, 25 per cent had annual incomes under £4,000, 36 per cent were under 25, and 55 per cent paid a deposit of under £1,000.[24] In some localities it is much easier to become a home-owner than in others. Consequently, younger people, lower-income groups and working-class households have more opportunity to enter the tenure. In other areas a shortage of dwellings and high house prices precludes owner-occupation as an effective tenure choice for many households, including some with relatively high incomes.

These examples, and the information provided in Table 14.3, suggest that although class is still strongly associated with tenure, significant numbers of home-owners are working-class people. However, these groups are less likely to be able to take advantage of the physical and economic benefits accruing to owner-occupation, as enjoyed by relatively affluent middle-class families in the tenure. Townsend has summed up the situation well:[25]

> With the rapid increase in home ownership tenure itself is becoming less strongly associated with class. As part of a historical process such ownership is becoming less a symbol of high non-manual class and more a system itself consisting of distinctive strata.

As we have seen, these hierarchies within the tenure often have a clear spatial manifestation. This also partly applies to another particularly important differentiation between home-owners - on the basis of whether they are mortgagors (i.e. those in the process of buying) or outright owners. As Table 14.2 demonstrates, almost one in two outright owners live in dwellings over 60 years old. Much older housing (and hence many outright owners) is located in the older urban areas, often in environmentally disadvantaged localities. In contrast, mortgaged dwellings are spread relatively equally across the age of building spectrum (less than a quarter are over 60 years old) and, by implication, in inner cities, suburban and rural areas.

By the late 1970s 43 per cent of home-owners in England were outright owners and 57 per cent were mortgagors. The information in Tables 14.2 and 14.3 indicates that in many respects the differences between these two groups operates as a major divide between home-owners, and are greater than those between owners and tenants discussed in section two.[26]

A majority of outright owners are relatively old and members of small families. Over half of household heads are at least 65 years old, and only one in ten under 45. In contrast, two-thirds of mortgagors are in this latter age group, and 68 per cent of mortgagor households are large or small family units or 'large adult households'. Most people do not become outright owners until they near retirement, and past the child-rearing stage of the family cycle. Not surprisingly, given their age and socioeconomic group, a majority of outright owners had no opportunity to take part in the expansion of higher education of the post-war period, and consequently have few qualifications. Similarly, because of their age, a majority of outright owners are economically inactive (57 per cent) and are unlikely to have any 'earners' in their household. In contrast, 94 per cent of mortgagors are economically active, and 61 per cent have two or more earners in the household.

Nevertheless, since for most economically active people, incomes peak in the years before retirement, we would at least expect *economically active* outright owners (who tend to be older than mortgagors) to have higher incomes than those in the process of buying. Significantly, the reverse is true. A greater proportion of economically active mortgagors have incomes of £4,000 or more than outright owners (65 per cent and 44 per cent respectively). This probably reflects the differences in socioeconomic group distribution between mortgagors and outright owners – with the latter group containing a greater proportion of manual heads of households whose incomes tend to be both lower and to peak earlier. In general, then, whether or not they are economically active, outright owners have lower incomes and are in a relatively disadvantaged economic position when compared with mortgagors.

This situation is closely related to differences in dwelling characteristics between the two groups of owners. The former group tend to occupy smaller and older properties, with lower rateable values, which are also more likely to lack central heating and basic amenities. Such dwellings may have relatively high maintenance, repair and running costs. In this way, the tenure system tends to be regressive. It allocates the best dwellings to those households that are already advantaged in educational, income and socioeconomic group terms. Critical in this are the lending practices of mortgage-lending institutions[27] which facilitate inequalities in the distribution of dwellings. The most disadvantaged households will be excluded from the tenure altogether, or allocated the worst of the owner-occupied stock.

Mortgagors, who by definition have access to mortgage finance, are able to acquire the funds necessary to occupy much of the better-quality dwelling stock in the tenure. By implication, the figures also suggest that despite perhaps owning a financial asset of some value, some outright owners are either unwilling (perhaps because they are satisfied with their existing dwelling) or unable (either because of insufficient net worth on their existing dwelling or because of their failure to obtain mortgage finance) to trade up to higher cost and quality dwellings.

To conclude this section it is useful to re-emphasise the fact that the internal differentiation within the owner-occupied sector is considerable. At times it outweighs the contrasts between tenures. The tenure is not, as is typically assumed, homogeneous. Being a home-owner has different meanings and carries with it different connotations from place to place and group to group. For some, and particularly for relatively

affluent, middle-class families with a mortgage who live in the
suburbs, home-ownership does ensure good housing which in
turn confers a variety of physical, social and economic benefits
(see chapter 5). For other groups the reverse is often true.
Being a low-income, old, working-class or economically marginalised home-owner, perhaps in the inner city, often carries
with it (even if a person owns outright) the burden of poor
and extremely restricted housing opportunities, and little
chance of moving to better dwellings. It is the issue of the
mobility or immobility of households that the following section
considers.

4 RESIDENTIAL MOBILITY

The geographical movement of households from one dwelling
to another is of considerable significance for a number of
reasons. At least in theory, mobility should be an important
force allowing for a closer alignment between dwellings and
households. The evolving needs and demands of households,
for example as a family expands or contracts or employment
changes, can, through residential mobility, be met by moves
to dwellings of particular sizes, types or locations. Movement
may help increase dwelling satisfaction, at least if the decision
to move is made by the household itself, and the financial and
other constraints on mobility opportunities are not so severe
as to force a move to inferior housing.

Cumulatively, household mobility is important in forming
and evolving socio-spatial patterns in residential areas: the
mix of people and social groups in particular groups of dwellings and specific areas, according to factors such as class,
occupation, income, age and household size. In turn, such
patterns influence the structure of social relations from place
to place. For example, the middle-class suburbs with specific
patterns of family behaviour and social relationships described
by authors such as Bell[28] and Connell[29] are, in an immediate
sense, the product of selected in-migration of certain social
groups. Similarly, gentrification[30] of inner-city housing (and
concomitant changes in the social structure of a neighbourhood,
the composition and activities of community organisations, the
class origins of pupils in local schools, and so on) typically
involves the movement out of working-class families and their
replacement by middle-class households.[31]

In aggregate, the mobility (and immobility) of households,
and the precise character of movement according to factors
such as distance, frequency and the dwelling and tenure of
departure and destination, help create the particular dwelling
and household associations between and within tenures detailed
in sections two and three.

Murie provides perhaps the most|elegant and realistic descrip-
tion of the mobility process and its consequences. He writes

that any particular housing situation should *not* be seen[32]

> as a static ordering of households, but as a dynamic chang-
> ing process under which households with different demands
> are constantly *competing* and changing their situation. The
> residential ordering which emerges is unlikely to reflect an
> optimum situation for all households. Rather, it reflects a
> series of economic and social constraints which limit the
> opportunity space for households. The process through
> which such limitation is implemented reflects the priorities
> and methods of operation of organisations which allocate
> housing resources and facilities in both public and private
> sectors.

The basic features of residential mobility in Britain are fairly
well known.[33] Most moves tend to be over a fairly short distance,
often within a local authority area. Moves between tenures
are most likely to be from the private rented sector into either
owner-occupied or public sector housing. Households moving
within the owner-occupied sector often improve their dwelling
characteristics on moving - for instance in terms of comparisons,
between past and present dwelling price, type and size. However, significant proportions of owner-occupied households do
occupy either similar or lower-quality dwellings on moving. For
example, the Housing Policy Review indicates that 50 per cent
of households traded up to significantly higher priced dwellings
on moving, 27 per cent experienced no substantial change,
and 23 per cent traded down to dwellings with a significantly
lower selling price.[34] Typically, it is already advantaged households, for example in terms of economic activity, income, and
socioeconomic group, that gain most from moving within the
owner-occupied sector.

By far the single most important set of reasons given by
mobile households for longer distance moves from one urban
area to another is related to employment, generally when the
head of household's job changes.[35] In contrast, the impetus for
moves within urban areas when they are not forced (for
instance, because of slum clearance) are often, according to
the respondents to various surveys, because of changes in
household type, age, size and social status. Such moves can
be seen to represent families adapting their dwellings to changing household circumstances.

Who moves, when, why and where from and to, is related to a
series of factors. Some are associated with household characteristics. Younger households around the time of marriage and as
household size increases are particularly likely to move. Similarly, non-manual groups, and especially professional workers,
employers and managers, and educationally successful higher-
income households who have some previous mobility experience,
tend to move further and more often than other households.
In contrast, older, smaller and economically inactive households,

manual workers, and those on relatively low incomes tend to move less frequently and over shorter distances. For the majority of manual workers, employment changes, which tend to be within rather than between urban areas, do not necessitate a change of home. Consequently moves, when they do take place, are often for 'family' or social status reasons and tend to be restricted to the 'home town' area.

Housing tenure itself is associated with the frequency and nature of residential mobility, although whether this is in a causal fashion is more difficult to ascertain. Clearly, the owner-occupied sector contains a majority of the households, described immediately above, that are likely to move most frequently and over longer distances. In contrast, the public sector houses many of the households who are less mobile and, when they do move, cover shorter distances.[36]

One piece of research that does indicate that tenure may have an independent effect on mobility is that of Gleave and Palmer. They argue: 'The local authority housing sector is characterised by a low proportion of migrants moving outside their area of origin even when variations in socioeconomic structure have been accounted for.'[37] Consequently: 'A manager, no less than a foreman or unskilled worker, is less likely to move for job reasons if he is resident in local authority housing.'[38] The nature of local authority housing policy restrictions, such as length of residence qualifications, is often argued to be the cause of such differences. One difficulty with this conclusion, as Gleave and Palmer themselves point out, is that other dimensions of structural variation not examined in their analysis, such as age, may also account for the differences between tenures. In any event, the socioeconomic group categorisation employed in the analysis may miss relatively subtle, yet crucial, job characteristics of many of the small proportion of local authority tenants who are professional workers, employers or managers. Whatever the constraints imposed by local authority selection policies, such households may be tied into a particular local employment market with little opportunity of inter-urban movement. Finally, the analysis ignores the extent to which the costs and difficulties of selling and buying owner-occupied dwellings may restrict the mobility of home-owners.[39]

Given the preceding discussions, it is perhaps superficially surprising that the distributions of length of residence between owner-occupiers and households in other tenures are broadly similar (Table 14.6). This dilemma - that the owner-occupied sector houses many households that have been shown to have a particularly strong propensity to be residentially mobile, and yet that survey evidence also shows that households in other tenures tend to be at least a little more mobile than home-owners - is partly resolved by looking at mobility experiences of outright owners and mortgagors. Much more significant than the mobility contrasts between tenures are those between the two groups of home-owners. Some 30 per cent of mortgagors had lived at their present address for less than three years, and 73 per cent for a decade or less. On the other hand, 68 per cent of outright owners had lived in their present dwelling for eleven or more years, and one in four for at least thirty-one years (clearly a considerable proportion of the life of any household).

Table 14.6 Length of residence by tenure in 1978

Length of residence of head of household (years)	Tenure			
	Outright owners %	Mortgagors %	All owner-occupiers %	Other tenures %
Under 1	2.0	10.0	6.6	8.1
1 but under 3	6.0	20.0	14.1	13.7
3 but under 5	6.0	14.0	10.6	9.8
5 to 10	18.0	29.0	24.4	20.2
11 to 20	26.0	21.0	23.3	30.2
21 to 30	17.0	4.1	9.6	8.9
31 or more	25.0	1.0	11.4	9.1

Source: OPCS (1980), *General Household Survey 1978.*

Mobile home-owners are clearly a non-random section of the total population in the tenure. Studies of residential mobility in the tenure tend to bypass the significant proportion of home-owners who are immobile, and who considerably lessen the aggregate mobility rates in the tenure.

These very significant differences in mobility are closely linked to the dwelling and household characteristics of the two groups of home-owners discussed in section three. Mortgagors, who are much more likely to be more mobile than either out-right owners or the universe of non-owners, tend to be at the child-rearing stage of the family cycle, economically active, with high incomes, and more than proportionately drawn from the non-manual socioeconomic groups. These households are likely to occupy relatively high-quality housing. In contrast, outright owners are often geographically immobile for very long periods, and have housing standards inferior to mort-gagors. Generally, they are drawn from older, small households, the economically inactive and those on relatively low incomes in comparison with the majority of mortgagors. Similarly, they are more likely to be in the various manual socioeconomic groups. Outright owners are not only disadvantaged when com-pared to mortgagors, but have vastly less opportunity to improve their housing circumstances through residential mobil-ity within the owner-occupied sector.

In part, the high rates of mobility apparent for mortgagors is a consequence of their socioeconomic and employment

characteristics. It is suggested that their work more often
necessitates moves from one urban area to another. Similarly,
their stage in the family cycle creates demands for changes
in a household dwelling which, in turn, results in a move to a
larger and higher-quality house. Seemingly irrefutable evidence of the importance of both employment and household
changes in inducing mobility can be found in the responses
to questionnaires asking why households moved home.

However, we also need to ask why households going through
the same stage in the family cycle may have very different
mobility experiences, with some moving and others remaining
immobile. This question pushes attention on to the operation
of the owner-occupied housing market itself. In this light a
particularly crucial factor in who moves and who does not is
access to mortgage finance. By definition, mortgagors have
such access, which considerably facilitates household movement.
Loan finance facilitates households trading up to better dwellings. In such circumstances, moves may occur without radical
or significant changes in family circumstances or employment.[40]
It is, consequently, a hazardous task to interpret or put causal
importance on the responses to questionnaire surveys. Similarly, 'care should be taken not to assume that because movement coincides with family changes this is the cause of movement'.[41] Respondents' answers may be post-move rationalisations
and explanations of mobility, which was actually inspired by
the ideology inherent in the owner-occupied housing market
and made possible by the operation of that system, rather than
because of the stresses created by changes in employment or
household characteristics. Seen in this way, higher-income
households and those in various non-manual groups not only
move more frequently for job or family reasons, but also
because they are advantaged by the operation of the mortgage
finance system and are best able to acquire the cream of the
dwelling stock through mobility: 'market forces, market position
and the nature of constraints arising from the institutional
operation of the housing market are important factors in determining housing access'.[42]

Households without access to building society finance or
other loans for house purchase typically have far less opportunity to trade up or, indeed, to move for other reasons.
Unless they have access to additional sources of capital, or are
prepared to trade down, most outright owners may remain
immobile simply because they have little realistic alternative.
As Murie says:[43]

> Both within the owner-occupied sector, and for those out-
> side, the operation of the market confers benefits differen-
> tially, unrelated to the needs of households, and in a manner
> which may actively prevent housing adjustment to meet such
> needs.

Variations in access to mortgage finance is also often of crucial importance in determining who gets which house in the owner-occupied sector. This is because 'accommodation in the owner-occupied sector represents a hierarchy of prices which households compete for. Increases in income or the capacity to obtain higher mortgage loans will, in many cases, lead to movement.[44] Bell graphically describes the end result of the process whereby house price differentials and variations in access to mortgage loans act to sift and sort significant sections of the total population of home-owners into distinct socio-spatial groupings: 'the prices of the houses act as a social sieve, with graduated meshes as it were, through which drop each homogeneous segment of the population around the edge of towns....The geographically mobile members of the middle class move from one spatially segregated estate to another where they settle among people of similar status and wealth.[45] Home-owners without access to mortgage finance will typically remain immobile. Households able to obtain relatively small loans will be restricted in their mobility and housing opportunities. Mortgagors able to secure larger sums will have a wider choice of housing available that they can move to. In consequence, distinctive socioeconomic patterns emerge in specific areas of owner-occupied housing.

Table 14.7 *Previous tenure by present tenure in 1978 (continuing heads of households who had lived at their present address for less than one year) (percentages)*

| Previous tenure | Present tenure | | | |
	Owner-occupied	Rented from local authority/ new town	Privately rented	Total
Owner-occupied	72	11	22	43
Rented from local authority/new town	8	64	11	26
Privately rented	20	25	67	31
Total	100	100	100	100
Percentage of all moves by continuing households	49	30	21	100

Source: OPCS (1980), *General Household Survey 1978*.

Residential mobility is also clearly of considerable importance in the evolution of housing tenures. Table 14.7 shows that continuing households moving *to* and *within* the owner-occupied sector account for almost one-half of all moves by such households over a twelve-month period. This is somewhat less than might be expected given both the overall size of the tenure and also its rapid expansion through the addition of new dwellings to the existing stock. Much of the mobility potential

created in the sector by the addition of new dwellings or households vacating the tenure (for example through death or household dissolution) is utilised by new and not continuing households.[46] The tenure has expanded quickly and recruited households, but this expansion has not facilitated increased mobility
opportunities for significant groups of existing home-owners.[47]

Nonetheless, Table 14.7 does indicate that of all *continuing*
households existing home-owners have by far the best opportunity of acquiring an owner-occupied property on moving;
continuing households from other tenures have much less
chance of purchasing a home of their own. Thus the flow of
continuing households from other tenures into owner-occupied
dwellings is much less than what would be expected if all
continuing households, whatever their previous tenure, had
equal access to the sector. As Murie suggests: 'The prospect
of gaining access to owner-occupation probably declines progressively with age and length of residence in other tenures.[48]
Indeed, *when the sizes of tenures are controlled for*, Table 14.7
suggests that continuing households have a better chance of
being mobile by moving to a rented dwelling than they do by
moving to an owner-occupied dwelling.

The owner-occupied sector functions as a tenure of termination. Once a home-owner, a household is unlikely to move to
another tenure. To a lesser extent, the council sector also
functions to retain its households. In contrast, the private
rented sector acts as what Murie[49] calls a 'sector of passage'
for a majority of households, feeding both the two main housing
tenures.

Residential mobility would appear to do little to break down
the existing contrasts either within the owner-occupied sector,
or between home-owners and people in other tenures. In this
process, socioeconomic grouping assumes great significance.
On moving from one dwelling to another, professional workers,
employers and managers have by far the best chance of becoming or remaining owner-occupiers. Other socioeconomic groups,
and in particular non-manual workers and the economically
inactive, are much less likely to move to an owner-occupied
dwelling. Residential mobility makes the extent of social segregation by tenure more marked: 'Through movement, differences
in the probability of different socio-economic groups using the
owner-occupied and public sectors becomes sharper.[50]

5 HOUSING CHAINS AND FILTERING

A central component in the structuring of residential mobility
is the supply of vacant dwellings. As suggested in chapter 9,
in any particular housing system (defined, for example, by
national or regional boundaries, the spatial extent of a labour
market, or by tenure itself) vacancies are created when *either*
additional dwellings are added to the existing stock (for

instance, building of new dwellings) *or* existing households leave the housing system and vacate a dwelling (for instance, through death, certain types of household dissolution or out-migration). These initial vacancies, when used by mobile households, form housing or vacancy chains. For example, when the initial vacant dwelling is occupied by a continuing household moving from another dwelling in the housing system, the vacancy is transferred from the first to second dwelling, and a second link in the chain completed. Eventually the vacancy will be extinguished and the chain terminated. This occurs through the reverse of the processes that create new vacancies: either the addition of new households to the housing system (through household formation or in-migration) or the with-drawal of dwellings from the existing stock (through demoli-tion, closure or conversion of two or more units into a single unit).

Closely related to the concept of housing chains is the notion of 'filtering', which has a very long pedigree in academic, government and housing institution circles.[51] Filtering is gener-ally used to refer to the downward movement of dwellings in value and quality over time and/or the upward movement of households from lower- to higher-quality dwellings. Through taking part in a housing chain, it is often argued that house-holds can filter up into better dwellings, thus releasing their old homes for other families who can also improve their housing in the process by moving from inferior dwellings.

The Building Societies Association has perhaps made the most non-academic use of the filtering notion. It has suggested, for example, that:[52]

The housing market must be seen as a ladder. People join at the bottom end; they move gradually upwards until they reach old age when they may move down again. Eventually they die and leave the ladder completely. The important point is that there is no room for people to come in at the bottom of the market unless people already there are moving upwards.

With such sentiments the BSA has justified the allocation of significant financial resources (such as mortgage loans and tax relief) to the upper end of the owner-occupied market - to higher-income home-owners in expensive dwellings.[53] The BSA has, for example, opposed either limiting or withdrawing tax relief, arguing 'that policy measures which, directly or indirec-tly, are aimed at particular sectors of housing are likely to create distortions in the market'.[54] In this view curtailing the construction or finance of expensive and high-quality dwellings would also curtail the mobility and housing opportunities of low-income people, perhaps in considerable housing need, who would use vacancies at later stages in housing chains.

What, then, is the reality of filtering and housing chains?

Table 14.8 presents aggregate data concerning vacancy creation, continuation and termination in the owner-occupied sector
in 1971.[55] Vacancies created are of crucial importance in any
housing system, since they provide the original mobility opportunities for all households wishing to move. Some means of
vacancy creation fluctuate wildly over time. For example, private
and public building may slump, as it did for a number of years
from the late 1970s, and restrict both the opportunities for
households to move to new houses in the owner-occupied sector
and to transfer to other tenures. Similarly, households that
might have made use of the second-hand dwellings, released
by the first set of mobile households, may also be thwarted in
their attempts to move.

*Table 14.8 Vacancy creation, continuation and termination in the owner-
occupied sector in 1971*

	('000)
New vacancies created	
New houses completed	192
Conversions	2
Dissolution of households	140
Moves to other tenures	58
Emigrants	27
Rented homes sold for owner-occupation[a]	60
Total	479
Vacancy transfers within the owner-occupied sector	
Existing home-owners both selling and buying	410
Vacancies terminated	
Demolition, etc.	20
Remaining vacant	5
Formation of households	177
Moves from other tenures	259
Immigrants	15
Total	486

Source: Derived from *HPTV*, part I, Tables III.10 and III.18, and part II, Table VI.1.

[a] Excludes sitting purchasers.

Apart from vacancy creation, the other factor that determines
the total mobility in a housing system is chain length – the
number of dwellings each vacancy occupies before termination.
Table 14.8 indicates that in 1971 the mean chain length (the
total number of residentially mobile households divided by the
total vacancies created) in the owner-occupied sector was
1.87; for each new vacancy 1.87 households moved before the
vacancy terminated. This figure is surprisingly low given the
assertions of organisations such as the BSA and the popular

mythology shared by many home-owners that chains of moves
are often long and complex. As might be expected given mean
chain length, the distribution of lengths are heavily biased
towards shorter chains. For example, one study[56] of chains
originating in the private sector (largely owner-occupied
housing) in the Hull urban area during 1972 revealed that chain
length varied from one to six links, with 45 per cent being of
one link; 36 per cent two links; 12 per cent 3 links; 6 per cent
4 links; and less than 1 per cent of 5 or more links.

It may be argued that the aggregate data in Table 14.8 arti-
ficially reduces chain length because vacancies that move to
other tenures are not traced to their termination. However, a
number of studies that traced vacancies originating in the
owner-occupied sector through tenure transfers, reveal very
similar lengths to that suggested using the data in Table 14.8.
The Hull research found a chain length of 1.83; a study of
chains resulting from building for home-ownership in west
central Scotland, 2.09[57]; similar work in Northern Ireland,
1.64[58]; and, a nationwide sample survey[59] of private newbuild
vacancies in 1969, 1.88.

It is therefore apparent that the majority of vacancy chains
originating in the owner-occupied sector are short; they do not
create an immense amount of mobility. The reason for this is
clear. For every 100 new vacancies, typically substantially less
than 100 continuing owner-occupied households are able to move
before other households new to the housing system step in to
extinguish the vacancy. Nevertheless, chain lengths might be
expected to vary over time and space according to variations in
the nature of housing market processes. For example, where
house prices are very high, new households may find it difficult
to compete for vacancies (against selling buyers who can rely
on using net worth from their previous dwelling) and the length
of chains may therefore tend to be longer.

Two crucial issues in what happens to a vacancy are the
nature of mortgage finance allocation and the exchange process.
Most households cannot move unless they have access to adequate mortgage finance. Households new to the owner-occupied
sector have a good chance, in comparison to the total body of
existing home-owners, of gaining such finance. For example,
between 1970 and 1980 the proportion of building society mortgages granted to first-time buyers ranged from 61 to 45 per cent
annually.[60] Similarly, the exchange process for each individual
dwelling determines what happens to a vacancy. In theory
estate agents could encourage longer chains and hence more
total mobility. Indeed, one advantage of public sector housing
is that the exchange process may be explicitly managed with
this in mind.[61] However, estate agents are not so much concerned with maximising chain length as with maximising the selling price and speed of each individual sale. Moreover the total
exchange process in the owner-occupied sector is so complex,
time-consuming and thwart with difficulty (see chapter 13 for

a detailed discussion), that many chains of sales that are lined up never materialise. As with other types of chain, a housing chain is only as strong as its weakest link: a single seller or purchaser dropping out of a potential chain, perhaps because of difficulties in obtaining an adequate mortgage, will invariably destroy the complete chain. New home-owners are inevitably advantaged since they have no dwelling to sell, and are so more likely to be able to purchase a dwelling (and extinguish a vacancy) quickly and without difficulty.

Apart from typically being terminated fairly rapidly, most vacancies remain within the urban area where they originated. In the Hull study only one in five vacancies were identified as leaving the urban area. The National Movers Survey of 1971[62] provides similar, if indirect, evidence, finding that 72 per cent of continuing home-owners moved to dwellings within one hour's usual travelling time of the vacated dwelling.

Perhaps the most central issue to discuss, particularly in view of the beliefs of organisations such as the BSA, is whether households are able to filter up to better dwellings through the operation of owner-occupied housing chains, and whether such chains do contribute to solving the housing needs of disadvantaged households. Since chains are short, the extent of filtering is in fact slight. From this perspective it seems unlikely that building or releasing high-quality owner-occupied dwellings will indirectly benefit (as a vacancy passes down a chain) the inadequately housed. However, those vacancies that survive the first links of a chain do often occupy progressively lower-cost and quality housing. In the Northern Ireland study the average price of a dwelling bought at link one was £4,950, declining to £3,107 at link three. The Hull study showed that rateable values for chains initiated in new suburban dwellings varied from £235 at link one to £156 at link four. The Scottish research revealed that the proportion of dwellings that were *not* detached or semi-detached houses increased from 16 per cent at link one to 79 per cent at the third and subsequent link. However, a considerable majority of vacancies do not survive the second link of chains.

In policy terms, more important than the decline in dwelling quality is the extent to which disadvantaged households are able to utilise vacancies and improve their housing conditions. Do disadvantaged households benefit from filtering?

Taking first continuing home-owners, as we have already seen, data for the early 1970s suggest that about one in four made sideways moves to similar quality dwellings (often for employment reasons) and another quarter actually traded down. Nonetheless, about one in two mobile continuing owner-occupiers benefited by moving to substantially higher-quality houses. However, such owners tend to be already advantaged in, for example, income and occupation. For reasons suggested earlier in this chapter, disadvantaged continuing home-owners are frequently immobile and rarely benefit from joining vacancy chains in the tenure; those who do move may actually filter down and not up.

Turning to new home-owners, we have seen that they are able to make considerable use of housing chains, often early on in the life of a vacancy. Both the Northern Ireland and west central Scotland studies found that 26 per cent of new dwellings were occupied directly by newly formed households without further moves being generated. Similarly, the Hull study of a wider range of initial vacancies revealed that 26 per cent of chains were extinguished at link one by the movement of new households. As with the case of continuing owner-occupiers, new home-owners tend to constitute a relatively narrow and already advantaged group. Two-thirds of the household heads moving into new owner-occupied houses in the Hull area were in non-manual occupations, as were 60 per cent of households occupying similar dwellings studied in Northern Ireland.

Rather than introducing greater equality into housing provision, the operation of housing chains originating in the owner-occupied tenure tends to be regressive. Higher-income and more credit-worthy households are able to outbid disadvantaged households for the best housing at all positions in chains of moves, leaving only inferior and sometimes extremely low-quality dwellings to be competed for by the disadvantaged. The BSA view of the owner-occupied sector on a ladder of housing opportunity and accessibility is inaccurate. As Murie and his co-authors argue:[63]

> filtering is an idealised conception of the operation of the
> housing market under certain conditions. As those condi-
> tions do not obtain in practice filtering ceases to be a
> representation of what happens in the housing market.
> The implication that filtering does or can occur becomes an
> untestable assertion which is inseparable from the political
> associations of the idea. In other words, it becomes an
> assertion used to justify a reliance on the market process
> and the capacity of that process to meet policy ends. It is
> an assertion which is difficult to sustain in theoretical or
> empirical debate.

Many new households - instead of coming 'in at the bottom of the market ... [when] people already there are moving upwards' - join immediately either in the middle or at the top end of the market. Some continuing home-owners are able to trade up, but this is not so for many disadvantaged owner-occupiers who will either be completely excluded from the chance of joining an owner-occupied housing chain, or left with extremely restricted and inadequate mobility opportunities. The operation of filtering through housing chains does not, in the case of the owner-occupied market, extend to all groups or enable all households to improve their housing through mobility. Indeed disadvantaged households in housing need stand a far better opportunity of improving their housing by joining chains in the public sector. Housing chain research[64] has identified that local authorities, through the management of vacancies, are able to satisfy the housing needs of many low-income households who would otherwise remain immobile and, in consequence, to at least partially tackle problems of inadequate housing, sharing and overcrowding typically left untouched in the operation of owner-occupied housing chains.

15 OWNER-OCCUPATION AND SOCIAL RELATIONS

by Fred Gray

1 INTRODUCTION[1]

For a number of decades, and particularly during the post-war
period, there has been an increasing tendency to fetishise the
impact of owner-occupation - as a tenure form - on social relations. The phrase 'social relations' is here taken to mean the
economic, social and political attitudes and aspirations, and
actions and behaviour, of people in the tenure. As such the
term denotes the nature and quality of the lives of people who
are home-owners; their relationships with other groups,
particularly tenants; and, how people in the tenure think about
and act in wider society.

The concept of fetishism is also central to this chapter. It is
used to describe a variety of work that has treated the tenure
itself as a powerful and essentially independent influence on
social relations. In particular, a considerable body of literature
has assumed that owner-occupation necessarily involves and
determines specific patterns and structures of social relations.
A stress is often placed on the internal characteristics of the
tenure in, sometimes almost automatically, producing distinctive
forms of thought, behaviour and actions amongst home-owners.
In subsequent sections of this chapter, a number of reasons
are put forward to support the argument that this general view
of owner-occupation and social relations is limited and inaccurate.
Rather than fetishising the tenure as an object with necessarily
distinctive qualities which, in turn, confer upon home-owners
specific social relations, it is argued that both the tenure itself,
and the social relations of owner-occupiers, should be seen to
be dependent on a host of external variables and processes that
are not uniform either over time or space. For this reason we
should expect neither owner-occupation as a tenure form nor
the social relations of home-owners to be monolithic or homogeneous. A variety of evidence is presented to support this
contention, and the notion that both tenure and social relations
are a product of processes such as economic change, the evolution of state form and activity, and class struggle.

The general tendency to fetishise owner-occupation and social
relations is apparent amongst many politicians and policy-makers
in government, and also in the statements made by key individuals of housing institutions such as building societies. More
recently, the notion that owner-occupation is an independent
variable of major causal importance in the lives of individuals

267

and the formation and nature of social groups has been taken
up by social scientists of a variety of persuasions, including
a number of Marxists and Weberian urban sociologists. It is,
then, possible to differentiate three alternative conceptualisations of the relationship between owner-occupation and social
relations: (i) *status quo* views of politicians, policy-makers
and housing institutions; (ii) normative Marxist views; and
(iii) Weberian views. In part, these three conceptualisations
vary because of simple differences in terminology and emphasis.
There are, however, important differences in theoretical starting point and orientation. Initially, this chapter describes in
some detail the nature of the three views. A critique is then
provided of each view in turn, and the chapter concludes with
a number of comments aimed at uniting the discussion and at
suggesting a more appropriate view of the relationships between
home-ownership and social relations.

2 THREE VIEWS OF THE IMPACT OF OWNER-OCCUPATION ON SOCIAL RELATIONS

Since the 1930s government policy-makers and politicians, partly
at least because of an assumed electoral advantage, have often
argued the central place of owner-occupation in the well-being
of individual, family and society.[2] During the interwar period
one of the key parliamentary figures, Neville Chamberlain, saw
home-ownership as 'a revolution which of necessity enlisted
all those who were affected by it on the side of law and order
and enrolled them in a great army of good citizens'.[3] Similarly,
following the war, the 1953 Conservative White Paper, *Houses -
the Next Step*, in discussing the role of owner-occupation
argued, 'Of all forms of saving, this is one of the best. Of all
forms of ownership this is one of the most satisfying to the
individual and the most beneficial to the nation.'[4]

More recently, the theme was developed in the 1971 White
Paper, *Fair Deal for Housing*:[5]

Home ownership is the most rewarding form of housing tenure. It satisfies a deep and natural desire on the part of
the householder to have independent control of the home
that shelters him and his family. It gives him the greatest possible security against the loss of his home; and particularly
against the price changes that may threaten his ability to
keep it. If the householder buys his house on mortgage he
builds up by steady saving a capital asset for himself and
his dependants.

Such ideas, only slightly modified, could jump party boundaries. For example, the Labour government's 1977 *Housing Policy
Review* argued:[6]

A preference for home ownership is sometimes explained
on the grounds that potential home owners believe that
it will bring them financial advantage. A far more likely
reason for the secular trend towards home ownership is
the sense of greater personal independence that it brings.
For most people owning one's home is a basic and natural
desire.

And in the same document:[7]

The widening of entry into home ownership for people with
modest incomes will help solve housing problems which
used to be faced by the public sector, as well as satisfying deep-seated social aspirations.

Despite a new Conservative government and new decade, the
following statement by Environment Minister, Michael Heseltine,
made in January 1980 gives one a certain déjà vu feeling:[8]

There is in this country a deeply ingrained desire for home
ownership. The Government believe that this spirit should
be fostered. It reflects the wishes of the people, ensures
the wide spread of wealth through society, encourages a
personal desire to improve and modernise one's home,
enables people to accrue wealth for their children, and
stimulates the attitudes of independence and self reliance
that are the bedrock of a free society.

Increasingly, then, the view that owner-occupation propagates
individual and societal well-being has been accepted by both
Labour and Conservative governments. In turn, this has been
related to the relegation of council housing as a second-best
welfare tenure for those unable or unwilling to accept the challenge of owner-occupation.[9] It has gone hand in hand with
financial and other policies favouring owner-occupation (see
chapters 1-3) and with, for example, the more recent Conservative drive towards council house sales (see chapter 8).

Turning to housing institutions and agencies, a similar picture emerges of owner-occupation being seen as a positive influence on social relations. As noted in chapter 13, the exchange
lobby and associated professional organisations have often
stressed the value of home-ownership. Similarly, this is true
of the building society movement over a long period of time.
Indeed, the building societies may be seen as a formative force
and pressure group on the approaches and assumptions of
successive British governments.

Harold Bellman, one of the central figures of the building
society movement during the interwar years, was also amongst
the most vocal concerning the benefits of home-ownership:[10]

The man who has something to protect and improve - a
stake of some sort in the country - naturally turns his
thoughts in the direction of sane, ordered, and perforce
economical government. The thrifty man is seldom or
never an extremist agitator. To him revolution is anathema;
and, as in the earliest days Building Societies acted as a
stabilising force, so to-day they stand, in the words of
the Rt. Hon. G.N. Barnes, as 'a bulwark against Bolshevism and all that Bolshevism stands for'.

The theme developed following the Second World War. For
example, John Dunham, Chairman of the BSA in 1964, argued
that home-ownership:[11]

is an essential part of one's life. It satisfies a basic human
need to surround oneself with something that is absolutely
personal and private between members of one's family.
   When one talks about it becoming the background of
family life one thinks of it as an anchorage or harbour from
which one emerges each day. Night after night one returns
and becomes part of the family again.

A decade later the BSA reasserted what by now was an old
and familiar story:[12]

The point where more than half the houses in the country
have become owner-occupied was a significant milestone
because even a small stake in the country does affect political attitudes. The greater the proportion of owner-
occupiers the less likely were extreme measures to prevail.

In another publication of the same organisation issued in 1980,
Gilchrist echoes and amplifies the recurrent argument. For
example, discussing the reasons for people to become owner-
occupiers, he states: 'Motivations are not purely financial.
People want to buy because buying gives them freedom, choice,
security, mobility, pride, maybe extra status, and extra
borrowing power.'[13]
   Status quo views suggest, then, that owner-occupation acts
as if it were a fairy godmother's wand. When waved, the wand
transforms an ordinary pumpkin and insignificant white mice
(a rented house) into a glittering coach and horses (a home of
one's own). Similarly, a previously ragged and unhappy Cin-
derella (a tenant) is changed into a beautiful and desirable
person (an owner-occupier) who can then join with similar
fortunate people (to use Anthony Eden's 1946 phrase - 'a nationwide property owning democrácy') in all the fun and joy of
the ball.
   How then have social scientists responded to these *status quo*
views about the influence of owner-occupation on social relations? A first line of criticism is against the supposedly innate

'natural desire' and 'basic human need' that home-ownership is argued both to derive from and, in turn, nurture. Thus comparative studies[14] show that the development and nature of home-ownership varies widely from country to country, bearing no clear relationship to per capita GNP, and not showing a general tendency to increase over time. For example, although one might suppose the 'desire' and 'need' for owner-occupation to be more easily fulfilled the greater the wealth of a nation, West Germany, Switzerland and Sweden (all economically more successful than Britain) have lower levels of owner-occupation. Similarly, at times during the post-war period, home-ownership has actually fallen in countries such as Canada, Australia and Switzerland. The 'ingrained', 'natural' and 'basic' 'desire' and 'need' may, on this basis, correctly be exposed as a myth. As Boddy notes,[15] this myth 'functions by projecting on to *individuals* the characteristics of the particular socio-economic system in which they are located - a system largely founded on private ownership of property'.

Turning away from comparative analysis, perhaps the most sustained response to *status quo* views has come from a number of scholars working in the Marxist tradition of urban political economy.[16] One of the strengths of Marxist approaches is the recognition of the social, economic and political (rather than individualistic and 'natural') origins of owner-occupation as a tenure form. Thus home-ownership is located within, and understood as part of, specific capitalist societies. However, many (although not all) Marxists have seen the links between owner-occupation and social relations in an essentially *normative* fashion. Thus the tenure is argued to produce functional social relations which have the effect of helping to sustain capitalism itself. Despite a number of changes in terminology, the arguments made in normative Marxist approaches are essentially the opposite side of the same coin as used in *status quo* views.[17]

Ball, for example, has argued that:[18]

Ideologically, home-ownership emphasises the desirability of the private ownership of property and the philosophy of individual 'self-help' and generates a group with a vested interest in maintenance of private property....Another advantage of owner-occupation for the capitalist economy is argued to be the division it creates among groups who might otherwise organise together.

In this set of ideas Ball is following Clarke and Ginsburg:[19]

The capitalist class as a whole has a clear commitment to owner-occupation on ideological grounds....This ideological commitment has two dimensions. Firstly...continuing to legitimate private property by reference to its socially useful character...[and secondly],...both in fragmenting the working class and in giving the individual workers a 'stake in the system'.

More recently, Boddy has stressed that 'the structure of housing tenure has a particular social impact and definite political and ideological implications'.[20] He goes on to argue that owner-occupation increases support for the ownership of private property and 'anaesthetises' social conflict in housing. In particular:[21]

> at the level of political struggle, home-ownership eliminates both the overtly antagonistic class relations of tenant versus profit-seeking private landlords and the equally conflict-ridden relationship of council tenant to local authorities.... Home owners have no obvious opponent against which to struggle.

In his own inimitable manner, Harvey has developed this perspective. He argues that home-ownership is a major source of defusing class struggle and of transforming it to intra-class community conflict. Owner-occupation promotes[22]

> the allegiance of at least a segment of the working class to the principle of private property; an ethic of 'possessive individualism'; and a fragmentation of the working class into 'housing classes' of homeowners and tenants....A worker mortgaged up to the hilt is, for the most part, a pillar of social stability.

He continues that owners will be concerned to preserve and enhance the value of their property, and may become petty landlords, so engaging 'in the appropriation of values at the expense of other workers'.[23] More importantly, he argues, every home-owner because of his equity in property will struggle against changes that adversely affect that equity; this tends to fragment the working class and puts owner-occupiers 'on the side of the principle of private property'.[24]

Marxists following this normative perspective add that homeowners do not constitute a distinct class or 'social category',[25] but argue that owner-occupation obscures the basic conflict between labour and capital by ideologically fragmenting the working class. Some Marxists also suggest that the tenure may not be entirely beneficial to capitalist society. For example, home-owners in defending their net worth may resist property speculation by financial institutions, and the fragmentation of urban landownership may create problems for industrial and finance capital.[26]

Despite these qualifications, there is, however, perhaps little to choose between normative Marxist and *status quo* views of the role owner-occupation plays in structuring social relations. Clearly the language is different, as is the tone - pessimistic against optimistic. It is as if the government's and building societies' fairy godmother has changed her clothes to become an evil stepmother set on killing Snow White - working-class unity. Owner-occupation is no longer a heroine but a villain, but the story stays the same.

It should be stressed, however, that the variety of Marxist analysis of owner-occupation and social relations described above is but one aspect of Marxist-inspired work on housing. At a purely intellectual level, much Marxist work has been of immense value in advancing understanding and explanation of 'the housing question' in capitalist societies.[27] Furthermore, authors working in this tradition, such as Rose, have moved away from a normative approach to owner-occupation and social relations[28] to see housing tenures in a less rigid and functional manner. In drawing on some of this more recent material, subsequent sections of this chapter attempt to provide a more complex and realistic view of home-ownership and social relations.

In contrast to normative Marxist views of housing tenure and social relations is the work of academics following a Weberian perspective. Rex and Moore were the first sociologists to formulate clearly a concept of 'housing class',[29] with the underlying assumption that 'where men's housing situation changed, their interests and hence their behaviour would change'.[30] The notion of housing class as formulated by Rex and Moore has been subject to considerable criticism, largely conceded by Rex himself.[31]

More recently, the concept has been revised by Saunders.[32] He attacks the Marxist stress on the ideological role of owner-occupation, and emphasises that owner-occupation is an accumulative form of tenure that brings real material gains that form the basis for the formation of housing classes and political divisions. Owner-occupiers that have an asset usable for real returns, and hence both live off property and live in it, are seen as a middle property class between the 'positively privileged' class of housing suppliers and the 'negatively privileged' class of non-owners. Because of their 'objectively distinct' class position, home-owners may align with either other class, according to the nature of the issue. 'When owner-occupiers mobilize politically their actions reflect a concern with their own material situation and cannot be dismissed as "false consciousness".'[33]

Saunders makes use of a variety of empirical material to support his case, and in particular his own study of the residents' associations of wealthy owner-occupiers living to the south of Croydon. These associations carried out a variety of successful campaigns to preserve the quality of their residential environment. From this evidence owner-occupation is seen to produce unique social relations and 'a very strong collective class awareness'[34] since 'the objective interests of each individual owner-occupier are in maintaining and enhancing his material advantages and opportunities for realising capital gains through inflation of house market values'.[35]

To sum up this long series of extracts from a variety of sources, despite considerable diversity in terminology and differences in theoretical starting point, the central and uniting theme is that owner-occupation is seen to have a powerful and independent impact on social relations. Effectively, it creates particular patterns of individual and family life and leads to the formation of a distinct social group sharing common interests. It results in particular sets of individual attitudes and aspirations, and clear modes of household behaviour and social group activity.

How accurate, then, is this set of assumptions and the underlying idea that housing tenure creates and reinforces new forms of social relations? The issue is important. In policy terms, if we accept the *status quo* argument, a drive towards owner-occupation will surely benefit all those who are included,[36] even if the excluded are increasingly deprived. In academic terms, if owner-occupation is viewed as a key determinant of social relations then many existing theories of class and power in society need at least to be reassessed.[37] For those politically on the Left, as Rose has observed, such assumptions imply a major limitation on the space available within everyday life for resistance to the logic of capitalism. 'In a society where more than half the population are already homeowners, the prospects offered so far by this perspective seem dismal'.[38] Similarly, 'the over-riding political implication of the theoretical framework that has so far dominated such research is that no progressive changes in the social relations of everyday living can be made without first of all creating a Revolution in the sphere of production'.[39]

The most appropriate manner to discuss the validity of *status quo*, normative Marxist and Weberian approaches is to examine each set of assumptions in turn,

3   A CRITIQUE OF *STATUS QUO* VIEWS

Status quo views suggest that home-ownership confers upon owner-occupiers a variety of positive characteristics which, in turn, lead to distinctive social relations beneficial to society as a whole. These characteristics include independent control of one's home; security of tenure; the building up of a capital asset; mobility; a freer and fuller life; and, considerable choice in housing.

A considerable array of empirical material does indicate that, during the post-war period in particular, many owner-occupiers have at least partially benefited in the manner suggested by the *status quo* view. The important point though, is that this has not always been the case in the past, nor is it true of the universe of owner-occupiers today.

Historically, some individuals working in the housing market have, unlike much building society propaganda today, been prepared to recognise that the tenure does not necessarily lead to a full and freer life. For example,[40]

for those who lack any capital and whose job has no permanence, to try to purchase a dwelling is asking for trouble... haphazard purchase by people who were so ill-advised as to 'sign-up' upon the dulcet tones of a selling agent working his magic, has been the cause of much misery in the past.

Similarly, the Central Housing Advisory Committee in a 1944 report, *Private Enterprise Housing*, found it necessary to examine and (despite the fact that membership of the Committee included building society personnel) found some truth in the following criticisms of pre-war owner-occupation:[41]

(1) That the standard of construction was not always satisfactory.
(2) That in order to obtain a house young marrieds had no alternative owing to the scarcity of houses for letting, but to undertake the purchase of houses on mortgage lending at a cost which imposed an undue strain on their means.
(3) That owner-occupation on the scale on which it developed during the inter-war period held a danger to national well-being, in that it tended to restrict the mobility of labour.

The final point is especially noteworthy given the continuing government emphasis on the role of council housing in restricting household mobility in contrast to the mobility presumed to be a benefit of owner-occupation.

These contemporary statements indicate that between the wars owner-occupation did not always bring in train a set of clear benefits. Indeed, for some groups the reverse was more likely. Since that period the nature of owner-occupation has changed in a variety of ways. Yet, as chapter 14 demonstrated, considerable evidence exists that the present owner-occupied sector is not homogeneous, and that many owners are disadvantaged when compared both with other households in the sector and some people in other tenures. Indeed, some homeowners receive few if any of the advantages presumed of the tenure. There appear to be two related sets of reasons for this. The first concerns the nature of particular housing markets or sub-markets; and the second, the characteristics of certain groups of home-owners.

The most well-researched examples of housing market processes working against the interests of owners concerns inner-city areas.[42] Dwellings in such areas are effectively isolated from the mainstream of the housing market. Typically, they are low-quality and old dwellings in environmentally poor locations.

The redlining policies[43] of building societies tend to exclude
these areas from the most advantageous mortgage facilities (the
source of a major set of benefits for most owners) forcing borrowers to seek short-term high-interest loans from a variety
of sources including fringe banks and money lenders (see
chapter 7).[44]

As the Benwell Community Project publication, *Private Housing and the Working Class*, demonstrates, in inner areas such
as Benwell in Newcastle and Saltley in Birmingham, the basic
housing problem is one of physical obsolesence: 'however long-
lived housing may be, sooner or later it begins to wear out.
Resources must increasingly be put into repairs and maintenance, or into upgrading old houses to modern standards.'[45]
Many of the advantages of the tenure depend on specific housing market processes and general house price inflation. Yet:[46]

> in the older housing areas, there is a growing possibility
> that the price of these houses will cease to rise in line with
> others unless there is massive investment in upgrading
> them. At the same time, the owners of these houses are
> increasingly likely to be those who cannot afford to make
> such an investment, either because they are long-standing
> residents now retired or on low incomes, or because they
> are new owner-occupiers with large mortgage repayments
> relative to their income, leaving little to spare for other
> housing expenditure.

In the long term, where the price of dwellings declines relative
to general trends, owners 'face a position in which their home
becomes obsolete, and even compensation based on full market
value proves grossly inadequate as a basis for their next
purchase'.[47] Such owners are likely to become trapped in housing of declining quality and value, and receive none of the
supposed advantages of the tenure. The extent of these problems is likely to increase in the future, because of growing
inner-city obsolescence, the unwillingness of the state to intervene on a radical scale, and the developing economic crisis
which reduces the incomes of poor home-owners.

One group particularly likely to experience these sorts of
problems are black people. As we saw in chapter 14, there is
a much higher proportion of home-owners amongst both West
Indians and Asians with 'working-class' occupations than for
white people with similar jobs. Smith suggests that 'for a
substantial proportion of Asians, buying their home is not a way
of getting superior housing at a premium price ... but a way
of getting poor housing cheaply'.[48] This, however, is to underestimate the housing costs associated with low-quality dwellings.
Rex and Tomlinson argue that both West Indians and Asians
become trapped in home-ownership, which represents 'a new
bottom of the housing system' and denies 'them the chance of
moving to the privileged rented sector'.[49] In their study of

Handsworth in Birmingham, an area containing some of the poorest housing and the most depressed conditions in the city, these two authors suggest:[50]

> The whites were there because they had stayed on while their property deteriorated. The West Indians were encouraged or constrained to go there by the kinds of housing finance available to them or not available to them. The Asians were there because they were the cheapest houses available.

Groups of both black and white households are pushed into certain sections of the market, but denied access to the supposed advantages of the tenure. Often people have no choice at all in determining their tenure (see chapter 5). In general, people forced into this sort of owner-occupation, and consequently barred from the full benefits of the tenure, fall into a variety of groups defined by a related set of factors such as class, occupation, age, educational success and race. However, from the viewpoint of who gets what housing in the owner-occupied sector perhaps the most decisive issue, springing from this series of factors, is the level, regularity and security of income.

Neither the low-quality dwellings nor the disadvantageous loan finance (see chapter 7) available to people with inadequate income represent security or independence. High and inflexible repair and running costs (see chapter 12) and mortgage payments are a considerable, sometimes unbearable, burden for such occupiers.[51] Moreover, since the late 1970s, growing economic recession and associated interest rate rises, unemployment, short-time working, and a decline in real wages for some groups will have undoubtedly 'marginalised' increasing numbers of other home-owners. These pressures may force borrowers to let rooms, cease the maintenance and repair of dwellings, default on mortgage payments or take out a second mortgage, and perhaps eventually leave the tenure altogether.

The supposed option of trading down to a cheaper dwelling, so realising the net worth of the first house, is not available.[52] Such dwellings already represent the bottom of the owner-occupied sector, and because of the property's obsolescence the price may be extremely low. Sideways moves to similar property have little to offer. In any event, the high transaction costs the vast majority of owner-occupiers are forced to bear (see chapter 13) in buying and selling property is another restriction on movement. Furthermore, if the occupier's present dwelling has fallen in relative value moves may be precluded, since many owner-occupiers depend to some extent on realising part of the net worth of their previous dwelling to finance transaction costs.

These situations are very different from the optimistic *status quo* vision of owner-occupation. Indeed, far from leading to a

fuller or freer life, the demands of the tenure may exert a
depressing control on social relations. As Rose[53] argues,
'for women in their domestic role the "ideal" single family home
has always been primarily a workplace, and often a very oppres-
sive and isolating one, rather than a haven of any kind'. This
clearly applies to other tenures as well as owner-occupation.
However, home-ownership often brings particularly intense
problems of isolation, especially in suburbia, because of the
physical nature of the tenure (see chapter 14). Moreover,
owner-occupation may have a detrimental impact on other members of a household apart from women. For example, high housing costs may reduce the number of children young couples
plan and have.[54] In addition, 'courtships have been extended
while saving for house and furniture, marriages postponed or
brought forward according to the availability of a house, and
wives continued to work after marriage'.[55] These sorts of
relationships between the demands of home-ownership and family
life-styles may also be extended to relatively high-income households, particularly in regions of high house prices where the
income and deposit requirements for tenure entrance are considerable. As Whitehead notes:[56]

> someone who is only just able to afford to become an owner-
> occupier may find in practice that he has no greater choice,
> and sometimes even less, than many council tenants...local
> authorities...do not, for instance, restrict space just because
> the tenant is poor.

It may be objected, of course, that the vast majority of owner-
occupiers do not experience such difficulties and disadvantages.
Indeed, many households enjoy considerable financial benefits,
and good secure material housing conditions, by being in the
tenure. But this argument misses what, in the context of this
discussion, is a more fundamental point. It may certainly be
the case that the majority of owners have gained considerably
from living in the tenure. This, when combined with the ideology stressing the immense benefits of owner-occupation over
other tenures, helps explain the preferences expressed by
most people for the sector (see chapter 14). Yet this is so only
because of a series of much wider factors. Whitehead has
developed this theme most comprehensively, and argues that
'many of the so-called benefits of owner-occupation depend on
wealth and secure income rather than ownership as such'.[57]
A prime example concerns building society mortgage finance
and related subsidies in the form of tax relief. It is the already
advantaged, in terms of income, wealth and employment, who
gain most from this sort of finance market. In turn, for successful households this confers high-quality, saleable property
which is an asset of increasing value. Many of the advantages
enjoyed by the majority of owner-occupiers lie in factors that
are independent of the tenure *per se*.

It is not in itself owner-occupation that confers advantage to individuals, but existing wider-based social and economic processes affecting the distribution of income, wealth and power in society, and the particular characteristics of spatially and temporally specific housing policies and housing market processes. Having recognised this, it would be absurd to argue that the supposed societal advantages – such as the maintenance of *status quo* political attitudes – can be said to spring from simply conferring the status of owner-occupation on to an individual or family. Most individuals are owner-occupiers because to some extent they have already become part of the *status quo*, and achieved a relatively secure place in the wider class and economic system. Equally, deprived home-owners may often stand no more chance of becoming part of the *status quo* – for example in class, occupational or income terms – because of their housing tenure, which may indeed actually confirm and reinforce their existing class position. This theme is developed in the following section.

4 A CRITIQUE OF NORMATIVE MARXIST VIEWS

The variety of Marxist analysis described earlier emphasises that owner-occupation creates normative social relations functional for capital. A stress is placed on the ideological nature of home-ownership. Debt encumbrance induces social docility. Ownership legitimates private property and turns inter-class conflict into intra-class and community conflict. The working class is divided into tenants and owners. Workers are given a 'stake in the system', and the class conflict underlying housing provision is obscured. In general, the tenure acts to maintain the stability of the existing social structure and social order.

There are a number of difficulties with this analysis. A particular problem is to find empirical evidence to support a largely theoretical construction. Western capitalist countries have experienced general social and political stability for much of the post-war period. However, the long period of relatively sustained growth – at least until a decade ago – was combined with rising affluence and increasing living standards for large sections of the population. Under these circumstances the likelihood of major political and social upheaval was remote with or without owner-occupation. Indeed, the examples of Western countries such as Sweden, West Germany and the Netherlands, where despite comparatively low levels of owner-occupation[58] the population – relative to the situation in Britain – was, if anything, more not less docile and politically stable, and less challenging to private property, suggests the relatively minor role of housing tenure in the process.

The majority of British home-owners have been drawn from those sections of the population who have, in any case, secured for themselves rising affluence and income levels independently of owner-occupation. So long as prosperity continued they were the groups less likely to threaten social and political stability. Home-ownership has given these groups a stake in the system, but only because of longer-term economic trends, prosperity, and broader social processes. Equally, tenants in good housing, and sharing in general prosperity, might also be expected not to push for radical change. At this level it is always possible, if somewhat false, to analyse the functionality for capital of particular tenures. However, the reverse may also be true. The potential for radical social and political change is likely to increase during periods of economic crisis for capitalism, and to exist both at the point of production, and in other arenas of class conflict including housing. In this situation, we might then recognise characteristics of all tenures that are dysfunctional for capital. The ability of capitalism to meet demands for adequate housing is reduced, and housing struggle more likely.

Housing struggles typically only take place when, first, people experience a real threat to their material housing conditions, and, second, this threat cannot be removed by work-place or wider political activity. It is possible to distinguish two levels of threat to material housing conditions. First, those that arise from changes in capitalist society in general. For example, economic crisis may lead the state to withdraw partially from its housing activity (for instance, rent subsidies may be cut or housebuilding curtailed). A second level are those threats that occur because of particular sets of local circumstances. For example, local housing institutions may introduce measures that adversely affect material housing conditions. At times the two levels of threat may mesh together. This was perhaps the case in Glasgow during the First World War.[59] Here men and women organised both at home and work against the exploitation of private landlords in a near monopoly position. The 'war effort' and the state itself was threatened, and, in consequence, central government was forced to take a number of measures to improve housing conditions. Ultimately, this housing struggle helped to destroy private renting as the major tenure form in Britain.

In many situations, potentially adverse housing change does not lead to direct housing struggle because of activity in the work-place or at the wider political level. For example, the effects of a rent or mortgage increase can be nullified by workers achieving a wage rise. Similarly, local or national political parties may act to reverse unfavourable policy changes. If and when these courses of action are ineffective, direct housing struggle is more likely to occur.

We can begin to understand the differences in the extent to which owner-occupiers and tenants have engaged in housing struggle in this light.

During the post-war period, the majority of home-owners

have not seen their material housing conditions threatened –
instead most have consistently enjoyed the protection and
enhancement of their homes through housing market processes
and government policies favouring home-ownership. In addition,
the majority of owner-occupiers have been drawn from those
groups whose work and incomes have been most stable and
secure. In most situations, increases in mortgage payments
arising from interest rate increases have, sooner rather than
later, been matched by wage or salary increases. In general,
then, home-owners have had little need to engage in housing
protest since their material housing conditions have not been
threatened. Furthermore, as a number of studies[60] have demonstrated, at the local level owner-occupiers have sometimes
experienced challenges to their existing housing situations,
and have often engaged in successful political campaigns and
housing struggles.

In contrast to owner-occupiers, during the post-war period,
tenants have had relatively more to struggle about and protest
against. In general tenants have experienced worse housing
conditions than owners (see chapter 14). Indeed, the development of inequalities between tenures appears closely related,
for, as Kemeny notes,[61] 'a fundamental prerequisite for the
maximum expansion of the home-ownership sector is that the
alternatives to it be as limited and as unattractive as possible'.
Thus demand for council housing has been restricted and closely
controlled, the tenure increasingly stigmatised, and the sector
so managed to produce often rigid and disadvantageous social
relations. In addition, increasingly, council tenants have been
drawn from the least powerful groups in society – including
semi- and unskilled workers, the unemployed, others on state
benefits including single women with children, and the elderly.
These groups have less opportunity to defeat threats to their
material housing conditions by either work-place or wider political activity, and so have been forced back on direct housing
struggle as their only recourse.

These 'marginalised' groups gained least from the general
post-war prosperity to the early 1970s – and were most affected
by the periodic recessions during the same period. Similarly,
these groups have been hit hardest in the more recent severe
economic crisis affecting British capitalism. Housing struggle
has occurred not only because of the overtly 'conflict-ridden'
tenant-landlord relationship, but also because tenants have
been most affected by wider economic and political changes
which have increasingly threatened their real material housing
conditions.

Nonetheless, despite these struggles, it remains the case
that during the post-war period public housing has been *comparatively* good. In addition, even the poorest households in
the council sector are helped with rent rebates. Housing struggles have remained muted, at least in terms of the threat posed
to the state, compared with the political and housing battles

over private rented housing occurring in Glasgow during
the First World War.[62]

This critique has attempted to deny the primacy of housing
tenure in determining social relations under capitalism, and,
in particular, the extent of manifest class conflict. Clearly in
capitalist societies, just as competition tends to force worker
against worker, so various segments of the population fight
against each other to maintain or enhance their housing situations. At this level home-ownership may involve intra-class
conflict – with 'community activity' by affluent owner-occupiers
perhaps acting to restrict the housing opportunities of poorer
people. But the same processes occur in other tenures. For
example, council tenants are fragmented into 'respectable'
and 'good' versus 'deviant' and 'poor', and groups of tenants
on particular estates may attempt to preserve or improve their
housing conditions at the expense of prospective tenants or
tenants in relatively low-quality dwellings.[63]

Given this analysis, it might be expected that the current
economic crisis will have resulted in increasing potential for
housing struggle in both rented and owner-occupied tenures,
not least because the state has a reduced ability to meet working-class demands for adequate housing. Some evidence of this
exists. The growing impoverishment of the council sector (partly
resulting from the 'financial necessity' on the state to reduce
its commitment to the tenure) has coincided with considerable
and widespread activity by council tenants protesting about
the adverse effects on their material housing conditions.[64] Hand
in hand with the state's withdrawal from public housing has
been an attempt to extend owner-occupation to lower-income
households. Yet, as we have seen, the state has been unable to
ensure that low-income home-owners have enjoyed the same
privileges as middle- and higher-income households in the
mainstream of the owner-occupied sector. The authors of *Private
Housing and the Working Class* suggest that they could not
'predict what response there will be to the political tensions
that these changes will generate. But as the system becomes
more regressive, housing struggles are more likely to be easily
seen by activists as class-bound and political in their origin.'[65]

Under these circumstances, low-income owner-occupation may
indeed become dysfunctional for capitalism. The legitimacy of
private property is, in theory, threatened for in some inner-
city areas it ceases to be seen by people living in obsolete dwellings as a socially useful good, but more as a disadvantaging
drain on financial and other resources, particularly in comparison to relatively advantaged tenants in good council houses.
Similarly, mortgage debt encumbrance may become a key political
problem if large numbers of working-class households are
unable to meet mortgage payments because of unemployment
and falling incomes. Whether or not these processes lead to
widespread housing struggle remains to be seen. The basis for
conflict and struggle exists, but the political organisation

necessary to activate it remains undeveloped.

A number of other points should be made against the 'functionality for capital' argument. The tenure does not always lead to 'possessive individualism'. McCulloch's work[66] on a series of widespread mortgage strikes around London in the late 1930s indicates that at times owner-occupation can throw people together with a common aim of defending themselves against the exploitation of builders and building societies. Indeed, McCulloch's analysis of Cabinet papers and other material suggests that this pattern of strikes may be viewed as a considerable success for working-class housing struggle. It forced the state and building societies to introduce a number of measures that altered the structuring of owner-occupation as a tenure form, providing safeguards against the building of excessively poor-quality houses for sale with building society money.

In a related manner, owner-occupation may also be a means for workers to partially withdraw and protect themselves from capitalist economic processes. This appears true of some groups of working people in Britain during the nineteenth century. Rose argues[67] that home-ownership 'was historically created, actively sought after, fought for - not usually through banner waving and organised campaigns, but rather through various less visible practices woven into the fabric of everyday life'. One case study Rose provides is of Northampton shoe workers, many of whom were home-owners who had[68]

a real and powerful motivation to maintain the home as 'a separate sphere' where time spent in capitalist production could be used to create a space for life-outside-capitalist-production - an explicitly non-capitalist environment.... A sense of security, autonomy and control over life at home, in the family, in the community, accompanied home-ownership....These were not purely illusory benefits, nor was there anything inherently 'reactionary' or 'divisive' about them...firmer local bases for struggles could be built up, with a view to achieving a greater degree of local political power in order to gain better housing, utilities, schools, public transport, recreational and cultural facilities, social security and so on.

Stretton[69] makes what is not a dissimilar argument about home-ownership today. He goes as far as to suggest that home-ownership should be viewed as socialist rather than capitalist because of the scope for co-operative inter-personal relationships and unalienated work in the 'domestic sector'. Rose, though, argues that this is true for men - who can escape from the capitalist work-place - rather than women, who are entrapped in their domestic roles 'as keepers of the home, socially and spatially isolated "as defined by capitalism"'.[70]

This partial freedom from capitalism is clearly likely to be

greater for higher rather than lower-income households, and
for outright owners rather than mortgagors. The political
awareness of home-owners is also of crucial and critical importance, sometimes cutting across both income level and the
nature of ownership (i.e. whether a dwelling is owned outright
or mortgaged). The mortgage strikes examined by McCulloch
were by people who were active members of trade union and
political organisations. Given political consciousness, even the
most exploited and constrained groups of home-owners may
begin to turn the tenure to their own benefit. For example,
some women, as domestic workers, have increasingly undertaken collective action in housing struggles.[71] Similarly, among
black people and particularly Asians, the high level of spatially
concentrated home-ownership allows for a more easy maintenance
of shared culture and tradition, and provides a physical base
for defence against racist attacks.

In summary, then, owner-occupation is not a switch which
when flicked suddenly and unavoidably produces a set of social
relations favourable to capitalism. Owner-occupation and its
role in structuring social relations has to be linked to broader
economic processes and wider social and political changes and
class struggle occurring at particular times and in specific
places. The particular variety of Marxist analysis criticised
here fetishises owner-occupation because of its failure to relate
the tenure to these processes and structures or to recognise
that owner-occupiers may be able to defeat or side-step the
functionality of the tenure for capital.

5 A CRITIQUE OF WEBERIAN VIEWS

The most elegant and detailed Weberian statement of the impact
of owner-occupation on social relations is that of Saunders.[72]
His basic argument is that home-owners constitute a distinct
class because of their ownership of an asset usable for real
returns. This financial lever produces 'a very strong collective
class awareness'. To support his case, Saunders uses a variety
of empirical material largely concerning the activities of relatively wealthy households in maintaining and enhancing the
quality of their residential locations. This is interpreted as
evidence of owner-occupiers acting according to their objective
housing class interests.

There is a considerable body of evidence that the majority of
people in the tenure do indeed live in a financial asset of considerable and generally increasing value (see chapter 11, and
particularly Table 11.7),[73] which has been of major importance
in redistributing wealth in Britain.[74] As Whitehead notes,[75]
'owner-occupation has certainly provided an investment with an
apparently high rate of return for almost all of those who have
so far entered the tenure'.

However, even for owner-occupiers, housing is not merely an

asset: the six major predicates associated with every dwelling were discussed in chapter 5. Here it is necessary to do no more than repeat Karn's point,[76] that 'more than any other service, housing influences many other aspects of social life: status in the community; contact with relatives and friends; quality of schooling; access to jobs; recreation facilities; aesthetic and social qualities of the environment'.

All households, whether owner or tenants, might be expected to respond to changes that threaten the role of housing in influencing such aspects of social life. People are concerned then to protect and enhance their housing conditions, defined in this broad sense, whether or not their dwellings are also a financial asset under their own ownership. It would seem particularly difficult to separate out the purely economic motivation for home-owners to engage in particular social relations from other non-economic motivations, such as a wish to preserve or better, for example, schooling or the nearby environment.

Indeed, much of Saunders's evidence concerns higher-income middle-class families in suburban or rural areas. For such groups, proposals to build council houses nearby may not only be seen to threaten the selling price of their dwellings, but also the local school system, the general quality of the environment, and social status of the neighbourhood. The activities of home-owners in fighting against such proposals is not simply reducible to a financial or economic imperative, but as part of the already existing division between the middle and working classes reflecting a broader range of processes that may have little to do with owner-occupation *per se*.

Support for the idea that some home-owners may have relatively little interest in the capital value of their dwelling may be found in Lambert *et al.*'s[77] work in inner Birmingham. They examine a General Improvement Area where the policy depended 'upon the economic rationality of owners and landlords to enhance their capital investment by grant-aided physical alterations to the fabric of the houses and the environment'.[78] For a variety of reasons neither the owners nor landlords 'could believe that it was rational to invest money even if they had it to invest'.[79]

Many home-owners were low-income families with high total housing costs that precluded additional borrowing for improvement. Others were elderly people used to relatively low housing standards, and with no interest in the price gains on their property - 'for them even their unimproved house was a home'. In addition, neither group of owners had faith in the permanency of the local authority policy.

A similar theme emerges in their discussion of residents' associations (very different from those examined by Saunders in Croydon) in another area of the city of mixed housing tenure. Lambert *et al.* suggest that the residents' campaign for a particular housing plan avoided[80]

any narrow representation of owner-occupiers engaged
simply in extending the availability of improvement-grant
aid in the area. Indeed, few, if any, of the members
seemed to be interested in the improvement of their capital
asset which the plan could bring. The plan was not seen
merely in terms of bringing material improvements to the
physical stock - the interest and attachment to the area
seemed to go deeper.

It may be objected that the Birmingham evidence is particular
to only a narrow range of owner-occupiers. However, other
support is available from surveys of the opinions of home-
owners. Thus Couper and Brindley[81] found that only one in
four home-owners interviewed in Bath primarily viewed the
home as a financial asset and investment. This general conclusion is also supported by Agnew's[82] survey of the opinions of
a broad range of home-owners in Leicester and Dayton in the
USA. Only three in twenty of those interviewed in Leicester
said that an 'important' reason for their purchase of a home was
so they could sell later at a profit. Some 85 per cent replied
that profit was either 'unimportant' or 'very unimportant' in
their decision to buy. 'The English [Leicester] home owners
were much less committed to their homes as investments than
their American [Dayton] counterparts.[83] Equally noteworthy
is Agnew's finding that only 39 per cent of Leicester respondents
believed that council housing should not be mixed with private
housing (45 per cent were in favour of mixing, and 17 per cent
were don't knows). Of the minority of owner-occupiers against
mixing, less than 10 per cent were so because they feared the
effect of council housing on property values - 'use' rather
than 'exchange' considerations dominated.
    In the context of both Weberian and normative Marxist views,
Agnew's research is of some importance, suggesting that in
Britain home-ownership is not such a divisive mechanism as
many authors believe. Agnew puts forward a number of explanations of his findings, including the idea that greater worker
class-consciousness and an active labour movement may have
'served to restrict the operation of private capital and prevented
the embourgeoisement of the working class, including that
fragment owning their homes'.[84]
    Saunders himself points to a further weakness of his analysis,
that it 'is based upon certain crucial historical conditions...if
these conditions were to alter so as to prevent continuing
accumulation through house ownership, then the logic of the
Weberian position is that the different tenure categories would
no longer constitute distinct property classes....This is perhaps the most serious weakness of this whole approach.[85]
Perhaps particularly important, then, is the analysis made
earlier of obsolete and inner-city dwellings, owned by low-
income households. Such home-owners, 'while paying a larger
share of their income to meet growing maintenance costs of older

housing, face a relative (and eventually absolute) decline in its market value as it approaches the final stage of deterioration'.[86] The proportion of owner-occupiers in this position is likely to increase, *both* as the state pushes owner-occupation on the ever-lower income groups who are forced to purchase physically inadequate and financially disadvantageous dwellings, *and* as the current economic crisis makes it less possible for either the state or individual home-owners to rectify the situation.

In summary, then, Saunders's Weberian approach can be criticised on a number of essentially empirical grounds. Other non-economic processes may lead households to try to protect or enhance their residential situations, apart from the economic imperative unique to home-owners. For example, all households may be expected to react to threats to the wider set of services and attributes housing offers. Similarly, the broader division between middle and working class may partly at least explain the attempts of affluent home-owners to exclude lower-income tenants from residential areas. In any event, home-owners in Britain sometimes appear relatively uninterested in the financial value of their dwellings. Moreover, some owners live in dwellings where they have little if any opportunity either to maintain, or increase, the already low selling price of their home.

Saunders's approach has also been criticised by Dunleavy[87] who moves away (although not completely) from fetishising the impact of owner-occupation on social relations. Dunleavy rejects Saunders' distinction of the basic division and conflict between 'owners' and 'non-owners', and also the stress on the role of 'capital accumulation' in determining 'class position'. Instead, he states that the conflicts between home-owners and council tenants 'around relative state subsidization of the two tenures[88] is a more appropriate way to view housing cleavages.

Moreover, Dunleavy argues that housing 'is not the only or the dominant pattern of consumption cleavage in contemporary Britain'.[89] In the specific instance of political alignment (as indicated by voting patterns) 'housing locations do not have a distinctive influence on alignment; rather housing and transport effects are broadly comparable'.[90] Clearly, this argument is to be welcomed in so far as it moves away from treating tenure (and home-ownership in particular) as the major and independent force producing specific patterns of social relations outside the sphere of production.

Saunders, in his more recent work,[91] largely accepts Dunleavy's argument that consumption cleavages, based on distinctions between public/collective and private/individualistic modes of consumption, are relatively independent of and cannot be explained in terms of 'occupational class', and instead often cut vertically through 'social grade' creating intra-class conflicts of interest.

Dunleavy's work is valuable in that it presents a more realistic account of the importance of housing tenures on social relations. Nevertheless, the approach is open to a number of criticisms. At one level, Harrop[92] makes a number of essentially empirical arguments against Dunleavy's use of survey material to support his theoretical construction. He argues, for example, that Dunleavy's analysis was unable to take account adequately of differentiations within 'social grade' (i.e. on the basis of income) and the confusing factor of age, both of which are associated with housing tenure. It is therefore, he argues, difficult to establish the 'residual' effect of housing tenure on voting. He also suggests that the attitudes of people in different tenures reveals 'a surprising degree of consensus between tenure groups',[93] and as such does not appear to support Dunleavy's view about the importance of housing and other consumption cleavages in political alignment: 'we may doubt whether housing tenure in particular or consumption locations in general are the same order or importance (as class) in structuring the electorates' perception of the political world'.[94]

Clearly, though, housing tenure is often associated with voting patterns and, indeed, with other patterns of social relations. One theme of this chapter, however, has been that owner-occupation is not, as is so often assumed, a monolithic and homogeneous tenure, and that we should expect (and find) historical and spatial variations in the quality and nature of both owner-occupation and in the social relations of people in the tenure. Dunleavy's work on consumption cleavages - as far as it relates to housing - may be criticised for this reason. As we have seen, owner-occupation does not have a single connotation and meaning, but rather a variety for different groups of home-owners.

On this basis the political alignment associated with the tenure is unlikely to be unitary, but will hinge instead on the nature of the specific form of owner-occupation enjoyed or endured in particular places and at particular times, and on other factors such as the general political awareness of groups of home-owners.[95] Dunleavy's work on consumption cleavages may indeed be a useful representation of the general (but not the universal) pattern of associations between housing tenure and political alignment (as a specific instance of social relations) in recent years. However, this portrayal of the general misses what, for reasons discussed above, are increasingly important contrasts within the owner-occupied sector.

Another, associated, difficulty in Dunleavy's analysis is his definition of the role of dominant ideological structures in producing and sustaining consumption cleavages. Dunleavy's view is that[96]

there is no very significant local social processes influencing a process of individual-level value formation....Instead, powerful (national) ideological structures are socially created and sustained by dominant classes, groups or institutions, and make available to individuals in different social locations particular perceptions of their interests vis-à-vis state policies and the interests of other social groups. These ideological structures are not amenable to individual construction, alteration or interpretation but are quite general in their application.

Drawing on this, Dunleavy goes on to describe the 'dominant perceptions' associated with particular tenure, and in turn tends to assume a homogeneity of owner-occupation resulting in a specific form of social relation, and consequently home-ownership as one side of *the* major housing cleavage in Britain. As we have seen, such assumptions are not always appropriate, and may lead to neglecting other important forms of housing and social relation differentiation. Moreover, Dunleavy's view of ideological structures implies a major limitation, indeed an inability, on the part of home-owners either to understand or transcend the ideology surrounding the tenure.[97] In contrast, and as we have seen elsewhere in this chapter, home-owners do not always hold these dominant perceptions, and in fact may (partly on the basis of their housing experiences) engage in explicit housing struggle, much against what might be expected from the dominant ideology concept.

6 SOME CONCLUDING COMMENTS

The central theme of the preceding discussion has been that *status quo*, normative Marxist and Weberian views fetishise the impact of owner-occupation on social relations. Saunders's Weberian analysis puts undue stress on the 'capital' value of property in creating particular housing classes and hence social relationships. Such an economic imperative is far from evident in all situations, and even where it does play a role it is but one of a range of factors that may influence home-owners to particular forms of social relations. Many Marxists assume a normative approach and present a relatively crude analysis of the functionality of owner-occupation for capital in inducing social stability, ignoring both that the major sources of social stability lie outside tenure forms *per se*, and that owner-occupation may, in some situations, be an arena for housing struggles or a means of partially stepping outside purely capitalist relationships. *Status quo* views, in contrast, may be criticised for going to the other extreme of asserting the value of owner-occupation for the well-being of individual, family and society. The supposed benefits of owner-occupation are neither internal to the tenure itself nor available to all home-owners.

As with the view through the wrong end of a pair of binoculars, the range of explanations discussed here tend to obscure more than they reveal. Owner-occupation does not have a simple independent effect on social relations. The tenure itself is not monolithic, but varies spatially and temporally. Neither is it

independent of society-wide economic, social and political processes. Similarly, the social relations of home-owners are not
homogeneous, and are not the consequence of owner-occupation
per se.

Owner-occupation can perhaps best be seen as a property form
that can combine with a range of social relations. Sometimes
these relationships may support the existing social order, but
at other times owner-occupation may be an arena for housing
and wider political struggle. Similarly individual families may be
either advantaged or disadvantaged in living in the tenure.
They may be able to lead a 'full and freer life' either, depending on one's political stance, as an individual integrated into
capitalist society, or as someone who has partially withdrawn
from that system. Equally, owner-occupation may act to reinforce an individual's poverty and general class position in
society. Under these circumstances, home-owners with similar
interests may unite together in a common housing struggle;
or people may remain as alienated, isolated and exploited individuals.

In an immediate or direct sense, housing tenure does have
an important influence on social relations - on the economic,
social and political attitudes and aspirations, and actions and
behaviour of those who live in a particular tenure. Yet the
influence of owner-occupation on home-owners cannot be simply
reduced to a cause and effect process which uniformly affects
all home-owners in a unitary manner. Instead, the influence of
owner-occupation is spatially and temporally specific, affecting
different groups of owners in different ways and to varying
degrees.

In turn, the manner in which owner-occupation relates to
social relations is dependent on a host of external variables that
are part of changing processes occurring in wider society. The
state's housing and related policies have operated to give
owner-occupation specific sets of characteristics (such as
particular financial implications) at certain times, in certain
areas, and for particular groups of people. Historically and
spatially specific housing market processes (such as house
price inflation and dwelling decay) have similarly acted differentially to structure owner-occupation in a multitude of ways,
with concomitant implications for social relations. The class
structure of society, and the wider distribution of wealth,
income and power have likewise enabled specific groups to gain
from the tenure. For other groups the same structure and distributions, when combined with owner-occupation, has contorted
and generally harmed their social relations.

Longer-term economic change, the roller-coaster of the capitalist economic system, has also affected the role of owner-occupation in determining social relations. During periods of prosperity shared by the majority of the population many people
have had a better material life, and a freer range of social
relationships through home-ownership, particularly in contrast

to tenants of state housing as it presently exists in Britain. The reverse is also true. Economic crisis increasingly impinges on the ability of the tenure to provide people with satisfactory housing or to produce a stable social structure. Under these conditions the potential grows for housing or wider political struggle by home-owners. Yet, in turn, this potential may only be realised through political awareness and activity arising through wider class-consciousness.

In this sense *status quo*, normative Marxist and Weberian views tend to fetishise owner-occupation by isolating the tenure and its occupiers from wider social, political and economic structures and processes. At least for those holding *status quo* or Marxist views, the deficiency of their approaches may be of more than academic significance. Those in government and housing institutions with *status quo* views may experience an unpleasant shock if the failure of the tenure to live up to its promise results in the spread of housing problems, mortgage failure, the ghettoisation of segments of the tenure and perhaps political discontent and housing struggle. Marxists may also do a disservice to home-owners by abandoning them as a lost cause. Indeed, increasingly those on the Left may combine with at least sections of home-owners to fight political battles in and around the tenure and over its implications for working people.

16 PERTURBATION AND DECLINE

1 INTRODUCTION

In chapters 4 to 15 this study has limited itself to partial analyses of specific dimensions of the British system of owner-occupation in the 1970s. Moreover, in most cases, the year-by-year passage of events has been touched upon only lightly. My purpose here is to take up the story again where chapter 3 left off, in 1970, and to run it on for the following years up to 1981. This also presents the opportunity of more systematically cross-relating the partial analyses. Unless otherwise stated - and excessive notes are avoided - the facts, concepts and arguments have in the main already been presented in the preceding text. In the rest of this section the broader demographic and macro-economic context of developments in housing is sketched out. Thereafter sections two, three and four deal with the events of 1970-4, 1974-9 and 1979-81 respectively.

The salient feature of the demography of the period is that the total population of Britain changed very little, although the size of the 15-44 age group and the total number of households both grew at the modest rate of a little less than 1 per cent per annum. House purchases are made by three dominant groups: continuing household selling buyers, continuing household former tenants and married couple new household first-time buyers. With respect to the last group the net demand effect derives, I suggest, from the marriages of spinsters to bachelors and here the demographic statistics are more interesting. The age group that is the chief source of female partners for such marriages rose rapidly in the early 1960s and then remained remarkably stable in the years 1967-71 inclusive at about 2.83 million. It then arced down to 2.68 million in 1974 and up again to 2.85 million in 1979 (see Graph 4.1). First marriages fell significantly almost throughout the decade, from their peak in 1970 of 340,000 down to 241,000 in 1979. The much higher rate, after 1971, in marriages where at least one partner was widowed or divorced is likely to have had no substantial net effect on demand: such unions may create more vacancies than they fill. Finally we should note that the long-term ageing of the British population and the secular expansion in the scale of home-ownership brought with it a massive and probably steadily growing stock supply of vacancies as a result primarily of the dissolution of elderly one-person households.

The macro-economic context of the period was one of more or

less continuing crisis. The rate of inflation was unprecedentedly
high: the general index of retail prices, for example, increased
from 54 in 1970 through 100 in 1975 to 166 in 1979.[1] There was
considerable volatility in the balance of payments on both current and capital account until the late 1970s when the inflow
of North Sea oil improved the aggregate payments situation.
Interest rates were high with the Bank of England's minimum
lending rate moving often violently about a distinct upward
trend.[2] Money wages and salaries grew rapidly, stimulating
housing demand in terms of current prices and at the same time
driving up the long-run supply price of new output, given the
slow (if not negligible) developments of housing production
technology.

Graph 16.1 Personal disposable income per capita in the UK at
1975 prices 1970-9

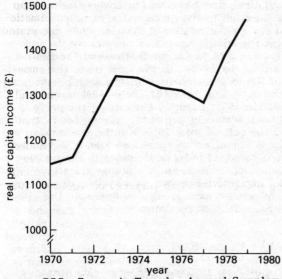

Source: CSO, *Economic Trends*, Annual Supplement

The movement of real personal disposable income tells a different story. As Graph 16.1 shows, there was a clear upward
trend in real per capita income for the period as a whole but
the annual movement was very irregular. There were powerful
surges in 1972 and 1973 and also in 1978 and 1979 as money
incomes net of tax advanced even more rapidly than retail
prices. However, in 1974-7 real income fell continuously and
more substantially than at any time since the data series began
in 1948. Real income increases in an inflationary context are
particularly favourable in their effect on the demand for owner-
occupied dwellings. I believe they encourage many households
merely to maintain their real expenditure on non-housing

consumption in order to switch the family budget into a greater
proportionate outlay on housing on a temporary basis. First-time
buyers burden themselves with an onerous impact ratio confident
that it will fall as money incomes continue to advance. Similarly
selling buyers are encouraged to trade up, even though this
brings with it upward steps in the generally downward sweep
of their impact ratio.

The most ominous statistic of this twelve-year period was the
rate of growth in unemployment which was associated with the
increasing size of the available labour force and an astonishing
decline in British capital's ability to compete in international
markets. The total number of unemployed in the UK, including
school-leavers, rose from 555,000 in 1970 to 1,344,000 in 1979.[3]
It then soared in the most dramatic fashion to 3 million in the
autumn of 1981. On the demand side unemployment and the
associated fall in earnings check access to the owner-occupied
sector in the case of first-time buyers, frustrates trading up,
and probably leads to a fall in the gross value of rehabilitation
production carried out on the houses of existing home-owners,
particularly amongst the middle-aged and the elderly.

Finally, I wish to highlight two major features of the British
housing system itself in the 1970s. In the first place the annual
number of starts in the local authority housing sector had
witnessed an enormous decline from 192,000 in 1967 down to
approximately 30,000 in 1981. Second, the size of the privately
rented sector had been seriously depleted, largely because of
slum clearance and the sale of some 70,000 units per annum
into home-ownership. The effect of these two trends was powerfully to constrict the range of individual choice in the housing
market in comparison with a situation of a stable privately
rented sector and an undiminished rate of state housing output.
The consequence, of course, was greatly to underpin the effective demand for owner-occupied dwellings.

2 1970-4: THE GREAT INFLATION

The general election of June 1970 had brought - for Harold
Wilson at least - an unexpected Conservative victory. Tory
housing policy had changed in a number of ways in comparison
with the early 1960s. The party wholeheartedly welcomed the
shift away from large-scale public redevelopment foreshadowed
in Labour's 1968 White Paper. Policy now sought much more
systematically to divert away from the local authority sector
any household that could conceivably pay off a mortgage. Above
all, the government sought to increase the rate of sales of
council houses to sitting purchasers because of its perceived
strategic political advantage to the Right and, in the long run,
to reinforce tenure stratification.

The Conservative objective can be conceived as the division
of the British working class, in its broadest sense, into 'two

nations', two 'housing classes'. The majority, with modest real
and financial assets and earning real wages and salaries close
to or in excess of the average, would be in the tenure of owner-
occupation. The minority, the modern poor, that is to say the
sick, the disabled, the unemployed, the single-parent families
and many of the elderly, would be in the state sector. The first
group would increasingly adopt a conservative political and
social outlook and, in the main, would vote Tory. The second
group might not vote at all. In addition, there was a half-
hearted desire to see the privately rented sector making profits
and a modest role was foreseen for the housing associations,
supplying philanthropic services and subsidised rental accommodation. The continuing dominant role for owner-occupation
was demonstrated in the government's first White Paper, *Fair
Deal for Housing*, in which home-ownership is associated with
subconscious preference, independence, control, shelter, the
role of the master within the family, security, saving, asset
appreciation and powerful institutional support.[4]

Within this broad context of tenure stratification, four specific policy measures are worth describing. First, with respect
to council rents, the 1972 Housing Finance Act initiated sharp
increases and at the same time channelled a decreasing proportion of the state's subsidy towards the higher-wage council
tenants, thereby providing them with a greater incentive to
choose home-ownership.[5] *Fair Deal for Housing*, shedding
crocodile tears over unfairness in the distribution of subsidies
to council and private tenants without applying the same criterion to owner-occupation, conceived this as establishing 'a
fairer choice between owning a home and renting one'.[6] Second,
government promotion of the sale of state housing, combined
with the powerful presence of Tory administrations at the local
level, led to an unprecedented increase in this form of stock
supply to 61,000 units in 1972. Third, and of less ambiguous
relevance to speculative building, was the dissolution in 1971
of the Land Commission and the abolition of the betterment levy.
Fourth, rehabilitation production was encouraged by maintaining the higher level of discretionary and standard grants available to private owners under Labour's 1969 Housing Act and
new legislation in 1971 made the grant provisions substantially
more generous in the development areas. The number of grants
to home-owners multiplied from 57,000 in 1969 to 186,000 in
1973 and was associated with a huge decline in the first half of
the 1970s in the degree of amenity deficiency in the owner-
occupied sector. It was the 1973 White Paper *Better Homes: The
Next Priorities* which blessed the supposed 'switch' from redevelopment to rehabilitation. In retrospect, the 'switch' led to a
major withdrawal of production resources from housing renewal
as a whole.[7]

The macro-economic policy of the Heath government in its
initial phase sought to raise industrial profits by means of
restrictive policies which, through increasing unemployment,

would hold down wages and raise the profit-wage ratio.[8] Simultaneously work began on formulating a new and more flexible regime of monetary controls and this made its appearance in April 1971 when the Bank of England published *Competition and Credit Control*. Implementation began five months later, in September. All existing ceiling limits on lending were removed although the banks and finance houses were required to observe a fixed minimum reserve ratio. In return the banks were to abandon the practice of non-competition over interest rates. The Bank of England was to control the aggregate volume of credit by increased intervention in the gilt-edged market. In both 1970 and 1971 the balance of payments was unusually favourable and this had permitted from March 1970 successive reductions in bank rate until in September 1971 it had fallen to a mere 5 per cent, the lowest for seven years.

However, the failure of the government's restrictive policy to lead to a renewed accumulation of capital in productive investment led to the famous U-turn. In April 1972 the Chancellor of the Exchequer, Anthony Barber, introduced an expansionary Budget with tax cuts and an increase in planned government expenditure. The intention was that growth in demand would itself be the basis for business confidence and investment. The combination of low interest rates, flexible credit controls and the budgetary stimulus did lead to a huge increase in private capital expenditure, but this was primarily in real estate, the famous property boom of 1971-3. One immediate although short-lived effect was a very substantial increase in 1972 and 1973 in the banks' net advances in loans for house purchase, including loans on down-market properties in inner areas. The boom also stimulated the break-up of flatted blocks so that the money appropriated in this form of stock supply could be recirculated into office property and commercial premises.

Throughout these years, indeed from the second quarter of 1969 until the second quarter of 1973, the rate of interest recommended by the BSA on new mortgage advances had remained remarkably stable at 8-8½ per cent. As bank rate and market rates in general fell in 1970-1, this permitted the societies to open up a very attractive differential between the rate they offered to rentiers and the rates offered by their competitors. As a consequence the societies experienced in 1971 and 1972 a considerable net inflow of funds. Table 16.1 shows that as a consequence there was an increase of one-fifth in the total number of advances in 1971 alone and a further small expansion in 1972. New dwellings cannot be pulled out of a hat and speculative completions in 1971 were only 13 per cent greater than those in 1970. This differential was partially responsible for an increase in average house prices in 1971 of 13 per cent. Thereafter the rapid increase in the general price index, the sharp upward movement in real disposable income in 1972 and 1973 as earnings outstripped retail prices, the large fall in the numbers totally unemployed in 1973 all helped to create

conditions for a general expectation of rises in house prices.
The exchange professionals did not hesitate to play their part
in reinforcing these tendencies. These market expectations
proved to be correct for prices rose in 1972 and 1973 at the
unprecedented rate of 31 and 35 per cent respectively.

*Table 16.1 The number of building society advances per quarter to first-time
buyers and to selling buyers in the UK 1970-4*

Year	Quarter	Advances to first-time buyers ('000)	Advances to selling buyers ('000)	Total ('000)	Proportion to first-time buyers
1970	1	68	39	107	64
	2	85	52	137	62
	3	90	59	149	60
	4	88	59	147	60
1971	1	84	49	133	63
	2	101	63	164	62
	3	110	71	181	61
	4	101	74	175	58
1972	1	95	66	161	59
	2	105	74	179	59
	3	102	77	179	57
	4	93	69	162	57
1973	1	86	71	157	55
	2	71	65	136	52
	3	71	69	140	51
	4	55	57	112	49
1974	1	49	44	93	53
	2	44	39	83	53
	3	61	58	119	51
	4	66	72	138	48

Source: BSA, *A Compendium of Building Society Statistics*, 3rd edn., London, BSA, 1980,
Tables E3 and E4.

Indeed, the only factor that did *not* favour the great house
price inflation was the demographic one. Of course, the total
number of marriages leaped in 1972 but the source of this was
second marriages, following the reform of the divorce law in
1969. It was suggested in section three of chapter 4 that second
marriages may even have a net supply effect in the owner-
occupied sector. The critical non-hybrid variable, the set of
females aged 17-24, had remained stable in 1967-1 and *fell* in
the following three years.

A fall in the rate of interest on personal assets, increased
council rents and the anticipation of short-term price rises are
all stimulants to the asset motive to enter owner-occupation.
This undoubtedly accounts for the strong demand amongst first-
time buyers for advances throughout most of 1971 and 1972
which is revealed in Table 16.1. Purchase by selling buyers
was also encouraged, both by the availability of mortgage funds

as well as by the incentive house price rises bring for trading
up. At this point in time, then, the rise in the price of the
housing commodity had a perverse effect on effective demand.
The relaxed criteria on society loans and the intervention of
the banks in the mortgage market led to a growth in the transfer finance available for the pre-1919 stock supply which,
combined with the quickening pace of government-funded
rehabilitation, was associated with the gentrification of some of
our inner-metropolitan areas, particularly in London.

These events were a godsend to the speculative housebuilder.
As Tables 11.7 and 11.8 show, in the three years following
1970 house prices rose by 100 per cent whilst the combined
cost index increased by 'only' 37 per cent. The differential
movement had a powerful positive effect on land prices and
improved the profitability of land banking firms in particular.
There was a massive growth in the number of active firms in
1970-3 and probably an acceleration in the average rate of
construction per house. Total starts jumped from 165,000 in
1970 to 228,000 two years later, whilst the commercial press
screamed that planners were making insufficient land available
for new building, and academics like myself 'demonstrated'
that the principal source of housebuilders' profits was speculation in land.

Let me return now to the changing macro-economic situation.
In 1971 the US government under President Nixon was still fully
committed in its wars against the Indochinese peoples, a by-
product of which was a continuing net outflow in the capital
account of their balance of payments. After severe speculation
against the dollar, in August 1971 Nixon unilaterally terminated
the right of those holding dollars to convert them into gold.
At the same time the British abandoned fixed exchange rates
and began to float the pound against gold, the dollar and the
other major currencies. Barber's reflationary budget was accompanied by a rapid deterioration in the balance of payments and
in June 1972 a run on the pound had been followed by an effective 7 per cent devaluation and the raising of bank rate to 6
per cent. In mid-October bank rate was replaced by the minimum
lending rate which initially was set at $7\frac{1}{4}$ per cent and then
quickly rose to 9 per cent by the end of December 1972. For
six months MLR then drifted downwards. However, in 1973
inflation was running at an annual rate of 9 per cent and a very
serious balance of payments deficit had arisen, partly as a
result of the increases beginning in 1971 in the price of our
imported oil supplies. In July 1973 sterling's floating rate began
to sink and this led to a huge increase in MLR from $7\frac{1}{2}$ per cent
at the beginning of the month to 13 per cent by mid-November,
at this time the most punitive terms on which the Bank was
prepared to lend to the money market for the entire century.

These events had extremely serious repercussions on the
supply of mortgage finance. The giddy upward shift in interest
rates between mid-1972 and the end of 1973 forced the building

societies to follow suit. The BSA recommended rate on ordinary shares rose from 4.75 per cent in September 1972 to 7.5 per cent in October 1973. But this was insufficient to prevent an erosion in their competitive position and as a result the net inflow of funds became increasingly unfavourable. The deposit rate might have been raised more sharply but this would have driven up the mortgage rate even more rapidly than was happening in any case. The BSA recommended rate on new mortgages had been raised from 8 to $8\frac{1}{2}$ per cent in September 1972. Then in March 1973 the building societies witnessed an extremely low net inflow of funds and in April, in spite of intense government pressure, the mortgage rate was raised to what was then a record level of $9\frac{1}{2}$ per cent. In the same month, in an extraordinary action, the government announced a temporary bridging grant to check the lending rate from moving into double figures within three months.[9] In the early summer the Bank of England 'requested' the clearing banks to limit the interest paid on deposits of less than £10,000 to $9\frac{1}{2}$ per cent, in order to stifle the competitive process.

The effective demand for dwellings, whether for the stock or the newbuild supply, thus came under a triple threat. In the first place, the deterioration in the building societies' flow of funds led to reductions in the number of advances they could make. Moreover the immense acceleration in prices implied that £1 million of expenditure on house purchase was sufficient to sell 50 per cent fewer dwellings in 1973 than was the case in 1970. (The decline in the purchasing power of mortgage finance was partially offset by a fall in the cover ratio in the two years following 1973.) Building society advances peaked in mid-1972, as Table 16.1 shows, and then fell almost without interruption until the second quarter of 1974 when they were running at only 46 per cent of this 1972 maximum.

The second threat to effective demand came as a result of a huge acceleration in what I shall call the access index. This is plotted in Graph 16.2. The indicator is a measure of the relative ease or difficulty in economic terms of *entering* owner-occupation for those who are able to secure a mortgage. The graph measures on a quarterly basis, for first-time buyers entering the market in each time-period, the ratio of the average mortgage repayment to the borrowers' average income.[10] The graph shows that the index lay in the range of 18.5 to 20.1 per cent from the beginning of 1969 until the second quarter of 1972. However, after the last quarter of 1971 it increased continuously for more than two years, peaking at 27.7 per cent at the beginning of 1974. Initially the change was the result of the faster rate of growth in house prices than in incomes, but subsequently it was the effect of increases in the mortgage rate, particularly from April 1973, with its corresponding intensification of the income frontloading effect.

The third threat to effective demand came from changing price expectations. We have seen that building society advances

Graph 16.2 The access index 1969–81

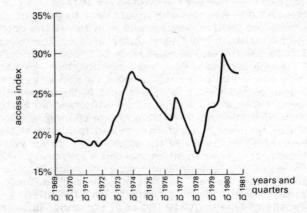

began to fall in the fourth quarter of 1972 and the recommended mortgage rate rose particularly sharply in the second quarter of 1973. The combined effect, one can postulate, was to bring about downward revisions in the anticipation of house price rises. Careful examination of BSA house price data suggests that the rate of growth in prices did indeed slow down very sharply at around the mid-point of 1973 and in the second quarter of 1974 prices actually fell.[11] It has already been shown that expectations of rapid price rises, through the financial predicate, positively influence the desire to enter the tenure on the part of first-time buyers. Conversely, a weakening of such expectations diminishes the eagerness to become a house-owner, at least in the short run.

So the milk really began to turn sour about the middle of 1973, and as this happened it became apparent to speculative housebuilders that the prospects for the industry were catastrophic. If they maintained output at the current high levels and then were forced into selling at whatever price a depressed market would bear, certain ruin lay in store. Their reaction was swift and decisive. Starts fell from 216,000 in 1973 to 106,000 in 1974, the largest peace-time fall in private housing output in British history. The number of active firms itself diminished by 2,500 over the same period. In 1974, also, there was a dramatic slump in solicitors' fees from conveyancing.

Graph 16.2 shows that from 1972 not merely was there a very sharp rise in the access index, but that compared with 1969–72 the mean of the index was very much higher in 1973–80. The respective unweighted averages were 19.4 and 24.1 per cent. Increasing house prices have an inconsistent effect on potential purchasers. For first-time buyers it makes entry more difficult. For selling buyers it facilitates trading up. Conversely, when prices are stable but sharp rises are anticipated, the entry of the rational first-time buyer is accelerated whilst the selling

buyer delays moving house, at least if the argument on real
and paper gains is correct. On the other hand an increase in
the mortgage rate favours neither group. In any case, the
upward shift in the mean of the index had the effect, it would
seem, of changing the ratio between first-time and selling
buyers for the rest of the decade. Table 6.4 showed that first-
time buyers as a proportion of all buyers fell from an average
of 60 per cent in 1970-2 down to 48 per cent in 1973-80.

Since selling buyers can plough into their newly purchased
houses their own net worth as well as a larger advance than
other buyers enjoy from the mortgage institutions, it should
not surprise us that in the 1970s there has been a spectacular
proportionate increase in the construction of houses (as distinct from flats) with at least four bedrooms. Table 11.6 showed
the proportion of such dwellings within speculative output
increased from 8 per cent in 1969 to 20 per cent in 1979.

Another aspect of the decline of the first-time buyer is its
effect on vacancy chains. The first-time purchase is the absolutely dominant means by which vacancy chains terminate within
the owner-occupied sector and the reduced flow of such households has meant an increase in average chain length, reinforced
by the higher use-value of speculative output just described.
The longer the chain the greater its complexity and the more
frequently it collapses, to the considerable cost and psychological distress of those buyers and vendors shackled to each
other. I believe it is not mere chance that a drawing room
comedy, Stanley Price's *Moving*, based entirely on the selling
buyer's exchange predicament, was launched on the London
stage for the first time in 1981. The response of the audience
was hysterical for more than one reason. In the days of George
Bernard Shaw the laughter (and the hisses) turned on *Widowers'
Houses*.

We have noted at a number of points in the preceding text the
bipartisan objective of Conservative and Labour governments
in promoting home-ownership within increasingly wider strata
of the working population. The remarkable shift in the access
index after 1971 clearly constituted a barrier to this policy. As
a consequence low-start mortgage schemes multiplied in the
1970s, including the NEDC proposal of 1972, the DoE/BSA
scheme of 1975, the option lease and finally the measures contained in the 1978 House Purchase Assistance Act. None of
these has been particularly successful.

Finally, in this section, let me turn back to the political
events of 1973-4. The decision by the OPEC countries at the
end of 1973 to quadruple oil prices threatened to have (and did
have) a real deflationary impact on the British economy and
simultaneously made a short-term generalised price inflation
absolutely certain. At the same time it put the British miners
in an extremely powerful political position if their leadership
sought to grasp the opportunity. The Conservative government's attempt to go for growth without generating substantial

increases in wages and salary rates had led them to introduce
in late 1972 a statutory freeze on pay, prices and dividends.
Phase II of this incomes policy was initiated in early 1973 and
phase III in November 1973. In the same month the miners began
an overtime ban over a wage dispute and this led the government
to bring in the three-day working week.[12] In February 1974,
three days before the date fixed by the miners for national strike
action, Edward Heath held a general election on the theme: who
runs the country? It was not to be Heath. He was replaced in
March 1974 by a minority Labour government led by Harold
Wilson. This political catastrophe for the Tories engendered a
powerful surge in the party's Right-wing which was to bear
strange and bitter fruit five years later. After a second general
election in October, the Labour government held office until
May 1979.

3   1974-9: THE HOUSING CRISIS AND THE STATE

Labour's return to power came at a time of crisis not merely in
the housing system but in the national and international economy as a whole. The 1970s, as we have already seen, were a
time of extremely wide fluctuations in interest rates as the pace
of world inflation increased and as government set its own
rate more and more to control the flow of hot money across
national boundaries. Internally, prices and money wages moved
upwards with unprecedented rapidity as the 1973 OPEC quadrupling of oil prices took effect and British workers fought
to maintain their real incomes by gaining massive improvements
in money wage rates, thereby further fuelling the fires of inflation. All this was combined with the worst recession since the
war. In 1960-73, UK manufacturing output had increased on
average by 3 per cent each year; in 1973-8 it *fell* by an average
of almost 1 per cent per year. There was a corresponding
upward movement in unemployment.
  With the formation of the new government in March 1974, the
administration immediately turned its attention to the extraordinary realisation crisis described in section two. This time
there was to be no national housing plan. Four distinct measures
were put into operation. First, the Exchequer made a short-
term loan of £500 million to the building societies. In order to
restore their competitive position, they had been considering
raising the mortgage rate to the unheard-of level of 13 per cent.
The government's move - Labour was in a minority in the
Commons and anticipated a second general election by the
autumn - checked this ghastly possibility.[13] Second, local
authority mortgage lending was increased massively: the number
of advances went from 45,000 in 1972 up to 102,000 in 1975 and
the sum loaned practically quintupled over the same period.
For one year, 1974-5, the priority categories were even expanded to embrace first-time buyers of the newbuild supply. Third,

district councils were encouraged to buy up unsold speculatively built houses to rescue construction companies from bankruptcy. Finally, a reversal was made in the decline of municipal housing starts, an action that perhaps owed as much to the construction slump as to Labour's commitment to state housing. Starts were increased from 87,000 in 1973 up to 134,00 in 1975.

A shift in policy towards the sale of council houses was also apparent. This, too, was probably welcome to the developers, although it was not introduced on their account. The Secretary of State at the DoE, Anthony Crosland, maintained the general consent to sell but strongly discouraged policies of indiscriminate disposal. In any case, sales had fallen from their 1972 peak as demand conditions turned sour and as Labour displaced Tory councils in country-wide local elections in that year. By 1974-6 total sales had fallen to only 2,000-5,000 per annum.

A related issue is the stock supply from the privately rented sector. We do not have accurate annual data, but the temporary rent restrictions of 1972, 1974 and 1975, the 1973 extension of security of tenure for unfurnished tenants and Labour's 1974 Rent Act, which gave security in furnished lettings except those with a resident landlord, all of these measures must have stimulated the flight of the absentee landlord from the ownership of residential property. The house price rise of 1971-3 had, of course, reduced his rate of return. The growth in the supply of local authority mortgage finance after 1972 must also have encouraged this tenure metamorphosis, although the decline in building society advances worked in the opposite direction.

The experience of 1971-4 had convinced the civil service and the Cabinet that the looseness of the relationship of the government with the building societies had been made obsolete, even politically dangerous for the ruling party in the new turbulent conditions of the economy. Not without reason the state attributed much of the perturbation in private house prices and housing starts to instability in the societies' rate of lending. Even before the output collapse of 1974 a new mechanism of government control had been introduced. In October 1973 a Memorandum of Agreement was signed between the government and the BSA establishing a number of objectives: continued support for owner-occupation; maintenance of a flow of mortgage finance sufficient for a high and stable level of new housebuilding (!); the stabilisation of house prices; the maintenance of housing choice; and the BSA were to encourage a system of mortgage rationing when the supply of loans to mortgagors was inadequate. The Memorandum also led to the formation of the Joint Advisory Committee on Building Society Mortgage Finance. After the events of 1974 the JAC prepared a new memorandum of agreement between the institutions and the state. The fundamental proposition was that when the societies took in a substantial flow of receipts, they were not to increase their lending

to the maximum extent possible nor necessarily to reduce the
inflow by cutting the investment rate. Instead, such receipts
were to be used to build up their liquid funds which could be
drawn on to maintain lending when net receipts fell in a later
stage of the cycle.

The same agreement set up, for the first time, the mortgage
lending guideline. Under this the government and the building
societies together decided how much should be lent (in terms
of net new commitments) and the BSA asked its members to
adhere to this figure. The monthly lending figure, usually set
at half-yearly intervals, was based on estimates provided by a
technical sub-committee. The agreed figure was seen as the
amount of mortgage lending that would most effectively promote
the objectives of 1973. The main consideration, undoubtedly,
was seen as the stabilisation of house prices in order to provide
a secure basis for housebuilding. At the same time it must be
stressed that the government enjoyed no formal control over
building society lending, only the mechanism of discussion
through the JAC.[14]

In 1974 competing rates of interest began to fall and this
continued during 1975 and into the early months of 1976. A very
substantial recovery took place in the societies' net receipts
and in their rate of lending in 1975. But now the inflow was
also used to build up the institutions' liquidity - to 22 per cent
by the spring of 1976, 6 to 7 per cent above normal. As MLR
rose precipitously to 15 per cent in the last quarter of that
year, the societies' ran down their liquidity to 18 per cent and
thereby managed, in 1976 as a whole, to lend more than in
1975. In 1977 MLR slid again, to 5 per cent in the last quarter,
but the societies' lending was increased only fractionally whilst
liquidity was once more allowed to rise. The new approach to
the stabilisation of exchange finance seemed to be working well.
I return to the effect of the guideline below.

The four years following 1973 were not happy ones for the
speculative housebuilding industry. Marriages between batche-
lors and spinsters were falling (almost) without interruption.
Per capita real disposable income also declined and Tables 11.7
and 11.8 show that over these years the average selling price
of all dwellings rose by 'only' 37 per cent whilst the combined
cost index rose by 106 per cent. Margins were squeezed fiercely
as a consequence. Land prices, too, were in the doldrums:
ignoring transaction lags, appendix 3 shows they peaked in
1973 and 1974 at £2,700 per plot and then fell to a stable
£1,800-1,900 in the three years 1975-7.

Yet we should also recognise that the relative stability in the
flow of realisation finance was associated with a remarkable
consistency in output. Graph 16.3 shows that annual dwelling
completions in the six years 1974-9 lay in a very narrow range
either side of the average of 145,000 and, after 1974, starts
were very nearly as stable. These output levels, of course,
were far below those of the second boom which, in the wisdom

of retrospect, we can consider to have terminated in 1968.
Appendix 2 shows that private completions in Britain in the
five years 1964-8 averaged 212,000 per annum whilst in the
five years 1969-73, i.e. *before* the collapse of 1974, they averaged only 185,000.

Graph 16.3 Dwellings constructed for private owners in Great
Britain 1970-80

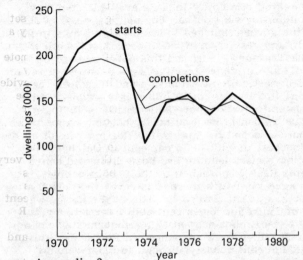

Source: Appendix 2.

The reduction in the newbuild supply was reflected in the
distribution of new mortgage advances made by the building
societies. The proportion of advances in the UK devoted to new
dwellings fell from 25 per cent in 1970 to 16 per cent in 1979,
as Table 6.6 showed. The words 'building society' as distinct
from 'mortgage society' were becoming increasingly obsolete.
A situation was fast approaching when the mobility of owner-
occupiers within the sector, critically dependent on the creation
of vacancies, was becoming dependent primarily on the dissolution of households rather than the construction of new output. Owner-occupation abhors a vacancy reserve since the costs
of holding vacancies in this tenure, ignoring the completion-
sale lag of speculative builders, falls entirely on the shoulders
of individual private households. The costs of the vacancy
reserve are not socialised as they are in the case of state housing. Any reduction in vacancies created as a proportion of the
total newbuild and stock supply must imply an increase in
average chain length, a phenomenon I have already discussed
with respect to new household formation and the up-market
trend of speculative output.

At this point, it is necessary to backtrack a little in order to

understand the turn of events with respect to municipal construction. The national economic crisis, particularly marked
from 1973 onwards, brought with it a major reversal in government economic policy in the summer of 1976. In that year the
country was running a huge current account deficit which,
along with purely speculative pressures, brought a striking
collapse in March–April of sterling's floating exchange rate. In
June this was temporarily staved off by the agreement of the
international banking community to make available stand-by
credits of $5 billion for six months. The political price of the
loan was that the government had to make massive cuts in public
expenditure. In any case, many British economists, both within
and without the Treasury, welcomed this policy change because,
so they argued, cuts in state spending were essential in reducing the rate of domestic credit expansion and therefore the
rate of inflation. In July cuts of £1 billion in previous public
spending estimates for 1977-8 were announced, including a
reduction of £150 million in local authority housing expenditure.[15]

In the autumn, a second collapse in the floating rate of sterling led to an increase of MLR to 15 per cent in October; the
effect on building society lending has been discussed above.
Meanwhile, Denis Healey, on behalf of the Labour cabinet, was
seeking a loan agreement with the IMF to cover the period after
the June credit was due to be repaid. The final package was
based on a $3 billion reduction in the PSBR over a two-year
period, mainly to be achieved by slashing government expenditure.[16] Cuts of £1 billion were announced in December 1976.
Thereafter MLR fell continuously through to 5 per cent by
October 1977. The new expenditure regime had a catastrophic
effect on state housing completions. Under Peter Shore, the
new Secretary of State at the DoE, these fell from 129,000
in 1976 to 76,000 in 1979. The latter figure was the lowest
strictly peace-time figure since 1935, and constituted a clear
breach with Labour's election mandate, the October 1974 manifesto.

The government also reduced the municipal budget for mortgage finance. With the recovery in the supply of building society
funds after 1974, the DoE had already announced in May 1975
a cut-back in the local authority mortgage allocation. The lagged effect of this, alongside the Draconian measures of July
1976, brought a fall in the number of advances in England and
Wales from 102,000 in 1975 to only 24,000 in 1976. As a consequence of these cut-backs, the government negotiated support
lending for house purchase by the societies to supplement the
direct lending of the districts. The principal effect may well
have been to legitimate the cuts rather than offsetting them.

Even more disquieting was the trend in owner-occupier rehabilitation, although our understanding of this, to say the least,
is incomplete. After peaking in 1973 at 186,000, rehabilitation
grants to home-owners fell to around 60,000 each year in
1976-9. For this decline the reduction in 1974 of the percentage

grant payment in the development areas and the fall in the
number of first-time buyers after 1972 was primarily responsible
and possibly also the restrictions on grant availability to
check gentrification.[17] The proportion of grants approved in
the GIAs, and in the HAAs introduced by the 1974 Housing Act,
was marginal. However primitive, the data on dwelling decay
suggest that in spite of huge reductions in amenity deficiency
there was a most disturbing growth in serious disrepair. The
fall in average real income after 1973 and the upward trend in
unemployment after 1974 must have been determining factors
in this. The obsolescence of the housing stock in all tenures
was bidding fair to become the central variable in housing
poverty in Britain in the 1980s.

Another casualty of 1976 was the much-heralded housing
policy review that had been in preparation since 1975. The
Consultative Document was eventually published in 1977.[18] Its
strategic importance in the positive development of Labour's
policies on housing can hardly be underestimated. In fact the
review is destined to be remembered only for the splendid
Technical Volume that accompanied it. Written in the midst of
state expenditure cuts it ignored the questions of land, the
housebuilding industry and spatial planning, determined that
a national appraisal of housing need and the resources necessary to meet it was neither necessary nor possible, and promised to leave the housing system largely unchanged. The
amateur psychoanalyst who appears to have had a hand in
writing all major housing policy statements since 1953 once more
conjured up the fundamental drive for home-ownership. However, at last, tax relief on mortgage interest was conceived
in the same terms as non-rebate council housing subsidies as
one form of 'general assistance', which 'meets some part of
housing costs without regard to an individual householders'
ability to pay'.[19] The Green Paper argued that access to owner-
occupation should be facilitated (see below) and that new forms
of tenure such as housing co-operatives, co-ownership associations and 'equity-sharing' should be encouraged both for
their own sake and as stepping stones to home-ownership.

With respect to mortgage finance, the government expressed
the desire to see a continuing growth trend matching demand
and hoped that the building societies might in future secure
an investment inflow from the pension funds and life assurance
companies, possibly through a financial intermediary. It was
also proposed that the societies could develop the stabilisation
arrangements of 1975 by building up their stabilisation funds to
more than 6-7 per cent of assets; by adopting a more flexible
relationship between their investment and mortgage rates; and
by raising short-term loans on the money market at times of
'famine'. The government, it was said, could help by taking
in stabilisation funds at no loss to the institutions and, very
rarely, by lending to the societies. On the subject of land
supply, the Green Paper merely stated that the land authorities

would come to play an increasingly important role as suppliers
of land to the housebuilding industry as the Community Land
Scheme developed.

Concerning state housing provision, the Green Paper was
decidedly ambiguous. In general it confirmed the residualism
first adopted in 1965.[20] Yet, in a much more positive manner, it
also pointed to the need for local authorities to provide for a
far wider range of household types in their letting and building
policies.[21] The necessity for such a shift arose from the continuing decline in the supply of privately rented accommodation,
the secular increase in headship rates and the consequential
expansion of what elsewhere I have called 'housing minorities'.[22]
On the sale of council houses, the consultative document maintained the general consent to sell provided that this was done
neither in areas of housing stress nor so as to reduce the
quality of the municipal stock - as if sales and a fall in quality
composition of the stock were separable![23] With respect to registered housing associations, the government wanted to see a
continuing growth in their activities. In Britain in 1977 as much
as 10 per cent of all new housing starts came from this tenure
category.

With respect to the ever-more apparent difficulties facing the
first-time buyer, proposals for new building society lending
practices and a government savings bonus and loans scheme
were made. (The latter was stolen from the Tory election manifesto of August 1974!) With respect to the institutions, the
document urged that the difficult situation of the marginal
owner-occupier would be improved if the societies were more
able and ready to provide low-start mortgages, to offer higher
cover for those with an insufficient deposit and to extend
further their lending on older property. In return, said the
Green Paper, especially in areas of older housing, the local
authorities might top-up the societies' loans, provide improvement and repairs grants and provide private guarantees to
societies that older properties are acceptable security for
loans.[24] The Catch-22 problem on old properties requiring a
government grant for their rehabilitation - no mortgage without
improvement, no grant without prior purchase - had already
been ameliorated by BSA and local authority policy modifications.[25]

The new government initiative, the savings and loans scheme,
was intended to function like a low-start mortgage. A government grant was proposed, providing an extra incentive to saving for home purchase, and a loan, the repayment of which
would not begin until five years after it was made. In a general
reference to the effect of such measures, the document pointed
out that 'the widening of entry into home ownership for people
with modest incomes will help to solve housing problems which
used to be faced largely by the public sector'.[26] The new
scheme took its final form in the 1978 Home Purchase Assistance
and Housing Corporation Guarantee Act, the only piece of

legislation based on the consultative document that was to be
enacted.

Let us now turn to look at the little boom of 1978-9. Graph
16.2 shows that, with the exception of one brief period, the
access index fell continuously from its 1974 first quarter peak
of 27.7 per cent down to 17.5 per cent exactly four years
later. The exception occurred at the end of 1976 when the index
was driven up by an increase in the mortgage rate to $12\frac{1}{4}$ per
cent following the autumn crisis. With the mortgage rate stable
at either $10\frac{1}{2}$ or 11 per cent from the end of 1973 to the end of
1976, it was the faster rate of increase in borrowers' money
incomes than in house prices that reduced the index. This
effect was then buttressed with the successive cuts in the mort-
gage rate from $12\frac{1}{4}$ per cent in April 1977 down to $8\frac{1}{2}$ per cent
in January 1978. After the summer of 1977, then, the conditions
of entry to owner-occupation for the first-time buyer were
unusually favourable. Moreover, Graph 16.1 shows real per
capita income grew very rapidly indeed in 1978 and 1979, partly
as a result of the rejection by the Trades Union Congress in
1977 of the continuation of an incomes policy. Finally, advances
from the building societies after the second quarter of 1977 were
running at an extremely high level, averaging 197,000 per
quarter up to and including the third quarter of 1979. This
was well above the mid-summer peak of 1972. Consistently more
than one-half were made to selling buyers.[27]

This marked improvement in effective demand was, of course,
very welcome to the industry. Margins improved substantially
as average house prices rose by 47 per cent in the two-year
period following 1977 whilst the combined cost index increased
by only 22 per cent. The response of private starts was positive
enough in 1978, with an increase of 23,000 over their 1977 level,
but (as in 1973) they dropped by a similar amount in 1979 with
builders growing nervous about the possibility of a mortgage
shortage in the latter part of the year. The differential rate of
change in prime costs and prices brought a new surge in the
price of land which in 1979 (ignoring lags) was running at well
above the 1973 peak as a result of the absolutely higher levels
in all money prices. What strikes the observer most about this
mini-boom is its transience, its fragility, its hesitancy. In part
the memories of the collapse after mid-1973 must have weakened
expectations of a continuing boom in prices and production.
In part, too, the industrial turmoil of the winter of 1978-9 and
the high level of unemployment undermined an excessive optimism. Indeed the most significant quantitative change that
took place was a burst in the sale of council houses. From a
level of 5,000 in 1976 these rose to an annual rate of 50,000 in
the first quarter of 1979. The Tory victories in the district
elections of 1976 and in the GLC in 1977, the stimulus to effective demand and Labour's general consent to sell all combined
to generate the most active turnover since Labour first entered
government in January 1924.

The price escalation in 1978-9 seems to me to have served primarily to correct the previous four-year divergence between prime costs and prices. But many observers overestimated the degree of the inflation and immediately turned to condemn the attempt to design and implement the mortgage-lending guideline. Whitehead's views were more cautious.[28] She showed that in fact the guideline had never been fully implemented as net commitments had alternately overshot or undershot the government's target. In practice the government had neither the power nor the political will, in acting through the BSA, to determine the societies' lending practices. If it was to work and work well, government intervention required more effective sanction against over-lending as well as a deeper understanding of housing market processes and a more accurate forecasting ability. At the same time both the trebling of insurance company topping-up loans in 1978 and a sharp fall in the societies' cover ratio, permitting more advances per million pounds loaned, indicated the technical difficulties any planning instrument of this kind would face.

Now let us consider the final days of the Labour administration whose term of office was due to expire no later than the autumn of 1979. In 1978 in the teeth of the opposition of both the Trades Union Congress and Labour Party conferences, James Callaghan, the Prime Minister, proposed a Phase IV to incomes policy beginning in August with a 5 per cent norm. The attempt to implement this resulted in the winter of discontent and in October 1978 to March 1979 10 million working days were lost.[29] Moreover, successive increases in MLR between April 1978 and February 1979 had driven up market interest rates so that the mortgage societies, too, had increased the mortgage rate from $8\frac{1}{2}$ per cent in June 1978 to $11\frac{3}{4}$ per cent in November. A more direct measure to alienate the support of the first-time buyer and the existing mortgagor could hardly have been found. In May 1979 the Conservative Party under the leadership of Margaret Thatcher triumphed in the general election with the vote of 33 per cent of the electorate, 44 per cent of those who actually voted and an overall parliamentary majority of 43 seats. Jones has argued that one issue playing a decisive role in the electoral victory was the proposal to give every council tenant a statutory right to buy his (or her) dwelling at a discount on the market price.[30]

But before reviewing developments under the Thatcher administration, I want to conclude this section by updating the stock-tenure matrix already presented for earlier periods in Tables 1.3 and 3.1. Table 16.2 shows that over the years 1960-75 the dominant mode of addition to the housing stock came from private construction for sale. At the same time there had been a substantial loss of privately rented units both via transfer to owner-occupation and through demolitions. As a result the relative importance of home-ownership had grown to well over half of all dwellings in England and Wales, whilst private rental had diminished to less than one-fifth.

Table 16.2 The size and growth of the housing stock and its distribution between tenures in England and Wales 1960-75 (m)

	Owner occupied	Local authority and new town	Private landlord and misc.	Total
Stock of dwellings in 1960:				
Units	6.4	3.6	4.6	14.6
%	44	25	31	100
New building[a]	+2.6	+1.6	+0.3	+4.5
Purchases (+) or sales (−)	+1.1	+0.1	−1.2	0
Demolitions and changes of use	−0.2	−0.1[b]	−0.8	−1.1
Stock of dwellings in 1975:				
Units	9.9	5.2	2.9	18.0
%	55	29	16	100

Source: HPTV, Part I, Tables 1.23 and 24.

[a] Includes conversions.

[b] Mainly 'prefabs'.

4 MONETARISM, IDEOLOGY AND THE COLLAPSE OF HOUSING OUTPUT

In my understanding, the dominant objective of the Conservative administration that came to power in 1979 was to restore the fortunes of British capital. Considerable evidence exists to suggest that the rate of profit on domestic operations had been falling since at least the 1960s.[31] It was towards a reversal of that fall and towards the subsequent extended accumulation of capital in the country, that the Cabinet bent its main energies. One building block in the new economic policy was a diminution in the rate of inflation: not only did it promise a return to real rates of interest for the rentier class, it would also assist the drive to expand exports and limit imports. Margaret Thatcher and her inner circle broadly accepted the theories of Milton Friedman and the Chicago School that the rate of price change is essentially a lagged function of the rate of growth in the money supply. Thus the monetary target initially came to be regarded as the centrepiece of economic policy.

A second building block, perhaps the most important in strategic terms, was the imperative to reduce the rate of growth in unit labour costs, particularly in manufacturing. This required a slowing down in the rate of advance in money wages, an increase in the intensity of the labour process and an associated breakthrough in the use of technically advanced methods of production. Such a revolution, it was held, could only be achieved over the body of the organised labour move-

ment. To succeed this necessitated new legislative constraints
on union power and a permanent weakening in the strength of
working-class organisation in industry by means of a decisive
increase in unemployment and the creation of a permanent
industrial army of labour. Deflationary policies in the short run
would, of course, reduce the aggregate flow of profits but by
creating a long-term shift in the distribution of income in favour
of capital at the expense of labour they would ensure that when
growth was resumed it would take place on a firm foundation.
The repressed memory of the trauma of the Barber boom and
its aftermath were now buried deep in the Thatcherite Uncon-
scious.[32]

The third building block was to reduce state expenditure on
a huge scale. This was perfectly consistent with the *laissez-
faire* ideology of the party; it could be seen as the precondition
for the transfer of real resources from the state sector into
private industry; and – if Keynes was right – it was the perfect
tool to create mass unemployment.

Any definitive judgment on the implementation of the grand
strategy is made peculiarly difficult by the fact that I am writing
at the end of 1981 itself, with the temple crashing down all
about me. Nevertheless, a preliminary assessment of the experience is an absolute precondition for understanding the housing
catastrophe of 1979–81.

In the sphere of finance, the implementation of policy was
very soon in deep water. The government had set itself a 7–11
per cent target for the rate of growth of M3, the broadest of
the standard measures of money. But already by the autumn of
1979 it had become clear from the published banking figures
that the increase since the spring was more likely to be in the
range of 14–17 per cent on an annual basis. As early as a month
after the general election MLR had been raised to 14 per cent.
In order to restrain the growth in M3 and to offload the considerable volume of gilt-edged stock necessary to fund the
PSBR – a heavier burden because of the June Budget's cut in
the basic rate of income tax to 30 per cent – the government
in November increased MLR to 17 per cent, its highest level
ever. It did not fall again below 16 per cent until a year later
by which time the Chancellor of the Exchequer, Sir Geoffrey
Howe, was exhibiting a much weaker commitment to a short-
term target for a single money measure.

Three macro-economic consequences of the high level of
interest rates can be cited. First, it raised the cost of lending
to industry and so discouraged investment, particularly amongst
small businesses more dependent on bank finance. This exacerbated the downward trend in output and employment. Second,
it made sterling more attractive for international hot money
flows. This created a very strong pound, particularly in view
of the fact that the British enjoyed the rare privilege of a 'petro-
currency' because of our new-found self-sufficiency in oil. In
real terms the exchange rate was probably overvalued by 30

per cent during the first two years of the Thatcher administration and, as the New Cambridge School centred around Wynne
Godley pointed out, this had a terribly debilitating impact on
our ability to compete in export markets and also raised our
propensity to import. Both of these effects were also deflationary. Sterling did not seriously weaken until June 1981, following the world oil glut and the upward shift in American interest
rates. The third consequence was that the government began
to seek means by which to fund the PSBR without such excessive reliance on issues of gilt-edged stock. The argument was
that the government's borrowing in this form was driving up
the cost of long-term capital to industry whether in the shape
of loan stock, debentures or equity finance. This access problem had the additional disadvantage that it led to a greater
reliance on bank credit with a stimulant effect on the growth
of the money supply. The Treasury's solution was to attack the
personal savings market by raising from it £2 billion in 1980-1
and £3 billion in 1981-2. The most important instruments were
index-linked savings and placement schemes such as SAYE and
the so-called 'granny bonds', with their progressively falling
minimum age limit; the 19th issue of National Savings Certificates, particularly favoured by those on high marginal tax
rates; and the attractive rates of interest available from the
National Savings Bank Investment Account. The 1980-1 target
was over fulfilled by £400,000 and early indications were of
complete success in attaining the 1981-2 target.[33]

In the sphere of employment, output and income, events were
nothing short of sensational. The Cabinet's objective of increasing unemployment has been, to date, its one unmistakable success. The dole queues had already grown considerably longer
under the premierships of Wilson and Callaghan. But the
Conservative-engineered slump was by far the worst since the
1930s. By September 1981 total UK unemployment was 2.99 million,
12.4 per cent of the working population. This was more than
twice the level of May 1979. The figure would have been higher
but for the fact that special employment measures such as the
Youth Opportunities Programme kept more than 300,000 persons
off the register whilst earlier retirement among men and a marked
fall in the number of women seeking work reduced the size of
the labour force by nearly half a million since May 1979. In
terms of statistical unemployment it was the 16-24-year-old
age group that suffered disproportionately. The fall in employment led to a sharp decline in total membership of the trade
unions, an upsurge of violent racism with its divisive political
effects, and urban rioting in dozens of centres in the summer
of 1981.

Output also suffered. Real gross domestic product fell by 3
per cent in 1980 and manufacturing output was 9 per cent down
on the 1979 total. In spite of the planned cuts in state expenditure, there appeared to be no net gain in the real resources
employed by private capital. With respect to personal income,

the experience was quite different. The data on aggregate real
personal disposable income show that after the advances of
1978 and 1979 there was a further rise of 2.1 per cent in 1980.
This is ascribed to the favourable terms of trade because of
sterling's strength, tight competitive conditions, a deceleration
of the rate of inflation after 1979 and the substantial money
income increases of the 1980 pay round. However, by mid-1981
the government's new tax and price index at last began to show
a fall in real income. Contributory factors were a fall in the
rate of increase in earnings since the autumn of 1980 as well
as the decisions taken in the 1981 Budget to raise national
insurance contributions and not to index personal taxation allowances.

The financial developments of 1979-81 were closely associated
with an evolution in bank and building society mortgage policies
and I shall describe these briefly before going on to discuss
the overall development of the housing situation. Let us begin
with the banks. From the beginning of 1979 there is clear evidence that the commercial and savings banks were taking a
much greater interest in the provision of finance for house
purchase than at any time since 1972-3. In part their motivation
was that building society lending seemed to have left an opening at the top end of the selling buyer market; in part perhaps
they feared the recession would inhibit the normal commercial
channels for loans; and in addition doubtless they were attracted by the profitable spin-offs from mortgage provision, e.g.
house insurance, top-up and house rehabilitation loans. The
banks that were most prominent and innovative in the new
push included Lloyds, Barclays, Williams & Glyn's and the
Trustee Savings Bank. Initially the targeting was up-market
with minimum loans of £25,000-£30,000 in early 1979, cover
ratios at 80 per cent of valuation and an interest rate set at
bank rate plus 3 per cent. At this juncture the mortgage rate
was certainly not competitive with that of the societies. However, as the months passed and despite the big price rises of
1979 the banks reduced their minimum loans and house valuations, nudged up the cover ratio, in some cases on the basis
of an indemnity insurance policy, and the TSB, Barclays and
Williams & Glyn's eventually introduced their own 'home loans'
rate which was not simply a fixed addition to bank base rate,
although it was necessarily influenced by the latter. By the
end of 1980 the mortgage rate of some of the banks had become
genuinely competitive for mainstream purchasers, particularly
when we recall that the societies' rates understate even more
than do the banks' the true interest rate as defined by the
Consumer Credit Act. The banks recalculate interest payable
on a monthly basis whilst the societies in general do so only
annually, thereby forcing the mortgagor to pay interest on a
proportion of the principal that has already been repaid! The
new wave of competition drove Norman Griggs, Secretary
General of the BSA in 1981, to assert that the banks were

subsidising their mortgage rate out of their other commercial business.[34] Finally, we should note that the removal of the government's corset controls over bank lending in June 1980 was quickly followed by them launching new deposit instruments in an attempt to claw back some of the business in personal savings lost to the societies since the early 1950s. Their ambition was said to include the 40 per cent of building society depositors who have no bank account. In June 1981 a wholly new initiative was taken, first by the Co-operative Bank and then by Barclays: they began schemes whereby a person who saved regularly over a two-year period was *guaranteed* a home loan which was a multiple of the sum saved. The depositor's privileged access to mortgage finance, one of the foundations of the societies' strength, at last had been plagiarised by the banks.

Now let me review briefly the changing posture of the building societies. The much more vigorous competition from government for personal savings and from the banks for mortgage business offered the prospect in the 1980s of a system in which the forces of the market would be more powerful, even threatening to the movement. In fact already at the beginning of 1979, with the likelihood of a new government coming to power firmly committed to sweeping away public intervention and controls, the building societies themselves appeared to be seeking a more competitive and uninhibited framework. No one symbolised this more than Ralph Stow, chief general manager of the Cheltenham & Gloucester building society and in 1978-9 chairman of the BSA. Even before the general election, he had attacked certain government intrusions into the housing system: structure plans manifested an anti-growth philosophy; there was too much concentration on high-cost inner-city developments with low marketability; and the CLS had weakened the ability and motivation of the industry to maintain new housing output.[35] At the Association's annual conference in Eastbourne in May 1979 Stow mauled the watchdog bodies impinging on the societies' operations and called for the early termination of the Equal Opportunities Commission, the Commission for Racial Equality, the Office of Fair Trading and the National Consumer Council.[36] He did not, however, demand the cessation of the state's intervention in the form of the tax relief accorded on owner-occupiers' mortgage interest and life premiums.

Another sign of the times was the criticism made by some society chiefs of small savers who were using their share accounts 'like the current account of a bank'. Mason of the Provincial and Bradley of Nationwide made the running here. The argument took the following lines: in 1950 of every £100 paid into the societies only £13 was withdrawn but by 1978 this had risen to £37. This is the result of small savers continually placing then withdrawing money. The average saver's balance in real terms is falling and the smaller, busier accounts are driving up operating costs. The correct response is to introduce

differential interest rates with a lower rate being offered to
small savers who hold their money in for shorter periods of
time.[37] In any case, these accounts may not be lost since the
savers are tied into the building societies if they wish to gain
access to a mortgage.

The most explicit move in this direction occurred in 1980
when the Bradford and Bingley, the eleventh largest society
in the country, introduced a two-tier interest rate structure.
Holders of small accounts making frequent transactions and
with no growth in their balances were penalised. They received
an interest rate of only 7 per cent as against the 10.5 per cent
rate ruling at the time. The alternative offered was to close
their accounts. The same logic took a quite distinct form in the
summer of 1981 when the Halifax introduced a premium rate for
ordinary share accounts with a minimum balance of £1,000.
Withdrawals, however, require three months' notice.

A more significant development has been the growing importance of term shares, a shift the movement has done its best
to encourage. Whilst they made up only 13 per cent of total
savings balances at the end of 1979, they were said to have
accounted for nearly half of all net receipts in that year. These
placements enjoy a premium over ordinary shares and are seen
by the societies as a means of locking in large sums of money
for medium to long time-periods, thereby stabilising to some
extent the net flow of receipts. They are also well adapted to
competition between societies, lying as they do outside the
strictures of the BSA's recommended rate of interest on ordinary share accounts. Term shares appear in a bewildering
variety of shapes but in fact take only three major forms. First,
there is the traditional kind: a depositor agrees to place his
money for a fixed period of time, say four years, and therefore
enjoys a premium over the ordinary share rate which varies
directly with the agreed term. Second come the escalator bonds:
the premium rate rises for each additional year that money is
left undisturbed until a certain maximum rate of interest is
attained. Third are the open-ended shares: one chooses a
specific term and if the deposit is maintained after the end of
that period one continues to enjoy the premium. Open-ended
escalator bonds also exist. Perhaps the most widely advertised
term share has been Abbey National's 'Sixty Plus Bondshare'
which, over its full six-year term, gives clients 3 per cent
above the ordinary share rate. This was launched specifically
to compete with the government's index-linked savings scheme
for pensioners. Approximately one-quarter of all building
society depositors are aged 60 or more. Term shares certainly
do seem to have been instrumental until this point in helping
the societies successfully resist government competition for
personal savings. At the same time the increase in the rate of
saving out of personal disposable income to over 16 per cent in
1981 has meant that there has been more money in aggregate
for the banks, the societies and the state to share.

The new atmosphere of competition has inevitably led to fresh criticism of the building society cartel, through which the BSA recommends to its members a maximum rate of interest to be paid on ordinary shares and a minimum rate of interest to be charged on new mortgages. The Stow report, the most influential BSA policy document of recent years, certainly argued that the cartel should come to an end and that mortgage rates should be allowed to settle at a higher level which would clear the market. In this case the existence of mortgage queues, almost continuous since the Second World War, would cease. The report also maintained that the societies' traditional sources of funds would continue to predominate: direct long-term loans to the movement at a variable rate of interest were unlikely to be attractive to the pension funds and the insurance companies whilst fixed-interest stock at a premium over gilts was not attractive to the societies.[38] Michael Cassell has argued that the end of the cartel will mean a much more flexible response by the societies in the interest rates they offer depositors, so that in a volatile market context the violent swings in the flow of net receipts might diminish. Such a change is likely to be accompanied by more frequent shifts in mortgage rates. Cassell also states that there would be 'a major shake-out of those societies which, without the protection of their colleagues, can no longer stand the pace'. That is, there would be an accelerated trend towards centralisation of building society capital. The increase in price competition is likely to be matched by a reduction in non-price competition and thus reduce the proliferation of building society branches which has been widely criticised.[39] The initial response of the Conservative government, usually so eager to stimulate competition, was for Nigel Lawson, Financial Secretary of the Treasury, to threaten to review the societies' favourable tax structure if moves to end the cartel on the mortgage rate went ahead. But with the Halifax, the giant of them all, breaking out of the ordinary share convention in July 1981 (see above) and the Leicester offering five Ford Fiestas as prizes to lucky depositors, the cartel seemed indeed to be crumbling.

The preceding paragraphs have set out the broader context of the implementation of macro-economic policy and have also included a brief account of current trends in the provision of mortgage finance, thereby updating some of the material contained in chapters 6 and 7. The final pages of this section must deal with housing policy itself, particularly with reference to owner-occupation. At the most general level one can argue that the government of housing in 1979-81 had many of the strategic features of the years 1970-4 but that implementation took a far more extreme course. Nevertheless, the regime of Michael Heseltine, Secretary of State for the Environment, appears to me to be distinctive from that of all other previous administrations in its primary concern with the ownership of the housing stock rather than with regulating the flow of output (for what-

ever purposes) towards meeting the housing requirements of
the population. Thus we have the extraordinary and unprecedented situation of the state in its housing policy placing
neither housing production nor realisation finance at the heart
of its strategy but rather a transformation in the legal status
of existing households. As a result of the influence of the
monetarist philosophy and *status quo* theories of the relation
between the ownership of domestic property and political ideology, the state's primary housing objective has become the
promotion of the local authority stock supply to sitting purchasers. Little wonder the press swore that 70 per cent owner-
occupation was an aspiration very dear to Mrs Thatcher's
heart.[40]

The earliest actions of the government were to reduce or
terminate the state's intrusion into the market system. The
1979 Estate Agents Act was put on ice for three years. The
guidelines on building society lending were put into abeyance.
The CLA was repealed and the activities of direct labour curtailed. The rate of development land tax was reduced to 60 per
cent and new concessions to developers were introduced. Pressure was put on the land authorities to sell off their land
banks to speculative builders. In 1981 planning regulations on
housing extensions were relaxed. A new form of lease was
introduced in the 1980 Housing Act, shorthold, in order to
erode the controls exercised over the private landlord but this
appears to be a complete failure. All this was accompanied by
a swingeing reduction in housing research.

The chief innovation in Conservative policy was the 1980
Act's introduction for tenants of state housing and housing
association properties of the statutory right to buy. The content of the Act has already been discussed in chapter 8. The
right to buy actually took effect in October 1980. It was warmly
welcomed by BSA leaders although they made it clear that the
movement was not prepared to set aside a special fund earmarked for council-house purchasers. Resistance to the policy
came both from members of the National Association of Local
Government Officers employed by the housing authorities as
well as from Labour councils. Labour opposition always remained
within the letter of the law and consisted of political argument
against the right to buy combined with the maximisation of
bureaucratic delay. The latter was facilitated by the complexity
of the purchase forms tenants are required to complete.
Labour's National Executive Committee and the parliamentary
party led from behind, so that resistance was uncoordinated.
Many Tory councils were themselves unenthusiastic about the
policy and even authorities such as Kensington and Chelsea,
selling scattered flats in tower blocks, were concerned - as
the ground landlords they would continue to be responsible for
some of the servicing and management tasks. The total number
of sales of local authority and new town houses, whomsoever
the buyer, rose from 41,000 in 1979 to 87,000 in 1980, the

highest level on record at the time. In the first nine months of
the operation of the right to purchase, 380,000 applications to
buy were made.[41]

In the pursuit of the government's macro-economic objectives
the second main plank of policy was to introduce huge cuts in
state expenditure on housing. In April 1980, after the Budget,
Peter Riddell wrote that in real terms it was the government's
intention to make reductions in this of 48 per cent, or £2.58
billion, over the four years up to 1983-4. It was also reported
that by that year the fall in housing spending would account
for three-quarters of all public sector savings![42] These intended
cuts lay behind the 'one-week' moratorium on all new housing
expenditure commitments by local authorities announced by
Heseltine on 23 October 1980, a seven-day freeze that was to
last four months.

The specific effect on the newbuild supply of state housing
was shattering. Starts fell from 77,000 in 1978 to 35,000 in
1980, an extremely effective means for underpinning the 'natural
desire' for home-ownership. Moreover, council rents were
forced up at a rapid rate to bring down the level of subsidies
in the state sector. Michael Cassell wrote: 'The view in some
government circles is hardening along the lines that the "carrot"
of home ownership being offered to tenants may only be acceptable if a stick, in the shape of sharply rising rents, also
exists.'[43] Tax relief to owner-occupiers continued: the 1979
reduction in income tax rates in itself obviously reduced the
subsidy and so helped offset the rise associated with the upward movement in house prices. The £25,000 limit, for the time
being, was left unchanged.

The cuts also seemed likely to have a negative effect on
owner-occupier rehabilitation. As authorities found their HIPs
slashed in real terms many of them, including the Tory GLC
for example, were forced to reduce their mortgage lending
and the provision of discretionary grants. Constraints on the
recruitment of local authority staff exacerbated processing
delays. At the same time the VAT increases of the 1979 budget
had made house repairs more expensive whilst the rise in
interest rates also raised the cost to the owner where production was financed by a loan.

Admittedly some changes worked in the opposite direction.
In 1980 the grants for installing basic amenities were raised to
75 per cent of maximum allowable cost in all areas. In addition
John Stanley, the Minister of Housing, was promoting by a
variety of means both homesteading as well as 'improvement for
sale' by local authorities and housing associations. But the
scale of such output was probably only a few thousand dwellings per year. Probably the most effective boost to rehabilitation was the substantial rise in real personal disposable income
in 1978-80. However, since we have no adequate measure either
of the flow of rehabilitation output or the scale of obsolescence
or the rate of decay, it seems impossible to make any firm

judgments on these issues. The decline in the volume of government housing statistics - apparently the monitoring of policy is
out of favour - ensures our knowledge is contracting rather
than expanding.

Finally let me consider developments in the flow of mortgage
finance and speculative housebuilding. The increase in interest
rates associated with the rise in MLR in June 1979 had led the
BSA to seek a corresponding shift in its own recommended
rates in order to defend the flow of net receipts and to maintain the societies' borrowing-lending margin. But tremendous
pressure was imposed on the BSA leadership by the government
which forced a delay in the mortgage rate increase until January
1980. This decision was 'greeted with undisguised and intense
relief by Ministers'.[44] Nevertheless the uncertainties created in
June and July, the surge in council house sales, the additional
costs of bank finance and the fall in the number of building
society advances were all responsible for a modest decline in
private starts in 1979 to 144,000, even though the differential
movement of prices and prime costs was very favourable to the
industry. The scars of 1974 were still showing.

The builders' caution was to prove justified. The November
increase in MLR to 17 per cent came as a hammer blow and an
emergency meeting of the BSA decided on an immediate increase
in the new mortgage rate to 15 per cent (a full $2\frac{3}{4}$ points above
the 1976-7 peak) and a rise in the ordinary share rate to $10\frac{1}{2}$
per cent. The combined effect of the 1979 house price acceleration and the new mortgage rate drove up the access index to
30 per cent, as Graph 16.2 showed. The number of unsold new
dwellings rose to 18,000 over the next half-year and the
response of the industry was to cut starts in 1980 to a miser-
able 97,000. *Judicial Statistics* showed that in 1980 27,000
home-owners were taken to court by mortgagees, for repossession of their properties! House prices increased by only
about 9 per cent in that year in spite of the continuing upward
movement in real incomes, a general rate of retail price inflation of some 15 per cent and the continuing increase shown in
Graph 4.1 of women in the 17-24 age group. Mortgage queues
disappeared and the average cover ratio went up. The total
number of building society advances in 1980 fell to only 679,000,
of whom 47 per cent were first-time buyers. Terminating chains
were becoming ever more difficult to construct.

The reduction in MLR in November 1980-March 1981 helped
improve the buyer's situation as the mortgage rate was then
brought down to 13 per cent in the latter month. But by now
the recession, the terrible surge in unemployment, the increased taxation of personal incomes and the prospect of increases
in money wages falling behind those of prices, particularly as
sterling fell against the dollar in the summer of 1981, all these
trends boded grimly for effective demand and the fortunes of
the speculative housebuilder.

The autumn of 1981 brought with it renewed perturbations.

In August the Bank of England had formally abandoned the continuous posting of MLR and stated it intended to operate by
keeping interest rates in an undisclosed band at the very short
end of the market. The world over-supply of oil and high US
interest rates brought a decline in sterling to only $1.77 in
September compared with $2.44 in October 1980. This was a
powerful inflationary force. In order to counter the pound's
weakness the Bank pushed up short-term interest rates by
about 1 per cent. This action and the market's response to
turbulence in share prices led the commercial banks to raise
their base lending rates by 4 per cent in September–October
and their seven-day deposit rate increased to $14\frac{1}{2}$ per cent. Not
surprisingly, the BSA recommended rates rose on 1 November:
the mortgage rate to 15 per cent, equalling its all-time high,
and the share rate to $9\frac{3}{4}$ per cent. House prices for 1981
appeared to be stagnant and fell short of retail price inflation
by about eleven percentage points. In order to sell, some
speculative builders had themselves to provide first-time
buyers with realisation finance at cheap rates and to purchase
the selling buyer's stock supply to finance up-market sales![45]
In November the pound stood at $1.91 but the Chancellor of the
Exchequer, the ineffable Sir Geoffrey Howe, had murdered
sleep for sterling M3, like Banquo's ghost, now haunted the
financial community: in February–October the Cabinet's chief
indicator of well-being had risen at an annual rate of 19 per
cent, compared with the target of 6–10 per cent.

The collapse of output both in the private and public sectors,
the associated decline in housing mobility, the fears that the
scale of obsolescence was advancing rapidly even on the speculatively built private estates of the 'first boom', the rise in
quantitative indicators of housing poverty such as local authority waiting lists, all demonstrated that in the sphere of reproductive production, housing would assert itself as one of the
most critical areas with which the next government would have
to deal.

17   A STRATEGY FOR THE FUTURE

1   INTRODUCTION

The object of inquiry in the preceding chapters has been the past. Hereafter my concern is the future and my wish is not to predict, but to shape it. The formulation of policy properly requires an explicit political perspective; here, it is to develop a socialist alternative housing strategy that is compatible with the alternative economic strategy so widely discussed within the British labour movement.

The objective of any socialist housing strategy must be to satisfy the housing needs of the working people of a country within the limits imposed by its overall political, economic and social development. The elimination of housing poverty requires action on the terrain of the appropriation of land, the production of new dwellings and the rehabilitation of existing ones, the supply of realisation and transfer finance, the allocation of vacancies and the provision of consumption subsidies. For each household, its housing need must be met, at a reasonable cost, in terms of the predicates of the physical character of the dwelling, the control exercised over it, its environmental and relative locus and the housing mobility it offers. The relevance of *tenure* is that it specifies the ownership of the dwelling and this is significant not merely to stock transfers but, in our social formation, is the critical link between production and consumption. For this reason housing tenure is a crucial concept in the implementation of strategy.

In Britain, I would suggest that the alternative housing strategy must address itself principally to the two dominant sectors, those of state housing and owner-occupation. With respect to the former my views have already been set out at length in *State Housing in Britain*. The modest proposals made there include the preparation of a rolling seven-year planning document to identify the changing scale of housing needs and the resources necessary to tackle them; the implementation of that plan by means of the expansion of state housing construction; the nationalisation of the land (excluding that of owner-occupiers and owner-occupier farmers) as well as the commanding heights of the building materials industry; the unshackling and promotion of the local authorities' direct labour organisations alongside improvements in their accountability; the re-introduction of construction licensing for medium- and large-scale projects; the municipalisation and rehabilitation of the obsolescent privately rented stock; the revival of the PWLB's post-war role as 100 per cent provider of the districts' capital funding requirements, moreover at a zero real rate of interest; the elimination in the medium term of general assistance housing subsidies in all tenures; rent-free accommodation for senior citizens in the state housing sector; no sale of council houses; and finally, the introduction of comprehensive reforms in access to and the allocation of council housing as well as major advances in tenants' rights and powers.[1]

Sections two to four below extend these strategic proposals to embrace the owner-occupied sector, dealing in turn with new building; rehabilitation; consumption subsidies and taxes; mortgage finance; and the exchange process. But before beginning that task three general remarks about tenure are in order. First, nothing in my researches during the past ten years has ever convinced me that there is something inherently socially progressive about owner-occupation. Nor has this work persuaded me that the tenure is inherently unjust. Thus no proposals are set out here urging an increase to 70 or even 100 per cent owner-occupation in Britain; nor, on the contrary, is the abolition of this property form suggested. The correct strategic approach, I insist, is not through the fetishism of tenure but through the evolution of effective policies on land, production, finance and consumption to transform the predicates of the accommodation possessed by households. In this light, as I say, the tenure question, however important, is conceived essentially as a dimension of strategy implementation.

Second, one of the fundamental principles of socialist action must be that of *tenure justice* between the property forms through which strategy is implemented. By this I mean that for any given level of accommodation payments, no such property form should suffer from an inherent disadvantage in terms of the variables defined by the predicative analysis. For example, if amongst a set of households making broadly similar net outlays on accommodation we discover that those in the council sector enjoy far less housing mobility than those in owner-occupation, then this would be inconsistent with the principle of tenure justice. How one could act to end such injustices would vary between its specific instances and in the example cited here the main advance would lie through an expanded state housebuilding programme as well as the allocation of a significant proportion of the vacancies appearing within the state sector (controlled for use-value) independently of households' residential qualifications.

Third, still on the issue of tenure, I am convinced that in a democratic socialist country state housing potentially enjoys certain advantages from a social point of view which have not been sufficiently recognised. These are:

(i)   In the state sector relative rent levels can be set to reflect relative use-values but, in an inflationary context, in the owner-occupied sector relative mortgage repayment levels will reflect the accident of differences in historic purchase costs. Similarly, in an inflationary world, income front-loading is an inherent feature of owner-occupation but not of pooled rents in the local authority sector, particularly because of the automatic index-linking effect of new building and major rehabilitation works.[2]

(ii)   The transfer of possession between households within the state sector is extremely simple in law, requires no 'capital finance' whatsoever, and is not dependent on the success-ful construction of terminating chains. This stands in sharp contrast with owner-occupation. The extremely high gross demand for transfer finance within owner-occupation has been the subject of considerable criticism, particularly for bleeding industry of much-needed investment funds. An able exponent of the case is Bernard Kilroy.[3] In this volume I do not explore the impact of owner-occupation on the macro-economy - my task has been onerous enough without that additional burden. However, in more than twenty years since I became an economics undergraduate I have heard everything with the exception óf sunspots (so far) used to explain the decline of British manufactur-ing profitability and I have now grown exceedingly cynical on this matter.

(iii) Because of the simplicity of its exchange process, the irrelevance of inter-regional house price differentials, and the socialisation of the costs of the vacancy reserve, the *potential* exists for much greater housing mobility within state housing in comparison with owner-occupation. For this potential to be realised, reforms of the kind described earlier in this section would have to be implemented.

(iv)   There are no regressive price gains to be won in the state sector.

(v)   Only in the state sector and in the housing association movement can the flow of production be channelled speci-fically to meet unsatisfied housing need.

One final remark is necessary before turning to specific dimensions of policy. In formulating these proposals no con-cessions are made to the possible political feasibility of the changes recommended. I believe judgments on practicality in electoral terms should be made by party and government, whilst academics in their scholarly work serve the labour movement best by avoiding any premature judgments on feasibility - a fickle creature - for this can only have the effect of narrowing the range of options the movement will consider. Thus there is a time and a place both for relatively unconstrained policy proposals as well as for the hammering out of commitments to be placed in a manifesto, and these distinct processes have a complementary relationship with each other.

2 HOUSING PRODUCTION

With respect to the newbuild supply, my recommendations can be set out very briefly. In the context of an alternative housing strategy, the state at central and local level would introduce a steady but powerful increase in the output of new, high-quality dwellings in the local authority sector. Speculative housebuilding would play a residualist role to the 'plannable instruments' of the district councils, just as it did in 1945-51. Both the building licensing system and land release by the land authorities would ensure that the speculative sector did not bid away the real resources required for the state housing programme. Land nationalisation implies the private industry's profits would be made essentially from the construction process, for the land would be sold with residential planning permission at market prices. No building firms would be nationalised. Annual starts could be expected to run at a few tens of thousands per year.[4]

A far more challenging problem is posed by the other mode of housing production for owner-occupation, that is to say, rehabilitation of the existing stock. A necessary preliminary observation is that the alternative economic strategy itself will contribute positively in this area. One of the major objectives of the strategy is a return to full employment in the medium term; the associated increase in the real income of numerous households will quite certainly strengthen the ability to purchase rehabilitation output. Moreover, if the central government were to end the current arrangements for basing local government finance on property taxation and switch to a local income tax, a beneficial side-effect would be to terminate the disincentive that domestic rates impose on owner-occupier improvement.

Policy analysis for rehabilitation must distinguish two dimensions where action is needed: the first concerns the access to the stock requiring such work and the second concerns the supply of and effective demand for output by established owner-occupiers. Let me take these in turn.

Access raises the issue of the allocation of mortgage advances. We know perfectly well from dozens of case studies that the building societies exacerbate the decay of the dwelling stock by their consistent discrimination against much of the older, inner-city housing stock and against the low-/middle-income group of first-time buyers who would seek to purchase down-market properties in disrepair. The solution to this lies in what I shall call the On-lending Scheme. All district councils would be required to set up their own mortgage departments, the chief function of which would be to channel mortgage finance into owner-occupier acquisition and rehabilitation of dwellings in serious disrepair or requiring basic improvement. The buyers would be required to satisfy reasonable criteria on their ability to pay, based on the ratio of repayments to household income.

The source of funds for these local authority mortgages would
be the PWLB which in its turn would raise them from the mortgage institutions, primarily the banks and building societies.
All such institutions would be required by law to supply to
the PWLB on a quarterly basis a (variable) proportion of the
value of their gross advances to home-owners in the previous
quarter. The PWLB would, in effect, be on-lending to the local
authorities a proportion of the funds originally raised by the
building societies and banks. The rate of interest charged on
local authority mortgages would be set in line with those of
the societies and banks, and this income, principal and interest
would be channelled through the PWLB back to the funding
source. Note that the greater the willingness of the mainstream
mortgage institutions to end their discrimination against obsolescent property, the fewer would be the potential mortgagors
approaching the local authorities for loans and therefore the
smaller the on-lending ratio applied to the institutions' quarterly
advances data! Since the purpose and effect of the On-lending
Scheme would be no more (and no less) than to recompose the
spatial pattern of mortgage advances funded directly and
indirectly by the societies and banks, local authority borrowing
from the PWLB for this purpose would be excluded from the
Public Sector Borrowing Requirement.[5]

Now let me consider the situation of the established owner-
occupier. The main lesson of chapter 12 was that the imbalance
in current policy needs to be corrected by giving more weight
to the supply side questions. Here I have just two main proposals. First, the unshackling and expansion of the direct labour
organisations should, amongst other objectives, be specifically
targeted on providing a quick, reliable, value-for-money service to owner-occupiers. In addition, each local authority
should draw up a list of local building firms and co-operatives
which, on the basis of their record, could be recommended to
local people for their rehabilitation work. Second, local councils
throughout the country should introduce agency agreements in
which, on the instructions of the owner, the local authority
would draw up and cost plans for repair, improvement and
adaptation, check these against the building regulations,
secure any necessary planning permission, manage the labour
process (often but not only using DLOs) and charge the whole
operation to the owner-occupier on a fixed price basis after
deduction of the appropriate rehabilitation grant.

With respect to the effective demand for rehabilitation, the
first point to make is that no evidence appears to exist that the
denomination of specific areas as GIAs and HAAs has any effect
in raising the aggregate rate of rehabilitation in a district above
what it would have been had the same resources been applied
without area-targeting. So, in my view, the area approach
should be abandoned in favour of a much simpler planning distinction between zones with a secure future and zones planned
for clearance in the short or medium term. On grants, I do not

believe there is any reasonable justification for making them available to households irrespective of their ability to pay. A sliding scale should therefore be applied to grant provision, running from zero to 100 per cent of maximum allowable cost, in an inverse relation with the household's income and its real and financial assets. There may also be a case, as SHAC has suggested, for a unified grant scheme in which the five separate grants currently available for rehabilitation are dropped in favour of a single grant intended to cover all the work necessary to raise dwellings to a ten-point standard, with a strong emphasis on securing the fabric of the dwelling.[6] These would be available only in zones with a secure future. Only patching grants would be available in the zones scheduled for clearance.

Finally, the municipalisation of owner-occupied property by agreement can also play a positive role in the fight against residential obsolescence. Particularly in the case of the elderly living in decaying homes, possibly far too big for their needs, local authorities should be willing to purchase the property (where appropriate with conversion specifically in mind) at a discount on its full market price in 'vacant possession'. In return for this discount the authority would provide the household with rent- and rate-free accommodation for life in council-owned property specifically designed for the elderly.[7]

3 CONSUMPTION SUBSIDIES AND TAXES

It is my strong conviction that the major fiscal weakness of British housing policy is the allocation of too high a proportion of the state's housing budget towards transfer expenditures and too low a proportion towards resource expenditures. Transfer expenditure redistributes housing outlays and income between government, housing consumers and the propertied classes involved in the housing system's land, production, finance and allocation mechanisms. Resource expenditure by the state consists of its purchase of the *output* of goods and services in the housing field, primarily housing production itself. In my view, in the short-medium term *all* housing transfer expenditures should be abolished except where they are strictly necessary to enable those with a limited ability to pay to secure access to decent local authority, new town and housing association rental accommodation. Supplementary Benefits Commission payments of owner-occupiers' mortgage interest would also continue. For this reason I attack all general assistance subsidies to tenants and propose, with respect to owner-occupiers, the complete removal of tax relief on mortage interest and on the life premiums associated with endowment mortgages as well as the termination of the option mortgage subsidy. Note that from the point of view of 'practical politics' it is perfectly possible swiftly to abolish owner-occupier subsidies without raising net mortgage payments, *provided* it is done at a time when the socialist government is reducing interest rates generally, with a consequent decline in the mortgage rate. The fall in state expenditure on general assistance to owner-occupiers could be regarded as releasing a huge funding source for the construction of high-quality state housing units. A beneficial short-term side-effect of general assistance abolition would be to discourage a sharp surge in house prices as interest rates fell. In the medium and long term it would also encourage the selling buyer to plough all his (or her) net worth into the purchase price of the 'new' house when trading up, so reducing the demand for transfer finance.

These remarks cover the question of subsidies. However, a considerable number of commentators have also suggested special taxes should be placed on owner-occupation, in particular a tax on price gains and a tax on the 'imputed income' from homeownership. Let me deal with these in turn. First, it goes without saying that a levy on house price gains would be political suicide. However, given the remarks on 'feasibility' in section one, that is totally irrelevant for my purposes. The arguments against the tax are:

(i)   These gains often partially reflect the rehabilitation labour and expenditure on a dwelling made by the household and this element, at least, it would be quite mistaken to tax.

(ii) The tax would significantly reduce housing mobility since the net worth appropriated on sale, of which the price gain can be a major component, is an important cash source from which the moving household meets its exchange and transport costs. Moreover the gain can be significant in funding the purchaser's deposit, under conditions of house price inflation, even when the household trades level.

(iii) Whilst it was argued in chapter 10 that price gains can be a real, not just a paper, advantage, nevertheless in periods of rapid house price inflation, when gains appear most dramatic, I do believe both households as well as the advocates of a tax suffer from price gain illusion.

(iv) The fact that price gains are appropriated by owner-occupiers and not by the tenants of state housing is *not* in itself inconsistent with the principle of tenure justice. The predicative analysis of chapter 5 demonstrated that despite this asymmetry the purely financial evaluation of tenure choice can still favour the rental sector.

For these four reasons I am opposed to a tax on price gains. However, with respect to argument (iv) above, one must recognise that in practice, particularly in periods when the real, post-tax rate of interest on personal savings is negative, the owner-occupier largely through his price gain does have access to a savings mechanism denied to the tenant. In recognition of

this I suggest an important innovation in fiscal policy that
can be referred to as the rental bonus plan. Quite simply this
would permit tenants of local authorities, new towns and housing associations to pay over certain sums of money, alongside
their rents, which would be placed in a special savings account.
The maximum weekly or monthly sum could be set, for example,
at 100 per cent of their net rent. This stream of savings would
be made available to the central government in meeting the
PSBR. Interest on the savings would be tax free and the rate
of interest would be set equal to the rate of retail price inflation plus, say, 1 or 2 per cent. The rental bonus would be
paid over to the tenant whenever he (or she) left his dwelling,
although in the case of transfers to another house within the
socially rented sector, the tenant could maintain his savings
account.

I believe this rental bonus plan or save-as-you-rent scheme
could be of very significant international interest. In any nation
with a commitment to a state housing programme yet which
exhibits negative, real, post-tax rates of interest on personal
savings, the rental bonus plan could have enormous potential
in improving the relative financial attractiveness of the state
housing sector.

Finally, the proposals to tax the 'imputed income' of owner-
occupiers must be discussed. This concept of 'imputed income'
from home-ownership is expressed in different and inconsistent
ways by different people and sometimes is simply assumed to
be self-explanatory. Its meaning to its proponents can, perhaps, best be set out in the following way:

> If we consider a dwelling in the possession of a household,
> then the family derives therefrom a flow of housing services.
> If the household rents the property, there is a money flow
> corresponding to the flow of services which we call the rent
> and this constitutes an income to the owner. It is, of course,
> liable to taxation as unearned income. But if the dwelling is
> owner-occupied, no rent is paid and therefore the owner
> receives no explicit income. But the flow of services has not
> disappeared and to this there corresponds (or this therefore
> constitutes) an 'imputed income' which goes untaxed.

Now in my view this concept is a piece of grotesque nonsense
and it is as much humbug when pronounced by distinguished
professors of economics as when it is used by members of the
International Socialists or the Labour Left. The philosophical
fault is that 'housing services' is a category of fantasy, as was
shown - I hope - in chapter 5, and because no real entity is
denoted by the term 'imputed income'. Since 'imputed income'
does not exist, it is logically impossible to tax it. If, however,
its protagonists merely argue that owner-occupiers should be
taxed as the owners of real property, real wealth, then of
course this deserves to be given the most serious consideration.

The principal observation to make on that line of attack is that we have been taxing the owner-occupier's property for several centuries. The British call it 'domestic rates'.[8]

4 MORTGAGE FINANCE AND THE EXCHANGE PROCESS

With respect to the flow of mortage finance from the banks and building societies, there are a number of important reforms I wish to propose. Public ownership of the major commercial banks is a central feature of virtually all versions of the alternative economic strategy and it is a socialist advance I support. However, it is not possible to speculate here on whether this would constrain aggregate bank lending for house purchase since that decision would be just one element within higher-order policies on the respective roles of the state and all the financial institutions, including the pension funds and insurance companies, in financing industrial and commercial investment. With respect to the building societies, their nationalisation is a measure I oppose. The lending policies any state building societies would pursue, given the structural economic location of these institutions as described in chapter 6, would not be sufficiently distinct from their current operations to justify taking them into public ownership. The reforms I do propose fall under eight heads.

First, the composite tax arrangements should be abolished, because of their regressive distributive character. Thereafter, interest would be paid to shareholders, etc. gross of income tax.

Second, the building society cartel would be terminated. This is no more than a progression on current trends. Price competition between societies would improve and interest rate changes, particularly on deposits, would become more frequent with a consequential stabilising effect on net inflows and gross advances.[9]

Third, the Joint Advisory Committee would be strengthened by including representatives from all the major mortgage finance institutions. The credit guidelines would be reintroduced, primarily with a view to checking violent upward movements in house prices as a result of a surge in advances. Reform two above would assist here. The societies would also be encouraged to allow their liquidity ratio to operate over a wider range in order to improve aggregate lending stability. Lastly, the Treasury would make available substantial short-term loans if these were necessary to offset an abrupt and temporary downward shift in the flow of advances.[10]

Fourth, all mortgage institutions would be required to describe their mortgage rates on the basis of a standard accounting practice along the lines of that laid down in the 1974 Consumer Credit Act.[11]

Fifth, the implicit sexual discrimination by mortgagees would be ended. This would include, in the case of couples, treating both their incomes on the same basis and not discounting the lower (usually the woman's) income.

Sixth, the On-lending Scheme would be introduced, as described in section two.

Seventh, the mortgage institutions would be required to introduce guarantees to first-time buyers that the rate of interest they pay on their mortgage would not rise above a specified amount in the early years of the repayment period. This would operate on a sliding scale whereby the greater the time that had elapsed since the advance was made, the greater would be the permitted maximum increase.[12]

Finally, that as a complement to existing low-start mortgage schemes which do not receive general assistance subsidies, the government consider the introduction of flexi-mortgages that relate repayments to income and already operate in Norway.[13]

Now let me turn to consider the exchange process where reform is long overdue. A major strategic objective of housing policy must be to increase housing mobility, in order to improve households' opportunities to match the use-value of their dwelling with their own perceived needs. By far the most significant change here concerns reform in the administrative control of access to and the allocation of vacancies in the stock of local authority housing. This issue has already been dealt with elsewhere.[14] But in the owner-occupied sector, the simplest advance will be to abolish the stamp duty on house purchase transactions which, of course, is a tax on mobility.

But the mobility of the owner-occupier is also constrained by the existing market relations themselves. Too many powerful and venal groups exist in this country which live off the charges imposed on those households buying and selling their homes. These interests include the surveyors and valuers, the solicitors and the estate agents, all of which are heavily represented in the Conservative Party as well as controlling strong professional institutions such as the Royal Institution of Chartered Surveyors and the Law Society. One line of attack on the structure of their monopoly and privilege will be through certain changes in the law itself, for example, by establishing an open public register of the ownership of all land and buildings.[15] In addition, do-it-yourself conveyancing should be encouraged as well as conveyancing services provided by persons other than solicitors.[16]

But whilst these groups have an interest in consolidating their parasitic relationship with the first-time buyer and the selling buyer, we should not forget that it is ownership itself, this particular property right, that in the housing field generates the need for certain functions. They include, of course, survey, valuation, conveyance of title and the development of a market nexus for vendors and purchasers. As long as owner-occupation exists, these functions will have to be carried out. It is for this reason I propose that a socialist government would establish, initially on an experimental basis in, say, a dozen cities and towns, a new local authority service. The district council, drawing on advice and centralised services provided by the DoE, would create a new department whose duty would be to serve the people living in the owner-occupied sector by carrying out, at cost, the exchange functions described above. The council's mortgage provision and rehabilitation agency services would also be located in the same department. Moreover, a municipal service would be provided which is absent in the private sector. We have seen in chapter 13 that one of the major blockages to owner-occupier mobility, and a source of considerable personal stress, is the necessity of constructing terminating chains. This particular Gordian knot would be cut clean through by the district acting as a buyer of owner-occupied dwellings which they would then resell at their earliest convenience. The holding costs could be covered by a fractional differential between buying and selling price. If this huge experiment of local authority enterprise prospered in the experimental areas, the scheme would be introduced on a nationwide basis.

5   FINAL COMMENT

It goes almost without saying that the civil service in the DoE will play an essential role in the implementation of any reforms of this kind. My reading and my own experience as a civil servant in the Ministry of Technology convince me that the great mass of workers will do their utmost to progress the political commitments of a Labour manifesto - and it is this party, warts and all, which I believe offers the only prospect of socialism in Britain in our time. However, some senior 'servants' at the Under-Secretary level and above will certainly try to block such advances. The Secretary of State will take pains to see their heads in a basket - in an administrative sense, that is. Moreover the party should establish a working group of its members within the Department, meeting on a regular basis, which would assist the Secretary in ensuring every effort was being made to carry out the manifesto. She (or he) would have better lines of communication with her staff than any minister has enjoyed heretofore.

These two volumes on the housing system of modern Britain are now complete. I swear I shall not write a third. Almost sixty years have passed since the first minority Labour government came to power. Housing conditions have changed very considerably during the intervening decades. Yet today there still exists housing poverty on a huge scale. In the medium and long term, there is no technical problem that prevents us eradicating such poverty, although I believe a period of as much as fifteen years would be required to do so, even with negligible total population growth. The critical barrier is the current relationships of political, economic and ideological power within our society. If a fundamental shift in these relationships can be won and if the Labour movement within Parliament and beyond it makes a sustained commitment to the solution of the housing question, then the end of housing poverty in Britain will be secured within a single generation.

APPENDICES

APPENDIX 1   Owner-occupation: a summary legislative chronology 1803 to 1981

The chronology is not a comprehensive précis of the entirety of
every Act but seeks to summarise the main provisions with
respect to owner-occupation in England and Wales. Scottish
legislation in most cases is broadly similar.

Income Tax Act, 1803. Income tax system set up. Annual
payments, such as interest and annuities, that were paid wholly
out of taxed income could be paid net of tax. The recipients
would not bear further tax on these sums. Those making the
payments, and deducting tax, could retain the tax so deducted
and in this way would obtain tax relief. The legislation was
repealed in 1816 and re-enacted with amendments in 1842.

Building Societies Act, 1836. For the first time, building
societies obtain specific legal recognition.

Building Societies Act, 1874. Together with the later Act of
1894 it gave societies a comprehensive legal framework within
which to conduct their business. They gained corporate status
and members enjoyed limited liability. Permanent societies were
permitted to issue small denomination 'paid-up' shares akin to
modern ordinary shares. Investment of surplus funds was
restricted to mortgages, or securities carrying a government
guarantee, thus prohibiting direct investment in land or other
property, companies, etc. Government exercised regulatory
powers.

Public Health Act, 1875. It was under this Act that local
authorities prepared building by-laws that set minimum standards for newly constructed dwellings.

Building Societies Act, 1894. Required wider disclosure of
information and extended Registrar's powers. Mortgage arrears
and property taken into possession by societies now had to be
declared and societies could not accept as security property
that was already mortgaged to another party.

Small Dwellings Acquisition Act, 1899. Local authorities were
permitted to lend sums of money not exceeding £400 per house
for dwelling purchase. The cover ratio was not to exceed 80
per cent.

Housing, Town Planning, etc. Act, 1909. Local authorities were permitted to prepare town planning schemes in order to control the development of new housing areas to secure proper sanitary conditions, amenity and convenience.

Finance Act, 1910. Introduced a 20 per cent betterment levy.

Housing, Town Planning, etc. Act, 1919. It became obligatory for all boroughs and urban districts with a population of 20,000 or more to prepare town planning schemes. The maximum loan for house purchase under the 1899 Act was raised to £800 and the maximum cover was raised to 85 per cent. Local authorities permitted to lend money to private owners for rehabilitation work.

Housing (Additional Powers) Act, 1919. A lump sum grant was payable to builders on new private sector houses not exceeding 1,400 square feet in area. The grant varied between £130 and £160 depending on the floor area. (Raised in May 1920 to £230 and £260.) The grants were available for the twelve-month period up to 23 December 1920. The aggregate subsidy paid was not to exceed £15 million in the UK. The builder required two documents: the 'A' certificate authorised construction in accordance with the local authority's standards and specified the grant; the 'B' certificate, issued after erection, recorded satisfactory completion.

Housing Act, 1921. Grants on new private dwellings were extended to completions up to 23 June 1922. The Minister of Health to issue Orders stating the rate of interest on loans under the Small Dwellings Acquisition Act.

Housing Act, 1923. Local authorities were to pay a subsidy to builders on dwellings built for private rental or sale provided they fell within certain minimum and maximum dimensions. The sum payable was not to exceed £6 per year per house over twenty years, or a lump sum of £75. This was available only for completions before 1 October 1925. The authorities' disbursements were funded by the Treasury. The scope of the SDAA was widened: the maximum loan was raised to £1,200 and the maximum cover to 90 per cent; advances could be made during construction up to 50 per cent of the value of the work done. Provisions were also made for local authorities to lend money to *builders*, for the purpose of constructing or acquiring houses after 25 April 1923. The maximum value of the house was £1,500 and the maximum cover was 90 per cent. Advances during construction up to 50 per cent of the value of the work done were permissible. Moreover the authorities were empowered to give guarantees to building societies on advances made to borrowers wishing to build or acquire houses of a value not exceeding £1,500 started after 25 April 1923.

Housing (Financial Provisions) Act, 1924. The 1923 Act subsidies continued to be available for houses completed before
October 1939. A new higher level of subsidies was also introduced but only for accommodation built for rental.

Land Registration Act, 1925. Established the current system
of land registration and was designed to simplify and cheapen
the process of conveying land. It replaced the complicated
and voluminous title deeds of property by a single land certificate. The purchaser now took the property free from any
encumbrance that was not entered on the register with the
exception of the list of overriding interests listed in Section 70.

Housing Act, 1925. A codifying measure.

Housing Act, 1930. Section 47 permitted local authorities to
make loans to persons or bodies of persons carrying out
repairs to a house.

Town and Country Planning Act, 1932. Extended planning
powers to almost any type of land, whether built-up or undeveloped.

Restriction of Ribbon Development Act, 1935. Designed to control the spread of development along major roads.

Housing Act, 1935. The maximum house value for loans to
builders was reduced from £1,500 down to £800. The maximum
loan for house purchase under the SDAA was also reduced
from £1,200 to £800. The rate of interest on SDAA advances was
henceforth to be set at $\frac{1}{4}$ per cent above the rate charged by the
PWLB for housing loans to the local authorities. Formerly the
rate had been fixed by the minister in consultation with the
Treasury.

Housing Act, 1936. A consolidating act. Local authorities were
empowered to sell council houses but required ministerial permission to do so. The best price obtainable had to be charged.

Public Health Act, 1936. It brought to an end building by-laws
made under earlier Acts and provided that subsequent by-laws
should have a life of not more than ten years.

Building Societies Act, 1939. Defined acceptable forms of collateral whose stringent conditions effectively terminated the
builder's pool.

Housing (Emergency Powers) Act, 1939. Empowered local
authorities to execute temporary or more permanent repairs to
dwellings damaged by enemy action. The costs were to be borne
by the owner or tenant. The Ministry of Health was authorised

to make loans to cover such costs.

Repair of War Damage Act, 1941. Waived all formalities for
first-aid repairs and widened their scope. Owners and tenants
were no longer charged, whilst the War Damage Commission
compensated the local authorities for their costs.

Supplies and Services (Transitional Powers) Act, 1945. Renewed
Defence Regulation 56A.

Building Materials and Housing Act, 1945. The advance permissible, under the SDAA and the 1936 Housing Act, to persons
wishing to buy their house or to build a house to live in was
raised from £800 back up again to £1,500. Local authorities
were permitted to fix maximum resale prices on dwellings built
or converted under licence. (This control was amended in the
1949 Housing Act and lapsed in December 1953.)

Town and Country Planning Act, 1947. It provided for two
major planning functions: (a) the preparation of a development
plan indicating the manner in which a local planning authority
proposed that land in its area should be used, including allocat-
ing areas for residential purposes. The plan was not binding.
(b) development control, that is, day-to-day controls to ensure
that proposals for individual development projects were properly
sited, both for their own needs and in relation to neighbouring
uses. This was implemented by making all development subject
to planning permission. Once-and-for-all compensation for the
loss of development rights was to be made on the basis of 1947
valuations and paid out of a national fund. Where development
was permitted, the developer was to pay a development charge
equal to 100 per cent of the increase in the value of the land
resulting from the permission to develop.

Housing Act, 1949. Grants became available from local authorities to owner-occupiers and landlords wishing to improve or
convert their houses. The total improvement cost was to lie
between £100 and £600 and the grant covered 50 per cent of
this. (The upper limit was raised to £800 in 1952.) The dwelling
had to provide accommodation for thirty years at a sixteen-
point standard. Advances to persons wishing to buy or build a
house for their own use were permissible henceforth on dwellings up to £5,000 in value. Section 4 allowed mortgages under
the Act to be issued at variable interest rates before (but not
after) the contract was signed. Section 5 permitted the local
authorities to guarantee excess advances made by building
societies for house purchase.

Income Tax Act, 1952. Consolidated legislation of 1951 that had
recognised a special arrangement first arrived at in 1925-6
whereby interest on building society mortgages was payable in

full without deduction of tax. To balance this departure from
the normal arrangements (see 1803 Act) and to obtain the same
relief as would be available if tax were deducted and retained,
borrowers could set these interest payments against their own
liabilities for tax. Since the introduction of PAYE in 1944 this
relief is normally given to employees through the borrower's
PAYE coding.

Housing Act, 1952. It repealed the existing requirement that
the best price must be realised when council houses were sold.
Within five years of the date of disposal, the local authority
could limit the price at which a house could be re-sold and could
reserve to itself a right of pre-emption.

Town and Country Planning Act, 1953. Abolished development
charges on any development begun after 18 November 1952.

Town and Country Planning Act, 1954. Protection against compulsory purchase at value in existing use was given to speculative builders who had bought for early development.

Housing Repairs and Rents Act, 1954. With respect to grants
for improvement and conversion, a twelve-point standard and
fifteen-year life replaced the 1949 Act provisions; and the
upper limit on costs was waived although the maximum grant
stayed at £400.

Slum Clearance (Compensation) Act, 1956. Owner-occupiers
of unfit houses were compensated as if the property were fit
provided it had been purchased between September 1939 and
December 1955.

Housing Act, 1957. Consolidated the various enactments relating to housing other than on financial matters.

Housing (Financial Provisions) Act, 1958. Consolidated previous
financial legislation.

House Purchase and Housing Act, 1959. Previously all grants
had been conferred at the discretion of the local authority and
this system of provision was continued, whilst the grant conditions were relaxed. However, a new 'standard grant' was introduced, claimable as of right on pre-1945 houses. These were
for improvement to a five-point standard with a minimum property life of fifteen years. The maximum grant was £155 or half
the cost of the work, whichever was lower. Local authorities
were permitted to make loans for owner's share of the costs. A
second feature of the Act was that it raised the cover ratio of
local authority mortgages to 100 per cent and removed the
restrictions prohibiting advances on houses valued at more than
£5,000. An entirely novel section was that the Treasury should

provide money for the purchase of older houses. Under an agreement between the Exchequer and certain approved building societies the latter were to make loans of up to 95 per cent of the value or purchase price (whichever was lower) of any house built before 1919 and valued at not more than £2,500 (£3,000 in London), which in the normal way of business would have qualified for a 75 per cent advance. On such mortgages Exchequer loans were made payable to the building societies up to an aggregate value of £100 million.

Public Health Act, 1961. Permitted the drawing-up of the first national building regulations. This was done in 1965 and came into force in 1966.

Town and Country Planning Act, 1962. A consolidating measure.

Building Societies Act, 1962. The major statute governing the operations of the societies, consolidating and extending nine previous Acts. It provided for incorporation; limited liability; restrictions on powers of borrowing, lending and investing; annual audit and publication of accounts; and the regulatory powers of the Registrar.

Finance Act, 1963. Abolished Schedule A taxation.

Housing Act, 1964. Discretionary grants to owner-occupiers were made more attractive by raising the grant limit for standard amenities and reducing from ten years down to three the period during which the grant conditions attached to the dwelling. Local authorities were permitted to declare improvement areas.

Housing (Slum Clearance Compensation) Act, 1965. Continued the provision for home-owners of unfit property purchased between 1939 and 1955 to be compensated at market values.

Building Control Act, 1966. Introduced building licensing to give priority to housing construction.

Supplementary Benefit Act, 1966. An owner-occupier on benefit was entitled to an allowance for rates, insurance, repairs and 'reasonable' interest charges on a mortgage.

Land Commission Act, 1967. It gave the Land Commission wide powers to purchase, manage and dispose of land and it introduced a betterment levy which was charged on increases in the development value of land, paid by the owners when they sold the land.

Leasehold Reform Act, 1967. Enabled people who had lived for at least five years in houses within the rateable value limit of

£200 (£400 inside Greater London), which they held on long
tenancies at low rents, to purchase the freehold of their house.
The price payable was to equal the market value of the freehold
interest on the assumption that the lease had been extended
for fifty years.

Housing Subsidies Act, 1967. Introduced option mortgages
under which house purchasers could choose an option mortgage
receiving a government subsidy reducing the rate of interest
on the mortgage. In addition the option mortgage guarantee
scheme was initiated. Building societies agreed to entertain
applications from option mortgage borrowers buying houses of
not more than £5,000 in price, or valuation if that was less,
for loans of up to 25 per cent of the valuation of the property
over and above the amount normally lent. The additional amount
lent was guaranteed by insurance, half provided free by the
government and half by insurance companies.

Town and Country Planning Act, 1968. Established a new
framework for plan preparation. Counties and major towns were
to write 'structure plans', statements of policy accompanied by
diagrammatic illustrations, dealing with broad land-use policies
and indicating action areas where major change through develop
ment, redevelopment and rehabilitation might be expected. Thes
plans were to be approved by the minister. Lower-level authorities (from 1974 the district councils) were to produce local
plans. When development was undertaken privately, the local
plan had to provide broad guidelines, as it were a brief to the
developer and architect. The Act also provided for planning
permissions to lapse if development had not begun within five
years and allowed local planning authorities to serve developers
with completion notices.

Housing Act, 1969. Local authorities were given powers to
declare general improvement areas in which resources were to
be devoted to improving and prolonging the life of a selected
residential area as a whole. The emphasis was on voluntary
co-operation rather than compulsion. Government grants were
made available towards environmental improvement up to an
expenditure of £100 per dwelling. At the same time the arrangements for rehabilitation grants were substantially altered. The
standard grant maximum was raised to £200. Discretionary
grants were renamed improvement grants; their maximum was
raised to £1,000 (£1,200 in houses of three or more storeys);
and, as part of them, approved works of repair and replacement
became eligible for grant aid for the first time. The conditions
of grant approval were relaxed. 'Special grants' were introduced
for installing amenities in houses in multi-occupation. The cost
of funding grants was borne largely by the Exchequer which
paid an annual sum over twenty years equal to three-quarters
of the loan charges arising for the authorities. Local authorities

were also given powers to make loans repayable on maturity to help owners improve or repair their homes and to assist owners to carry out improvement works by taking over the job by agreement. Finally the code of compensation was changed so that henceforth virtually all owner-occupiers of unfit homes compulsorily acquired in slum clearance schemes received compensation at market value.

Finance Act, 1969. Abolished tax relief on loan interest with specific exemption to interest paid on loans for the acquisition or improvement of property.

Housing Act, 1971. In the intermediate and development areas rehabilitation grants were raised to cover three-quarters of approved costs.

Housing (Amendment) Act, 1973. Enabled the minister to authorise or require local authorities to control the resale of council houses for a period of over five years.

Housing Act, 1974. Housing action areas introduced, with a five-year life, to give priority to the improvement of living conditions in areas where the poor physical condition of houses was combined with social stress. The eligible expense limit on which grants were based was raised to £3,200 for discretionary grants and £1,500 for intermediate (i.e. standard) grants. In HAAs and GIAs repairs-only grants were made available on eligible expenses up to £800. In HAAs the grant could cover three-quarters of the expense limit or up to 90 per cent in hardship cases. For the first time the repairs element was extended to standard grants. Owner-occupiers were required not to sell their house within five years of grant receipt in breach of which the grant could be reclaimed at compound interest. Restrictions were introduced on grant approvals for owner-occupiers in GIAs, HAAs and Priority Neighbourhoods where the house had been tenanted in the previous twelve months. The Secretary of State was also given powers to specify a rateable value limit on owner-occupied properties eligible for improvement grants.

Finance Act, 1974. Ended tax relief on interest on most forms of personal loans other than for house purchase and improvement. Tax relief permitted on main residence of a borrower but not on second homes, and the size of the mortgage on which relief could be claimed was limited to £25,000. In addition, development gains on land transactions were henceforth taxed as income.

Community Land Act, 1975. It gave land authorities first the power and subsequently the duty to acquire all land needed for relevant development. The exemptions and exceptions included

land owned by builders or residential developers which had
planning permission for development on 12 September 1974.
Three implementation stages were foreseen, of which only
the first took place, i.e. by means of a five-year rolling programme, the land authorities were to consider requiring land
for relevant development to carry out their structure and local
plan intentions. Acquired land developed privately could either
be leased or resold.

Development Land Tax Act, 1976. Introduced a tax to be paid
by landowners on the realised development value (RDV) of land,
calculated as the difference between a base value and the selling price of the land when disposed of. When an owner himself
developed a site he was deemed to have disposed of it immediately
prior to the development. There were three methods of calculating the base value which all referred to expenditure on improvement by the owner plus either its cost of acquisition or its
current-use value. In 1976-9 for a single owner in a single year
the first £10,000 of RDV was tax exempt. The rest was charged
at a rate of 80 per cent save that in the period up to 31 March
1979 the first £150,000 of RDV carried a $66\frac{2}{3}$ per cent rate.

Home Purchase Assistance and Housing Corporation Guarantee
Act, 1978. First-time buyers who saved at least £600 over a
period of at least two years with a recognised savings institution
qualified for a £600 additional loan for house purchase. No
interest or capital payments were necessary on the loan for the
first five years after receipt. In addition a bonus of £40-110
was paid to those qualifying for the loan, the amount depending
on their rate of saving. The price of the property purchased
was not to exceed certain regionally defined limits.

Estate Agents Act, 1979. Aimed to protect home-owners in their
involvement with agents. Protection was provided for clients'
deposits. The Director General of Fair Trading could prohibit
'unfit' persons from working as agents. Agents were required
to give vendors details of the basis of their charges.

Local Government, Planning and Land Act, 1980. Repealed the
Community Land Act.

Housing Act, 1980. Secure tenants of public sector dwellings
enjoyed the right to buy their homes if they had been tenants
for more than three years. A discount was available on the
market price of 33 per cent with tenancies of less than four
years rising by 1 per cent for each further completed year to
a 50 per cent maximum. The purchaser could deposit £100 with
the local authority and complete the purchase at the original
valuation within two years. Tenants had a right to a local
authority or Housing Corporation mortgage. If a purchaser sold
within five years, the discount was repaid, reduced by one-

fifth for every year subsequent to purchase. In National Parks
and Areas of Outstanding Natural Beauty, the local authority
could restrict resale to someone who had lived or worked in the
area for three years.

With respect to rehabilitation grants, these could no longer
be reclaimed from owner-occupiers moving within five years of
receipt. Repair grants were extended to any area, not just
GIAs and HAAs. The Secretary of State was given the power to
change the allowable cost and the percentage met from grant
and was enabled to make grants to local authorities and housing associations to rehabilitate dwellings for sale. On mortgage
advances, the local authority's interest rate was to be limited
to the building society rate or the local pool rate, whichever
was higher. Switching between option mortgage subsidy and tax
relief was further simplified.

APPENDIX 2   Permanent dwellings constructed for private
owners in Britain 1919-80

Year a	Completions c	Year a	Starts b	Completions c
1919-20	)	1951	27,080	22,551
1920-1	)annual estimated	1952	52,327	34,320
1921-2	)average is	1953	83,226	62,921
1922-3	)25,727	1954	106,781	90,636
1923-4	74,097	1955	127,522	113,457
1924-5	119,903	1956	120,416	124,161
1925-6	134,847	1957	125,625	126,455
1926-7	151,032	1958	136,855	128,148
1927-8	141,017	1959	169,414	150,708
1928-9	118,833	1960	182,772	168,629
1929-30	146,826	1961	189,413	177,513
1930-1	132,504	1962	185,976	174,800
1931-2	135,517	1963	199,404	174,864
1932-3	151,101	1964	247,453	218,094
1933-4	221,542	1965	211,068	213,799
1934-5	294,748	1966	193,412	205,372
1935-6	279,829	1967	233,648	200,438
1936-7	282,480	1968	200,050	221,993
1937-8	267,609	1969	166,835	181,703
1938-9	237,220	1970	165,071	170,304
1939-40	151,921	1971	207,348	191,612
1940-1	30,822	1972	227,964	196,457
1941-2	6,293	1973	215,748	186,628
1942-3	2,718	1974	105,931	140,865
1943-4	1,171	1975	149,128	150,752
1944-5	2,022	1976	154,652	152,181
1945	1,390	1977	134,810	140,820
1946	30,315	1978	157,311	149,021
1947	41,860	1979	143,990	140,299

Year a	Completions c	Year a	Starts b	Completions c
1948	34,582	1980	97,421	125,894
1949	27,198			
1950	29,088			

Sources: 1919-39: *Statistical Abstract of the United Kingdom*; 1939-50: *Annual Abstract of Statistics*; 1951-66: *HSGB*; 1967-80: *HCS*.

a For the years 1919-20 through to 1944-5 the data run from 1 April to 31 March. From 1945 onwards the data are for calendar years. The 1945 figure is an estimate. For the years 1939-40 to 1944-5 the data for Scotland and for England and Wales are not compatible. Thus for 1939-40 (and similarly in the five subsequent years) I have had to add the April 1939 to March 1940 data for England and Wales to the January-December 1939 data for Scotland.
b Information on starts is not available before 1951.
c In the years 1919-20 to 1944-5, the data on England and Wales excluded dwellings with a rateable value greater than £78 (or £105 in the Metropolitan Police District). The figure for 1923-4 is an estimate derived by multiplying up the England and Wales total of 71,800. In the calendar years 1945-50 the data include war-destroyed houses that were rebuilt. Their numbers were, in these six years respectively, 51, 2,942, 9,469, 12,369, 5,477 and 2,508.

APPENDIX 3 Private sector housing land prices in England and Wales, 1963-80[a]

Year	Weighted average price per plot (£)	Weighted average price per hectare (£)	Price index per plot or hectare at constant average density
1963	413	9,444	46
1964	473	10,816	52
1965	525	12,005	58
1966	562	12,851	62
1967	575	13,149	63
1968[b]	664	15,184	73
1969	828	18,934	91
1970	908	20,763	100
1971	1,030	23,553	113
1972	1,727	39,491	190
1973	2,676	61,190	295
1974	2,663	60,900	293
1975	1,839	42,050	203

Year	Weighted average price per plot (£)	Weighted average price per hectare (£)	Price index per plot or hectare at constant average density
1976	1,848	42,260	204
1977	1,943	44,430	214
1978[c]	2,376	54,330	262
1979	3,395	77,640	374
1980	4,460	101,991	491

Source: Andrew Evans, 'Private sector housing land prices in
        England and Wales', *Economic Trends*, February 1974;
        HCS.

a Transactions in land with planning permission for housing
sold to private purchasers. Sites of at least four plots. There
is an approximate gap of five months between agreement of
price and reporting of the transaction.
b Before 1969 data were based only on 'pressure areas'.
c Change of weights after 1978.

APPENDIX 4   Subsidies received by owner-occupiers 1967-8 to
        1979-80[a]

Year	Tax relief on mortgage interest[b]	Tax relief on life premiums[c]	Option mortgage subsidy	Rehabilitation grants[d]
1967-8	180	9	nil	nk
1968-9	195	10	7	nk
1969-70	235	12	9	nk
1970-1	285	13	12	nk
1971-2	310	13	17	nk
1972-3	365	15	26	37
1973-4	507	17	49	70
1974-5	687	21	73	104
1975-6	856	25	105	48
1976-7	1,090	nk	140	49
1977-8	1,040	nk	150	47
1978-9	1,110	nk	140	62
1979-80	1,450	nk	190	86

Sources: *HPTV*, Table IV.20. House of Commons, *Parliamentary
        Papers*, Written Answers, 30 November 1981, c.47-8;
        HCS; DoE, *Housing and Construction Statistics
        1969-79*, London, HMSO, 1980.

a The main text has shown there are six different types of subsidy paid to owner-occupiers. Only four appear in this table

because no data is available on SBC payments of home-owners'
mortgage interest nor on the subsidies provided under the
1978 Home Purchase Assistance Act.
b The data for 1976-7 onwards includes relief on interest paid
by housing societies, about 1 per cent of the total.
c Premiums associated with endowment mortgages.
d This is my own estimate based on taking the grants paid in
England to private owners and multiplying this, for discretionary and other grants separately, by the ratio of grants
approved for owner-occupiers to approvals for all private
owners. The other three subsidy columns are for the UK.

APPENDIX 5 Building society advances by number and value
and the average building society mortgage rate and share rate
in 1918-80 in Great Britain[a]

Year	Advances Number ('000)	Advances Value (£m)	Mortgage rate %	Share rate %
1918		7		
1919		16		
1920		25		
1921		20		4.26
1922		23		4.36
1923		32		4.33
1924		41		4.37
1925		50		4.35
1926		52		4.39
1927		56		4.39
1928	116	59		4.54
1929	141	75		4.54
1930	159	89		4.65
1931	162	90		4.62
1932	159	82		4.52
1933	197	103		3.95
1934	238	125		3.80
1935	241	131		3.64
1936	252	140		3.45
1937	241	137		3.38
1938	232	137	4.82	3.37
1939	167	95	4.79	3.40
1940	43	21	4.76	3.27
1941	22	10	4.74	2.83
1942	32	16	4.77	2.48
1943	48	28	4.80	2.40
1944	75	53	4.71	2.36
1945	121	98	4.68	2.34
1946	207	188	4.35	2.15
1947	243	242	4.29	2.15
1948	259	264	4.24	2.16

Year	Advances Number ('000)	Advances Value (£m)	Mortgage rate %	Share rate %
1949	301	276	4.20	2.15
1950	302	270	4.18	2.22
1951	299	268	4.19	2.22
1952	284	266	4.32	2.38
1953	307	299	4.55	2.45
1954	353	373	4.58	2.45
1955	342	394	4.66	2.61
1956	276	335	5.32	3.08
1957	296	374	5.98	3.45
1958	289	375	6.13	3.48
1959	370	517	5.98	3.43
1960	387	560	5.89	3.37
1961	364	546	6.28	3.54
1962	378	613	6.61	3.70
1963	477	849	6.27	3.56
1964	535	1,043	6.16	3.50
1965	457	955	6.63	3.78
1966	536	1,245	6.95	4.01
1967	586	1,463	7.20	4.20
1968	595	1,590	7.46	4.37
1969	545	1,559	8.08	4.82
1970	624	1,954	8.58	4.94
1971	769	2,705	8.59	4.95
1972	893	3,630	8.26	4.88
1973	720	3,513	9.59	6.51
1974	546	2,945	11.05	7.53
1975	798	4,908	11.08	7.21
1976	913	6,183	11.06	7.02
1977	946	6,745	11.05	6.98
1978	1,184	8,808	9.55	6.46
1979	1,040	9,002	11.94	8.45
1980	937	9,506	14.94	10.37

Source: Annual Reports of the Chief Registrar of Friendly
Societies, London, HMSO. 1980: BSA estimate.

a The average annual value of advances in 1901–17 was £8m.
Publication of the number of advances, the mortgage rate and
the share rate only began in the years 1928, 1938 and 1921
respectively.

APPENDIX 6: Loans to private persons for house purchase in
England and Wales by local authorities 1945–80

Year	Number of dwellings	Amount loaned (£000)
1945–51	43.934	37,210

Year	Number of dwellings	Amount loaned (£000)
1951-2	21,209	23,380
1952-3	18,327	21,450
1953-4	23,905	28,856
1954-5	38,559	49,087
1955-6	53,182	69,170
1956-7	51,052	64,394
1957	48,175	56,007
1958	38,563	45,580
1959	44,699	55,498
1960	47,864	66,843
1961	62,318	99,205
1962	53,385	84,764
1963	57,617	103,865
1964	77,217	166,270
1965	87,112	220,398
1966	46,229	108,899
1967	56,598	144,390
1968	38,792	85,693
1969	19,096	42,156
1970	44,103	118,344
1971	47,174	126,682
1972	45,202	132,927
1973	59,421	292,668
1974	75,396	455,112
1975[a]	101,952	636,089
1976	24,420	136,500
1977	23,475	134,950
1978	27,315	154,500
1979	35,475	244,400
1980	16,375	134,500

Source: *MHLG Annual Reports*; *HSGB*; *HCS*.

a Up to and including 1975 figures are for loans reported by local authorities. Later figures are rounded estimates of loans made during the period, including adjustments for returns not received.

NOTES

1 THE FIRST BOOM

1 'HPTV', part I, table 1.23.
2 J.B. Cullingworth, 'Town and Country Planning in Britain', 5th edn, London, Allen & Unwin, 1974, pp. 18-23.
3 'HPTV', part I, pp. 3-4.
4 See Martin Boddy, 'The Building Societies', London, Macmillan, 1980, pp. 5-11. The standard text on the history of the building societies is E.J. Cleary, 'The Building Society Movement', London, Elek Books, 1965.
5 See 'HPTV', part II, p. 57.
6 See 'HPTV', part I, pp. 40-2.
7 See 'HPTV', part II, p. 62.
8 See Stephen Merrett, 'State Housing in Britain', London, Routledge & Kegan Paul, 1979, ch. 1.
9 Marian Bowley, 'Housing and the State: 1919-1944', London, Allen & Unwin, 1945, p. 22.
10 Ibid., p. 32.
11 These events are treated in detail with respect to state housing in Merrett, op. cit., ch. 2.
12 MoH, 'First Annual Report, 1919-1920', Cmd 917, London, HMSO, 1920, p. 11. The same report, on p. 35, cheerfully announced that the Ministry was preparing 'a model scheme' for the sale of council houses.
13 See MoH, 'Twelfth Annual Report of the Ministry of Health, 1930-31', Cmd 3937, London, HMSO, 1931, p. 114.
14 See Keith Feiling, 'The Life of Neville Chamberlain', London, Macmillan, 1946, p. 86.
15 'HPTV', part I, p. 11.
16 Ibid., pp. 12-14.
17 Bowley, op. cit., p. 279. Annual data on the value and number of advances for house purchase can be found in appendix 5.
18 See Boddy, op. cit., pp. 12-16; also H.W. Richardson and D.H. Aldcroft, 'Building in the British Economy between the Wars', London, Allen & Unwin, 1968; E.T. Nevin, 'The Mechanism of Cheap Money: A Study of British Monetary Policy 1931-1939', Cardiff, University of Wales Press, 1955; and Cleary, op. cit.
19 Merrett, op. cit., p. 52.
20 Bowley, op. cit., p. 277.
21 Ruth Issacharoff, 'The building boom of the inter-war years: whose profits and at whose cost?', in Michael Harloe (ed.), 'Urban Change and Conflict', London, CES, 1978, p. 315. This detailed study of the British building industry between the wars was the last paper written by Ruth before her untimely death in 1977.
22 Bowley, op. cit., pp. 278-9. This reduction was reflected in the increase in real incomes referred to under (a). I am not double-counting, however, because the income effect was brought about not only by the fall in accommodation costs.
23 MoH, 'Eleventh Annual Report of the Ministry of Health, 1929-30', Cmd 3667, London, HMSO, 1930, p. 77. It should be noted that in Scotland no changes were made in the 1923 and 1924 subsidies until they were

abolished in 1933.

24   MoH, 'Tenth Annual Report of the Ministry of Health, 1928-29', Cmd 3362,
     London, HMSO, 1929, p. 66. Similar messages were contained in circulars
     755/27 and 954/29.
25   MoH (1930), op. cit., p. 77.
26   See Ralph Miliband, 'Parliamentary Socialism: A Study in the Politics of
     Labour', London, Merlin Press, 1972, ch. 6.
27   MoH, 'Fourteenth Annual Report of the Ministry of Health, 1932-33', Cmd
     4372, London, HMSO, 1933, pp. 89-90.
28   See Paul Wilding, 'Government and housing: A study in the development
     of social policy 1906-39', D. Phil. thesis of the University of Manchester,
     March 1970, p. 315.
29   Marian Bowley suggests a net loss during redevelopment of 103,000 units
     in 1934-9. See Bowley, op. cit., pp. 172, 270.
30   See 'The Economist', 18 February 1939, p. 348. Also Issacharoff, op. cit.,
     p. 309.
31   See Noreen Branson and Margot Heinemann, 'Britain in the Nineteen
     Thirties', St Albans, Panther, 1973, pp. 206-10.
32   See Ministry of Labour Cost of Living Inquiry, 'Ministry of Labour
     Gazette', December 1940 and January 1941; and Philip Massey, 'The
     expenditure of 1,360 middle-class households in 1938-9', 'Journal of the
     Royal Statistical Society', 1942.

2 WAR AND RECONSTRUCTION

1   See Nathan Rosenberg, 'Economic Planning in the British Building Industry
    1945-49', Philadelphia, University of Pennsylvania Press, 1960, p. 39.
2   This point is made well by Michael Ball in British housing policy and the
    house-building industry, 'Capital and Class', no.4, spring 1978, p. 88.
3   The average annual number of marriages in England and Wales in 1931-8
    was 338,000 whilst in 1939 and 1940 it was 458,000! The average in 1941-
    50 was 367,000. See 'HPTV', part I, Table 1.3.
4   The framework of building controls is described in detail by Rosenberg,
    op. cit., ch. 2.
5   MoH, 'Report for the Year ended 31st March 1946', Cmd 7119, London,
    HMSO, pp. 159-60.
6   CHAC, 'Private Enterprise Housing', London, HMSO, 1944.
7   MoH, 'Report for the Year ended 31st March 1947', Cmd 7441, London,
    HMSO, 1948, p. 170.
8   'Let Us Face the Future', Labour Party, 1945.
9   See R.A. Sabatino, 'Housing in Great Britain 1945-49', Dallas, Southern
    Methodist University Press, 1956, p. 30.
10 See Rosenberg, op. cit., p. 69.
11 MoH, 'Report for the Year ended 31st March 1948', Cmd 7734, London,
    HMSO, 1949, p. 239. The council housing cuts are treated at greater
    length in Stephen Merrett, 'State Housing in Britain', London, Routledge &
    Kegan Paul, 1979, ch. 9, section two.
12 Rosenberg, op. cit., Table XIII.
13 The target of 200,000 units under construction is given in MoH, 'Housing
    Return for England and Wales 31st May 1948', Cmd 7442, London, HMSO,
    1948, p. 3; and by Aneurin Bevan, the minister, in 'Parliamentary Debates',
    House of Commons, 1947-8, vol. 453, 14 July 1948, c. 1321. Statements
    on 200,000 units completed per annum are given by Bevan in 'Parliamentary
    Debates', House of Commons, 1948-9, vol. 466, 4 July 1949, c. 1825; and,
    as a target, by Sir John Wrigley in Michael Foot, 'Aneurin Bevan 1945-60',
    St Albans, Paladin, 1975, p. 94.
14 MoH, 'Report for the Year ended 31st March 1949', Cmd 7910, London,
    HMSO, 1950, p. 319.
15 Rosenberg, op. cit., pp. 107-8.
16 MoH, 'Report for the Year ended 31st March 1950', Cmd 8342, London,

HMSO, 1951, p. 122.
17 'HPTV', part I, Tables I.5 and I.11.
18 Ralph Miliband, 'The State in Capitalist Society: the Analysis of the Western System of Power', London, Quartet Books, 1973, p. 96.

3 THE SECOND BOOM

1 See Stephen Merrett, 'State Housing in Britain', London, Routledge & Kegan Paul, 1979, pp. 102-3. The same source sets out the history of the period 1951-70 for local authority housing policy on pp. 246-59.
2 See MHLG, 'Report for the period 1950/51 to 1954', Cmd 9559, London, HMSO, 1955, pp. 11-13. Also see D.V. Donnison, 'Housing Policy since the War', Welwyn, Codicote Press, 1960, pp. 18-19.
3 MHLG, op. cit., pp. 6-7.
4 See Merrett, op. cit., Graph 9.1.
5 MHLG, op. cit., pp. 16-17.
6 On these matters, see circular 54/57 and the annual reports of the MHLG for 1955, 1956 and 1957, pp. 12-13, 13 and 14 respectively.
7 MHLG, 'House Purchase: Proposed Government Scheme', Cmnd 571, London, HMSO, p. 3. The White Paper should have said 'these 1919-1940 houses'.
8 This was in spite of an improvement in the terms of grant approval. From 1952 the cost range of work done on which grants could be claimed was raised to £150 minimum and £800 maximum (the minimum was reduced again to £100 in 1954). See Cmd 9559, p. 22.
9 MHLG, 'Houses: The next Step', Cmd 8996, London, HMSO, 1953, pp. 3-4.
10 Ibid., p. 4.
11 See 'HPTV', part III, p. 117.
12 MHLG, 'Housing in England and Wales', Cmnd 1290, London, HMSO, 1961, p. 10.
13 Ibid., p. 10.
14 See Dave Burn, 'Rent Strike: St Pancras 1960', London, Pluto Press, 1972.
15 See Merrett, op. cit., p. 252.
16 MHLG, 'Housing', Cmnd 2050, London, HMSO, 1963, p. 15.
17 Ibid., p. 11.
18 See 'HPTV', part I, p. 48, footnote 43, and part II, pp. 62-3. I return again to the taxation of the owner-occupier's so-called imputed income in ch. 17.
19 In fact the concept of 'housing class' itself originates much later, in the work of John Rex. See 'Race, Colonialism and the City', London, Routledge & Kegan Paul, 1973, especially ch. 3.
20 MHLG, 'The Housing Programme 1965 to 1970', Cmnd 2838, London, HMSO, 1965, pp. 7-8.
21 Evelyn Sharp, 'The Ministry of Housing and Local Government', London, Allen & Unwin, 1969, p. 82.
22 See 'HPTV', part I, p. 30.
23 MHLG, 'Report of the MHLG 1965 and 1966', Cmnd 3282, London, HMSO, 1967, p. 66.
24 DoE, 'Report of the MHLG 1969 and 1970', Cmnd 4753, London, HMSO, 1971, p. 6.
25 Ibid., p. 10.
26 MHLG, 'Help towards Home Ownership', Cmnd 3163, London, HMSO, 1966, p. 2.
27 MHLG, 'Old Houses into New Homes', Cmnd 3602, London, HSMO, 1968, p. 10.
28 MHLG (1965), op. cit., p. 17.
29 A fuller account is given in Merrett, op. cit., pp. 254-9.
30 MHLG (1965), op. cit., p. 11, 13.
31 J.B. Cullingworth, 'Town and Country Planning in Britain', 5th edn, London, Allen & Unwin, 1974, pp. 159-60.

THE DEMOGRAPHIC CONTEXT

1   Note that this definition of first-time buyers excludes sitting buyers but
    includes, for example, a purchaser leaving rented accommodation in order
    to buy but who had been a home-owner before taking up his current
    rented house or flat. It also includes house purchases by households
    immigrating into the country within the defined time-period, even though
    they may have owned a house abroad. The dwellings these categories refer
    to are all assumed to be located in Britain.
2   See 'HPTV', part I, p. 13.
3   Ibid., p. 77-8.
4   Ibid., p. 81. The point is made in the 'HPTV' with respect to the stock of
    owners, not the flow of purchasers.
5   The starting point of gross flows analysis is A.E. Holman's article, 'A
    forecast of effective demand for housing in Great Britain in the 1970s',
    'Social Trends', no. 1, 1970, pp. 33-42. I have not, however, used his
    new/immigrant/moving household classification as the basis for effective
    demand analysis since it formally excludes sitting purchasers and the
    purchase of second homes.
6   'HPTV', part I, p. 93.
7   Ibid., Table II.46. The same document suggested that at 1971 rates of
    movement to owner-occupation, some 65 per cent of married couples would
    become owner-occupiers either directly they set up house or after a
    temporary spell as tenants. See 'HPTV', part II, p. 34.
8   See 'HPTV', part I, Table A.3, p. 158.
9   See OPCS, 'Marriage and Divorce Statistics', Marriage Series FM2, no. 2.
10 A more sensitive ratio would be the number of first marriages by women
    aged 17-24 as a proportion of all spinsters in the 17-24 age group. Un-
    fortunately these data are not available to me.
11 See 'HPTV', part I, Table II.48.

THE WILLINGNESS TO PURCHASE

1   On access to and the allocation of local authority dwellings see Fred Gray
    Council house management, in Stephen Merrett, 'State Housing in Britain',
    London, Routledge & Kegan Paul, 1979, ch. 8. A useful article on the
    constraints faced by young households is Rosemary Mellor, Planning for
    housing: market processes and constraints, 'Planning Outlook', New
    Series, vol. 13, autumn 1973, pp. 26-42.
2   The need to understand 'the house as a home', fulfilling the requirements
    for a multitude of activities, is particularly stressed by the Socialist
    Housing Activists Workshop in their publication 'Socialism and Housing
    Action: The Red Paper on Housing', Gateshead, SHAW, 1979, pp. 2-5.
3   I prefer this neologism to the term 'equity' both because the latter, quite
    inappropriately, is a synonym for 'fairness' and also because even in its
    strictly financial sense 'equity' is used with a variety of meanings, although
    the most common of these coincides with net worth. I also prefer 'price
    gain' to 'capital gain' because, in deference to a higher authority, I use
    'capital' as far as is practicable to refer to outlays on real and financial
    assets made specifically to appropriate the surplus product of society.
4   See Jim Kemeny, 'The Myth of Home-Ownership: Private versus Public
    Choices in Housing Tenure', London, Routledge & Kegan Paul, 1981, p.8.
5   Joan Robinson and John Eatwell, 'An Introduction to Modern Economics',
    rev. edn, London, McGraw-Hill, 1974, p. 38.
6   DoE, 'Fair Deal for Housing', Cmnd 4728, London, HMSO, 1971, p. 4.
7   See Stephen Merrett, Some conceptual relationships in 'Capital', 'History
    of Political Economy', vol. 9, no. 4, December 1977. This article con-
    stitutes the basis of my rejection of Marxist value theory on philosophical
    grounds, quite apart from the theory's total uselessness for empirical
    research.

8   See Karl Marx, 'Capital', New York, International Publishers, 1967, vol. 3, p. 774. Commodity fetishism is discussed in vol. 1, ch. 1, section 4.
9   See Christine Whitehead, Why owner-occupation?, 'CES Review', no. 6, May 1979, pp. 33-41. This excellent article does not itself use the term 'Whitehead's law' to sum up the main thrust of the argument.
10 See Gray, op. cit., pp. 202, 220-2.
11 See, for example, 'HPTV', part I, pp. 90-6.
12 Arthur Miller, 'Death of a Salesman', Harmondsworth, Penguin Books, 1980, p. 10. On the inheritance of owner-occupied dwellings see Malcolm Clarke, Homes as heirlooms, 'New Society', 9 June 1977, p. 507.
13 See for example C.B. Macpherson, The meaning of property, in C.B. Macpherson (ed.), 'Property, Mainstream and Critical Positions', Oxford, Blackwell, 1978, pp. 1-13.
14 See Justinian, How the married woman's rights prevailed, 'Financial Times', 23 June 1980.
15 See MHLG, 'Houses: The Next step', Cmd 8996, London, HMSO, 1953, pp. 3-4; DoE (1971), op. cit., p. 4; DoE 'Housing Policy: A Consultative Document', Cmnd 6851, London, HMSO, 1977, p. 50.
16 See 'HPTV',part I, pp. 97-8. The source is the DoE National Movers Survey.

6 THE CAPACITY TO PURCHASE AND THE BUILDING SOCIETIES

1   The failure of this mode of output realisation to ensure the health, productivity and quiescence of the working people is described elsewhere. See Stephen Merrett, 'State Housing in Britain', London, Routledge & Kegan Paul, 1979, ch. 1.
2   From the point of view of a flow analysis of the cost of alternative tenures the neatest way to deal with that portion of the purchase price met out of personal assets is as a loss of (post-tax) unearned income. This approach was employed in ch. 5.
3   Martin Boddy, 'The Building Societies', London, Macmillan, 1980, p. 52.
4   See 'HPTV', part II, p. 85.
5   Ibid., p. 84.
6   Boddy, op. cit., p. 27.
7   See 'BSA Bulletin', no. 27, July 1981, Table 1.
8   See Boddy, op. cit., pp. 31-2, for a fuller account of the process of concentration.
9   Ibid., pp. 33-4.
10 For a fuller account of reserves see 'HPTV', part II, pp. 98-102.
11 Many commentators adopt the curious and misleading convention of treating the interest that is credited to depositors' accounts as a source of funds for mortgage advances. This is mistaken because such interest simply is not an inflow at all and therefore cannot be a source of lending. Nevertheless it is true that of the interest due each half-year (usually) on deposits the more that is credited to accounts then the less must be paid out - thus permitting a correspondingly greater outflow of mortgage advances. If in Figure 6.1 I included this fictitious inflow of interest credited to accounts and altered 'regular payments of interest to depositors' to 'interest owed to depositors', then the final net effect would be the same. Interest owed minus interest credited to accounts is exactly what 'regular payments of interest to depositors' means. In practice about two-thirds of interest is in fact credited to accounts. This is almost always the case with small sums; larger depositors are offered a choice.
12 See 'HPTV', part II, p. 119. The argument on principal repayments that follows is drawn entirely from paras 74-87 of this document.
13 Ibid., p. 125.
14 For a fuller account of deposits and subscription shares see Boddy, op. cit., pp. 42-5.
15 I have assumed people whose income is so low that they are zero-rated

are poorer than those who pay the basic rate. This is not always true. Note, too, that taxpayers on higher rates than the basic one are in a quite different position. For them the deposit rate of interest net of tax is recalculated gross of tax at the basic tax rate and the interest thus earned is taxed at the depositor's own (higher) tax rate. It can be shown that the net rate of interest received by this group equals $j(1-h)/(1-b)$ where j is the composited share rate, h is the tax rate of this group, and b is the basic rate of tax.

16 Note that the argument assumes that the discrimination against zero-rated taxpayers does not create a disinclination among them to hold deposits with the societies, which precisely offsets the higher inflow from basic-rate taxpayers. Assuming no such counter-tendency, then if the deposit rate *net* of tax is the same for placements in the societies and in 'the money market', then the before-tax rates are related as follows: $i= i*(1-b)/(1-c)$ where i is the societies' rate, $i*$ is the money market rate, and b and c are respectively the basic and composite rate of tax. In an example where $i*$ is 12 per cent, b is 35 per cent, and c is 27.75 per cent (as in 1975), i would only have to equal 10.8 per cent. Note, too, that in their advertising material the societies often quote two deposit rates: the societies' share rate net of tax and the before-tax rate that their competitors would have to offer the basic-rate taxpayer to make the respective net rates equal.

17 'HPTV', part II, p. 129.
18 Boddy, op. cit., p. 49.
19 Ibid., Figure 4.6.
20 See, for example, 'HPTV', part II, ch. 7; Boddy, op. cit., ch. 6, and G. Hadjimatheou, 'Housing and Mortgage Markets: The UK Experience', London, Saxon House, 1976.
21 See pp. 2-3 and 36-7.
22 See ch. 3, pp. 36-7.
23 See Boddy, op. cit., p. 53.
24 This fall in the impact ratio is, in principle, quite distinct from simple 'frontloading' which refers to the falling real value of a constant money stream of payments over time under inflationary conditions, irrespective of their relation to income. When incomes and prices both rise at a constant rate and the rate of interest is stable we get both 'frontloading' and 'income frontloading'. For a fuller account of the former see Stephen Merrett, op. cit., pp. 164-5.
25 This argument is well expressed in 'Profits against Houses: An Alternative Guide to Housing Finance', London, CDP Information and Intelligence Unit, 1976, p. 42. I return to the question in ch. 16.
26 Ibid., pp. 47-8.
27 No single text in the philosophy of science has influenced me more than the magnificent final essay of E.P. Thomspon's, 'The Poverty of Theory and Other Essays', London, Merlin Press, 1978, pp. 193-397.
28 See 'HPTV', part II, p. 98.
29 Ibid., pp. 45-6.
30 See 'HPTV', part I, p. 129 and part II, pp. 42-9. Note that by defining trading up as a move to a house of higher-ranked use-value I thereby include cases where the household moves to a better but cheaper house as a result of moving from a region with relatively high house prices to one with relatively low prices. With this exception, trading up is, I believe, always correlated with a move to a more expensive dwelling. However, the exception is important enough to invalidate the use of simple price comparisons in examining trading up if the regional variable has not been controlled for. Data for 1973 show that the selling price of the existing house of selling buyers averages just 93 per cent of their 'new' one, ibid., p. 74. Longitudinal research would be of great value in advancing our understanding of trading up.
31 Boddy, op. cit., pp. 60-1.
32 Ibid., p. 64.

33 There is an interesting discussion in the 'Housing Policy Technical Volume' that is related to this net cash question but neither poses it nor provides data permitting it to be answered. There the excess of house purchase loans (net of repayments of principal) over the value of new houses is attributed primarily to the purchase of second-hand houses from sellers who are not buying other houses and, also, to cash proceeds taken out by selling buyers. See 'HPTV', part II, pp. 112-16. Incidentally, the same source (p. 46) shows realisation and transfer purchases cross-classified by selling and first-time buyers. The data are rather uninteresting since there is very little difference between them in their proportionate purchases of new or second-hand houses.

34 Boddy, op. cit., pp. 65-6.

35 Using the notation of note 16, let us suppose the mortgage rate would equal i^* in the absence of compositing and tax relief. Compositing reduces this to $i^*(1-b/(1-c))$. Relief further reduces the rate to $i^*(1-b)(1-b)/(1-c)$. Let $b = .30$ and $c = .255$ then the effective rate paid is equal to $.66i^*$.

7 OWNER-OCCUPATION AT THE MARGIN

1 A brief account of the principles of local authority 'capital expenditure' is given in Stephen Merrett, 'State Housing in Britain', London, Routledge & Kegan Paul, 1979, ch. 6.

2 See Michael Harloe, Ruth Issacharoff and Richard Minns, 'The Organization of Housing: Public and Private Enterprise in London', London, Heinemann, 1974, pp. 47-50.

3 See pp. 30-2.

4 See 'HPTV', part II, Table A-3, and DoE, 'Housing and Construction Statistics 1969-1979', London, HMSO, 1980, Table 139.

5 See Valerie Karn, 'Priorities for Local Authority Mortgage Lending: A Case Study of Birmingham', CURS Research Memorandum 52, Birmingham, 1976, pp. 5-13, and 'HPTV', part II, pp. 108-9.

6 See Steve Clark, The last resort? How councils make home loans, 'Roof', October 1976, pp. 138-40, and Harloe *et al.*, op. cit., p. 46.

7 DoE, 'Local Authority Advances for House Purchase', Circular 22/71, 7 April 1971.

8 'HPTV', part II, p. 154.

9 Karn, op. cit., p. 34.

10 Martin Boddy, 'The Building Societies', London, Macmillan, 1980, p. 75.

11 Neil McIntosh, Mortgage support scheme holds the lending lines, 'Roof', March 1978, pp. 44-7.

12 Boddy, op. cit., p. 76.

13 Mark Boleat, Support lending on target, 'Roof', January 1979, p. 6.

14 'HCS', London, HMSO, no. 31, Table 40, and part 1, June quarter 1981, Table 1.9.

15 Boddy, op. cit., pp. 77-8. The insurance companies and building societies also make mortgage finance available to their staff on favourable terms.

16 Karn, op. cit., p. 18.

17 Harloe, Issacharoff and Minns, op. cit., pp. 55-8. Other relevant material is included in Geoff Green, Property exchange in Saltley, in M. Edwards *et al.* (eds), 'Housing and Class in Britain', London, Political Economy of Housing Workshop, pp. 50-63; Valerie Karn, 'Local Authority Mortgages in Saltley', Birmingham, Birmingham CDP, 1975; and Benwell Community Development Project, 'Private Housing and the Working Class', Final Report Series no. 3, Newcastle-upon-Tyne, Benwell Community Project, 1978.

18 'HPTV', part II, pp. 78-9.

19 Karn (1976), op. cit., pp. 19-20.

20 The argument in this paragraph follows on naturally from the material contained in this chapter and the preceding one. See also Valerie Karn, 'The Impact of Housing Finance on Low Income Owner Occupiers', CURS Working Paper 55, Birmingham, 1977.

21   The material in the next two paragraphs is drawn from DoE, 'Housing Policy: A Consultative Document', Cmnd 6851, London, HMSO, 1977, pp. 52-7, and 'HPTV', part II, pp. 143-9.
22   See David Hughes, Half and half mortgages: what they're about, 'Roof', November 1976, pp. 164-7.
23   See DoE (1977), op. cit., pp. 58, 103-5.
24   See Hughes, op. cit., and Stuart Weir and Bernard Kilroy, Equity sharing in Cheshunt, 'Roof', November 1976, pp. 168-70.
25   'HCS', no. 32, 4th quarter 1979, Table 42 and March quarter 1981, part 2, Table 2.15.
26   See DoE (1977), op. cit., p. 60.
27   'HCS', no. 32, 4th quarter 1979, Supplementary Table XXIX.
28   See, for example, Jo Tunnard, Marriage breakdown and the loss of the owner occupied home, 'Roof', March 1976, pp. 40-3; Nick Finnis, Mortgage arrears: tomorrow's problem, 'Roof', January 1978, pp. 10-11; Valerie Karn, Pity the poor home owners, 'Roof', January 1979, pp. 10-14. A study of the Scottish situation, which unfortunately does not include any analysis of the reasons for default, is contained in LAMSAC, 'Mortgage Arrears in Scotland', London, LAMSAC, 1979.
29   Karn (1979), op. cit., p. 11.
30   Finnis, op. cit., p. 10.

8   THE SALE OF COUNCIL HOUSES

1   Stephen Merrett, 'State Housing in Britain', London, Routledge & Kegan Paul, 1979, pp. 307-9.
2   Alan Murie, 'The Sale of Council Houses: A Study in Social Policy', Birmingham, CURS, 1975, pp. 13, 41. This monograph gives a very much more detailed account of the developments in state policy over the period 1952-75 than space permits here and thus I have drawn on it extensively.
3   House of Commons, 'Parliamentary Debates', 5th series, vol. 494, session 1951-2, c. 2251.
4   Murie, op. cit., p. 62.
5   See Alan Budd, 'The Politics of Economic Planning', London, Fontana, 1978, chs 1-3.
6   Alan Murie, Council house sales mean poor law housing, 'Roof', March 1977, p. 49. There have been a number of other publications critical of the social effects of sales policy. See Ray Forrest and Alan Murie, 'Social Segregation, Housing Need and the Sale of Council Houses', Birmingham, CURS, 1976; E.A. McHugh, The sale of rented housing in East Kilbride new town, in John English and Colin Jones (eds), 'The Sale of Council Houses', Glasgow, University of Glasgow Department of Social and Economic Research, 1977, pp. 76-81; J.T. Burns, House sales to council tenants: the situation in Edinburgh, in English and Jones, op. cit., pp. 82-9; Ray Forrest and Alan Murie, Paying the price of council house sales, 'Roof', November 1978, pp. 170-3; Steve Schifferes, 'Facts on Council House Sales', London, Shelter, 1979; Labour Party Research Department, 'The Sale of Council Houses', London, The Labour Party, 1979. In 1980 the proceedings of a symposium on council house sales appeared. See 'Policy and Politics', vol. 8, no. 3, August 1980, pp. 287-340.
7   House of Commons, 'Parliamentary Debates', vol. 967, session 1979-80, c. 1223.
8   This point is made by Fred Gray in Merrett, op. cit., p. 230. Chapter 11, section seven of the same book outlines some feasible lines of advance in improving the quality of management practices.
9   See the arguments reported by Murie (1975), op. cit., p. 29 and also John English, Council house sales in local areas, in English and Jones, op. cit., pp. 62-3.
10   Forrest and Murie (1976), op. cit.
11   The point is made by English and Jones in Reflections and conclusions,

in English and Jones, op. cit., pp. 93-4. A similar astigmatism was referred to in the discussion of subsidies on p. 34.

12　Alan Murie, Financial aspects of the sale of council houses, in English and Jones, op. cit., p. 59.

13　Nottingham Housing Action Group, 'Where have all the assets gone? A study of the financial effects of council house sales in Nottingham', Nottingham, Nottingham Alternative Publications, 1979. Also see Murie in English and Jones, op. cit.; and Bernard Kilroy, No jackpot from council house sales, 'Roof', May 1977, pp. 74-80.

14　See Steve Schifferes, Counter sales, 'Roof', November 1979, pp. 184-6.

15　Policy shifts in 1970-4 are dealt with in much greater detail in Murie (1975), op. cit., pp. 47-53.

16　See Merrett, op. cit., pp. 187-91.

17　Murie (1975), op. cit., p. 37. By 1976 the government view was that sales could be resumed where the average waiting period for those eligible for a new-town rented house was less than three months.

18　Forrest and Murie (1978), op. cit.

19　Nottingham Housing Action Group, op. cit., p. 49.

20　Labour Party Research Department, op. cit., p. 3.

21　Michael Jones, The Tories: Bringing the house down, 'Marxism Today', May 1980, p. 11. The election manifestos of March and October 1974 also promised the right to buy.

22　Murie (1975), op. cit.

23　The only published figure I have seen is in McHugh's article on sales in East Kilbride new town where by August 1976 of 2,214 properties sold, 68 per cent were to sitting purchasers. See McHugh, op. cit., p. 81.

24　Henry Aughton, Play safe on sales advice, 'Roof', July 1979, p. 109.

25　Murie (1975), op. cit., p. 103.

26　Ibid., p. 82.

27　See Pat Niner, 'Local Authority Housing Policy and Practice - a Case Study Approach', Birmingham, CURS, 1975; Forrest and Murie (1976), op. cit., p. 8; McHugh, op. cit., p. 79; Burns, op. cit., pp. 84, 89; Labour Party Research Department, op. cit., p. 13; Nottingham Housing Action Group, op. cit., pp. 48-9.

28　Steve Billcliffe, Leading evidence, 'Roof', November 1979, pp. 187-8. This survey thereby refutes the contention by John Stanley, Minister of Housing in the Thatcher government, that in Leeds it was not only the best houses that were sold.

29　Murie (1975), op. cit.

30　Ibid., pp. 119-24.

31　Ibid., p. 32.

32　Ibid., p. 124.

9　THE SALE OF PRIVATELY RENTED ACCOMMODATION

1　'HPTV', part III, p. 61.

2　Ibid., Table IX.1.

3　'HPTV', part I, p. 37, and A.E. Holmans, Housing tenure in England and Wales: the present situation and recent trends, 'Social Trends', no. 9, 1979, p. 11.

4　The classic text on these years is Marian Bowley's 'Housing and the State 1919-44', London, Allen & Unwin, 1945. See also 'HPTV', part III, ch. 9. An important recent article on the 1915 Act is Dave Byrne and Sean Damer, The state, the balance of class forces, early working class housing legislation, in M. Edwards *et al.* (eds), 'Housing, Construction and the State', London, Political Economy of Housing Workshop, 1980, pp. 63-70.

5　For a fuller account see 'HPTV', part III, pp. 66-8.

6　See Table 1.3.

7　See the discussion in ch. 5, pp. 67-8.

8　'HPTV', part III, pp. 75-6.

9   Ibid., p. 75.
10 Deduced from 'HPTV', part III, p. 75, para. 42.
11 Bobbie Paley, 'Attitudes to Letting in 1976', London, HMSO, 1978, Table 2.9.
12 Ibid., Table 2.15. In a subsequent chapter including material on the sale for owner-occupation of dwellings that had been wholly let in 1971, it appeared that these were predominantly pre-1919 in age; most were whole houses but a substantial minority were converted flats. Ibid., p. 44.
13 Ibid., Table 3.18 and pp. 2 and 10.
14 Ibid., Tables 3.16 and 3.18.
15 Ibid., Tables 3.19 and 4.5.
16 Ibid., p. 41.
17 On re-letting see John Short, Landlords and the private rented sector: a case-study, in Martin Boddy (ed.), 'Land, Property and Finance', Bristol, SAUS, 1979, pp. 72-4; 'HPTV', part I, pp. 133-4; 'HPTV', part III, pp. 79-80; Paley, op. cit., pp. 35-6.
18 Chris Hamnett, The flat break-up market in London: a case-study of large-scale disinvestment - its causes and consequences, in Boddy, op. cit., pp. 35-55.
19 See Hamnett, op. cit., pp. 41-5.
20 Ibid., p. 47. In some cases the blocks have been sold to tenants associations.
21 See Stephen Merrett, Gentrification, in M. Edwards et al., 'Housing and Class in Britain', London, Political Economy of Housing Workshop, 1976, pp. 44-9. A much more substantial account of gentrification in London that - unfortunately, from the point of view of these chapters - covers the 1960s rather than the 1970s, can be found in Chris Hamnett and Peter Williams, 'Gentrification in London in 1961-71: An Empirical and Theoretical Analysis of Social Change', Birmingham, CURS, 1979. Note that gentrification includes examples where low-income tenants are displaced in favour of high-income tenants as well as owner-occupiers.
22 See Merrett, op. cit., p. 47. Also see Short, op. cit., pp. 67-8. Note that the conversion of an existing structure may increase, leave constant or reduce the total number of dwellings contained within that structure.
23 See 'HPTV', part III, p. 83.
24 Unfortunately in the article referred to above I did not recognise that even in the unmediated case the original landlord might himself engage in rehabilitation and conversion before selling. Note too that developers may rehabilitate and sell a whole house without converting it.

10   THE STOCK SUPPLY FROM OWNER-OCCUPIER HOUSEHOLDS

1   'HPTV', part I, p. 20. How often in dealing with such questions does one turn to this admirable volume and how often one wishes that there existed a definitive text on the demography of housing in Britain!
2   See p. 50. The reader may also remember that the effect of second marriages on the demand for and supply of owner-occupied accommodation has already been discussed on p. 52.
3   See Jo Tunnard, Marriage breakdown and the loss of the owner-occupied home, 'Roof', March 1976, p. 40; and A.E. Holmans, Housing tenure in England and Wales: the present situation and recent trends, in 'Social Trends', no. 9, p. 13.
4   See 'HPTV', part I, p. 129.
5   In England and Wales in 1971 there were 8.23 million owner-occupier households and 385,000 moves by selling buyers. See 'HPTV', part I, Table II.40. The year 1971 was not untypical so this suggests that twenty-one years are necessary for all these households to have moved on average once. Since the average length of time that selling buyers exist as owner-occupiers is of the order of forty-five years, the average number

of moves as selling buyers is probably something over two.
6 See for example I.C.R. Byatt, A.E. Holmans and D.E.W. Laidler, Income
   and the demand for housing: some evidence for Great Britain, in M. Parkin
   and A.R. Nobay (eds), 'Essays in Modern Economics', London, Longman,
   1973, pp. 65-84; and R.K. Wilkinson, The income elasticity of demand for
   housing, 'Oxford Economic Papers', November 1973, pp. 361-77.
7 See Byatt et al., op. cit., p. 84, and DoE, 'HPTV', part II, p. 47.
8 See D. Stanton, Income and the demand for housing: further evidence
   for the UK, 'DoE Economic and Statistical Notes', no. 16, 1973; and
   Michael Ball and R. Kirwan, 'The Economics of an Urban Housing Market:
   Bristol Area Study', London, CES, 1975, chs 5 and 6.
9 See Christian Topalov, 'Capital et Propriete Fonciere', Paris, Centre de
   Sociologie Urbaine, 1973. Jim Kemeny is in the same camp. See his 'The
   Myth of Home Ownership: Private versus Public Choices in Housing
   Tenure', London, Routledge & Kegan Paul, 1981, pp. 36-7.
10 Michael Ball is a 'real gains' proponent. See his article on Owner occupation, in M. Edwards et al. (eds), 'Housing and Class in Britain', London,
   Political Economy of Housing Workshop, 1976, p. 25. Published data on
   encashment can be found in DoE, 'HPTV', part II, pp. 112-16. Note that
   the treatment of price gains when one compares an owner-occupier with
   a tenant has already been completed in ch. 5.

11 THE SPECULATIVE HOUSEBUILDING INDUSTRY

1 Central Statistical Office, 'National Income and Expenditure: 1981 Edition',
   London, HMSO, 1981, Table 1.9.
2 Andrew Cullen, An analytical account of takeovers, acquisitions and joint
   ventures by building capital during the 1970s, in BSAP, 'The Production
   of the Built Environment', Proceedings of the Bartlett Summer School
   1979, London, BSAP, 1980, p. 123.
3 DoE Housing Development Directorate, 'Starter Homes', Occasional Paper
   2/80, London, HMSO, 1980.
4 See Michael Harloe, Ruth Issacharoff and Richard Minns, 'The Organization of Housing: Public and Private Enterprise in London', London,
   Heinemann, 1974, p. 137. On house-types one medium-sized builder informed me that with flats and some of the new 'urban designs', a financial
   disadvantage in a discounted cash-flow situation is that you cannot sell
   any of the dwellings in such a development until all of them are ready.
5 See Economist Intelligence Unit, 'Housing Land Availability in the South
   East', London, HMSO, 1975, pp. 42-3; and National CDP, 'Profits against
   Houses: An Alternative Guide to Housing Finance', London, CDP Information and Intelligence Unit, 1976, pp. 21-2.
6 Cullen, op. cit., p. 122.
7 See Harloe et al., op. cit., p. 141.
8 See Doreen Massey and Alejandrina Catalano, 'Capital and Land: Landownership by Capital in Great Britain', London, Edward Arnold, 1978,
   pp. 109-13. A similar transfer can occur when a housebuilder forms a
   joint company with a financial institution.
9 See Economist Intelligence Unit, op. cit., p. 40; Cullen, op. cit., p. 124;
   Inter Company Comparisons Ltd, 'Business Ratio Report: Housebuilders',
   London, ICC Business Ratios, 1980.
10 See Harloe et al., op. cit., pp. 144-5; Harry Gracey, The planners:
   control of new residential development, in Peter Hall, Harry Gracey, Roy
   Drewett and Ray Thomas, 'The Containment of Urban England', vol. 2,
   London, Allen & Unwin, 1973, pp. 128-9; and Roy Drewett, The developers: decision processes, in Hall et al., op. cit., pp. 168-9.
11 See Cullen, op. cit., pp. 123-4.
12 Economist Intelligence Unit, op. cit., pp. 45-6.
13 Ibid., pp. 41-4; Harloe et al., op. cit., pp. 143-7.
14 This residualist approach is widely ascribed to in the academic literature

as well as amongst the developers I have talked to. See Drewett, op. cit., pp. 170-3; Harloe et al., op. cit., p. 143; Economist Intelligence Unit, op. cit., pp. 47-8; National CDP, op. cit., p. 13; Peter Ambrose, 'The Land Market and the Housing System', Working Paper 3, Urban and Regional Studies, University of Sussex, 1976, p. 19; Stephen Merrett, 'A Theory of the Capitalist Land Market', Town Planning Discussion Paper no. 33, BSAP, 1979; and Keith Bassett and John Short, 'Housing and Residential Structure: Alternative Approaches', London, Routledge & Kegan Paul, 1980, p. 64.

15 See Andrew Evans, Private sector housing land prices in England and Wales, 'Economic Trends', no. 244, February 1974, p. xii.

16 Ambrose, op. cit., p. 20 gives a neat example of such a downward shift with location and legal circumstances constant.

17 See Economist Intelligence Unit, op. cit., pp. 6-7; Ambrose, op. cit., p. 10; National CDP, op. cit., p. 23; Massey and Catalano, op. cit., pp. 110-11; and Stephen Merrett, 'State Housing in Britain', London, Routledge & Kegan Paul, 1979, p. 70.

18 See Evans, op. cit., p. xvi.

19 See Michael Edwards, Notes for analysis of land use planning, in BSAP, op. cit., p. 21.

20 An example of a generalised broadside can be found in an article by Roger Humber, Director of the House Builders Federation. See Can the private sector fill the gap?, 'Roof', September-October 1980, p. 156.

21 DoE, 'Oxfordshire Structure Plan: Examination in Public', May-June 1977, especially pp. 4, 25.

22 See Economist Intelligence Unit, op. cit., p. 35.

23 Ibid., p. 4. Also see pp. 46-7.

24 Ibid., p. 26.

25 Ibid., p. 2.

26 See p. 40.

27 See Martin Boddy, Community land scheme dying of neglect, 'Roof', May 1978, pp. 78-80. Also see Land Campaign Working Party, 'Lie of the Land: Community Land Act, or Nationalisation Betrayed', London, LCWP, 1976.

28 See Peter Dickens, The hut and the machine: towards a social theory of architecture, 'Architectural Design', vol. 51, no. 1/2, 1981, pp. 18-24; and Social science and design theory, in 'Environment and Planning B', vol. 7, 1980, pp. 353-60.

29 Gracey, op. cit.

30 Dickens (1981), op. cit., p. 23. Gracey's work illustrates the opposition of planners to land release for very small developments, infill sites excepted, because they prejudice the installation of an efficient physical infrastructure in terms of drainage, sewerage, highway access, etc. See Gracey, op. cit., pp. 135-7.

31 Essex County Council, 'A Design Guide for Residential Areas', Chelmsford, Essex County Council, 1973.

32 See Graham Ive, Fixed capital in the British building industry, in BSAP, op. cit., p. 112. Ive tells me that there is a third mode of organising the building process in which the developer directly hires a number of firms and gangs on a trades contract basis, the form in which building in Scotland has traditionally been carried out.

33 See Terry Austrin, Unions and wage contracts: the case of the Lump in the construction industry; and John Sugden, The nature of construction capacity and entrepreneurial response to effective demand in the UK, both in BSAP, op. cit.

34 Richard Hill, The industrialisation of housebuilding in Britain, in BSAP, op. cit., p. 128.

35 Ibid., p. 128.

36 Ive, op. cit., pp. 107, 109.

37 Hill, op. cit., p. 128. Compare this well-researched view with Whitehead's unquestioning acceptance of myth. 'Housebuilding . . . is done mainly by

craftsmen with traditional materials and few tools.' See Christine Whitehead, 'The UK Housing Market: an Econometric Model', Farnborough,
Saxon House, 1974, p. 123.

38   See Ive, op. cit., p. 112 and Hill, op. cit., p. 129.
39   See, for example, R.K. Wilkinson and Catherine Archer, Measuring the
     determinants of relative house prices, 'Environment and Planning', vol. 5,
     1973, pp. 357-67; R.K. Wilkinson, House prices and the measurement of
     externalities, 'Economic Journal', vol. 83, March 1973, pp. 72-86; Michael
     Ball, Recent empirical work on the determinants of relative house prices,
     'Urban Studies', vol. 10, 1973, pp. 213-33; John Cubbin, Price, quality
     and selling time in the housing market, 'Applied Economics', vol. 6, 1974,
     pp. 171-87; and Harry Richardson, Joan Vipond and Robert Furbey,
     Determinants of urban house prices, 'Urban Studies', vol. 11, 1974,
     pp. 189-99.
40   See, for example, Ambrose, op. cit., pp. 17-18 and National CDP, op.
     cit., p. 13.
41   The index is described in 'Building', 3 January 1975, p. 41. The data for
     1973-80 are given in the issues of 6 January 1978, p. 57, and 5 September
     1980, p. 23. In Graph 11.1 I have used the data for June 1974 as the 1974
     entry and similarly for other years. I have also converted the base of
     100 from 'Building''s December 1973 date to June 1975 for consistency with
     the other data.

12   OWNER-OCCUPIER REHABILITATION

1   See Bev Nutt, Bruce Walker, Susan Holliday and Dan Sears, 'Obsolescence
    in Housing: Theory and Applications', Farnborough, Saxon House, 1976,
    p. 11.
2   'HPTV', part III, p. 89.
3   See for example T.L.C. Duncan, 'Housing Improvement Policies in England
    and Wales', Birmingham, CURS, 1974, p. 113; Tim Mason, 'Inner City
    Housing and Urban Renewal Policy: A Housing Profile of Cheetham Hill,
    Manchester and Salford', London, CES, 1977, p. 59; Chris Paris and Bob
    Blackaby, 'Not Much Improvement: Urban Renewal Policy in Birmingham',
    London, Heinemann, 1979, p. 30; and Elizabeth Monck with Gillian Lomas,
    'Housing Action Areas: Success and Failure', London, CES, 1980, p. 48.
4   Richard Kirwan and D.B. Martin, 'The Economics of Urban Residential
    Renewal and Improvement', London, CES, 1972, p. 14.
5   Peter Cowan, Depreciation, obsolescence and ageing, 'Architects Journal',
    16 June 1965, pp. 1395-1401.
6   Roland Watkins and John Shutt, 'From Failure to Facelift', Saltley,
    Birmingham CDP, 1980, p. 24.
7   On these price-outlay relationships see A.J. Harrison, The valuation gap:
    a danger signal?, 'CES Review', December 1977, pp. 101-3; Paul Balchin,
    'Housing Improvement and Social Inequality: Case Study of an Inner City',
    Farnborough, Saxon House, 1979, p. 221; Paris and Blackaby, op. cit.,
    p. 28; Monck with Lomas, op. cit., pp. 49, 94; and Watkins and Shutt,
    op. cit., p. 17.
8   Kirwan and Martin, op. cit., pp. 30, 38-40, 126-7. The same argument
    can be applied to the decisions of first-time buyers considering whether
    to purchase and rehabilitate. In this case, however, the 'HPTV' has
    pointed to a different chain of events leading to the purchase of a new
    suburban house. It argues that older houses tend to sell for lower prices
    than 'comparable' new ones and says that some first-time buyers only
    purchase starter houses because they cannot get mortgages on older semi-
    detached and terraced houses. See 'HPTV', part II, p. 150. Here, then,
    we have three distinct ways in which speculative building can undermine
    the rehabilitation of the older housing stock.
9   The Family Expenditure Survey publishes data on estimated weekly average
    household expenditure on payments to contractors, repair, maintenance

and decoration, classified by tenure and income range. The problem here is that rehabilitation is a much more comprehensive term than repair and maintenance and is extremely uneven over time so that the concept of an average weekly sum tells us very little about the real life situation. The FES, of course, provides no information on the sources of rehabilitation expenditures. Data based on the FES appear in Table 12.1 for the years 1967-75.

10 See, for example, Duncan, op. cit., p. 138; Paris and Blackaby, op. cit., pp. 109, 115-16; Monck with Lomas, op. cit., ch. 6; and Watkins and Shutt, op. cit., p. 31.
11 See p. 113.
12 Kirwan and Martin, op. cit., p. 126.
13 See Kirwan and Martin, op. cit., p. 87; Duncan, op. cit., pp. 85, 101-2, 155, 171; Paris and Blackaby, op. cit., p. 116; Monck with Lomas, op. cit., p. 97; and Watkins and Shutt, op. cit., p. 23. The elderly, and low-income owner-occupiers more generally, may also be dissuaded from major improvements by the consequent increase in the rateable value of their house and therefore their rate payments. The evidence on this is not, however, very convincing. See Robert McKie and W.K. Kumar, House improvement and rateable values, 'Urban Studies', June 1971, pp. 147-50, and Jim Wintour and Ros Franey, Are improvement grants tied up in the town halls?, 'Roof', May 1978, pp. 82-3.
14 I hasten to add that not only have the relevant elasticities never been calculated, but no one has ever attempted to estimate the difference in total rehabilitation output which has, presumably, resulted from the introduction since 1949 of rehabilitation grants.
15 See 'HPTV', part III, Table X.29.
16 For example Wintour and Franey, op. cit.
17 On inflexibility in standards and the burden of costs see Duncan, op. cit., pp. 131, 142, 178; CDP Political Economy Collective, 'The Poverty of the Improvement Programme', Newcastle upon Tyne, CDPPEC, 1977, p. 11; Wintour and Franey, op. cit., pp. 81-2; Paris and Blackaby, op. cit., pp. 28-9; Monck with Lomas, op. cit., pp. 46-8, 52, 94-6; and Watkins and Shutt, op. cit., pp. 11, 29.
18 See Wintour and Franey, op. cit.; Paris and Blackaby, op. cit., pp. 119-20; Monck with Lomas, op. cit., pp. 53-4; and Watkins and Shutt, op. cit., p. 16.
19 Monck with Lomas, op. cit., p. 56.
20 The most important exception to the rule is the outstanding work of that unique woman, one time Professor of Political Economy in University College London, Marian Bowley. P.A. Stone is also acquitted of all such crimes. In recent years some important work has begun to develop amongst those such as Michael Ball, Richard Hill and Graham Ive, associated with the Political Economy of Housing Workshop or the Bartlett School of Architecture and Planning, at University College London.
21 Paris and Blackaby, op. cit., assign it 2 pages out of 198!
22 Some confirmation for these hypotheses is to be found in Kirwan and Martin, op. cit., pp. 97-106 and in Murie's description of rehabilitation by the sitting buyers of council houses, see Alan Murie, 'The Sale of Council Houses: A Study in Social Policy', Birmingham, CURS, 1975, pp. 119-21.
23 See articles by A. Taylor, A. Kransdorff and P. Taylor in the 'Financial Times' of 20 January, 15 May and 21 May 1979.
24 Paris and Blackaby, op. cit., p. 113. Also Duncan, op. cit., pp. 123, 142, 184-5.
25 See Paris and Blackaby, op. cit., pp. 113-15, 196-7; Watkins and Shutt, op. cit., pp. 19-20; and Duncan, op. cit., pp. 98, 158.
26 See Watkins and Shutt, op. cit., p. 30.
27 John Young, Newport wraps up improvements package, 'Roof', July 1979, pp. 116-17.
28 See, for example, Stephen Merrett, 'State Housing in Britain', London,

Routledge & Kegan Paul, 1979, ch. 5.

29 A point made forcibly by Duncan, op. cit., ch. 3. The quotation by
Lord Brooke comes from 'Parliamentary Debates', House of Lords Official
Report, 25 July 1969, c. 1192.

30 'HPTV', part I, p. 34. The statistic specifically refers to standard grants,
however.

31 The earlier figure is calculated on the basis of 'HPTV', part III, Table
X.31 and 'HCS', no. 32, Table 29. The later figure is based on 'HCS',
no. 31, Supplementary Table II. Grants paid are assumed equal to 80 per
cent of those approved. Trevor Roberts in his 'General Improvement
Areas', Farnborough, Saxon House, 1976, p. 152, noted for 1970-4 'the
almost complete irrelevance of GIAs within the national progress towards
improved housing'. He tactfully makes this point towards the end of his
book, the subject-matter of which is, precisely, GIA rehabilitation.

32 'HPTV', part III, p. 89.

33 The data are taken from 'HPTV', part III, Tables A.3 and B.1. The last
point is reinforced when we remember that houses formerly owner-occupied
and then left vacant but not sold are not classified as owner-occupied but
as vacant.

34 On central heating see 'HPTV', part I, pp. 59-60; on the relative importance of clearance and rehabilitation in amenity deficiency reduction see
'HPTV', part III, p. 111 which refers to all tenures.

35 'HPTV', part II, p. 114. At the end of 1977 a national survey of dwellings
and households was carried out in England and the results published in
1978. It contains information for owner-occupiers, subdivided between
those with and those without a mortgage, on a number of variables including the use of basic amenities, type of central heating and main form
of room heating. See DoE, 'National Dwelling and Housing Survey', London,
HMSO, 1978, Table 6.

   However, for comparisons over time, the data already set out in this
section for the years 1971 and 1976 are preferable.

13 THE EXCHANGE PROCESS

1 The terms 'merchant capitalist' and 'merchant professional' are taken
from S. Merrett, Gentrification, in M. Edwards et al. (eds), 'Housing
and Class in Britain', London, Political Economy of Housing Workshop,
1976, pp. 44-9.

2 Illustrations of this are provided by M. Harloe et al., 'The Organization
of Housing: Public and Private Enterprise in London', London, Heinemann,
1974, ch. 5.

3 RICS, 'Buying and Selling a House', London, RICS, 1975.

4 G. Lee, 'The Services of a Building Society', London, Hodder & Stoughton,
1964, pp. 94-5.

5 Community Development Project, 'Profits Against Houses', London, CDP
Information and Intelligence Unit, 1976, pp. 50-1.

6 Benwell CDP, 'Benwell's Hidden Property Companies', Newcastle upon
Tyne, Benwell CDP, 1977.

7 One of the most comprehensive discussions of the relationships between
building societies and exchange professionals is provided by National
Consumer Council (NCC), 'Building Societies and the Consumer', London,
NCC, 1981, ch. 5.

8 Birmingham Community Development Project, 'From Failure to Facelift',
Birmingham, Birmingham CDP, 1980, p. 48.

9 See for example, E. Milne, 'No Shining Armour', London, John Calder,
1976.

10 Royal Commission on Legal Services (Benson Report), 'Final Report',
vol. 2, Cmnd 7648, London, HMSO, 1979, p. 494.

11 Ibid., p. 118.

12 C. Wolmar, Getting in on the Housing Act, 'Roof', January-February

    1981, p. 3.
13 G. Green, Property exchange in Saltley, in Edwards et al. (eds), op. cit.,
    pp. 50-63.
14 A. Stewart, 'Housing Action in an Industrial Suburb', London, Academic
    Press, 1981.
15 'HPTV', part I, pp. 225-30.
16 Ibid., p. 196.
17 Price Commission, 'Charges, Costs and Margins of Estate Agents', Cmnd
    7647, London, HMSO, 1979, p. 34.
18 Monopolies Commission, 'Estate Agents', London, HMSO, 1969, p. 6.
19 Price Commission, op. cit., pp. 61-3.
20 Another way of presenting the inaccuracy of the 'Housing Policy Review'
    figure is as follows. Accepting the figure of £73 million and dividing by
    the very conservative total of 11,500 estate agents in Britain produces
    £6,350 as the average income of agents from domestic property sales in
    1975. This seems most unlikely given the Price Commission research indi-
    cation that two years later, in 1978, income from domestic property
    sales varies from an average of £23,100 for single office firms to £46,000
    per office for large firms.
21 Royal Commission on Legal Service (Benson Report), op. cit., p. 118.
22 Consumers' Association, Moving home, 'Which?', May 1979, pp. 305-13.
    For a discussion and examples of transaction costs in Scotland, with its
    somewhat different exchange process, see Royal Commission on Legal
    Services in Scotland (Hughes Report), 'Volume One, Report', Cmnd
    7846, London, HMSO, 1979.
23 At least 30 per cent of buyers make one or more offers that fall through.
    Price Commission, op. cit., p. 31.
24 See, for example, ch. 8 of S. Merrett, 'State Housing in Britain', London,
    Routledge & Kegan Paul, 1979.
25 Green, op. cit.
26 Quoted in Monopolies Commission, op. cit., p. 4.
27 See here the comments of the Monopolies Commission, suggesting that the
    practice of estate agency has undergone a particular historical develop-
    ment, with it being most developed in the south of England, less developed
    in the north of England and relatively undeveloped in Scotland. Ibid.,
    p. 66.
28 Price Commission, op. cit., p. 19.
29 Ibid., p. 16.
30 'The Residential Attractions of Crawley', c. 1920 (author and publisher
    not stated).
31 'The Ifield Estate, Ifield, Sussex', c. 1930 (author and publisher not
    stated).
32 Monopolies Commission, op. cit., p. 5.
33 Price Commission, op. cit., p. 1.
34 P. Williams, The role of financial institutions and estate agents in the
    private housing market: a general introduction, 'University of Birming-
    ham Centre for Urban and Regional Studies, Working Paper 39', p. 51.
35 The most recent national estimate is that from the Price Commission
    survey, of 73 per cent of vendors selling through estate agents (Price
    Commission, op. cit., p. 15). In 1979, the 'Which?' survey reported a
    figure of 71 per cent (Consumers' Association, op. cit.). The 'Housing
    Policy Review', using the DoE's 1972 and 1974 Movers Surveys, suggested
    a lower proportion of six out of ten vendors using estate agents (quoted
    in Price Commission, op. cit., p. 15). In 1969 the Monopolies Commission
    reported that at least 25 per cent of sellers did not use estate agents
    (Monopolies Commission, op. cit., p. 7).
36 Price Commission, op. cit., p. 17.
37 Ibid., part II, p. 17.
38 Ibid. See also K. Bassett and J. Short, 'Housing and Residential Struc-
    ture', London, Routledge & Kegan Paul, 1980, p. 86.
39 Price Commission, op. cit.

40 For discussion of gentrification see Merrett (1976), op. cit.; and Williams, op. cit.
41 Quoted in Merrett (1976), op. cit., p. 48.
42 Quoted in ibid., p. 44.
43 Williams, op. cit.
44 A similar point is made by Harloe et al., op. cit.
45 Green, op. cit.
46 Price Commission, op. cit., p. 30.
47 E. Burney, 'Housing on Trial', London, Oxford University Press and Institute of Race Relations, 1967, p. 41.
48 Ibid., p. 39.
49 Ibid., p. 38.
50 S. Hatch, 'Estate agents as urban gatekeepers', unpublished paper presented to the British Sociological Association, Urban Sociology Group, University of Stirling, October 1973. Quote on p. 13.
51 D.J. Smith, 'Racial Disadvantage in Britain', Harmondsworth, Penguin Books, 1977, p. 286.
52 Ibid.
53 Commission for Racial Equality, 'Cottrell and Rothon Estate Agents', London, CRE, 1980.
54 Williams, op. cit., p. 58.
55 Price Commission, op. cit., p. 45.
56 Ibid.
57 Ibid., p. 3.
58 Ibid., p. 43.
59 Ibid., p. 15.
60 Ibid., part II, p. 25.
61 Ibid., ch. 4. See also Monopolies Commission, op. cit.
62 Ibid., p. 62.
63 Fees range from an average of 1.5 per cent of the selling price of dwellings in Scotland to 2.4 per cent in Greater London. Price Commission, op. cit., p. 5.
64 Monopolies Commission, op. cit., p. 68.
65 Price Commission, op. cit., p. 35.
66 RICS, op. cit.
67 Price Commission, op. cit., p. 19.
68 Ibid., p. 35.
69 Ibid., pp. 38-9.
70 For a description of parliamentary attempts to regulate estate agency, see D. Card, 'Estate Agents Act 1979', London, Butterworth, 1979.
71 D. Hirsch, Law to limit agents, 'Roof', November-December 1981, p. 3.
72 Monopolies and Mergers Commission, 'Surveyors Services', London, HMSO, 1977, p. 7.
73 Ibid., p. 10.
74 Membership of the RICS increased from less than 200 in 1868 to 49,628 in 1975. Ibid., p. 93.
75 Ibid., p. 13.
76 The term 'chartered surveyor', however, may only be used by members of the RICS.
77 Price Commission, op. cit., p. 14.
78 Monopolies and Mergers Commission, op. cit., p. 14.
79 Ibid., p. 187.
80 Ibid., pp. 190-1.
81 C. Lambert, Building societies, surveyors and the older areas of Birmingham, 'University of Birmingham, Centre for Urban and Regional Studies, Working Paper 38', 1976.
82 Ibid., p. 64.
83 Ibid., p. 67.
84 Royal Commission on Legal Services in Scotland (Hughes Report), op. cit.
85 RICS, 'Purchaser Beware', London, RICS (undated).
86 Ibid.

87 Quoted in Monopolies and Mergers Commission, op. cit., p. 11.
88 Royal Commission on Legal Services in Scotland (Hughes Report), op. cit., p. 124, and Housing Research Unit, University of Surrey, 'Purchasers' Opinions of House Buying', Surrey, University of Surrey, 1978.
89 T. Didman, New-style house report for buyers, 'Financial Times', 16 May 1981.
90 NCC, op. cit., p. 15.
91 Ibid., pp. 24-7.
92 Full descriptions of the conveyancing process are provided by the Royal Commission on Legal Services (Benson Report), op. cit., Royal Commission on Legal Services in Scotland (Hughes Report), op. cit., and M. Joseph, 'The Conveyancing Fraud', London, Michael Joseph, 1976.
93 Scottish solicitors are in a relatively unique position, also being involved in the various activities and negotiations leading up to the purchase and sale of dwellings. For example, of Scottish vendors 56 per cent use solicitors at the time of advertising property, and 61 per cent in dealing with prospective buyers and offers. In contrast, estate agents are used in these two activities by only 21 and 17 per cent of Scottish sellers respectively. Royal Commission on Legal Services in Scotland (Hughes Report), op. cit., p. 128.
94 Ibid., p. 131.
95 Consumers' Association, op. cit.
96 Royal Commission on Legal Services (Benson Report), op. cit., p. 271.
97 Quoted in ibid., p. 244.
98 Quoted in Joseph, op. cit., pp. 60-1.
99 Ibid., p. 71.
100 The data in this and the following paragraph come from the Royal Commission on Legal Services (Benson Report), op. cit.
101 Joseph, op. cit.
102 Ibid., p. 90.
103 Ibid., p. 24.
104 Royal Commission on Legal Services in Scotland (Hughes Report), op. cit.
105 R. Parker, Fight goes on for cut-price conveyancing, 'The Times', 17 January 1976.
106 Royal Commission on Legal Services (Benson Report), op. cit., p. 245.
107 Quoted in ibid., p. 271.
108 A similar restriction applies in Scotland, Royal Commission on Legal Services in Scotland (Hughes Report), op. cit., p. 130.
109 Ibid., and Royal Commission on Legal Services (Benson Report), op. cit.
110 See Royal Commission on Legal Services in Scotland (Hughes Report), op. cit., pp. 146-8.

14 STOCK AND FLOW

1 Peter Dickens and Simon Duncan provided helpful comments on the first draft of this chapter.
2 Central Statistical Office, 'Social Trends', no. 11, London, HMSO, 1980, p. 145.
3 Ibid.
4 See the chapters by E. Craven on private developers in R.E. Pahl, 'Whose City?', 2nd edn, Harmondsworth, Penguin Books, 1975.
5 K. Young and J. Kramer, 'Strategy and Conflict in Metropolitan Housing', London, Heinemann, 1978.
6 See part 2 of P. Saunders, 'Urban Politics', Harmondsworth, Penguin Books, 1980.
7 For example, 80 per cent of dwellings with a rateable value of over £300; 89 per cent of detached and 63 per cent of semi-detached houses; and 70 per cent of six-room dwellings and 84 per cent of seven or more room dwellings were in the owner-occupied sector in the late 1970s. See DoE,

'National Dwelling and Housing Survey', London, HMSO, 1979.

8 For a review see A. Harrison and G. Lomas, Tenure preference: how to interpret the evidence, 'CES Review', vol. 8, 1979, pp 20-3. Quote on p. 23.

9 See, for example, the comparison with Sweden, provided by J. Kemeny, 'The Myth of Home Ownership', London, Routledge & Kegan Paul 1981, and S.S. Duncan, Housing provision in advanced capitalism: Sweden in the 1970s, 'University of Sussex, Working Paper in Urban and Regional Studies, no. 10, 1978.

10 See p. 9, P. Gilchrist, The growth of owner-occupation, in BSA, 'The Housing Market in the 1980s', London, BSA, 1980, pp. 9-18. A detailed discussion of tenure transfers is provided in chs.1-3 of this book.

11 'Hansard', 27 July 1979, c. 643.

12 DoE, op. cit.

13 Central Statistical Office, op. cit.

14 M. Pawley, 'Home Ownership', London, Architectural Press, 1978, p. 143.

15 Quote on p. 116, D. Harvey, The urban process under capitalism: a framework for analysis, in M. Dear and A.J. Scott (eds), 'Urbanization and Urban Planning in Capitalist Society', London, Methuen, 1981, pp. 91-121.

16 For example, Peter Saunders argues that Harvey's basic failure is not relating 'the questions of production and reproduction, capital accumulation and class struggle'. See p. 231 of P. Saunders, 'Social Theory and the Urban Question', London, Hutchinson, 1981.

17 D.J. Smith, 'Racial Disadvantage, in Britain', Harmondsworth, Penguin Books, 1977.

18 House of Commons, 'Home Affairs Committee, Race Relations and Immigration Sub-Committee, Minutes of Evidence Thursday 17th July 1980, (Commission for Racial Equality)', London, HMSO, 1980, p. 308.

19 Smith, op. cit.

20 J. Rex and S. Tomlinson, 'Colonial Immigrants in a British City', London, Routledge & Kegan Paul, 1979.

21 DoE, op. cit.

22 S. Merrett, 'State Housing in Britain', London, Routledge & Kegan Paul, ch. 8.

23 P. Townsend, 'Poverty in the United Kingdom', London, Allen Lane, 1979, p. 493.

24 Building Societies Association, 'Studies in Building Society Activity 1974-79', London, BSA, 1980, p. 93.

25 Townsend, op. cit, p. 398.

26 G. Lomas, Aspects of owner-occupation: a statistical note, 'CES Review', no. 4, 1973, pp. 62-7.

27 M. Boddy, 'The Building Societies', London, Methuen, 1980; and also see ch. 6 of this book.

28 C. Bell, 'Middle Class Families', London, Routledge & Kegan Paul, 1968.

29 J. Connell, 'The End of Tradition', London, Routledge & Kegan Paul, 1978.

30 C. Hamnett and P. Williams, 'Gentrification in London 1961-71', Research Memorandum 71, Centre for Urban and Regional Studies, University of Birmingham, 1979.

31 J. Pitt, 'Gentrification in Islington', London, Barnsbury Peoples Forum, 1977.

32 A. Murie, 'Household Movements and Housing Choice', Occasional Paper no. 28, Centre for Urban and Regional Studies, University of Birmingham, 1974, p. 106. This perspective is in direct contradiction to the extremely inadequate view of authors such as Pennance and Gray who assume, for example, that 'only households know their own needs, means and preferences, and so only they can choose the price, location, quantity and quality of housing that suits them best'. F.E. Pennance and H. Gray, 'Choice in Housing', London, Institute of Economic Affairs, 1968, p. 6.

33 See, for example, Murie, op. cit., and A. Murie et al., 'Housing Policy and the Housing Systems', London, Allen & Unwin, 1976, ch. 2; and HPTV, part I, pp. 90-101.

34 'HPTV', part II, p. 44.
35 See, for example, J.H. Johnson et al., 'Housing and the Migration of Labour in England and Wales', Farnborough, Saxon House, 1974, pp. 112-14.
36 D. Gleave and D. Palmer, Mobility of labour: are council tenants really handicapped?, 'CES Review', no. 3, 1978, pp. 74-7.
37 Ibid., p. 77.
38 Ibid., p. 78.
39 See, for example, the comments on the restrictions on owner-occupied mobility in 'HPTV', part I, p. 96.
40 See Murie, op. cit., p. 117.
41 Ibid.
42 Ibid.
43 Ibid., p. 110.
44 Ibid., p. 117.
45 Bell, op. cit., p. 129.
46 In 1971, 176,000 households new to the housing system in England and Wales moved into owner-occupied dwellings, compared with 625,000 continuing households moving into the tenure, either from owner-occupied dwellings or accommodation in other tenures. 'HPTV', part II, p. 93.
47 Ibid.
48 Murie, op. cit., pp. 108-9.
49 Ibid.
50 Murie et al., op. cit., p. 47.
51 For a full discussion see F. Gray and M. Boddy, The origins and use of theory in urban geography: household mobility and filtering theory, 'Geoforum', vol. 10, 1979, pp. 117-27.
52 Building Societies Association, 'Evidence Submitted by the BSA to the Housing Finance Review', London, BSA, 1976, quote on p. 11.
53 See Boddy and Gray, op. cit., p. 45.
54 Building Societies Association, op. cit., p. 12.
55 Since housing chains are no respecters of calendars, some households moving during 1971 will have utilised vacancies created in earlier years. Similarly, some vacancies created in 1971 will have provided mobility opportunities for some households after the end of the year. Nonetheless, Table 14.8 is useful in given quantitative approximations of vacancy creation, continuation and termination over a particular time-period.
56 F. Gray, Housing chains and residential mobility in an urban area, unpublished Ph.D. thesis, University of Cambridge, 1977.
57 C.J. Watson, 'Household Movement in West Central Scotland', University of Birmingham, Centre for Urban and Regional Studies, 1973.
58 A. Murie, P. Hillyard et al., New building and housing needs, 'Progress in Planning', vol. 6, no. 2, 1976.
59 Building Statistical Services, Chains of sales in private housing, unpublished report to the Housing Research Foundation and the DoE, 1972.
60 See ch. 6, especially Table 6.4.
61 See Gray, op. cit., ch. 7.
62 Quoted in 'HPTV', part I, p. 94.
63 Murie et al., op. cit., p. 91.
64 Ibid., and Gray, op. cit., ch. 7.

15 OWNER-OCCUPATION AND SOCIAL RELATIONS

1 Peter Dickens, Simon Duncan and Peter Saunders made a number of stimulating comments on the first draft of this chapter.
2 See, for example, Benwell Community Project, 'Private Housing and the Working Class', Newcastle upon Tyne, Benwell Community Project, 1978, ch. 2; and M.J. Boddy, 'The Building Societies', London, Macmillan, 1980, ch. 2.
3 Quoted in H. Bellman, 'The Silent Revolution', London, Methuen, 1928, p. 31.

4   MHLG, 'Houses - the Next Step', London, HMSO, 1953, para. 7.
5   DoE, 'Fair Deal for Housing', Cmnd 4728, London, HMSO, 1971.
6   DoE, 'Housing Policy: A Consultative Document', Cmnd 6851, London,
    HMSO, 1977, p. 50.
7   Ibid., p. 68.
8   'Hansard', 15 January 1980, 1445.
9   See S. Merrett, 'State Housing in Britain', London, Routledge & Kegan Paul,
    1979.
10 H. Bellman, 'The Building Society Movement', London, Methuen, 1927, p. 54.
11 G. Lee, 'The Services of a Building Society', London, Hodder & Stoughton,
    1964, p. 11.
12 Quoted in Boddy, op. cit., p. 24.
13 D. Gilchrist, The growth of owner-occupation, in BSA, 'The Housing
    Market in the 1980s', London, BSA, 1980, p. 16.
14 See J. Kemeny, 'The Myth of Home Ownership', London, Routledge & Kegan
    Paul, 1981, especially ch. 1.
15 Boddy, op. cit., p. 25.
16 For a review of this work see P. Saunders, 'Urban Politics', Harmondsworth,
    Penguin Books, 1980, pp. 76-83.
17 Although, as described in this chapter, I now criticise normative Marxist
    approaches on a number of grounds, in some of my earlier work I employed
    and accepted this view of owner-occupation and social relations.
18 M. Ball, Owner-occupation, in M. Edwards et al. (eds), 'Housing and
    Class in Britain', London, Political Economy of Housing Workshop, 1976,
    p. 29.
19 S. Clarke and N. Ginsburg, The political economy of housing, in Political
    Economy of Housing Workshop, 'Political Economy and the Housing Question',
    London, PEHW, 1975, p. 25.
20 Boddy, op. cit., p. 21.
21 Ibid., p. 24.
22 D. Harvey, Labor, capital, and class struggle around the built environment
    in advanced capitalist societies, in K.R. Cox (ed.), 'Urbanization and
    Conflict in Market Societies', London, Methuen, 1978, p. 15.
23 Ibid., pp. 15-16.
24 Ibid., p. 16.
25 Ball, op. cit., p. 28.
26 See ibid., p. 29, and K. Bassett and J. Short, 'Housing and Residential
    Structure', London, Routledge & Kegan Paul, 1980, p. 210.
27 See, for example, Edwards et al., op. cit., and Political Economy of
    Housing Workshop, op. cit.
28 See, for example, D. Rose, Toward a re-evaluation of the political signifi-
    cance of home-ownership in Britain, in Political Economy of Housing Work-
    shop, 'Housing, Construction and the State', London, PEHW, 1980; and
    D. Rose, Home-ownership and industrial change: the struggle for a
    'separate sphere', 'University of Sussex, Urban and Regional Studies,
    Working Paper, 25', 1981.
29 J. Rex and R. Moore, 'Race, Community and Conflict', London, Oxford
    University Press and Institute of Race Relations 1967.
30 J. Rex and S. Tomlinson, 'Colonial Immigrants in a British City', London,
    Routledge & Kegan Paul, p. 155.
31 P. Saunders, Housing tenure and class interests, 'University of Sussex,
    Urban and Regional Studies, Working Paper, 6', 1977; and Rex and
    Tomlinson, op. cit.
32 Saunders (1977), op. cit.; and, Saunders (1980), op. cit., ch. 2.
33 Saunders (1980), op. cit., p. 100.
34 Saunders (1977), op. cit., p. 15.
35 Ibid., p. 14.
36 During the mid-1970s the then chairman of the Child Poverty Action Group,
    Frank Field, suggested that as a means of redistributing wealth, council
    houses should be transferred to the ownership of their tenants.
37 See, for example, Saunders (1980), op. cit., pp. 98-102; and P. Dunleavy,

'Urban Political Analysis', London, Macmillan, 1980, ch. 3.
38   Rose (1980), op. cit., p. 71.
39   Rose (1981), op. cit., pp. 9-10.
40   N. Wiltshire, 'Rent, Rates and Housing (The Existing Problems and the Solution', London, Estates Gazette Ltd, 1944, quoted in Benwell Community Project, op. cit., p. 63.
41   Central Housing Advisory Committee, 'Private Enterprise Housing', London, HMSO, 1944, p. 25.
42   Benwell Community Project, op. cit., and A Murie and R. Forrest, 'Housing Market Processes and the Inner City' (Report commissioned by the SSRC Inner Cities Working Party), London, SSRC, 1980.
43   Boddy, 1980, op. cit., pp. 68-71 and 120-5, and S. Weir, Redline districts, 'Roof', July 1976.
44   See Rex and Tomlinson, op. cit., pp. 146-8, and S.S. Duncan, Self-help: the allocation of mortgages and the formation of housing sub-markets, 'Area', vol. 8, no. 4, 1976.
45   Benwell Community Project, op. cit., p. 14.
46   Ibid.
47   Ibid., pp. 106-8.
48   D.J. Smith, 'Racial Disadvantage in Britain', Harmondsworth, Penguin Books, 1977, p. 213.
49   Rex and Tomlinson, op. cit., p. 129.
50   Ibid., p. 148.
51   V. Karn, Pity the poor home owners, 'Roof', January 1979, pp. 10-14, Quote on p. 14.
52   C. Whitehead, Why owner-occupation, 'CES Review', vol. 6, 1979, pp. 35-41. Quote on p. 36.
53   Rose (1981), op. cit., p. 28.
54   R. Mellor, Planning for housing: market processes and constraints, 'Planning Outlook', vol. 13, autumn 1973, pp. 26-42. Quote on p. 32.
55   Ibid., pp. 29-30.
56   Whitehead, op. cit., pp. 35-6.
57   Ibid., p. 36. Thorns makes a similar point about New Zealand. He argues that 'when capital gains are examined for specific groups of owner-occupiers it is clear that the rates of gain are highly varied and not assured. . . . The ability to capitalize on the gains within the property market relates also to the individual's position with regard to the labour market and to inherited wealth and position.' D.C. Thorns, The implications of differential rates of capital gains from owner occupation for the formation and development of housing classes, 'International Journal of Urban and Regional Research', vol. 5, no. 2, 1981, pp. 205-17, Quote on p. 215.
58   C. Pugh, 'Housing in Capitalist Societies', Farnborough, Gower, 1980.
59   D. Byrne and S. Damer, The state, the balance of class forces, and early working-class legislation, in Political Economy of Housing Workshop, op. cit.
60   Saunders, 1980, op. cit., and, J. Kramer and K. Young, 'Strategy and Conflict in Metropolitan Housing', London, Heinemann, 1978.
61   Kemeny, op. cit., p. 76.
62   Benwell Community Project, op. cit., p. 110.
63   See Merrett, op. cit., ch. 8.
64   See, for example, 'Community Action' magazine 1979 and 1980.
65   Benwell Community Project, op. cit., p. 110.
66   A. McCulloch, Mortgage strikes and working class owner-occupiers, unpublished paper presented to the Political Economy of Housing Workshop, London, October 1980.
67   Rose (1981), op. cit., pp. 3-4.
68   Rose (1980), op. cit., p. 73.
69   H. Stretton, 'Capitalism, Socialism and the Environment', London, CUP, 1976.
70   Rose (1980), op. cit., pp. 74-5.
71   Rose (1981), op. cit., pp. 30-1.

72 Saunders (1978), op. cit., and Saunders (1980), op. cit.
73 See, for example, P. Townsend, 'Poverty in the United Kingdom', London, Allen Lane, 1979; M. Pawley, 'Home Ownership', London, The Architectural Press, 1978; and, S. Lansley, 'Housing and Public Policy', London, Croom Helm, 1979.
74 Royal Commission on the Distribution of Income and Wealth, 'Third Report of the Standing Conference', London, HMSO, 1977, ch. 7.
75 Whitehead, op. cit., pp. 37-8.
76 V. Karn, Public sector demolition can seriously damage your wealth, 'Roof', January-February 1981, pp. 13-23. Quote on p. 15.
77 J. Lambert, C. Paris, and B. Blackaby, 'Housing Policy and the State', London, Macmillan, 1978.
78 Ibid., p. 113.
70 Ibid., p. 115.
80 Ibid., p. 128.
81 M. Couper and T. Brindley, Housing classes and housing values, 'Sociological Review', vol. 23, 1975, pp. 563-76.
82 J.A. Agnew, Market relations and locational conflict in cross national perspective, in Cox, op. cit.
83 Ibid., p. 132.
84 Ibid., p. 133.
85 Saunders (1980), op. cit., pp. 97-8.
86 Benwell Community Project, op. cit., p. 110.
87 Dunleavy, op. cit., and, P. Dunleavy, The urban basis of political alignment: social class, domestic property ownership, and state intervention in consumption processes, 'British Journal of Political Science', vol. 9, 1979, 9 pp. 409-43.
88 Ibid., p. 443.
89 Ibid., p. 442.
90 Ibid., p. 443.
91 P. Saunders, 'Social Theory and the Urban Question', London, Hutchinson, 1981, pp. 274-6.
92 M. Harrop, The urban basis of political alighment: a comment, 'British Journal of Political Science', vol. 10, 1980, pp. 388-98. See also Dunleavy's reply: P. Dunleavy, The urban basis of political alighment: a rejoinder to Harrop, 'British Journal of Political Science', vol. 10, 1980, pp. 398-402.
93 Harrop, op. cit., p. 395.
94 Ibid., p. 396.
95 As Harrop notes (ibid., p. 397) 'the single most striking change over the last fifteen years in the relationship of class to party has in fact been the steady increase in Labour's support among the middle class.' Many of these voters will be home-owners with relatively good housing.
96 Dunleavy (1980), op. cit., p. 74.
97 Elsewhere Dunleavy suggests that ideological structures 'may often be rejected on the basis of collective experience' (Dunleavy, (1979), op. cit., p. 422) although he does not exemplify this brief statement.

16 PERTURBATION AND DECLINE

1 CSO, 'Economic Trends', Annual Supplement, London, HMSO, 1981, Table 114.
2 Ibid., Table 192.
3 Ibid., Table 99.
4 DoE, 'Fair Deal for Housing', Cmnd. 4728, London, HMSO. 1971. See the quotation on p. 268 of this volume.
5 See Stephen Merrett, 'State Housing in Britain', London, Routledge & Kegan Paul, 1979, pp. 188-9.
6 DoE, op. cit., p. 1.
7 See Merrett, op. cit., pp. 138-41.
8 See Andrew Glyn and John Harrison, 'The British Economic Disaster',

London, Pluto Press, 1980, ch. 3.

9   See Mary Smith, 'Guide to Housing', 2nd edn, London, Housing Centre Trust, 1977, pp. 117-18.

10 The indicator was calculated by taking, in each quarter, the average price paid by first-time borrowers from building societies, multiplying this by a constant cover ratio of 0.8, calculating the mortgage repayment over a twenty-five year term due on such an advance at the BSA recommended rate operating at the midpoint of the quarter, and then dividing this by the average income of the borrowers. The raw data were taken from two BSA sources, 'A Compendium of Building Society Statistics', 3rd edn, London, BSA, 1980, and 'Mortgage Repayment Tables', London, BSA, undated. I hope this indicator will become a permanent tool in the analysis of housing dynamics. Its specification could be improved, were the data available, by using repayments net of subsidy and income net of tax and by using the income of the set of potential rather than actual buyers since in the latter case a rise in repayments may squeeze out low-income buyers and thereby have a perverse effect on the indicator by raising the denominator. Note that I prefer to assume a constant cover ratio since variations in the cover from formal mortgage finance institutions may be offset by informal loans.

11 See BSA (1980), op. cit., Table E5. The increase in average UK house prices at the mortgage completion stage over their level in the previous quarter, in the sixteen quarters from 1971 to 1974 inclusive, were, in percentages: 2.2, 3.0, 7.0, 3.9, 5.5, 8.0, 15.3, 7.3, 9.1, 4.5, 7.2, 3.6, 1.5, -0.9, 2.7, 0.6. Allowing for the lag between exchange of contracts and mortgage completion, the turning point must have been about the midpoint of the year.

12 See Glyn and Harrison, op. cit., pp. 84-90.

13 See Martin Pawley, 'Home Ownership', London, The Architectural Press, 1978, p. 123.

14 See Christine Whitehead, House prices: what determines them and can they be controlled?, 'CES Review', no. 3, May 1978, p. 8 and also What should be done with the guideline?, 'CES Review', no. 7, September 1979, p. 37.

15 See Merrett, op. cit., pp. 265-8.

16 See Glyn and Harrison, op. cit., pp. 111-13.

17 The peak in building society advances to first-time buyers took place in 1972 one year before the peak in grants to owner-occupiers. Allowing for the lag between house purchase and grant approval, the turning points are wholly consistent.

18 DoE, 'Housing Policy: A Consultative Document', Cmnd 6851, London, HMSO, 1977. There is an accompanying 'Technical Volume' in three parts.

19 Ibid., pp. 4,32. This shift may have reflected the influence of Anthony Crosland, Secretary of State at the DoE from 1974 until his death in 1977. In an earlier Fabian pamphlet he had specifically argued that tax relief was an 'indiscriminate subsidy to the owner-occupier'. He also argued that the Labour Party strongly favoured home-ownership because it is 'good' for savings, 'good' for self-reliance, encourages DIY, makes an essential contribution to 'good' planning, helps produce a balanced community in areas of urban renewal, contributes to wider environmental objectives and is what many people want. See Anthony Crosland, 'Towards a Labour Housing Policy', Fabian Tract 410, Fabian Society, London, 1971, pp. 18-19. The indiscriminate character of tax relief was partly modified by the 1974 Finance Act which limited to £25,000 the size of the mortgage on which relief could be claimed and terminated relief on second homes. In spite of the state expenditure crisis of 1976, however, subsidies to owner-occupation remained unchanged. Their growth over time is summarised in appendix 4.

20 DoE (1977), op. cit., p. 44.

21 Ibid., pp. 46-7.

22 Merrett, op. cit., pp. 286-7.

23 DoE (1977), op. cit., pp. 106-7.

24 Ibid., pp. 52-3, 58-9.

25 Ibid., pp. 96-7.

26 Ibid., p. 68. Also see p. 45.
27 See BSA (1980), op. cit., Tables E3 and E4.
28 See Whitehead (1979), op. cit., pp. 37-50.
29 See Glyn and Harrison, op. cit., pp. 118-19.
30 Michael Jones, The Tories: bringing the house down, 'Marxism Today', May 1980, p. 10.
31 See Andrew Glyn and Bob Sutcliffe, 'British Capitalism, Workers and the Profits Squeeze', Harmondsworth, Penguin Books, 1972.
32 See Glyn and Harrison, op. cit., p. 74.
33 The 1981-2 target was later revised to £3.5 billion, of which £1.76 billion was raised in the first five months of that financial year. My reading of current financial events has been enormously assisted by that excellent newspaper, the 'Financial Times', particularly the columns of Michael Cassell, Tim Dickson, Peter Riddell and Andrew Taylor.
34 The competitiveness of bank loans in the middle of 1981 is well illustrated in Tim Dickson, Feeding hungry house-buyers, 'Financial Times', 6 June 1981.
35 See Andrew Taylor, Building societies warning on shortage of land, 'Financial Times', 10 April 1979.
36 See Michael Cassell, Building societies chief hits at watchdogs, 'Financial Times', 24 May 1979.
37 See Michael Cassell, The dangers of borrowing short and lending long, 'Financial Times', 2 March 1979.
38 BSA, 'Mortgage Finance in the 1980s', London, BSA, 1979. In fact the Alliance building society did launch a fixed-rate, marketable yearling bond, for institutional investors only, in September 1980. It came in tranches of £50,000 and the intention was to raise £60 million with it in 1980. This was said to be the first-ever building society placement in the wholesale money market. In August 1981 the Nationwide issued £5 million of negotiable bonds on the Stock Exchange, the first building society to obtain a Stock Exchange listing.
39 See Michael Cassell, The cartel begins to crumble, 'Financial Times', 11 April 1981.
40 See 'Financial Times', 13 June 1979, and 12 November 1979.
41 See 'Financial Times', 20 June 1981 and 29 June 1981.
42 See Peter Riddell, Questions for the Treasury, 'Financial Times', 1 April 1980; and 'Financial Times', 23 October 1980.
43 See Michael Cassell, The missing link in the government's new package on housing, 'Financial Times', 11 August 1979.
44 'Financial Times', 14 July 1979.
45 See June Field, Give-aways to boost sales, 'Financial Times', 24 October 1981. Development in mortgage market competition by the autumn had witnessed: a growth in 1981 in the banks' net advances to an estimated 18 per cent of recorded home loans; the abandonment of differentially high rates on large mortgages, first by the banks and thereafter by many building societies, including the Woolwich, the Halifax and Nationwide; the wider use by the banks of mortgage rates not directly linked to their own base rate; and continued pressure on the cartel, for example with the Cheltenham's reintroduction of its 'Gold Account'. By September 1981 the commercial banks were quite sure that the Bank of England's quantitative credit guidelines, which were supposed to discourage lending to persons and were still nominally in force, had in practice been suspended.

17 A STRATEGY FOR THE FUTURE

1 See Stephen Merrett, 'State Housing in Britain', London, Routledge & Kegan Paul, 1979, pp. 283-302. On the sale of council houses I would now argue that the essence of the case against sales is that it leads to tenure stratification and that it implies an end to the socialised allocation of the flow of vacancies generated within what was the local authority stock.

Since 1979 I have also become convinced of the value of a national rent pooling scheme. See Bernard Kilroy, 'Housing Finance - Organic Reform?' London, Labour Economic, Finance and Taxation Association, 1978, pp. 19-20, 31, 42-4.

2   The advantages of pooled historic rents with state housing under inflationary conditions is one of the main themes in Jim Kemeny's 'The Myth of Home Ownership: Private versus Public Choices in Housing Tenure', London, Routledge & Kegan Paul, 1981.

3   See Bernard Kilroy, Housing finance - why so privileged? 'Lloyds Bank Review', July 1979, pp. 37-52.

4   In 'State Housing in Britain', pp. 288-90, I suggested the only land not nationalised would be that of owner-occupiers and owner-occupier farmers. In the case of development of any such land, it would first be compulsorily purchased by the Central Land Board. Note that I do not argue for the release of sites to the speculative industry at existing-use prices since the effect would be merely to swell the producer's profit rather than reduce the price to the purchaser (see chapter 11).

5   I conceived this idea as a result of thinking about Frank Allaun's bulk-lending proposals (see p. 105).

6   SHAC, 'Good Housekeeping: An Examination of Housing Repair and Improvement Policy', London, SHAC, 1981. Also see John Perry and Mike Gibson, Pause for renewal, 'Roof', July-August 1981, pp. 23-4.

7   See David Webster, House prices and allocation: the case for action on the demand side of the market, 'Housing Review', January-February 1975, pp. 12-15.

8   Domestic rates are also paid, of course, by tenants or, alternatively, their landlords. Protagonists of a tax on 'imputed income' (the reintroduction of Schedule A in fact) include M.A. King and A.B. Atkinson, Housing policy, taxation and reform, 'Midland Bank Review', spring 1980, pp. 7-15; Hugh Kerr and John Phillips, 'Tory Rent Robbery and How to Fight it', London, Socialist Worker Pamphlet, 1972; and Martin Boddy, 'The Building Societies', London, Macmillan, 1980, pp. 133-4. See also Webster, op. cit., p. 14.

9   See T.J. Gough and T.W. Taylor, 'The Building Society Price Cartel', London, Institute of Economic Affairs, 1979.

10   See Christine Whitehead, House prices: what determines them and can they be controlled? 'CES Review', no. 3, May 1978, pp. 5-9; and also What should be done with the guideline?, 'CES Review', no. 7, September 1979, pp. 37-50.

11   In March 1981 the Labour MP Ken Weetch introduced a Private Member's Bill to achieve this.

12   Leonard Williams of the BSA is reported to have suggested a two-year period of this kind. See 'Financial Times', 21 December 1979.

13   See Boddy, op. cit., p. 117.

14   See Merrett, op. cit., pp. 300-2 as well as Fred Gray's contextual material in chapter 8 of that book.

15   See Michael Jones, The Tories: bringing the house down, 'Marxism Today', May 1980, p. 16.

16   See Michael Joseph, 'The Conveyancing Fraud', London, Michael Joseph, 1976. Many of the recommendations in the Hughes Report provide a basis for the reform of the legal aspects of the exchange process. See Royal Commission on Legal Services in Scotland, 'Report', vol. 1, Cmnd 7846, London, HMSO, 1979.

SELECT BIBLIOGRAPHY

BOOKS, RESEARCH PAPERS, PAMPHLETS AND ARTICLES

Ambrose, P.J., 'The Land Market and the Housing System', Urban and Regional Studies Working Paper no. 3, Brighton, University of Sussex, 1976.

Ashmore, G., 'The Owner-Occupied Housing Market', Research Memorandum no. 41, Birmingham, CURS, 1975.

Aughton, H., 'Housing Finance: A Basic Guide', London, Shelter, 1981.

Austerberry, H., and Watson, S., A woman's place: a feminist approach to housing in Britain, 'Feminist Review', no. 8, summer 1981, pp. 49-62.

Balchin, P., 'Housing Improvement and Social Inequality: Case Study of an Inner City', Farnborough, Saxon House, 1979.

Ball, M., Recent empirical work on the determinants of relative house prices, 'Urban Studies', vol. 10, no. 2, June 1973, pp. 213-33.

Ball, M., British housing policy and the house-building industry, 'Capital and Class', no. 4, spring 1978, pp. 78-99.

Ball, M., The development of capitalism in housing provision, 'International Journal of Urban and Regional Research', vol. 5, no. 2, June 1981, pp. 145-77.

Ball, M., and Kirwan, R., 'The Economics of an Urban Housing Market: Bristol Area Study', London, CES, 1975.

Barrett, S., Boddy, M., and Stewart, M., 'Implementation of the Community Land Scheme', Bristol, SAUS, 1978.

Barrett, S., Stewart, M., and Underwood, J., 'The Land Market and Development Process: A Review of Research and Policy', Bristol, SAUS, 1978.

Barrett, S., and Whitting, G., 'Local Authorities and the Supply of Development Land to the Private Sector', Bristol, SAUS, 1980.

Bassett, K., and Short, J., 'Housing and Residential Structure: Alternative Approaches', London, Routledge & Kegan Paul, 1980.

Bell, C., 'Middle Class Families', London, Routledge & Kegan Paul, 1968.

Bellman, H., 'The Building Society Movement', London, Methuen, 1927.

Bellman, H., 'The Silent Revolution', London, Methuen, 1928.

Bellman, H., 'Bricks and Mortals: A study of the Building Society Movement and the story of the Abbey National Society 1849-1949', London, Hutchinson, 1949.

Benwell, CDP, 'Private Housing and the Working Class', Final Report Series no. 3, Newcastle upon Tyne, Benwell Community Project, 1978.

Billcliffe, S., Leading evidence, 'Roof', November 1979, pp. 187-8.

Bloor, J. et al., 'Housing Improvement Handbook: A Self-Help Approach for Residents' Groups', Manchester, Manchester Polytechnic, 1978.

Boddy, M., Community land scheme is dying of neglect, 'Roof', May 1978, pp. 78-80.

Boddy, M. (ed.), 'Land, Property and Finance', Bristol, SAUS, 1979.

Boddy, M., 'The Building Societies', London, Macmillan, 1980.

Boddy, M., and Gray, F., Filtering theory, housing policy and the legitimation of inequality, 'Policy and Politics', vol. 7, no. 1, January 1979, pp. 39-54.

Boleat, M., 'Building Society Branching', London, BSA, 1981.

Bowley, M., 'Housing and the State: 1919-1944', London, Allen & Unwin, 1945.

Branson, N., and Heinemann M., 'Britain in the Nineteen Thirties', St Albans, Panther, 1973.

British Market Research Bureau, 'Building Societies and the Savings Market', London, BSA, 1979.

BSA, 'Mortgage Repayment Tables', London, BSA, undated.

BSA, 'Co-operation between Building Societies and Local Authorities', London, BSA, 1978.

BSA, 'Mortgage Finance in the 1980s', London, BSA, 1979.

BSA, 'A Compendium of Building Society Statistics', 3rd edn, London, BSA, 1980.

BSA 'Studies in Building Society Activity 1974-79', London, BSA, 1980.

BSA, 'The Housing Market in the 1980s', London, BSA, 1980.

BSA, 'The Determination and Control of House Prices', London, BSA, 1981.

BSAP, 'The Production of the Built Environment: The Proceedings of the Bartlett Summer School 1979', London, BSAP, 1980.

BSAP, 'The Production of the Built Environment: The Proceedings of the Barlett Summer School, 1980', London, BSAP, 1981.

Burnett, J., 'A Social History of Housing 1815-1970', London, Methuen, 1980.

Burney, E., 'Housing on Trial', London, Oxford University Press and Institute of Race Relations, 1967.

Byatt, I.C.R., Holmans, A.E., and Laidler, D.E.W., Income and the demand for housing: some evidence for Great Britain, in Parkin, M., and Nobay, A.R. (eds), 'Essays in Modern Economics', London, Longman, 1973, pp. 65-84.

Card, D., 'Estate Agents Act 1979', London, Butterworth, 1979.

CDP Political Economy Collective, 'The Poverty of the Improvement Programme', Newcastle upon Tyne, CDPPEC, 1977.

Clark, S., The last resort? How councils make home loans, 'Roof', October 1976, pp. 138-40.

Clarke, M., Homes as heirlooms, 'New Society', 9 June 1977, p. 507.

Cleary, E.J., 'The Building Society Movement', London, Elek Books, 1965.

Collison, P., 'The Cutteslowe Walls: A Study in Social Class', London, Faber, 1963.

Consumers' Association, Moving home, 'Which?', May 1979, pp. 305-13.

Coppock, J.T., 'Second Homes: Curse or Blessing?', Oxford, Pergamon Press, 1977.

Couper, M., and Brindley, T., Housing classes and housing values, 'Sociological Review', vol. 23, 1975, pp. 563-76.

Cowan, P., Depreciation, obsolescence and ageing, 'Architects Journal', 16 June 1965, pp. 1395-401.

Cox, K.R. (ed.), 'Urbanization and Conflict in Market Societies', London, Methuen, 1978.

Crosland, A., 'Towards a Labour Housing Policy', Fabian Tract 410, London, Fabian Society, 1971.

Crossman, R.H.S., 'The Diaries of a Cabinet Minister, Volume I: Minister of Housing 1964-66', London, Hamish Hamilton, 1975.

Cubbin, J., Price, quality and selling time in the housing market, 'Applied Economics', vol. 6, no. 3, September 1974, pp. 171-87.

Cullingworth, J.B., 'Essays on Housing Policy: The British Scene', London, Allen & Unwin, 1979.

Cullingworth, J.B., 'Town and Country Planning in Britain', 7th edn, London, Allen & Unwin, 1979.

Dear, M., and Scott, A.J. (eds), 'Urbanization and Urban Planning in Capitalist Society', London, Methuen, 1981.

Dickens, P., Social science and design theory, 'Environment and Planning B', vol. 7, 1980, pp. 353-60.

Dickens, P., The hut and the machine: towards a social theory of architecture, 'Architectural Design', vol. 51, no. 1/2, 1981, pp. 18-24.

Donnison, D.V., 'Housing Policy since the War', Welwyn, Codicote Press, 1960.

Duncan, S.S., Self-help: the allocation of mortgages and the formation of housing sub-markets, 'Area', vol. 8, no. 4, 1976.

Duncan, T.L.C., assisted by Curry, J., 'Housing Improvement Policies in England and Wales', Birmingham, CURS, 1974.

Dunleavy, P., The urban basis of political alignment: social class, domestic property ownership, and state intervention in consumption processes, 'British Journal of Political Science', vol. 9, 1979, pp. 409-43.

Dunleavy, P., 'Urban Political Analysis', London, Macmillan, 1980.

Dunleavy, P., The urban basis of political alignment: a rejoinder to Harrop, 'British Journal of Political Science', vol. 10, 1980, pp. 398-402.

Economist Intelligence Unit, 'Housing Land Availability in the South East', London, HMSO, 1975.

Edwards, M., Merrett, S., and Swann, J., 'Political Economy and the Housing Question', London, Political Economy of Housing Workshop, 1975.

Edwards, M., Gray, F., Merrett, S., and Swann, J. (eds), 'Housing and Class in Britain', London, Political Economy of Housing Workshop, 1976.

Edwards, M., Gray, F., Ive, G., and Paddon, M. (eds), 'Housing, Construction and the State', London, Political Economy of Housing Workshop, 1980.

English, J., and Jones, C. (eds), 'The Sale of Council Houses', Glasgow, University of Glasgow Department of Social and Economic Research, 1977.

Evans, Alan W., 'The Economics of Residential Location', London, Macmillan, 1973.

Evans, Alan W., Economic influences on social mix, 'Urban Studies', vol. 13, 1976, pp. 247-60.

Evans, Andrew W., Private sector housing land prices in England and Wales, 'Economic Trends', no. 244, February 1974, pp. xiv-xxxvii.

Evans, Andrew W., 'The Five per cent Sample Survey of Building Society Mortgages', Studies in Official Statistics, no. 26, London, HMSO, 1975.

Fenton, M. 'Asian Households in Owner-Occupation: A study of the Pattern, Costs and Experiences of Households in Greater Manchester', Birmingham, SSRC Research Unit on Ethnic Relations, 1977.

Ferris, J., 'Participation in Urban Planning: The Barnsbury Case. A Study of Environmental Improvement in London', London, Bell, 1972.

Finnis, N., Mortgage arrears: tomorrow's problem, 'Roof', January 1978, pp. 10-11.

Foot, M., 'Aneurin Bevan 1945-60', St Albans, Paladin, 1975.

Ford, J., The role of the building society manager in the urban stratification system; autonomy versus constraint, 'Urban Studies', vol. 12, 1975, pp. 295-302.

Ford, J., Building society managers: their limited powers, 'Roof' October 1976, pp. 141-4.

Forrest, R., and Murie, A., 'Social Segregation, Housing Need and the Sale of Council Houses', Birmingham, CURS, 1976.

Forrest, R., and Murie, A., Paying the price of council house sales, 'Roof', November 1978, pp. 170-3.

Forsyth, J., Nice house - shame about the place, 'Roof', November 1979, p. 171.

Foster, J., 'The Demand for Building Society Shares and Deposits 1961-73', discussion papers in Economics no. 9, Department of Social and Economic Research, University of Glasgow, 1974.

Foster, J., 'The Re-distributive Effects of the Composite Income Tax Arrangement and Building Society Behaviour', discussion papers in Economics no. 5, Department of Social and Economic Research, University of Glasgow, 1974.

Ghosh, D., 'The Economics of Building Societies', Farnborough, Saxon House, 1974.

Gleave, D., and Palmer, D., Mobility of labour: are council tenants really handicapped?, 'CES Review', no. 3, 1978, pp. 74-7.

Goudie, J., 'House Agents', London, Fabian Society, 1966.

Gough, T.J., Determinants of fluctuations in private housing investment, 'Applied Economics', vol. 4, no. 2, June 1972, pp. 135-44.

Gough, T.J., Phases of British private housebuilding and the supply of mortgage credit, 'Applied Economics', vol. 7, no. 3, September 1975, pp. 213-22.

Gough, T.J., and Taylor, T.W., 'The Building Society Price Cartel', London, Institute of Economic Affairs, 1979.

Gray, F., and Boddy, M, The origins and use of theory in urban geography: household mobility and filtering theory, 'Geoforum', vol. 10, 1979, pp. 117-27.

Green, G., 'Leasehold Loopholes', Oxford, Birmingham CDP Research Team, 1979.

Greer, R., 'Building Societies?' London, Fabian Society, 1974.

Hadjimatheou, G., 'Housing and Mortgage Markets: The UK Experience', London, Saxon House, 1976.

Hall, P., Gracey, H., Drewett, R., and Thomas, R., 'The Containment of Urban England', vol. 2, London, Allen & Unwin, 1973.

Hammond, D., 'The Home Ownership Game and How to Win it', Newton Abbot, David & Charles, 1981.

Hamnett, C., and Randolph, W., Flat break-ups, 'Roof', May-June 1981, pp. 18-24.

Hamnett, C., and Williams, P., 'Gentrification in London in 1961-71: An Empirical and Theoretical Analysis of Social Change', Birmingham, CURS, 1979.

Harloe, M., Issacharoff, R., and Minns, R., 'The Organization of Housing: Public and Private Enterprise in London', London, Heinemann, 1974.

Harrison, A.J., The valuation gap: a danger signal?, 'CES Review', December 1977, pp. 101-3.

Harrison, A.J., and Lomas, G., Tenure preference: how to interpret the survey evidence, 'CES Review', no. 8, January 1980, pp. 20-3.

Harrison, M.L., 'The Local Authorities/Building Society Support Scheme in Leeds', Housing Research Paper no. 1, Department of Social Policy and Administration, University of Leeds, 1977.

Harrison, M.L., 'Local Authority Mortgages in Leeds after Local Government Re-organisation', Housing Research Paper no. 2, Department of Social Policy and Administration, University of Leeds, 1977.

Harrop, M., The urban basis of political alignment: a comment, 'British Journal of Political Science', vol. 10, 1980, pp. 388-98.

Hicks, J.R., 'The Renter Prospects: A Survey of the Households who Rent but Could Afford to Buy', London, Housing Research Foundation, 1971.

Hirsch, D., How to limit agents, 'Roof', November-December 1981, p. 3.

Holmans, A.E., A forecast of effective demand for housing in Great Britain in the 1970s, 'Social Trends', no. 1, 1970, pp. 33-42.

Holmans, A.E., Housing tenure in England and Wales - the present situation and recent trends, 'Social Trends', no. 9, 1979, pp. 10-19.

Housing Monitoring Team, 'The Structure and Functioning of Building Societies: A Head Office View', Birmingham, CURS, 1978.

Housing Monitoring Team, 'New Housebuilding and Housing Strategies: A Report of the Public/Private Sector Housing Forum', Birmingham, CURS, 1980.

Housing Research Unit, 'Purchasers' Opinions of House Buying', Surrey, University of Surrey, 1978.

Hughes, D., Half and half mortgages: what they're about, 'Roof', November 1976, pp. 164-7.

Hughes, D., The law of equity sharing, 'Roof', January 1977, pp. 19-21.

Hughes, G.A., 'Inflation and Housing', London, Housing Research Foundation, 1974.

Humber, R., Can the private sector fill the gap?, 'Roof', September-October 1980, p. 156.

Ineichen, B., Home-ownership and manual workers' life-styles, 'Sociological Review' (new series), vol. 20, August 1972, pp. 391-412.

Ineichen, B., 'A Place of Our Own', London, Housing Research Foundation, 1973.

Ineichen, B., Home-ownership: a neglected social revolution, 'Town and Country Planning', vol. 41, no. 9, September 1973, pp. 406-8.

Inter Company Comparisons Ltd, 'Business Ratio Report: Housebuilders', London, ICC Business Ratios, 1980.

Issacharoff, R., The building boom of the inter-war years: whose profits and at whose cost?, in Harloe, M. (ed.), 'Urban Change and Conflict', London, CES, 1978.

Jackson, A.A., 'Semi-detached London: Suburban Development, Life and Transport 1900-1939', London, Allen & Unwin, 1973.

Johnson, J.H., Salt, J., and Wood, P.A., 'Housing and the Migration of Labour in England and Wales', Farnborough, Saxon House, 1974.

Joint Advisory Committee on Building Society Mortgage Finance, 'The Guideline System', Report of the Technical Sub-Committee, London, BSA, 1980.

Jones, C., 'Household Movement, Filtering and Home Ownership', Urban and Regional Discussion Paper no. 23, University of Glasgow, 1975.

Jones, M., The Tories: bringing the house down, 'Marxism Today', May, 1980, pp. 10-17.

Joseph, M., 'The Conveyancing Fraud', London, Michael Joseph, 1976.

Karn, V., 'Local Authority Mortgages in Saltley', Birmingham, Birmingham CDP, 1975.

Karn, V., 'Priorities for Local Authority Mortgage Lending: A Case Study of Birmingham', CURS, Research Memorandum 52, Birmingham, 1976.

Karn, V., 'The Impact of Housing Finance on Low Income Owner Occupiers', CURS Working Paper 55, Birmingham, 1977.

Karn, V., Pity the poor home owners, 'Roof', January 1979, pp. 10-14.

Karn, V., Public sector demolition can seriously damage your wealth, 'Roof', January-February 1981, pp. 13-23.

Kemeny, J., Home ownership and privatization, 'International Journal of Urban and Regional Research', vol. 4, no. 3, September 1980, pp. 372-87.

Kemeny, J., 'The Myth of Home-Ownership: Private versus Public Choices in Housing Tenure', London, Routledge & Kegan Paul, 1981.

Kilroy, B., No jackpot from council house sales, 'Roof', May 1977, pp. 74-80.

Kilroy, B., 'Housing Finance - Organic Reform?', London, Labour Economic, Finance and Taxation Association, 1978.

Kilroy, B., Housing finance - why so privileged? 'Lloyds Bank Review', July 1979, pp. 37-52.

King, M.A., and Atkinson, A.B., Housing policy, taxation and reform, 'Midland Bank Review', spring 1980, pp. 7-15.

Kirwan, R., and Martin, D.B., 'The Economics of Urban Residential Renewal and Improvement', London, CES, 1972.

Lambert, C., 'Building Societies, Surveyors and the Older Areas of Birmingham', Birmingham, CURS, 1976.

Lambert, J., Paris, C., and Blackaby, B., 'Housing Policy and the State', London, Macmillan, 1978.

LAMSAC, 'Mortgage Arrears in Scotland', London, LAMSAC, 1979.

Land Campaign Working Party, 'Lie of the Land: Community Land Act, or Nationalisation Betrayed', London, LCWP, 1976.

Lansley, S., 'Housing and Public Policy', London, Croom Helm, 1979.

Lee, G., 'The Services of a Building Society', London, Hodder & Stoughton, 1964.

Llewellyn, D.T., Do building societies take deposits away from banks?, 'Lloyds Bank Review', January 1979, no. 131, pp. 21-34.

Lomas, G., Aspects of owner occupation: a statistical note, 'CES Review', no. 4, 1973, pp. 62-7.

McIntosh, Mortgage support scheme holds the lending lines, 'Roof', March 1978, pp. 44-7.

McKie, R., and Kumar, W.K., House improvement and rateable values, 'Urban Studies', June 1971, pp. 147-50.

Maclennan, D., Information, space and the measurement of housing preferences and demand, 'Scottish Journal of Political Economy', vol. 24, no. 2, June 1977, pp. 97-115.

Madge, J., and Brown, C., 'First Homes': A Survey of the Housing Circumstances of Young Married Couples', London, Policy Studies Institute, 1982.

Mahon, D., 'No Place in the Country: A report on Second Homes in England and Wales', London, Shelter, 1973.

Mason, T., 'Inner City Housing and Urban Renewal Policy: A Housing Profile of Cheetham Hill, Manchester and Salford', London, CES, 1977.

Massey, D., and Catalano, A., 'Capital and Land: Landownership by Capital in Great Britain', London, Edward Arnold, 1978.

Mellor, R., Planning for housing: market processes and constraints, 'Planning Outlook' (new series), vol. 13, autumn 1973, pp. 26-42.

Merrett, S., 'A Theory of the Capitalist Land Market', Town Planning Discussion

Paper no. 33, London, BSAP, 1979.

Merrett, S., 'State Housing in Britain', London, Routledge & Kegan Paul, 1979.

Monck, E., with Lomas, G., 'Housing Action Areas: Success and Failure', London, CES, 1980.

Munby, D.L., 'Home Ownership', London, Fabian Society, 1957.

Murie, A., 'Household Movements and Housing Choice', Birmingham, CURS. 1974.

Murie, A., 'The Sale of Council Houses: A Study in Social Policy', Birmingham, CURS, 1975.

Murie, A., Council house sales mean poor law housing, 'Roof', March 1977, pp. 46-9.

Murie, A. et al., Proceedings of a symposium on council house sales, 'Policy and Politics', vol. 8, no. 3, August 1980, pp. 287-340.

Murie, A., and Forrest, R., 'Housing Market Processes and the Inner City', London, Social Science Research Council, 1980.

Murie, A., Niner, P., and Watson, C., 'Housing Policy and the Housing System', London, Allen & Unwin, 1976.

National CDP, 'Profits against Houses: An Alternative Guide to Housing Finance', London, CDP Information and Intelligence Unit, 1976.

National Consumer Council, 'Building Societies and the Consumer', London, NCC, 1981.

Nevin, E.T., 'The Mechanism of Cheap Money: A Study of British Monetary Policy 1931-1939', Cardiff, University of Wales Press, 1955.

Notting Hill People's Association Housing Group, 'Losing-out: A Study on Colville and Tavistock', London, NHPAHG, 1972.

Nottingham Housing Action Group, 'Where Have all the Assets Gone? A Study of the Financial Effects of Council House Sales in Nottingham', Nottingham, Nottingham Alternative Publications, 1979.

O'Herlihy, C.S.J., and Spencer, J.E., Building societies' behaviour, 1955-70, 'National Institute Economic Review', no. 61, August 1972, pp. 40-52.

Pahl, R.E., 'Whose City?', 2nd edn, Harmondsworth, Penguin Books, 1975.

Paley, B., 'Attitudes to Letting in 1976', London, HMSO, 1978.

Paris, C., and Blackaby, B., 'Not Much Improvement: Urban Renewal Policy in Birmingham', London, Heinemann, 1979.

Parsons, H.K., 'Recent Private Development in Older Areas of Birmingham', Birmingham, CURS, 1973.

Pawley, M., 'Home Ownership', London, The Architectural Press, 1978.

Pennance, F.E., and Gray, H., 'Choice in Housing', London, Institute of Economic Affairs, 1968.

Pepper, S., 'Housing Improvement: Goals and Strategy', London, Lund Humphries, 1971.

Perry, J., and Gibson, M., Pause for renewal, 'Roof', July-August 1981, pp. 23-4.

Pitt, J., 'Gentrification in Islington', London, Barnsbury Peoples Forum, 1977.

Power, A., 'David and Goliath: Barnsbury 1973', London, Holloway Neighbourhood Law Centre, 1973.

Price, S.J., 'Building Societies: Their Origin and History', London, Franey, 1958.

Revell, J., 'The British Financial System', London, Macmillan, 1973.

Revell, J., 'UK Building Societies', Economic Research Papers no. 5, University College of North Wales, 1973.

Revell, J., UK building societies, in Organisation for Economic Co-operation and Development, 'Housing Finance: Present Problems', Paris, OECD, 1974, pp. 66-99.

Rex, J., 'Race, Colonialism and the City', London, Routledge & Kegan Paul, 1973.

Rex, J., and Moore, R., 'Race, Community and Conflict', London, Oxford University Press, 1967.

Rex, J., and Tomlinson, S., 'Colonial Immigrants in a British City', London, Routledge & Kegan Paul, 1979.

Richardson H.W., and Aldcroft, D.H., 'Building in the British Economy between

the Wars', London, Allen & Unwin, 1968.
Richardson, H., Vipond, J., and Furbey, R., Determinants of urban house prices, 'Urban Studies', vol. 11, 1974, pp. 189-99.
RICS, 'Purchaser Beware', London, RICS, undated.
RICS, 'Buying and Selling a House', London, RICS, 1975.
Roberts, T., 'General Improvement Areas', Farnborough, Saxon House, 1976.
Robinson, R., 'Housing Economics and Public Policy', London, Macmillan, 1979.
Rose, D., Home-ownership and industrial change: the struggle for a 'separate sphere', Falmer, University of Sussex, 'Urban and Regional Studies Working Paper 25', 1981.
Rosenberg, N., 'Economic Planning in the British Building Industry 1945-49', Philadelphia, University of Pennsylvania Press, 1960.
Sabatino, R.A., 'Housing in Great Britain 1945-49', Dallas, Southern Methodist University Press, 1956.
Saunders, P., Housing tenure and class interests, Falmer, University of Sussex, 'Urban and Regional Studies Working Paper 6', 1977.
Saunders, P., Domestic property and social class, 'International Journal of Urban and Regional Research', vol. 2, no. 2, June 1978, pp. 233-51.
Saunders, P., 'Urban Politics', Harmondsworth, Penguin Books, 1980.
Saunders, P., 'Social Theory and the Urban Question', London, Hutchinson, 1981.
Schifferes, S., 'Facts on Council House Sales', London, Shelter, 1979.
Schifferes, S., Counter sales, 'Roof', November 1979, pp. 184-6.
SHAC, 'Good Housekeeping: An Examination of Housing Repair and Improvement Policy', London, SHAC, 1981.
Sharp, E., 'The Ministry of Housing and Local Government', London, Allen & Unwin, 1969.
Shelter Community Action Team, 'The Great Sales Robbery: The Case against Selling Council Houses', London, SCAT, 1979.
Shoults, T., The re-development of low-density areas in London, 'Housing Review', March-April 1975, pp. 50-3.
Sigsworth, E.M., and Wilkinson, R.K., Constraints on the uptake of improvement grants, 'Policy and Politics', vol. 1, no. 2, pp. 131-41.
Skeffington, A., 'Leasehold Enfranchisement', London, Fabian Society, 1956.
Smith, D.J., 'Racial Disadvantage in Britain', Harmondsworth, Penguin Books, 1977.
Socialist Housing Activists Workshop, 'Socialism and Housing Action: The Red Paper on Housing', Gateshead, SHAW, 1979.
Southwark CDP and Joint Docklands Action Group, 'Alternative Forms of Tenure: Preferences and Costs', London, Southwark CDP, 1975.
Stanton, D., 'Income and the Demand for Housing: Further Evidence for the UK', DoE Economic and Statistical Notes, no. 16, 1973.
Stewart, A., 'Housing Action in an Industrial Suburb', London, Academic Press, 1981.
Stone, P.A., 'Housing, Town Development, Land and Costs', London, Estates Gazette, 1962.
Stone, P.A., 'Urban Development in Britain: Standards, Costs and Resources 1964-2004', Cambridge, Cambridge University Press, 1970.
Stretton, H., 'Capitalism, Socialism and the Environment', London, Cambridge University Press, 1976.
Thomas, A., 'Area-based Renewal: Three Years in the Life of an HAA', Birmingham, CURS, 1979.
Townsend, P., 'Poverty in the United Kingdom', London, Allen Lane, 1979.
Tunnard, J., Marriage breakdown and the loss of the owner occupied home, 'Roof', March 1976, pp. 40-3.
Tunnard, J., The mortgage vows, 'Roof', November 1978, p. 192.
Tunnard, J., and Whately, C., 'Rights Guide for Home Owners', London, SHAC, 1977.
Turvey, R., 'The Economics of Real Property', London, Allen & Unwin, 1957.
de Vance, R., 'Second Home Ownership: A Case Study', Bangor Occasional Papers in Economics, University of Wales Press, 1975.

Vipond, J., Fluctuations in private house building in Great Britain 1950-66, 'Scottish Journal of Political Economy', June 1969, pp. 196-211.

Watkins, R., and Shutt, J., 'From Failure to Facelift', Saltley, Birmingham CDP, 1980.

Watson, C.J., 'Household Movement in West Central Scotland', Birmingham, CURS, 1973.

Weber, B., A new index of residential construction, 1838-1950, 'Scottish Journal of Political Economy', vol. 2, no. 2, June 1955, pp. 104-32.

Webster, D., House prices and allocation: the case for action on the demand side of the market, 'Housing Review', January-February 1975, pp. 12-15.

Webster, D., Financial consequences of council house sales: why do assessments vary? 'CES Review', no. 9, April 1980, pp. 39-46.

Weir, S., Red line districts, 'Roof', July 1976, pp. 109-14.

Weir, S., and Kilroy, B., Equity sharing in Cheshunt, 'Roof', November 1976, pp. 168-70.

Whitehead, C., 'The UK Housing Market: An Econometric Model', Farnborough, Saxon House, 1974.

Whitehead, C., House prices: what determines them and can they be controlled?, 'CES Review', no. 3, May 1978, pp. 5-9.

Whitehead, C., Why owner-occupation?, 'CES Review', no. 6, May 1979, pp. 33-41.

Whitehead, C., What should be done with the guideline?, 'CES Review', no. 7, September 1979, pp. 37-50.

Wilkinson, R.K., House prices and the measurement of externalities, 'Economic Journal', vol. 83, March 1973, pp. 72-86.

Wilkinson, R.K., The income elasticity of demand for housing, 'Oxford Economic Papers', November 1973, pp. 361-77.

Wilkinson, R.K., and Archer, C., Measuring the determinants of relative house prices, 'Environment and Planning', vol. 5, 1973, pp. 357-67.

Wilkinson, R.K., and Sigsworth, E.M., Attitudes to the housing environment: an analysis of private and local authority households in Batley, Leeds and York, 'Urban Studies', vol. 9, no. 2, June 1972, pp. 193-214.

Williams, P., 'The Role of Financial Institutions and Estate Agents in the Private Housing Market: A General Introduction', Birmingham, CURS, 1976.

Williams, P., Building societies and the inner city, 'Transactions of the Institute of British Geographers', vol. 3, no. 1, 1978, pp. 23-34.

Williams, P., and Wintour, J., Doing well or doing good, 'Roof', November 1979, pp. 188-95.

Wiltshire, N., 'Rent, Rates and Housing (The Existing Problems and the Solution)', London, Estates Gazette, 1944.

Wintour, J., and Franey, R., Are improvement grants tied up in the town halls?, 'Roof', May 1978, pp. 82-3.

Wishlade, R.L., 'Home Ownership in England and Wales', London, Housing Research Foundation, 1970.

Wolmar, C., Getting in on the Housing Act, 'Roof', January-February 1981, p. 3.

Young, J., Newport wraps up improvements package, 'Roof', July 1979, pp. 116-17.

Young, K., and Kramer, J., 'Strategy and Conflict in Metropolitan Housing: Suburbia versus the Greater London Council 1965-75', London, Heinemann, 1978.

STATE PAPERS

CHAC, 'Private Enterprise Housing', 1944.

Commission for Racial Equality, 'Cottrell and Rothon Estate Agents', 1980.

DoE, 'Fair Deal for Housing', Cmnd 4728, 1971.

DoE, 'Widening the Choice: The Next Steps in Housing', Cmnd 5280, 1973.

DoE, 'Better Homes, the Next Priorities', Cmnd 5339, 1973.

DoE, 'Housing Policy: A Consultative Document', Cmnd 6851, 1977.

DoE, 'Housing Policy Technical Volume', parts I, II and III, 1977.
DoE, 'Scottish Housing: A Consultative Document', Cmnd 6852, 1977.
DoE, 'National Dwelling and Housing Survey', 1978.
DoE, 'Starter Homes', Occasional Paper 2/80 of the Housing Development Directorate, 1980.
DoE, 'Housing and Construction Statistics, 1969-1979', 1980.
Essex County Council, 'A Design Guide for Residential Areas', Chelmsford, Essex County Council, 1973.
House of Commons Expenditure Committee, '10th Report: House Improvement Grants', House of Commons Paper 349-I, 1973.
MoH, 'Report of the Departmental Committee on the Valuation for Rates' (Fitzgerald Report), 1944.
MoH, 'Report of a Committee chaired by J.W. Morris on Control of Selling Price of Houses', Cmd 6670, 1945.
MHLG, 'Houses: The next Step', Cmd 8996, 1953.
MHLG, 'House Purchase: Proposed Government Scheme', Cmnd 571, 1958.
MHLG, 'Housing in England and Wales', Cmnd 1290, 1961.
MHLG, 'Residential Leasehold Property', Cmnd 1789, 1962.
MHLG, 'Housing', Cmnd 2050, 1963.
MHLG, 'The Housing Programme 1965 to 1970', Cmnd 2838, 1965.
MHLG, 'Leasehold Reform in England and Wales', Cmnd 2916, 1966.
MHLG, 'Help towards Home Ownership', Cmnd 3163, 1966.
MHLG, 'Old Houses into New Homes', Cmnd 3602, 1968.
Monopolies Commission, 'Estate Agents', 1969.
Monopolies and Mergers Commission, 'Surveyors Services', 1977.
National Board for Prices and Incomes, 'Rates of Interest on Building Society Mortgages', Cmnd 3136, 1966.
Price Commission, 'Charges, Costs and Margins of Estate Agents', Cmnd 7647, 1979.
Royal Commission on the Distribution of Income and Wealth, 'Third Report of the Standing Conference', 1977.
Royal Commission on Legal Services, 'Final Report', Cmnd 7648, 1979.
Royal Commission on Legal Services in Scotland, 'Report', Cmnd 7846, 1979.

JOURNALS AND SERIES

'Building'
'BSA Bulletin'
'Building Societies Yearbook'
'Census of Production'
'CES Review'
Chief Registrar of Friendly Societies, 'Annual Reports'.
'Economic Trends'
'Family Expenditure Survey'
'General Household Survey'
'Housing and Construction Statistics'
'Housing Return for England and Wales'
'Housing Statistics Great Britain'
MoH, 'Annual Reports'
'MHLG Reports'
Private Contractors' Construction Census
'Roof'
'Social Trends'

NAME INDEX

GENERAL INDEX